Travel & Tourism

A2

Lindsey Taylor

Collins

William Collins' dream of knowledge for all began with the publication of his first book in 1819. A self-educated mill worker, he not only enriched millions of lives, but also founded a flourishing publishing house. Today, staying true to this spirit, Collins books are packed with inspiration, innovation and practical expertise. They place you at the centre of a world of possibility and give you exactly what you need to explore it.

Collins. Do more.

Published by Collins
An imprint of HarperCollins*Publishers*
77–85 Fulham Palace Road
Hammersmith
London
W6 8JB

Browse the complete Collins catalogue at
www.collinseducation.com

© HarperCollinsPublishers Limited 2006

10 9 8 7 6 5 4 3 2 1

ISBN-13 978 0 00 720038 2
ISBN 0 00 720038 2

Lindsey Taylor and Nicki Stephenson assert their moral right to be identified as the authors of this work.

British Library Cataloguing in Publication Data
A Catalogue record for this publication is available from the British Library

Commissioned and edited by Graham Bradbury
Cover design by Blue Pig Design Limited
Cover picture courtesy of BAA Aviation Photo Library
Series design by Patricia Briggs
Book design by Ken Vail Graphic Design
Indexed by Patricia Baker
Picture research by Thelma Gilbert
Production by Sarah Robinson
Printed and bound by Butler and Tanner Ltd, Frome

This high quality material is endorsed by Edexcel and has been through a rigorous quality assurance programme to ensure that it is a suitable companion to the specification for both learners and teachers. This does not mean that its contents will be used verbatim when setting examinations nor is it to be read as being the official specification – a copy of which is available at www.edexcel.org.uk

Contents

Unit 7

Unit 8

4

Travel & Tourism

5

Travel & Tourism

About this book

Welcome to A2 Travel and Tourism. This textbook is written specifically for students taking the Edexcel GCE Travel and Tourism awards and provides you with the underpinning knowledge to be successful in either the single or double award. To gain a single award you must successfully complete AS units 1–3, plus A2 units 7–9. To gain a double award, you must successfully complete all the AS units and all the A2 units.

Unit	Title	How is this unit assessed?
7	Responsible Tourism	External test
8	Current Issues in Travel and Tourism	Internal assessment
9	Working in Travel and Tourism	Internal assessment
10	Promotions and Sales in Travel and Tourism	External test
11	Special Interest Holidays	Internal assessment
12	Travel Organisations	Internal assessment2

Explanatory introduction outlines what you will need to learn about each topic.

Real examples from the industry support and clarify all the explanations in the text.

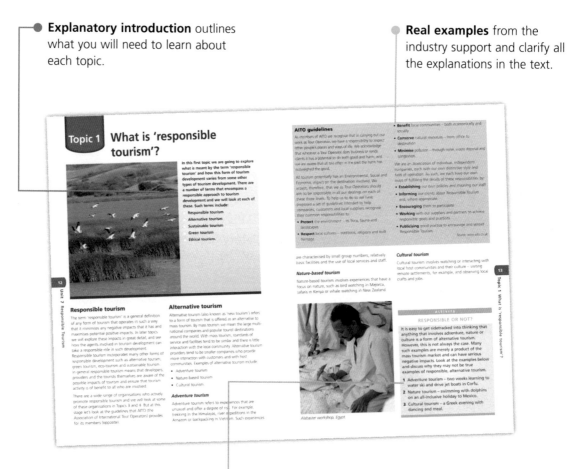

Activities provide you with an opportunity to develop your understanding about specific aspects of a topic and practise your skills. Most activities are designed for you to work on your own, with a partner or with a small group.

The assessment of your knowledge and understanding of the different units will follow the same pattern as your AS level award:

- an assignment that is written and marked by your teacher (internal assessment) or
- a written examination lasting one and half hours, which is written and marked by Edexcel, your awarding body (external assessment).

Case studies support your learning and help put it into context.

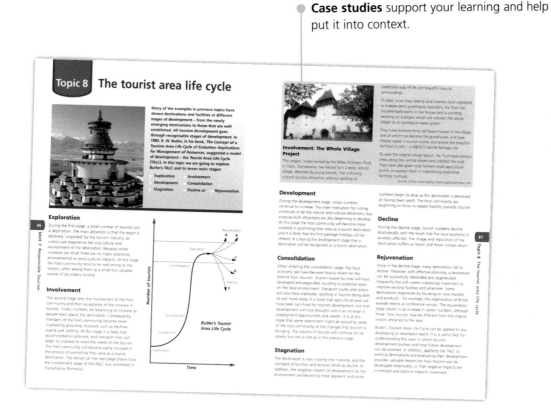

Collins Travel and Tourism A2 for Edexcel is divided into six units, each corresponding to a unit of the Edexcel A2 specification. The units in this book are divided into topics, and each topic provides a manageable chunk of learning covering the subject content of the Edexcel unit. The contents lists at the beginning of this book and at the start of each unit will show you how the topics correspond to the Edexcel specification.

Good luck with your A2-level Travel and Tourism studies. This book provides you with interesting, supportive and motivating learning materials that we hope will help you to succeed in your course.

Organisations and destinations referred to in this book

Tourism is a global industry that impacts on the lives of everyone. Developments in tourist destinations have the potential for being forces for good, in terms of providing improved living standards, infrastructure and environment for host communities. There are many examples throughout the world where responsible tourism development has resulted, not only in maintaining local communities, but also, tangible improvements in the quality of life for all.

When poorly managed, however, the impacts of tourism can be catastrophic – exploitation of local work forces, destruction of the natural environment, loss of traditional employment and culture, and tourism revenue leaking out of the host community to the large international tourism organisations. Frequently this occurs when tourism development takes place rapidly with little regard or planning for the future impact of such development. This is a particular problem in poorer countries where local communities may initially view the tourism industry as a lifeline to increased wealth. By the time that they realise that this is not necessarily the case, it is often too late to correct the damage that has already been done.

It is the moral duty of anyone involved in tourism development to ensure that the products and services that they offer are based on the principles of responsible tourism, and bring real benefits to everyone involved. Failure to do so will eventually threaten the very industry that they seek to develop.

In this unit you will gain an understanding and appreciation of the principles of responsible tourism, including green tourism, alternative tourism, sustainable tourism and eco-tourism. We will also explore the range of agents that are involved in tourism development and the specific objectives that they set themselves to ensure that they behave responsibly. In addition, we will examine the impacts that tourism development can have on key destinations, and how these impacts can be managed to ensure that negative impacts are minimised and positive impacts maximised.

The industry focus interview (at the end of Topic 9) is with Maryanne Mills of the responsible tourism tour operator, Naturetrek. Her interview highlights the ways in which organisations such as hers are striving to ensure that tourism development abides by all of the guiding principles of responsible and sustainable tourism.

Unit 7

Responsible Tourism

What is 'responsible tourism'?

In this first topic we are going to explore what is meant by the term 'responsible tourism' and how this form of tourism development varies from some other types of tourism development. There are a number of terms that encompass a responsible approach to tourism development and we will look at each of these. Such terms include:

- Responsible tourism
- Alternative tourism
- Sustainable tourism
- Green tourism
- Ethical tourism.

Responsible tourism

The term 'responsible tourism' is a general definition of any form of tourism that operates in such a way that it minimises any negative impacts that it has and maximises potential positive impacts. In later topics we will explore these impacts in great detail, and see how the agents involved in tourism development can take a responsible role in such development. Responsible tourism incorporates many other forms of responsible development such as alternative tourism, green tourism, eco-tourism and sustainable tourism. In general responsible tourism means that developers, providers and the tourists themselves are aware of the possible impacts of tourism and ensure that tourism activity is of benefit to all who are involved.

There are a wide range of organisations who actively promote responsible tourism and we will look at some of these organisations in Topics 3 and 4. But at this stage let's look at the guidelines that AITO (the Association of International Tour Operators) provides for its members (opposite).

Alternative tourism

Alternative tourism (also known as 'new tourism') refers to a form of tourism that is offered as an alternative to mass tourism. By mass tourism we mean the large multi-national companies and popular tourist destinations around the world. With mass tourism, standards of service and facilities tend to be similar and there is little interaction with the local community. Alternative tourism providers tend to be smaller companies who provide more interaction with customers and with host communities. Examples of alternative tourism include:

- Adventure tourism
- Nature-based tourism
- Cultural tourism.

Adventure tourism

Adventure tourism refers to experiences that are unusual and offer a degree of risk. For example, trekking in the Himalayas, river expeditions in the Amazon or backpacking in Vietnam. Such experiences

AITO guidelines

As members of AITO we recognise that in carrying out our work as Tour Operators we have a responsibility to respect other people's places and ways of life. We acknowledge that wherever a Tour Operator does business or sends clients it has a potential to do both good and harm, and we are aware that all too often in the past the harm has outweighed the good.

All tourism potentially has an Environmental, Social and Economic impact on the destination involved. We accept, therefore, that we as Tour Operators should aim to be responsible in all our dealings on each of these three levels. To help us to do so we have proposed a set of guidelines intended to help companies, customers and local suppliers recognise their common responsibilities to:

- **Protect** the environment – its flora, fauna and landscapes
- **Respect** local cultures – traditions, religions and built heritage

- **Benefit** local communities – both economically and socially
- **Conserve** natural resources – from office to destination
- **Minimise** pollution – through noise, waste disposal and congestion.

We are an Association of individual, independent companies, each with our own distinctive style and field of operation. As such, we each have our own ways of fulfilling the details of these responsibilities by:

- **Establishing** our own policies and involving our staff
- **Informing** our clients about Responsible Tourism and, where appropriate,
- **Encouraging** them to participate
- **Working** with our suppliers and partners to achieve responsible goals and practices
- **Publicising** good practice to encourage and spread Responsible Tourism.

Source: www.aito.co.uk

are characterised by small group numbers, relatively basic facilities and the use of local services and staff.

Nature-based tourism

Nature-based tourism involves experiences that have a focus on nature, such as bird watching in Majorca, safaris in Kenya or whale watching in New Zealand.

Cultural tourism

Cultural tourism involves watching or interacting with local host communities and their culture – visiting remote settlements, for example, and observing local crafts and jobs.

Alabaster workshop, Egypt.

activity

RESPONSIBLE OR NOT?

It is easy to get sidetracked into thinking that anything that involves adventure, nature or culture is a form of alternative tourism. However, this is not always the case. Many such examples are merely a product of the mass tourism market and can have serious negative impacts. Look at the examples below and discuss why they may not be true examples of responsible, alternative tourism.

1 Adventure tourism – two weeks learning to water ski and drive jet boats in Corfu.

2 Nature tourism – swimming with dolphins on an all-inclusive holiday to Mexico.

3 Cultural tourism – a Greek evening with dancing and meal.

Sustainable tourism

Alternative tourism embraces many of the principles of sustainable tourism. The concept of sustainable development first arose from a number of movements in the 1980s. In 1987, the World Commission on Environment and Development defined sustainable development as:

'Development that meets the needs of the present without compromising the ability of future generations to meet their own needs'.

This was followed in 1992 by the Rio Earth Summit, involving 152 major world leaders. At the summit, sustainability was defined in 'Agenda 21' a global plan that required all countries to produce and implement their own strategy for sustainability.

Sustainability is concerned with ensuring that the interests of local host communities are considered and that they will continue to benefit economically, environmentally and culturally in the long-term. For example, development needs to such that the host community will continue to thrive should the tourism trade decline. We look at sustainability in more detail in Topic 10.

Fair Trade and tourism

One of the most important initiatives in sustainable and responsible tourism was the Fair Trade movement. This should establish a Fair Trade label and ethical trading arrangements – you may have seen the Fair Trade logo on branded goods such as tea and coffee.

The motivation for the movement was based on the fact that there are large inequalities in wealth between the poorer tourist destinations and the tourist-generating countries. This had the potential for exploitation of the poorer countries, with much of the profits from tourism going back to wealthier countries through the international travel companies. This concept, known as 'tourism leakage', will be explored further in Topic 5.

Fair Trade Tourism established five main criteria:

1. Fair trade partnerships between tourism and hospitality investors and local communities
2. Fair share of benefits for local stakeholders
3. Fair trade between tourist and local people
4. Fair and sustainable use of natural resources
5. Fair wages and working conditions.

A full explanation of each of these criteria can be found on www.tourismconcern.org.uk.

Green tourism

Green tourism refers to any tourism activity that takes place in an environmentally safe way. In other words, it does not have any negative impacts on the existing environment. It is particularly concerned with the use of natural resources and the disposal of waste. So, for example, installing solar-powered heating and using 'grey water' (recycling used water without processing it) can help preserve local resources. Whilst the term 'green tourism' tends to suggest tourism within remote areas, there is also considerable focus on applying the concept to urban areas. Urban green tourism is where cities and large towns encourage environmentally safe forms of transport. (An example of this is shown in Topic 10.)

The term 'green tourism' is often confused with what is known as 'eco-tourism'. Whilst largely similar, eco-tourism takes the concept of responsible tourism one step further and is defined by the International Ecotourism Society (TIES) as:

'Responsible travel to natural areas that conserves that environment and improves the well being of local people'.

In other words, whilst green tourism may not harm the destination's environment, eco-tourism actually creates some benefit, as well as not causing harm. These benefits may be in the form of raising environmental awareness of a destination or providing funding for improvements and protection of the natural environment.

Ethical tourism

Ethical tourism means that tourism development adheres to acceptable moral practices and behaviour. In other words, host countries and communities are treated in a fair and equitable way and not exploited. Examples of where tourism development is not ethical might include:

- Where a high level of new crime is generated as a direct result of tourism development
- Child labour or poor employment terms and conditions for the community as a whole
- Prostitution
- Exploitation of the local community in terms of paying very low prices for land and local produce.

nor the excitement of safari, but meeting the people and culture of Africa, which has been one of the most moving and profound experiences of my life.'

Amanda Marks, director of the fair trade tour operator Tribes, charts the growing importance of people in eco-tourism. 'When Tribes started four years ago our customers thought mainly of wildlife and habitat. Now they're asking just as much about communities. Everyone's

Africa has been at the forefront of the evolution from nature-tourism to eco-tourism. In the 1980s, the authorities faced dire prospects such as rhino extinction, and recognising the fragility of the continent's wildernesses, moved people like Kenya's Maasai off their lands to create National Parks. But this heightened the conflict over land between people and wildlife. The new National Parks were ringed by resentful communities. Unable to graze their herds alongside the wildlife, as they had done for centuries, they turned to poaching and illicit hunting for the pot. Conservation didn't stand a chance, until far-sighted individuals realised that if African people were given a stake in the safari industry and allowed to benefit from the income that wildlife generated, game would have a higher value to them alive than dead.

realising that people have a right to benefit from tourism activities on their lands, and that they have customs and traditions as interesting and worthy of protection as the natural world.'

A glance at the global context emphasises the importance of this development. Thirty per cent of international tourists visit developing countries, and long-haul travel is growing faster than any other sector in the industry. Africa is in the front line: between 1995 and 2000, annual arrivals in Egypt increased from 2.9 million to 5.1 million; in South Africa, they rose from 4.7 to 6 million. British tourists alone spent £3billion holidaying in developing countries in 2000 – about the same as their government gave in aid that year.

Source (adapted): www.eco-resorts.com

So, primarily to help conservation, Africans were brought into the tourist industry. It's only in recent years that tourists and operators have given local communities a different role in tourism, one based on their right to benefit from tourism and on the priceless value of their interactions with travellers. This has been key in enabling African tourism to help reconcile people and wildlife in their competing claims for land.

'People often come to Africa very goal-oriented,' says Gavin Bate, director of Adventure Alternative, which leads small groups up Kilimanjaro. 'They arrive wanting only to make the summit, but when they leave, the strongest impression they take with them is invariably of Africa's people.' One client wrote to Gavin saying 'The memories the group will take away from our trip are not the challenge of Kilimanjaro,

activity

AFRICAN EXAMPLES

Read the case study above on Africa. In pairs, identify and discuss whether there are any examples of the following:

- **Responsible tourism**
- **Alternative tourism**
- **Adventure tourism**
- **Nature-based tourism**
- **Cultural tourism**
- **Sustainable tourism**
- **Green tourism**
- **Eco-tourism.**

Impacts, benefits, conservation and respect

In the last topic we discussed different types of responsible tourism, including eco-tourism, sustainable tourism and alternative tourism. In this section we are going to explore how specific principles of responsible tourism are applied to tourism development. These principles include:

- **Minimising negative impacts**
- **Creating economic benefits and improving the quality of life for local people**
- **Promoting the conservation of natural and cultural heritage**
- **Promoting respect between tourists and local people.**

Minimising negative impacts

We have already discussed the fact that responsible tourism requires the negative impacts of tourism to be minimised. In general negative impacts can occur in three ways:

- Economic impacts
- Environmental impacts
- Socio-cultural impacts.

Whilst we explore all three of these impacts in depth later in this unit, it is useful at this stage to define what we mean by each.

Economic impacts

In simple terms 'economic impact' means the amount of money generated (or lost) through tourism development. This does not just involve the profits made by large tourism providers but also employment and investment in the local community. One of the main principles of responsible tourism is to minimise any negative economic impact that tourism development might create within the host community. For example, the loss of traditional employment opportunities or money going outside the area to large companies.

Environmental impacts

'Environmental impacts' refers to any effect that tourism development might have on the environment. This includes plant and animal life, air and water quality, as well as landscapes. As we will discuss later, there are strict laws and guidelines that protect the environment from inappropriate development, and many organisations campaign strongly to prevent negative impacts. Planning permission for any major form of tourism development inevitably requires the developer to demonstrate that they have based their development on principles that will minimise negative impacts on the environment.

Socio-cultural impacts

'Socio-cultural' is short for 'sociological and cultural'. Most tourism development is closely linked to the location in which it takes place. Each location has its own society – its resident population with its own characteristics and culture. One of the guiding principles of responsible tourism is that it should not have a negative impact on the socio-cultural nature of the destination. This is particularly crucial where a new destination is being developed, because tourists could easily swamp a region with their own cultural expectations – and thus change the nature of the destination. This was witnessed in the early days of the package holiday and the development of the Spanish 'Costas', where large areas were transformed into mini-versions of British seaside resorts at the expense of the local Spanish culture. The case study below shows clearly how the organisation Tourism Concern is attempting to introduce principles that embrace minimising negative effects on a popular and growing area of tourism.

a c t i v i t y

MINIMISING NEGATIVE IMPACTS

Although we will look at negative impacts in greater detail later, at this stage it would be useful to clarify your own thoughts on the importance of minimising these impacts in view of what you learned about responsible tourism in the first topic. In pairs, discuss and describe all of the negative impacts that you think might arise from irresponsible tourism and share your ideas with the rest of the group.

Tourism Concern's campaign on working conditions for porters

Frostbite, altitude sickness and even death can be the cost for the porters carrying trekkers' equipment in the Himalayas, on the Inca Trail in Peru and at Mount Kilimanjaro in Tanzania. Tourism Concern's new campaign aims to put a stop to the abuse of porters' human rights.

Mountain trekking – it's exhilarating, it's beautiful, it's challenging. But how many of us could do it without the porters who carry our luggage and equipment? Porters are an essential part of treks, but the reality of their working conditions comes as a shock.

Think of Himalayan trekking, and many of us picture the famously hardy sherpas accompanying big-name mountaineers on Everest expeditions. But while the sherpas are from high-altitude areas, most Nepalese porters are poor farmers from lowland areas, and are as unused to the high altitudes and harsh conditions as western trekkers.

Many people don't know this, and a myth seems to

have been created that porters are superhuman – the massive weights they carry, the cold and the high altitudes are nothing to them – they're different. But this is madness. In fact, Nepalese porters suffer four times more accidents and illnesses than western trekkers. Making matters worse, there are many reports of porters being abandoned by tour groups when they fall ill. Porters have even been abandoned in life-threatening blizzards while trekkers were rescued by helicopter.

And it's not just the Himalayas – the problems are repeated worldwide. In the most extreme cases, porters believe they are simply seen as beasts of burden. In the words of a Peruvian porters' syndicate: 'We suffer humiliation upon humiliation, and are treated as less than human.' A tour operator in Pakistan is even more direct: the way porters are treated, he says, amounts to modern slavery.

So should people stop trekking? Definitely not – porters need the work. But the roots of this problem need to be tackled: the policies and practices of the tour operators who the porters ultimately work for. But here in the UK, the majority of operators are not yet addressing porters' rights and working conditions.

So what's the way forward? Tourism Concern believes that fair trade in tourism offers an opportunity for real change and that includes UK tour operators addressing the working conditions of their porters. We have worked with the trekking industry and tour operators within the UK – and got results. Forty-one out of eighty operators now have policies on porters – but more still needs to be done.

Source: Tourism Concern www.tourismconcern.org.uk

Creating economic benefits and improving the quality of life for local people

Just as one of the guiding principles of responsible tourism is to minimise negative impacts, so too, is the principle of creating positive impacts.

Creating economic benefits for the host community through increased employment and profits for local providers is a strong justification for responsible tourism development. Added to this, many tourism development projects can result in an improvement in the quality of life for local people by providing a rise in their standard of living and improvement in local facilities.

Promoting the conservation of natural and cultural heritage

Whilst we often tend to think of tourism development as a profit-making venture for larger organisations, there are many organisations who are guided by the principles of improving or conserving our natural or cultural heritage. Such organisations may still be keen to attract tourists and visitors, but their prime motivation is to be able to conserve natural features or heritage through tourism. For example, organisations such as English Heritage and the National Trust encourage people to visit their properties and rural destinations – but use the money raised to fund conservation and improvement programmes. Even organisations that are primarily profit-making also

need to embrace the issues of conservation if they are to be successful in their planning applications. For example, Eden Camp museum in Malton, North Yorkshire is housed in a Second World War prisoner of war camp – and its success has been largely based on the fact that conservation and renovation of the old camp was at the forefront of their original principles for development.

Promoting respect between tourists and local people

We saw earlier that one of the effects of irresponsible tourism can be a negative impact on the socio-cultural nature of the destination and its host community. A strong guiding principle for responsible tourism development is to ensure that any development takes into account the nature of the destination and actively encourages respect between the visiting tourists and the local people. Many responsible tour operators incorporate such principles into the advice that they give to their customers. For example, Naturetrek provides sound advice to travellers on how they can appreciate local socio-cultural values and foster a good relationship with the host community (see opposite).

Many organisations involved in tourism development state the guiding principles that need to be observed. The extract opposite, for example, shows some of the principles outlined by the South African Department of Tourism.

Eden Camp museum, North Yorkshire

Naturetrek's advice: some examples

- Remember, our so-called 'high standards' have come largely at the expense of our environment. If you cannot accept and enjoy the different standards and cultures of less affluent countries, you should stay at home!

- Before travelling, read widely to familiarise yourself with your destination's history, background, culture, customs, standards, etc. The well prepared tourist is likely to have a fulfilling holiday, with minimal problems and regrets.

- Dress practically and conservatively, paying particular attention to observe local dress codes to ensure that you are not offending your host country's cultural or religious beliefs (particularly in Hindu and Muslim countries). If in doubt, cover up (you'll also avoid sunburn, insect bites and consequential ill-health!).

- Be sensitive to local conditions, laws and customs, asking your local guide if in doubt. Seek advice and their permission before photographing local people, thus showing respect and awareness of another's culture and beliefs. At all times avoid the obvious display of cameras and other expensive items; you'll find more in common with the locals, and avoid becoming the victim of theft.

Leave only friendship behind in the countries you visit. Communicate with local people at all times in a friendly manner, and make an effort to learn a few words and phrases of the local language. Accept local foods or drinks when offered them, and indicate to your hosts your interest in, and support for, their wildlife, landscapes and culture to promote their value both to local people and ultimately their governments.

Source: www.naturetrek.co.uk

National Responsible Tourism Guidelines for South Africa

Economic

- Assess economic impacts as a prerequisite to developing tourism
- Maximise local economic benefits – increasing linkages and reducing leakages
- Ensure communities are involved in and benefit from tourism.

Social responsibility

- Involve the local community in planning and decision making
- Assess social impacts as a prerequisite to developing tourism
- Maintain and encourage social and cultural diversity
- Be sensitive to the host culture.

Environmental

- Assess environmental impacts as a prerequisite to developing tourism
- Use local resources sustainably, avoid waste and over-consumption
- Maintain and encourage natural diversity.

Source: www.icrtourism.org

activity

UNDERSTANDING THE PRINCIPLES

Read through the National Responsible Tourism Guidelines for South Africa above. In small groups, discuss the following:

1 What does the term 'a prerequisite to developing tourism' mean?

2 What is meant by 'linkages' and 'leakages'?

3 What is 'social and cultural diversity'?

4 What do you understand by the term 'over-consumption'?

5 What is 'natural diversity'?

For further information, visit www.icrtourism.org

Topic 2 Impacts, benefits, conservation and respect

Topic 3 — The private, public and voluntary sectors

The development of any tourism facility, service or destination frequently involves the participation of a number of different organisations. In this and the next topic we are going to explore the different types of organisations and agencies involved in tourism development and the reasons for their involvement. Broadly speaking, these can be categorised as:

- Private sector organisations
- Public sector organisations
- Voluntary sector bodies.

Private sector organisations

Private sector enterprises are those organisations that operate primarily to make a profit. Traditionally, the development of tourism has been dominated by the private sector, which has meant that many decisions on development have been based on profit-making objectives. For example, the growth and development of the accommodation and hospitality sector has been almost exclusively carried out by private hotel, restaurant and retail licensing companies. Likewise, the development of the foreign package holiday market has grown predominantly from the activities of private tour operators. There are several different categories of private sector enterprises which are explained below.

Landowners

Since most tourism development requires development land, landowners are often key agents. In many situations, landowners are keen to benefit from the large profits that can be made by selling land to developers. However, there are a number of laws and planning regulations that restrict the use of land for tourism development. Factors that are considered include the effect that development of land may have on the surrounding area and the number of similar developments in the area. For example, in the 1990s there was a rapid increase in the number of farmers wanting to convert large areas of farmland into golf courses. Many such applications were turned down because of similar developments within the region and the problems that would arise if too much farmland was lost to tourism development. Some landowners decide to develop their land for tourism purposes themselves, rather than sell it to developers. The rapid increase in 'farm tourism', for example, is indicative of this trend.

Development companies and consultancies

Development agencies, companies and consultancies are private organisations that initiate, advise or coordinate the development of tourism projects. They will usually rely on the cooperation and contribution of other tourism agents to ensure the success of the project. For example, the development of a multi-facility attraction such as an out-of-town shopping mall – where a wide range of tourist attractions, facilities and services are offered – may be co-ordinated by a development agency who bring together a number of tourism organisations such as catering, retailing, transport, visitor attractions, etc. to provide the actual facilities and services within the development.

Accommodation providers

The hospitality industry is generally rated as the single largest sector of the travel and tourism industry. The provision of accommodation – and food and drink – plays a leading role in much tourism development. For example, a large-scale development such as a conference venue will often require the participation of accommodation providers, such as hotels. Clearly, hospitality is a key component of products such as package holidays. However, other tourism products also rely heavily on hospitality to complement their main product. For example, theme parks such as Alton Towers and the Disney parks derive significant revenue from their accommodation and catering outlets.

Whilst there is a substantial volume of privately owned provision, the accommodation industry is dominated by large multi-national chains that tend to trade in a range of markets. For example, the two organisations below operate in a number of diverse branded markets:

Travel organisations

Travel organisations such as travel agents, tour operators and transport providers are often at the forefront of tourism development – particularly in the development of new destinations and package holidays. However they will work closely with many

public sector bodies in the development phase. For example, the development of a new resort destination will necessitate liaison with the country's government.

Leisure and entertainment organisations

Private leisure and entertainment organisations play a key role in the development of tourism products and services, and can include theatres and cinemas, events, tourist attractions, retailing, sporting activities and spa facilities.

Such organisations may operate independently or form part of a larger, multi-facility. Much of this sector of the industry is dominated by large multi-national companies that operate in a number of leisure and entertainment fields – the Rank Organisation, for example.

Bourne Leisure

Operating brands

- Warner
- Butlins
- Haven and British Holidays – caravan parks

History

Bourne Leisure bought the Rank Holiday Division in 2000 for £700m. This comprised of Haven, Butlins, Oasis and Warner. Bourne sold Oasis and also several of the smaller Haven Parks who now have a total of 35 Haven and British Holidays Parks across the UK.

Warner specialises in short breaks just for adults. It comprises six historic hotels (all Grade I or Grade II listed buildings with formal gardens), four coastal resorts and three character hotels making a total of around 5300 beds.

Source: Haven and British Holidays

Whitbread PLC

Welcome with a smile

Operating brands

- Beefeater
- Brewsters
- Pizza Hut
- Premier Travel Inn
- Brewers Fayre
- Costa
- TGI Friday

History

The holding company, Whitbread Holdings PLC, consists of the Whitbread Hotel Company, Whitbread Restaurants and David Lloyd Leisure. Founded in 1742, Whitbread was traditionally a brewer and pub operator, but it sold its brewing arm to a Belgian company in 2000 and its pubs and bars division the following year.

Whitbread bought 38 Swallow hotels in 2000 as part of its takeover of the Swallow Group. In 2003 it sold 13 Swallow hotels – and the Swallow brand name – and has converted its remaining Swallow hotels to the Marriott and Renaissance brands.

In 2004 Whitbread bought the 132-strong Premier Travel Inn chain of UK budget hotels, including 19 adjoining pub-restaurants.

COSTA *Source: Whitbread Plc*

activity

AGENTS WORKING TOGETHER

We have now looked at the main private sectors agents in tourism development. In small groups, identify a UK-based tourism development project that might include all of these agents, and explain how they might work together on the project. Present your suggestions to the rest of the group.

Public sector organisations

The wide-scale involvement of public sector organisations in the development of tourism has been relatively recent. In 1969, the Development of Tourism Act established the British Tourist Authority and the English, Welsh and Scottish Tourist Boards. This structure no longer exists. It has been replaced by the organisations discussed in the sections below. Since then both central government and local authorities have played an increasingly important role in tourism development, with many other public sector organisations being established.

Local authorities

In 1972, the Local Government Act gave local authorities the power to develop tourist facilities and services and to promote their area as tourist destinations. Many local authorities now have specific tourism departments who take responsibility for development and work closely with local groups and private sector organisations.

activity

YOUR LOCAL AUTHORITY

Find out what tourist facilities and services are provided by your local authority. Compare them with similar privately owned facilities in the area.

National governments

Central government supports many areas of tourism development through the provision of grants and support for specific projects. For example, the government's tourism strategy, 'Tomorrow's Tourism', aims to 'promote the development and uptake of visitor payback schemes to encourage tourists or businesses to contribute (financially or in kind) to local environmental protection and enhancement programmes. It also aims to encourage people to use alternative means of transport by identifying and publicising schemes such as park and ride, integrated ticketing schemes, discounts or other incentives for those arriving by public transport, and free or reduced price local bus or train services.'

The UK government department that has responsibility for government policy on tourism development and related leisure provision is the Department for Culture, Media and Sport (DCMS). Its areas of interest include the arts, sport and recreation, the National Lottery, libraries, museums and galleries, the built heritage – and tourism. The DCMS is responsible for tourism policy and sponsoring the tourism industry in England and for ensuring that tourism is promoted in Great Britain as a whole. The Scottish and Welsh Offices, and the Department for Economic Development (Northern Ireland) are responsible for tourism policy for Scotland, Wales and Northern Ireland respectively. The DCMS has many other areas of responsibility including heritage, museums and the arts which also make a considerable contribution to the development of tourism products and destinations.

National and regional tourist boards

There are four National Tourist Boards – the Welsh Tourist Board, Scottish Tourist Board, Northern Ireland Tourist Board and VisitBritain. Each Tourist Board is responsible for creating and implementing their strategy for tourism development within their country. VisitBritain also has additional responsibilities, based on Britain as a whole, rather than just England.

The Regional Tourist Boards (RTBs) are not government agencies but are funded from membership fees (for example from local authorities and private businesses), and by the National Tourist Boards, the DCMS and Regional Development Agencies (RDAs). The structure and nature of the RTBs are currently being reviewed in line with each region's individual strategy. In some regions, RTBs are working in partnership with the RDAs, whereas in others the role of the RTB is being taken over by the RDA. Alternatively, in some regions the RDAs have formed 'Destination Management Organisations' (or Partnerships) which oversee sub-regional development.

UK regional development agencies

The eight Regional Development Agencies (as well as the London Development Agency) were set up in 1998 under the Regional Development Agencies Act. As non-departmental public bodies, their main role is to be the strategic drivers of economic development within their region. Each RDA has five statutory purposes:

1. To further economic development and regeneration
2. To promote business efficiency, investment and competitiveness
3. To promote employment

Regional Tourist Boards and Destination Management Organisations/ Partnerships

- Tourism South East www.seeda.org.uk
- VisitLondon www.londontouristboard.com
- South West Tourism www.swtourism.co.uk
- East of England Tourist Board www.eetb.org.uk; www.visiteastofengland.com
- North West Tourist Board www.visitnorthwest.com; www.northwesttourism.net
- Heart of England Tourist Board www.visitheartofengland.com
- Northumbria Tourist Board www.visitnorthumbria.com
- Yorkshire Tourist Board www.ytb.org.uk
- Cumbria Tourist Board www.cumbria-the-lake-district.co.uk
- The Mersey Partnership www.visitliverpool.com
- Marketing Manchester www.destinationmanchester.com

- Cheshire & Warrington Tourism www.visit-cheshire.com
- Lancashire & Blackpool Tourist Board www.lancashiretourism.com

Please note that these organisations are evolving and changing over the coming years. To identify recent changes visit: www.culture.gov.uk

4. To enhance development and application of skills relevant to employment
5. To contribute to sustainable development.

The role of the RDAs has a strong focus on working with partners in both the private and public sectors. As such, they are firmly committed to regional tourism development based on responsible and sustainable tourism principles. The budgets of each RDA for the three years up to 2008 are:

RDA	Total allocation (£m)		
	2005–06	2006–07	2007–08
Advantage West Midlands	272	284	291
East of England Dev. Agency	129	134	138
East Midlands Dev. Agency	156	163	167
London Development Agency	373	391	400
North West Development Agency	382	400	409
One North East	240	251	258
South East England Dev. Agency	157	163	167
South West of England Dev. Agency	153	159	164
Yorkshire Forward	295	310	316
Totals	**2,157**	**2,256**	**2,309**

Source: www.consumer.gov

Non-governmental organisations (NGOs)

The Charity Commission defines an NGO as an organisation that:

- has some kind of formal existence
- is established for benevolent or philanthropic purposes, exclusively or primarily for the benefit of the public or a defined section of the public, whether in England and Wales or elsewhere
- does not belong to those who run it, are employed by it or who benefit from it
- is independent of central or local government or their agencies
- is independent from government control, but is not seeking to challenge governments, either as a political party or by a narrow focus on human rights
- is non-profit-making and non-criminal.

Under 'national governments' we looked at the DCMS and, in fact, many of its activities are carried out through non-departmental public bodies, which are funded by the DCMS. Such bodies include:

- Arts Council of England (www.artscouncil.org.uk)
- The British Library (http://portico.Bl.uk)
- The British Museum (www.british-museum.ac.uk)
- British Tourist Authority (www.visitbritain.com)
- Crafts Council (www.craftscouncil.org.uk)
- English Heritage (www.open.gov.uk/heritage/ehehome)
- English Tourist Board (www.visitbritain.com)

ENGLISH HERITAGE

It is our job at English Heritage to make sure that the historic environment of England is properly maintained and cared for. From the first traces of civilisation, to the most significant buildings of the twentieth century, we want every important historic site to get the care and attention it deserves. To protect the historic environment, planning and development must be based on informed decision-making. National policies need to reflect local issues, and local solutions must take account of national perspectives.

Designation

We identify sites, buildings and landscapes of special national and local significance.

Statutory advice

We advise the local authority on any implications of planning applications, and publish an annual Buildings at Risk Register, with information on Grade I and II* listed buildings and scheduled ancient monuments, which are 'at risk' from neglect.

Grants

We distribute grants to the owners of individual historic buildings. These funds are targeted at cases of real need, and they have ensured the survival of many of the most significant historic buildings and monuments in England.

Source: www.english-heritage.org.uk

- Millennium Commission (www.millennium. gov.uk)
- National Lottery Charities Board (www.nlcb.org.uk)
- Royal Commission on Historical Manuscripts (www.hmc.gov.uk)
- Royal Commission on the Historical Monuments of England (www.rchme.gov.uk)
- Sport England (www.sportengland.org)

There are many more examples of NGOs which are actively involved in responsible tourism development. One such organisation is English Heritage, as outlined above.

Voluntary sector bodies

Clearly, all tourism development has the potential to have both positive and negative effects on the community, and it is therefore vital that local communities are consulted and involved in the process of development. Whilst much of this involvement may be based on individual opinions and contributions there are an increasing number of community groups, pressure groups and charities involved in tourism development, such as the Ramblers' Association, the National Trust and Tourism Concern.

Community groups

Community groups are voluntary sector bodies that have formed with the objective of influencing or contributing towards specific tourism issues. They are differentiated from pressure groups in that they are localised, and therefore concerned with issues that affect a particular community. For example, many areas have tourism forum groups such as Stratford-upon-Avon's Residents' Week and the Cambridge Residents' Forum. In other areas there are partnerships between a number of different community groups to address tourism issues, such as the Canterbury City Centre Initiative and the Windsor and Maidenhead Visitor Management Strategy Partnership.

Pressure groups

Pressure groups exist to influence development plans and strategies. Many, such as Tourism Concern and VSO, are concerned with the negative impacts that tourism development can have on the environment. For example, many seaside resorts have local pressure groups that campaign for measures to minimise the harmful effects that tourism can have on beaches and bathing waters. Likewise plans for new large-scale tourist attractions can often result in pressure groups

Tourism Concern

Tourism Concern has a wide range of exciting and innovative projects. We work with communities in destination countries to reduce social and environmental problems connected to tourism and with the out-going tourism industry in the UK to find ways of improving tourism so that local benefits are increased.

Tourism for communities

Central to Tourism Concern's work is the fact that tourism often causes or exacerbates poverty. This is something that few people have fully realised, but which has received more credence over the last few years. Agencies working overseas are also increasingly finding that tourism development impacts on the lives of communities they work with, in just the same way as other multinational industries might, such as oil and mining companies.

Tourism Concern has been working since 1989 to raise awareness of the negative impacts of tourism – economic, cultural, environment and social. Advocacy is a major part of our work, and time and again the message from our Southern (Developing World) partners is the same: 'We want tourists, but at the moment we don't benefit from them'. Communities often find that they have tourism imposed on them by governments, foreign developers and tourism businesses; that there is little linkage between tourism (especially at a mass scale) and local industry, such as agriculture; that their land and natural resources are frequently co-opted, often illegally; and that their cultural traditions are appropriated and commercialised.

Our links with communities and agencies working in developing countries show that there is great concern that the trend in tourism is towards greater control by multinationals, more all-inclusive tourism which excludes local people and businesses, and greater numbers. The consequences of such trends could prove disastrous for local people.

Public awareness

We work hard to raise awareness amongst the public about tourism's impacts. We are frequently quoted in the media, and our website carries considerable information and is well used.

Source: © Tourism Concern www.tourismconcern.org.uk.

forming who are concerned at the effects that such a development might have on the visual appeal of an area.

Tourism Concern has been at the forefront of encouraging and promoting responsible tourism initiatives. Below is a brief outline of some of their activities. For more information on the projects that they are involved in, visit www.tourismconcern.org.uk.

Registered charities

In the UK, charities are regulated by the Charity Commission, which is a government agency. They explain what charities are:

'Charity is the short form for charitable trust, a charitable foundation, or a corporation set up entirely for charitable purposes. These are set up for specific causes, such as curing diseases; providing goods or services for people or areas that lack them; nature conservation; and many others. In some countries (including the UK, Canada, Australia, and the United States) a charitable organisation needs, by law, to register with the government. This is to reduce the possibilities of fraud and increase the opportunities for charities to receive tax breaks.'

It should be stressed that many of the pressure groups, such as Tourism Concern, are also charities. A wide range of charities exist, whose work influences responsible tourism development. One of the largest is the National Trust. This charity was set up in 1895 amidst growing concerns about the potential impacts of industrialisation and uncontrolled development. The main aim of the trust was to acquire and protect threatened buildings, and areas of countryside and coastline. They are currently guardians of over 200 historic buildings, most of which are open to visitors, as well as large areas of countryside and coastline. The trust is mainly funded through membership and entrance fees. One unique feature of the National Trust is that it has the statutory right to declare land 'inalienable'. This means that it cannot be sold against the wishes of the trust.

activity

EFFECTS OF A CAMPAIGN

Visit the Tourism Concern website (www tourismconcern.org.uk) and select one of their current campaigns. Analyse how this campaign may affect other tourism development agents in the private, public and voluntary sectors.

Topic 3 The private, public and voluntary sectors

Reasons for involvement and objectives

In the last topic we explored the range of organisations and agencies involved in tourism development. We are now going to look at the reasons why they become involved and what their objectives are likely to be. We will look first at the reasons for involvement of:

- Private sector organisations
- Public sector organisations
- Voluntary sector bodies.

Then we will consider the objectives that may be identified by each, such as:

- Economic objectives
- Environmental objectives
- Socio-cultural objectives
- Political objectives.

The reasons for involvement of private sector organisations

As we discussed in the last topic, private sector organisations are primarily commercial enterprises and therefore seek to make a profit from their products and services. As such, they are constantly looking for areas in which they can expand and develop. Large-scale tourism development projects frequently attract a great deal of interest from private sector organisations who are keen to be involved in new initiatives and reach new markets.

Whilst concern for the environment is an issue most often associated with the public and voluntary sectors, there is increasing pressure on private sector organisations to demonstrate their commitment to responsible tourism development. From a business perspective, this is good public relations since it enhances the image and reputation of the company, which in turn will usually result in increased sales. For example, Center Parcs use their commitment to the environment as a strong selling point in their sales literature as shown on the right.

Center Parcs' commitment to the environment

There's a lovely harmony between the ecology of Center Parcs and all the ways you can unwind in our 400 acres of woodland. You can't help relaxing in the natural forest setting. The environment that sustains such a rich diversity of flora and fauna is also a life force for our guests. Our beautiful, natural setting yields activities that fulfil all kinds of individual needs, whether it's sailing on the lake, getting quietly close to nature or taking up a new physical challenge.

Source: www.centerparcs.co.uk

The reasons for involvement of public sector organisations

Public sector organisations are largely non-commercial. However, their involvement in tourism development frequently aims to maximise the economic contribution of tourism locally and nationally in order to enhance the community experience. For example, as we discussed in the previous topic, regional tourist boards and Regional Development Agencies seek to initiate projects and development that will generate wealth and improve the environment for local communities through tourism.

The reasons for involvement of voluntary sector bodies

Voluntary bodies such as Tourism Concern, the National Trust and the World Wide Fund for Nature are usually involved in tourism development because of their concern for and commitment to responsible tourism principles. Much of their involvement will also be motivated by the desire to raise awareness of issues relating to tourism and educate people to take a more responsible approach. Whilst non-profit making, many will also seek to raise funds in order to finance their activities. For example, the National Trust's main motivation may be the preservation of our heritage but they also carry out commercial activities such as entrance fees, catering outlets and souvenir shops in order to fund their main activities.

Economic objectives

Where a range of agents are involved in a tourism development project it is likely that each will have specific and, possibly, different objectives. One of the main objectives of tourism development is often based on economic gains, particularly in the private sector. This does not simply mean making a profit for the tourism providers as there can frequently be economic objectives designed to benefit the community as a whole, as explained below.

To create employment

For many tourism development initiatives, a key objective will be to create more jobs within an area. This is particularly true in areas where traditional industries have declined, resulting in rising unemployment. For example, tourism regeneration projects have been developed in many former industrial cities and towns to replace the jobs lost through failing industry. Public sector organisations such as local authorities are especially likely to view employment creation as one of their main objectives when developing tourism. In many of the less affluent overseas destinations, employment creation will be a key objective of tourism development. Responsible developers will look at ways in which local skills can be utilised and encouraged to provide increased employment opportunities through providing for the tourism trade.

To increase foreign currency earnings

A further objective of many tourism development initiatives is to increase the level of foreign currency earnings by attracting foreign tourists to an area who then spend money on local products and services.

To maximise tourist contributions to the economic multiplier effect

The economic multiplier effect refers to the situation where original money spent on tourism products is then spent again on other goods and services. For example, part of the money that a visitor pays for hotel accommodation will go to staff in terms of their wages; this money is then spent on other goods, for example, in shops. In turn the money from the shops is then paid to retail staff as wages, which they then spend on other goods, and so on. In other words the original amount of money paid to the hotel can multiply many times. Maximising the multiplier effect is often one of the main objectives of tourism development agents, particularly in the public sector.

activity

DIFFERENT ECONOMIC OBJECTIVES?

A local council is working in partnership with a national hotel chain who have agreed to develop a 5-star hotel adjacent to the council's conference centre. Discuss what the economic objectives of each agent might be.

Environmental objectives

One of the key issues that arises with all tourism development is the potential effects that such development may have on the environment. This is because tourism is inextricably linked with the environment in which it is located. Some of the concerns are global issues such as the impact on the ozone layer following a rapid increase in air travel, or the problems of pollution associated with increased road and water transport. Other issues may be more localised such as erosion and overcrowding in popular countryside areas or the loss of natural landscapes due to building development. Growing awareness of the importance of preserving and improving the environment has led to many agents embracing the principles of sustainable tourism and incorporating them into their development objectives.

Apart from meeting their obvious environmental responsibilities, tourism providers also frequently find that planning applications meet with a more favourable response if they are able to show how the environment will be improved by a specific tourism development.

To educate locals and tourists

Many resort destinations have development strategies that aim to educate locals and tourists about ways in which they can help to preserve the environment. For example, a large number of seaside resorts display signs on beaches, covering issues such as the removal of litter and the banning of dogs from the sands.

 The growing concerns about protecting the environment have become so strong in recent years that some tourism development has been based on the prime objective of educating people about environmental issues through a tourist attraction. For example the National Parks offer a range of educational activities and visitor centres.

To preserve wildlife habitats

Tourism development can have serious effects on an area's wildlife, and many pressure groups have been established to safeguard the natural habitat of a wide range of wildlife species (habitat preservation). One of the most obvious examples of the potential effects on wildlife is the building of new attractions or facilities that disrupt or destroy the natural habitat of local wildlife. However, there are many more, less obvious, potential effects, such as the impact of an increase in visitor numbers, increased litter, pollution, noise, etc. Agents involved in new developments are required to state objectives that show that they have considered any negative impacts on wildlife habitats and sought to minimise them.

To facilitate regeneration

Regeneration refers to the process of improving and boosting a declining area's economy and environment through planned development.

Many agents involved in tourism development identify specific objectives that will encourage regeneration and benefit the local community. In areas that have become rundown there is the obvious objective of improving the physical environment for residents. This may involve eliminating unattractive buildings and wasteland or restoring them to their past glory.

To encourage conservation

In the last topic we looked at agents such as the National Trust and English Heritage. Such organisations will have conservation of the environment and buildings at the forefront of their development objectives. Private sector organisations will also frequently need to incorporate conservation into their development objectives – particularly where they are developing land or changing the nature and use of buildings.

To make environmental improvements

Many tourism development initiatives will identify environmental improvements as one of their main objectives. This might include the renovation or regeneration of rundown areas or buildings resulting in an improved environment with better facilities and services. Such improvements may benefit local people and wildlife as well as tourists.

Socio-cultural objectives

As we have already discussed, most tourism development is closely linked to the location in which it takes place. Each location will have its specific resident population with their own characteristics and culture. In addition, the local population will have a range of opinions on the desirability of tourism development and the extent to which it will improve or hinder the local culture and social make-up of the area. When planning tourism development, responsible providers will consider the socio-cultural impacts of their initiative and incorporate such concerns into their objectives. The issues that they may consider are detailed below.

To promote cultural understanding between hosts and tourists

There are often significant differences between the cultures of tourists and the host population, and responsible tourism development agents seek to promote an understanding between these cultures. There has been a rapid increase in recent years in tourism development agents embracing objectives that actively seek to promote cultural understanding. For example, many of the responsible tour operators such as Naturetrek state such objectives as part of their strategy.

To encourage positive host–tourist interactions

Encouraging positive host–tourist interactions takes the promotion of cultural understanding one stage further. It requires the tourism provider to ensure not only that the local culture is understood by visitors but also that they are actively involved with the local community and interacting on an equal basis. The case study about Tourism Concern's campaign for the mountain porters on page 17 demonstrates the ways in which some agents focus on this particular area.

To improve the local people's quality of life

Frequently, tourism development can create considerable improvements in the quality of life for local people. As well as improvements in the physical environment, tourism development also frequently provides a wider range of community facilities for locals. For example, populations in seaside resorts benefit all year round from the facilities and attractions that are primarily provided for visitors during the tourist season.

Political objectives

We have already discussed how public sector organisations such as local and central government are key agents in the development of tourism. Their involvement and support is often based on political objectives, such as the two below.

To enhance the image of an area

Agents such as local authorities may put the enhancement of their area's image at the forefront of their objectives for tourism development. The investment in new facilities and the regeneration of rundown areas – coupled with a marketing strategy that informs the public of the improvements – can all help to enhance the image of an area. Image enhancement can not only attract more tourists to the area, but also improve the environment and quality of life for the local population. For example, a better image will often result in increased outside investment in an area and the subsequent improvement of facilities and services, better employment prospects and increased prosperity.

To create a regional or national identity

Various agents in tourism development may aim to create specific identities. This may be on a national scale such as the creation of a 'positive national image of the UK as a tourist destination' that Visit Britain sets as one of its key objectives. Similarly, Regional

Tourist Boards and RDAs aim to create regional identities, and local authorities will strive to establish a unique identity for their area. This is adventure travel company Exodus' policy:

Responsible tourism policy

- We use locally owned and run accommodation by preference.
- We will aim, where possible, to purchase our equipment and food from local sources.
- We support local income generation and small business enterprises by supporting locally owned shops and restaurants, and using local guide services.
- We encourage clients through our leaders, the literature and presentations to act in a responsible way and with an insight and understanding of the host destination.
- We will work together with our business partners in the host destinations to implement the highest standards, and where necessary work out an agenda on how these standards can be met.
- We will take into consideration economic, environmental and cultural issues when looking at new destinations.
- We will aim to ensure that our type and scale of tourism is appropriate to local conditions, and operate within the limits set by local appropriate infrastructure and carrying capacity.
- We aim to minimise water and atmospheric pollution from tourism developments.
- We aim to achieve zero litter policies.
- We aim to integrate environmental considerations into all economic considerations.
- We will provide regular and ongoing training, in the principles and practices of responsible tourism, both to our staff in the office and those employed out of the office.
- We will try to ensure that foreign operators and guides are not used in preference to local operators and guides.
- We will provide financial support for local economic and environmental projects that will benefit the local communities, thereby actively encouraging local community involvement in tourism projects.

Source: www.exodus.co.uk

activity

IDENTIFYING OBJECTIVES

Read through the responsible tourism policy of the tour operator Exodus Travel, on the right.

1 In pairs, identify examples of: economic objectives, environmental objectives, socio-cultural objectives, and political objectives.

2 Discuss what other tourism agents Exodus might work with to achieve their objectives.

3 Analyse ways in which the objectives of Exodus Travel might conflict with other development agents that they work with.

The economic impacts of tourism development

Any form of tourism development will have a wide range of impacts. These can be positive – bringing benefits for people and destinations, or they can be negative – causing actual harm. Broadly speaking, tourism development impacts can be categorised as being economic, environmental or socio-cultural. This topic explores economic impacts, starting with the positive impacts:

- **Increased domestic income and foreign currency earnings**
- **Benefits of the multiplier effect**
- **Increased employment opportunities**
- **Improved infrastructure.**

We then go on to explore some negative economic impacts:

- **Leakage**
- **Changes to traditional employment**
- **Seasonal employment**
- **Increased living costs.**

Positive economic impacts

There is no doubt that the tourism industry generates huge sums of money (see below) and creates significant financial benefits for host communities, destinations and countries. This is particularly true in the poorer developing countries where tourism development can offer a substantial increase in the country's wealth and standard of living. Let's look at some of the ways in which responsible tourism development has a positive economic impact.

According to the World Travel and Tourism Council, 698 million people travelled to a foreign country in 2000, spending more US$ 478 billion. International tourism receipts combined with passenger transport currently total more than US$ 575 billion – making tourism the world's number one export earner, ahead of automotive products, chemicals, petroleum and food.

Source: WTTC

Increased domestic income and foreign currency earnings

Earnings in foreign currency from overseas visitors help to generate income for the host country as well as encouraging overseas organisations to invest. In

addition, the import and export of goods related to tourism also generate income.

An important indicator of the role of international tourism is its generation of foreign exchange earnings. Tourism is one of the top five export categories for as many as 83% of countries, and is a main source of foreign exchange earnings for at least 38% of countries.

Source: World Tourism Organization

In addition to foreign currency earnings, domestic spending (i.e. money spent by tourists within their own country) is equally important. Ideally, tourism development will aim to attract foreign tourists whilst also encouraging residents to take their holiday within their own country. The development of Benidorm in Spain is a good example of how both domestic and foreign markets can be targeted. Having experienced a decline in British holidaymakers in the early 1990s, the Spanish authorities undertook a process of development with the objective of increasing both foreign and domestic spending. This included the regeneration of rundown areas, up-grading of accommodation and a beach-cleaning initiative. Whilst British visitors to Benidorm have now risen again, more than 40% of the total visitors are Spanish tourists.

Benidorm

Benefits of the economic multiplier effect

We discussed the economic multiplier effect in the last topic. Generally, the multiplier effect has a positive economic impact on the host community and country if the money spent largely stays within the community or country (we will look at examples of how this might not happen under 'leakage' on page 32). Increased investment in an area and money coming in through tourist revenue means that local tourism providers will profit and employment opportunities increase. In turn this results in the host community having more disposable income to spend on local goods and services or to re-invest in new developments and improvements.

Many successful regeneration projects have witnessed the benefits of the multiplier effect. Torquay, for example, realised that its local economy was suffering as the traditional seaside holiday market declined, and refocused on developing the conference market. Local hotels, attractions, transport and entertainment providers adapted their products to suit the needs of this new market, and the whole local economy benefited.

Increased employment opportunities

The growth of the tourism industry has witnessed the rapid expansion of job opportunities within its range of sectors. Many of these opportunities are in areas that we would traditionally associate with tourism such as the hospitality industry, transport and tour operations. However, there are many more in ancillary industries that provide the products and services needed by the tourism industry, such as transport, construction and retailing. A further result of this expansion of job opportunities has been the growth of training courses and qualifications that are now available to those wishing to follow a specific career within travel and tourism. Whether it is tour guide, resort rep, cabin crew, call centre operative, travel agency adviser or customer service adviser, there are now a wide range of qualifications available.

Improved infrastructure

By 'infrastructure' we mean the framework of basic services and facilities that a community or area relies upon to function effectively. This framework would include systems for transport, energy, communication, waste and water. Large-scale tourism development frequently requires improvements in the existing infrastructure to meet the needs of increasing visitor numbers. For example, improvements to roads and public transport connections or improved water and sewage treatment. Such improvements do not only benefit the visitor but also provided a better environment and services for the host community.

The North Moors National Park Authority and their Developing Assets of Protected Areas scheme (DAPA) – Responsible Tourism award-winner 2004

DAPA has facilitated an effective link between the local rural economy and sustainable environmental management by encouraging cooperation among local businesses to work together and strengthen their economic position in ways that have a positive effect on conservation and the environment.

Examples:

- Formation of a cooperative of local charcoal burners, encouraging sustainable woodland management and longer-term development, and research with Leeds University into commercial uses for charcoal fires in treatments for air and water pollution.
- Supporting trials to grow native edible mushrooms in local woodland areas to provide an economic output from low-value timber whilst encouraging woodland management and increased biodiversity.
- Local Origin Seed Production – encouraging diversification opportunities for local farmers and securing the conservation of local grass and wildflower species.
- Formation of a cooperative of organic farmers to support and develop awareness of organic farming and marketing of their organic produce.

Source: Online travel agency www.responsibletravel.com

Negative economic impacts

Whilst tourism can generate many positive economic impacts it can also create negative effects. Such impacts are often felt more strongly in the poorer developing resorts. Let's look at some of these impacts and the reasons why they occur.

Leakage

One of the major concerns about income generation from tourism is 'leakage'. This refers to the situation where most of the income generated does not stay in the local economy but boosts profits for foreign airlines, tour operators, etc. Leakage has been identified as a particular problem in many less developed countries that have developed as tourist destinations. The problems associated with leakage have not been helped by the rapid growth in all-inclusive holidays where customers pay a single price for a holiday that includes all accommodation, facilities, food, drinks and often sporting activities.

A study of tourism 'leakage' in Thailand estimated that 70% of all money spent by tourists ended up leaving Thailand (via foreign-owned tour operators, airlines, hotels, imported drinks and food, etc.). Estimates for other less developed countries range from 80% in the Caribbean to 40% in India (*Source: Sustainable Living*).

Changes to traditional employment and the problem of seasonal employment

We have already identified increasing employment opportunities as a positive benefit, but one potential negative impact is the loss of traditional employment opportunities. For example, developments in rural areas can often encourage local people to leave traditional jobs such as farming to follow careers in tourism. When this happens on a large scale the end result can be the loss of traditional skills and a skills shortage in local areas of employment. In addition to this, much of the employment in tourism is seasonal. This may result in increased employment opportunities only being available for limited times during the year – with widespread unemployment during low season.

Increased living costs

A further negative impact that some tourism development can have is in increasing the local cost of living. This is a particular problem in poorer countries where the local population has a relatively low income. The development of such a country as a tourist destination will often result in prices rising – simply because visiting foreign tourists are wealthier

Tourism leakage in Bali

The island of Bali, Indonesia, always has been an enchanting place for foreigners. However, Bali's tourism development occurred quickly and without proper planning. The government wanted to make Bali the 'showcase' of Indonesia and to serve as the model of future tourism development for the rest of the country. But, instead of attracting the well-heeled to luxury hotels and resorts, the island drew many young and budget-conscious travellers, eager to see more of the island than just resort facilities. Consequently, the tourist industry in Bali unintentionally found itself catering for two types of tourism: the 'package-tour group high-spending tourists' on the one hand, and 'individual low-spending tourists' on the other. Although locally owned tourist facilities sprung up all over Bali to cater for the budget travellers, the real money was elsewhere. The big, luxury resorts that were pampering the upper-scale tourists were owned by the big multinationals, and not much of their money stayed on the island.

Source (adapted):www.american.edu

and can afford to pay more for products and services. Of course, it also means that the local population is faced with higher prices which they may not be able to afford. Local property and land prices can also experience a dramatic increase following tourism development. Prime areas of land in developing tourist resorts will often become valuable development land making it too expensive for local buyers. Likewise, house and property prices can increase as tourism developers look for premises to convert or use.

Like other countries, Thailand has promoted tourism as a major source of national income. However, tourism has had some destructive effects, not only at a national but also at a local level. Having suffered from uncontrolled tourism, Thailand is now searching for less destructive approaches.

One of the most intriguing sustainable tourism themes is rural tourism, which has lately become very popular. Although tourism has brought Thailand benefits – such as foreign exchange, employment, higher government revenues and the transformation of agriculture into a modern service industry – it has been a two-edged sword, which has damaged many indigenous societies. The economic benefits have brought prosperity mainly to urban communities and entreprenuers. The rate of economic return to rural communities has been low.

- Facilities such as resorts, hotels and tour companies belong mainly to investors from cities – who take most of the profits.

- Food, drink and other daily necessities used by tourists are normally imported from outside, not produced locally.

- Revenues in the form of taxes and fees do not go directly to the rural communities, but return to the central government.

- Local labour is employed only at a low level. Employment opportunities for local people are thus very limited.

- Over the past ten years, the development of local handicrafts and agriculture in rural areas have not benefited much from the multiplier effect, because of the weak linkage between tourism and local production.

Poorly planned tourism can mean that villages are invaded by foreign visitors with different values, disrupting rural culture. A decline in participation in rural traditional and cultural practices follows. Traditional houses are replaced by modern buildings, as the local culture is eroded. The agriculture which was the basis of traditional life is replaced by, and becomes secondary to, tourism. Coconut cultivation in Koh Samui, a popular tourist island in the south of Thailand, and traditional farming practices in Ayutthaya, a well-known historic capital, have both decreased in recent years.

The higher standards of living in urban tourist destinations have caused emigration from nearby rural neighbors, resulting in changes in the demographic structure and possible culture shock. Furthermore, employment in tourism can have a negative social impact. The younger generation may gain prestige that rivals that of their elders as they gain experience, jobs and money from tourism.

Though there are various training courses organised by universities, the number of personnel with specific skills such as the interpretation of nature, local culture, history and archeology, is still limited. In particular, local authorities do not have staff experienced in tourism management and development.

Although a large amount of funding is needed to develop rural tourism, only a limited budget is given because funding is determined by the size of the local population. As a result, essential developments such as human resource management, enforcement of regulations, building of physical structures, and land use management are not being implemented efficiently.

Source: www.fftc.agnet.org

activity

ECONOMIC IMPACTS IN THAILAND

Prepare a 5-minute presentation on the economic impacts of tourism in Thailand, describing how the various agents involved in Thailand's tourism are responsible for these impacts.

The environmental impacts of tourism development

This topic looks at the key positive and negative environmental impacts of tourism development. You will know from Topic 1, and the discussion of green and eco-tourism, that concern for the environment is high amongst many of the agents involved in tourism development. Issues that constitute positive impacts include:

- **Education for tourists and locals**
- **Improved assets**   **Landscaping**
- **Conservation and habitat preservation**
- **Regeneration of derelict areas.**

Negative environmental impacts may include:

- **Traffic congestion**   **Erosion of land**
- **Loss of natural habitats**
- **Decreasing biodiversity**
- **Pollution.**

Positive environmental impacts

As we have already discussed, responsible and effective management of tourism development can have a positive impact on the environment. For example, the landscaping of areas of wasteland into countryside attractions and outdoor centres, such as the Garden Festival projects in the 1980s and early 1990s,has often created an environment that is better than the original area. With the support of various conservation groups, many of these areas have been able to create entirely new habitats for wildlife and plants that did not previously exist.

Education for tourists and locals

Responsible tourism development can help to raise the public's awareness of environmental issues through education or simply bringing them into contact with specific aspects of the environment. In addition, the agents involved in tourism development can help by ensuring that customers realise the environmental consequences of their actions. At its best this will help to make people more environmentally concerned and form behaviour that actively protects the environment, as the case study from the Sumatran orang-utan conservation programme, right, shows.

The orang-utan viewing centre: awareness raising and alternative employment

Observing wild and semi-wild orang-utans in their natural habitat is a significant environmental education opportunity for large numbers of domestic visitors. To enhance this education experience, the existing station at Bohorok in North Sumatra (Indonesia) is to be transformed from a rehabilitation centre into an orang-utan viewing centre, thus offering another, crucial contribution to the sustainable conservation of the rainforest ecosystem. By developing ecotourism for orang-utan viewing under the new project, all visitors will gain a rewarding personal experience from orang-utans, wildlife and the rainforest ecosystem in general. This will increase their awareness of the importance of rainforest conservation. Moreover, tourism will continue to provide a major source of income for the local population, thus promoting sustainable forest utilisation as a genuine alternative to timber exploitation and the poaching and trade of wildlife.

Source: Sumatran orang-utan conservation programme

Find out more at www.sumatraorangutan.org

Improved assets

In the last topic we discussed how a positive economic impact of tourism was the increase in revenue and earnings. This can have a knock-on effect on the environment if some of the earnings are used to improve assets and conserve the environment. Voluntary groups are particularly active in this area, raising money from visitors and using it for conservation projects. However, private organisations also participate in using funds to improve assets, as the extract below shows.

Contributing to the Orang-utan Foundation

The tour operator Discovery Initiatives, which is a member of the Tour Operators Initiative for Sustainable Tourism Development, makes an annual financial contribution to the Orang-utan Foundation of some US$ 45,000. The money is earned from only five tour groups of ten people each visiting the Tanjing Putting National Park in Central Kalimantan. The park is under huge pressures from deforestation and river pollution from unrestricted gold mining. This money directly funds park staff and rangers, rehabilitation efforts for young orang-utans, and the care centre. It provides almost the only economic support for saving this park, where the official park fees are only the equivalent of 12 pence a day.

Source: www.uneptie.org

In many destinations, governments are also heavily involved in using money from tourism to improve assets – often in the form of a specific 'tourism tax' that is then used to develop tourism responsibly. For example:

* The Seychelles in the Indian Ocean is introducing a US$ 90 tax on travellers entering the Seychelles. Revenue will be used to preserve the environment and improve tourism facilities. (UNEP)

* In West Virginia (USA) a white-water rafting tax is collected from everyone who participates in a commercial rafting trip. The fee goes toward studying the environmental impacts of rafting. In addition, the rafting companies participate in several river clean-up days each year. (EPA)

* In Belize, a US$ 3.75 departure tax goes directly to the Protected Area Conservation Trust, a Belizean fund dedicated to the conservation of the barrier reef and rainforest. (The International Ecotourism Society)

Source: www.uneptie.org

Landscaping

Landscaping refers to the process of laying out grounds, plants and trees in a way that produces a pleasant and attractive effect. Many destinations such as areas of outstanding natural beauty are already attractive and in little need of formal landscaping. However, derelict and rundown regions of countryside and urban areas can frequently benefit hugely from tourism development that involves landscaping. Many of the traditional industrialised cities such as Leeds, Sheffield and Newcastle have seen substantial landscaping projects, with areas of the city transformed into parks and gardens or recreational areas. Even areas that we usually think of as beautiful already can benefit from some landscaping, as the case study below shows.

Restoring Barton Broad

Barton Broad, on the River Ant, is the second largest of the broads. Owned by the Norfolk Wildlife Trust, the whole area is also a National Nature Reserve, made up of the broad and the surrounding reed beds, fen, marshes and swamp woodland. In fact, it is so important for wildlife that it has a string of special protection measures, both national and international.

The restoration of the broad, as part of a major wetland complex, is a feat of national and international significance for nature conservation. The project draws together years of trials of water-quality restoration techniques. These include suction dredging to remove 300,000 cubic metres of nutrient-rich mud from the broad's bed, and biomanipulation, the temporary removal of fish to help balance the ecology of the water. The reed swamp fringe of the broad is being restored, and Pleasure Hill, a small island in the broad, which had almost disappeared by the mid-1990s, has been rebuilt and planted with reed.

Broads Authority staff and volunteers have built a boardwalk through the thick swamp woodland at the south end of the broad, with a viewpoint looking out over the water. After an absence lasting decades, otters are now re-colonising Barton Broad. The improvements to habitats are clearly already helping the return of the characteristic wetland wildlife.

Source: www.broads-authority.gov.uk

Conservation and habitat preservation

Responsible tourism development can play an important role in conservation and the preservation of natural habitats. Many organisations such as the National Trust, RSPB and the National Parks Authority are committed to ensuring that conservation and habitat preservation is at the forefront of their activities. Newly developing overseas destinations are also embracing sound environmental principles by actively seeking to protect and enhance indigenous plant and animal life.

A resort in the Dominican Republic (see below) offers an example of how luxury tourism development and conservation can be combined.

Tourism and conservation in the Dominican Republic

Grupo Punta Cana, a high-end resort, was established with the goal of catering to luxury-class tourists while respecting the natural habitat of Punta Cana. The developers have set aside 10,000 hectares of land as a nature reserve and native fruit tree garden. The Punta Cana Nature Reserve includes 11 freshwater springs surrounded by a subtropical forest where many species of unusual Caribbean flora and fauna live in their natural state. Guests can explore a 'nature path' leading from the beach through mangroves, lagoons of freshwater springs and dozens of species of Caribbean bird and plant life. The Punta Cana Ecological Foundation has begun reforesting some parts of the reserve that had been stripped of their native mahogany and other trees in the past. Other environmentally protective policies have been put into effect at the resort, such as programmes to protect the offshore barrier reefs and the recycling of wastewater for use in irrigating the grounds. The fairways of the resort's new golf course were planted with a hybrid grass that can be irrigated with sea water The grass also requires less than half the usual amounts of fertiliser and pesticides.

Source: www.uneptie.org

Regeneration of derelict areas

Over the last two decades, the regeneration of derelict areas has been one of the main focuses of many public sector bodies, such as RDAs and national and regional government. Frequently, this has meant working in partnership with the private and voluntary sectors to ensure that such development is responsible and sustainable. There are many instances of regeneration projects that have resulted in considerable improvements in the environment, with rundown areas and buildings being restored to their former state. In some initiatives, such areas and properties are actually improved upon, with further assets being developed.

Negative environmental impacts

When badly managed, tourism development can have serious negative impacts on the environment. One of the key problems is that tourists frequently travel long distances to get to tourist attractions or destinations. Advances in transport, coupled with increasing car ownership, has meant that we can now travel further and faster then ever before, which has opened a wide range of tourism options. For example, many people would think nothing of driving for two hours to visit a theme park for the day or getting on a flight for a weekend in Paris. However, all forms of transport, including walking, have a negative impact on the environment.

Traffic congestion

Traffic congestion from cars and coaches is a problem in areas that cannot handle a large volume of traffic, such as small narrow streets in historic towns or minor roads in rural areas. At peak periods this can lead to disruption for local road users, damage to roads and verges, visual intrusion of traffic jams and an increase in traffic-related accidents.

Damage to coral reefs

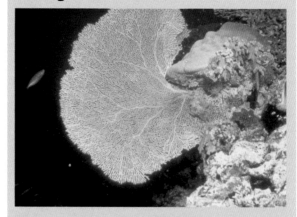

There are 109 countries with coral reefs. In 90 of them reefs are being damaged by cruise ship anchors and sewage, by tourists breaking off chunks of coral, and by commercial harvesting for sale to tourists. One study of a cruise ship anchor dropped in a coral reef for one day found an area about half the size of a football field completely destroyed, and half again as much covered by rubble that died later. It was estimated that coral recovery would take fifty years.

Source: Ocean Planet

Erosion of land

Large increases in visitor numbers can often impact on the environment by eroding land. For example, visitors to rural areas such as the Lake District have worn away paths – and caused even more damage to land when they have strayed from the designated pathways. Constructing new facilities in coastal locations can erode sand dunes and beaches. Likewise, the rise in popularity of winter sports holidays has caused large areas of forest to be cleared to enable the construction of accommodation. Ecosystems such as coral reefs are particularly fragile, and can be severely damaged through irresponsible tourism development (see box below, left).

The World Wildlife Fund's advice to travellers

- Boats and jet-skis create noise and chemical pollution which is disturbing to wildlife – don't keep the engine running unnecessarily.

- If you are sailing, surfing or windsurfing keep a distance of at least 100m from seal-resting and bird-nesting sites to avoid disturbing them.

- Only participate in hunting or fishing when it can be shown to be part of an effective management plan.

- When rock pooling, don't disturb animals, especially limpets as they can die if dislodged from the rock.

- Discard hooks, nets, lines and weights responsibly as they are a potential threat to wildlife.

- Don't damage or collect marine life when diving. A carelessly kicked fin can easily break coral that has taken 50 years to grow.

- Be careful what you choose to bring home as a holiday souvenir. Many species – from coral and conch shells to elephants and alligators – are endangered because they are killed for curios or souvenirs. It is illegal to import about 800 species into the UK, and over 25,000 more require a special licence.

- Don't be tempted to touch wildlife and disturb habitats – whether on land, at the coast or under water.

- Take all rubbish home from the beach – turtles are often killed by plastic bags they've mistaken for jellyfish, and many items take years to degrade as well as being dangerous.

Source: www.wwf.org

Loss of natural habitats

The construction of new tourist facilities can have a profound effect on ecosystems, often resulting in the loss of natural habitats of indigenous animal and plant life. In addition, large volumes of visitors can disturb the natural life of animals and result in them behaving differently. For example, Kenyan safaris with their accompanying noise and transport puts huge stress on the animals being observed. In some cases this has resulted in the animals failing to mate or abandoning their offspring. Some of the issues surrounding the negative impact that visitors can have on animals' natural habitat are outlined by the World Wild Fund for Nature's advice to travellers (see left).

Decreasing biodiversity

Friends of the Earth define biodiversity as

> 'the total web of all living things and ecosystems. Everything from whales to warblers and forests to coral reefs. It also includes the genetic variety within a species as well between species. It is the richness of life on Earth.'

Damaging biological diversity can have a serious negative impact on the environment. For example:

- It threatens our food supplies, our opportunities for recreation and tourism, and our sources of wood, medicines and energy.

- It interferes with essential ecological functions such as species balance, soil formation, and greenhouse gas absorption.

- It reduces the productivity of ecosystems, thereby shrinking nature's basket of goods and services, from which we constantly draw.

- It destabilises ecosystems and weakens their ability to deal with natural disasters such as floods, droughts, and hurricanes, and with human-caused stresses, such as pollution and climate change.

Irresponsible tourism development may often lead to a loss of biodiversity through the overuse of resources and land. In addition, the destruction of natural plant and animal habitats can destroy delicate ecosystems which then has a negative impact on other systems dependent upon them. For example, the destruction of particular plants may remove the food source for specific animals resulting in the animals being unable to thrive.

The UK Centre for Economic and Environmental Development (UK CEED) was asked to carry out a 'destination audit' to research the impacts of British Airways Holidays tourists in St Lucia in 1997. This Caribbean island was chosen because it has clearly defined geographical boundaries and it is a popular holiday destination in rapid transition. The project objectives were to: research the development of the holiday destination; assess the general impacts of tourism on the island environment; assess the specific impacts of the tour operator; and produce recommendations for the host government, tour operator and tourists as to how to develop sustainable tourism.

The holiday destination of St Lucia

St Lucia is a volcanic island with a land area of 610 km^2 located in the Windward Islands of the Eastern Caribbean. The natural environment is a key element in the promotion of the island as a holiday destination, which is marketed by the Tourist Board as 'Simply

Beautiful'. White sand beaches, natural harbours, coral reefs on the west coast, sulphur springs, rainforest and the spectacular Pitons mountains are important resources for the tourism industry. Tourism is emerging as the lead sector in the restructuring of the economy and is the primary generator of foreign exchange. The tourism sector is rapidly changing, with increasing foreign investment, the development of large-scale hotels (particularly all-inclusives) and significant cruise ship activity. Visitor arrivals to St Lucia in 1996 totalled 425,000, of which 56%) were stay-over visitors and 43% were cruise passengers. A key Government objective is the expansion of tourist accommodation from 4,000 rooms in 1995 to 5,200 rooms by 2003.

General impacts of tourism on the island environment

UK CEED's study provides clear indications that St Lucia's transitional phase from low-density to high-density, mass market tourism has been associated with increasing

Garbage in the Caribbean

The Wider Caribbean Region, stretching from Florida to French Guiana, receives 63,000 port calls from ships each year, and they generate 82,000 tons of garbage. About 77% of all ship waste comes from cruise vessels. The average cruise ship carries 600 crew members and 1,400 passengers. On average, passengers on a cruise ship each account for 3.5 kg of garbage daily – compared with the 0.8 kg generated by each of the less well-endowed folk on shore.

Source: Our Planet, UNEP magazine for environmentally sustainable development, vol. 10, no. 3, 1999

environmental stress.

Currently, the greatest environmental impacts of tourism arise from:

- Land consumption, habitat loss and disturbance to ecosystems for site and infrastructure development.
- Destruction of coral reef through increased sedimentation from land clearing for construction of hotels and roads and artificial beach maintenance.
- Water pollution as a consequence of hotel wastewater plants not working or operating below optimal capacity. There is evidence that certain areas of the coastline are periodically contaminated by sewage which poses environmental and health risks.
- Inadequate solid waste management and disposal systems, which have led to the leaching of pollutants from landfill sites.
- Water pollution and anchor damage to reefs from boating activities.

In the 1997 operating year, the majority of British Airways Holidays tourists visiting St Lucia stayed in all-inclusive resorts where all or most guest services are included in one pre-paid package price. Therefore a distinct focus of the research was the environmental and socio-economic impacts of the all-inclusive holiday relative to the conventional holiday.

All-inclusive resorts were generally found to be associated with significant environmental impacts, mainly because they tend to be larger-scale resorts which occupy land on the beachfront. However, the evidence suggests that the impacts of conventional hotels of a comparable size on the shoreline are of a similar scale. Furthermore, all-inclusive resorts may be in an advantageous position to improve environmental management. This is because they have well developed management systems, greater technical expertise and financial resources, and can achieve economies of scale (particularly with high year-round occupancy rates).

Conclusions and recommendations

Like many other emerging destinations, St Lucia's transition towards mass market tourism has been associated with increasing environmental stress. Issues which require attention include conservation of coastal habitats, especially beaches and reefs, improvements to sea water quality and the management of waste. UK CEED's research also suggests that there is an opportunity for the all-inclusive sector to be the driving force for the introduction of environmental management in the local tourism industry.

The strategies of tour operators are also crucial to the promotion of sustainable tourism. In particular, operators can influence the nature and level of demand for holidays in St Lucia, require the improvement of environmental management in hotels and provide environmental information to tourists. British Airways Holidays should monitor the capacity of the island's infrastructure to accommodate additional volumes of tourists; include environmental criteria in specifications when product managers select hotels; and work with the authorities, tourism associations and hotels to further develop best practice and establish mechanisms to transfer expertise in environmental management from the all-inclusive sector to smaller conventional hotels.

source: www.worldbank.org

Pollution

The obvious impacts of mass travel are pollution and fuel consumption, but there are other impacts that need to be considered. For example, travel results in noise; the traffic congestion of roads, air space and waterways; the building of transport terminals and car parks, etc. Water travel and water-based sports create water pollution. And any form of tourism development construction brings with it the potential to create visual pollution – when the landscape and views are blotted by inappropriate building development. The disposal of litter and solid waste can also add to the problems of pollution (see left).

activity

ENVIRONMENTAL IMPACTS IN ST LUCIA

In pairs:

1 Discuss the main negative environmental impacts that tourism is having in St Lucia and the reasons why you think they have occurred.

2 Explain ways in which tourism development in St Lucia could have positive environmental impacts.

3 Take one of these position statements each and argue and justify your case:

'All-inclusive holidays are the reason for the negative environmental impacts of tourism in St Lucia.'

'All-inclusive holidays can have many positive environmental impacts on tourism in St Lucia.'

The socio-cultural impacts of tourism development

In the last two topics we discussed some of the key positive and negative economic and environmental impacts of tourism development. In this topic we are going to look at socio-cultural impacts. Issues that constitute positive impacts include:

- Preservation of customs and crafts
- Revival of festivals and ceremonies
- Provision of community facilities and public services
- Improved infrastructure for the local community.

Negative socio-cultural impacts include:

- Conflicts with – and influence on – the local community
- Crime and prostitution
- Staged authenticity
- Loss of cultural identity.

We will also look at a case study on the Vietnamese town of Sapa.

Positive socio-cultural impacts

Tourism development can often result in positive benefits for the cultural and social characteristics of an area. Where an entire area or country is being developed, supporting and promoting the local culture may be a key feature of the tourism product being offered.

Preservation of customs and crafts

Observing local customs and crafts is often a major attraction for visitors, and many tourism development agents will be keen to promote this aspect. Grants and other means of support may be provided to allow local craftspeople to produce traditional products both for the visitors and for the local community.

Without such grants and support, the traditional products or methods of production may disappear. For example, visitors in Holland can visit clog-making factories where skilled craftspeople produce the traditional footwear by hand, using methods passed down through generations. In reality, clogs can now be produced much more cheaply and efficiently in a factory by employees with limited craft skills. Likewise, Greek islands such as Rhodes have been able to revive and maintain ancient crafts such as handmade fine lace because it provides an attraction for visiting tourists.

Revival of festivals and ceremonies

Many local ceremonies and festivals would have undoubtedly died out without the support of the tourist trade. Often such festivals have been revived and enhanced by tourism organisations or local government to encourage more visitors to an area. For example, many areas stage festivals such as morris dancing or traditional street entertainment. Within the UK there is a wide range of unique and unusual festivals and ceremonies, as the example on the opposite page shows.

The Dunmow Flitch

Five couples have been revealing the secrets of married bliss in an open court – in an attempt to win a side of bacon. This bizarre July event is part of the ancient ceremony of the Dunmow Flitch Trials, held in Great Dunmow, Essex.

For centuries, the ceremony has attracted couples from across the country who set out to prove they have not had a cross word for a year and a day.

Their revelations are made before a 'judge' in a mock court, and a 'jury' of maidens and bachelors decide if they deserve to win the flitch – a salted side of pork.

The successful couples are awarded their prize after swearing an oath, and are then carried through the town on chairs in front of cheering crowds. [Last year] was as much fun and as memorable as in previous years, so we must ensure that this unique local tradition continues for hundreds more years.

Source: www.dunmowflitch.co.uk

Provision of community facilities and public services

Further socio-cultural benefits include the development of additional facilities and services that can be enjoyed by the local community as well as tourists. For example, public services such as a tourist information centre in a town centre may be provided primarily for visitors to the area. However, local residents will also benefit from being able to use the centre to book theatre tickets and tickets to other events. Likewise, tourist destinations tend to have a wide range of restaurants, bars and entertainment venues to cater for the tourist trade. These facilities and services are also available for the local population.

Improved infrastructure for the local community

As we discussed in Topic 5, the term infrastructure refers to the framework of basic services and facilities that a community or area rely upon to function effectively, including systems for energy, communication, transport, waste and water. Where there is large-scale tourism development this will inevitably lead to a substantial increase in the population during peak season. Consequently, improvements to the existing infrastructure are often required to meet the needs of the visitors. For example, roads and public transport may need to be improved. Whilst these improvements are needed because of the numbers of visitors they also benefit for the host community.

Tourists in Venice

Negative socio-cultural impacts

In attracting tourists, a destination is inviting 'strangers' into their area. These strangers may have very different cultural and social standards, behaviour and expectations. Some tourists will expect the area to adapt to their culture. For example, many of Club 18–30's customers who are attracted by the brochure descriptions may make few concessions to local cultural values, and expect the local population to adjust to them. Other tourists may visit a destination because they want to experience the local culture and not expect the population to treat them any differently. Clearly the second type of tourist is going to have a far less negative impact on the socio-cultural values and behaviour of the host destination.

Conflicts with – and influence on – the local community

Any situation that brings different cultures together creates the potential for conflict. In addition, where the visitors' culture is allowed to dominate there is the risk that it will influence and change the culture of the host community. For example, countries with strict religious beliefs, such as Muslim countries, have stringent restrictions on alcohol consumption and expected dress. Visitors to such countries often have a more relaxed approach to such issues and can risk offending the host community. Differences in the wealth of visitors and the host community have also been shown to have a negative effect on a destination. This is particularly true in the poorer developing countries where the host community constantly see the relative wealth of visitors – and become dissatisfied with their own lifestyles.

Crime and prostitution

Because tourism usually means that more wealth is coming into a destination via its visitors, it can also lead to an increase in crime and prostitution in the area. This is a real problem in poorer destinations where the local community may aspire to the same level of wealth as their visitors. These visitors usually bring with them a range of belongings that make easy pickings for the criminal – such as jewellery, cameras, video recorders, designer goods, credit cards and, of course, large amounts of cash. Petty crime, such as mugging, pick-pocketing and burglary are rife in many tourist destinations. Added to this is the problem of increasing prostitution in areas that attract wealthy visitors. Poorer members of the host community may view prostitution as an easy way to finance a better standard of living.

Many areas in the Far East and South America have become notorious sex-tourism destinations. Of particular concern is the rise of child sex tourism (see below and right), defined by the United Nations as: 'Tourism organised with the primary purpose of facilitating the effecting of a commercial sexual relationship with a child.'

The statistics are disturbing enough, but perhaps the true impacts that sex tourism have can best be appreciated through the effects that it has on individual lives, as detailed on the next page.

Staged authenticity

Staged authenticity occurs when the visitors to a destination want to view aspects of the culture and the

Child sex tourism

While much of the initial international attention on sex tourism of children focused on Thailand and other countries of Southeast Asia, there is no hemisphere, continent, or region unaffected by this trade. As countries develop their economies and tourism industries, this form of tourism seems to surface.

Economic difficulties, civil unrest, poverty, and displacement of refugees all contribute to the growth of this industry. The United Nations International Children's Educational Fund (UNICEF) released a report in 1997 estimating more than 1 million children, overwhelmingly female, are forced into prostitution every year, the majority in Asia.

End Child Prostitution, Child Pornography, and Trafficking of Children for Sexual Purposes (ECPAT), however, also reports increasing evidence of children being exploited in former Eastern Bloc countries. Reports of children entering prostitution, being exploited by foreigners and aid workers, and trafficked to Western European brothels are coming from the Czech Republic, Poland, Romania, and Russia.

Unfortunately there are still numerous small travel companies throughout the world that promote sex tourism of children by identifying resorts where prostitution is widespread. Because these companies are so small, they rarely draw attention from law enforcement.

In addition, the advent of the internet has revolutionised the growth of the industry. Some internet chatrooms, message boards, and online organisations not only encourage this form of tourism, but give detailed instructions about how to partake in it.

Source: www.missingkids.com

Beli

Beli was only fourteen years old when she was sold into a life of prostitution. The brothel madams beat her, starved her, assaulted her both physically and mentally, and locked her in a room until she lost the will to escape. After nearly four years in a brothel, of never being allowed out on the street to buy anything, of living and working in a tiny room with four other people, servicing up to 45 men a day, Beli has finally escaped to a shelter in Bombay, rescued by Vinod Gupta, a millionaire social worker dedicated to helping these young girls escape the prostitution rings.

But Beli will never shake off the legacy of the brothel – now she has found out that she is HIV-positive. She doesn't want to return home, and she has refused to see her brother after he spat in her face when told she had AIDS.

Beli's story is not uncommon. The practice of selling the girl-child – bringing as much as 10 years' income – is so commonly accepted in some areas that entire villages have been depopulated of women. Girls are often recruited with promises of work, wealth, and freedom in the big city – a far cry from the life they would lead if they stay in the villages, where they are considered little more than chattels. Some are taken as early as nine years old. Younger girls are worked especially hard to get as much money out of them as possible before they become too old or disease-ridden.

Source: www.american.edu

host community 'stage' shows or demonstrations. Often the staged shows bear little resemblance to the actual culture of the community, and therefore lack authenticity. For example, many visitors to Greece will have been tempted by the 'traditional Greek night' with Greek food and dancing. Frequently the experience bears little resemblance to how the Greeks would spend such an evening – with Americanised food and entertainment that ends with the 'Birdie Song'! The negative impact of such staged authenticity is that it degrades the local culture and does nothing to foster a positive relationship and cultural understanding between visitors and the host community.

Loss of cultural identity

The combined effects of conflicts between the host community and visitors, rising crime and staged authenticity can have long-term negative impacts on the cultural identity of a destination. Sections of the host community can become used to the income that visitors bring to the extent that they are willing to sacrifice their own culture in order to satisfy the needs of the visitor. This can lead to conflicts and divisions between those within the host community who want to maintain the culture and those who are willing to

sacrifice it. Many of the destinations that have been developed for the young adult holiday package market have witnessed this trend – traditional members of the host community have been resistant to the development of this market as it has resulted in the loss of many of the strong cultural aspects of their society.

activity
IDENTIFYING THE REAL SOCIO-CULTURAL VALUES

Select a relatively new tourist destination such as the Dominican Republic, Slovenia, etc. Research the destination that you have selected and identify the key socio-cultural values and expectations – for example, the country's religion, customs, traditional crafts, etc. Can you identify any differences in the descriptions of socio-cultural values and behaviour between the different sources of information? Discuss the extent to which tourism development might conflict with the host community or lead to a loss of cultural identity.

Impacts of tourism in Sapa, Vietnam

High atop a beautiful valley near the border with China, Sapa town is one of northern Vietnam's most popular destinations for both domestic and international tourists. It is the centre of a mountain district of 40,000 people, almost half of whom are Hmong, followed by Dao, Vietnamese, and a small number of Giay. The Hmong, Dao and Giay are highland minority groups, with languages and cultures very different from the Vietnamese majority living in the lowlands of Vietnam.

French colonialists built the resort of Sapa in the 1920s. After 70 years of revolution and war, tourists again began to make the arduous journey to Sapa, and in less than ten years this small market town has boomed into a major draw for travellers.

Travellers arriving in Sapa are greeted by two groups of people: the Vietnamese owners of guesthouses, jostling for customers; and young Hmong girls looking to make 'friends' – their term for the tourists who will buy their trinkets, listen to their stories, and maybe even visit their villages.

The carefree life of travellers is a far cry from growing up in a poor village. As the girls learn to enjoy the freedom tourists have, they are pulled farther away from their families. In town, the village girls are used to people looking down on them – older Hmong, other minority groups, and the Vietnamese, and this only makes them more confused and isolated from their community.

Some have all but abandoned their villages, and on the cold, cloudy streets of Sapa they fall victim to abuse from foreigners and Vietnamese alike. Late nights of drinking and partying with tourists has led to sexual abuse and even prostitution.

The Vietnamese are generally not concerned with this plight. Many view the girls as obnoxious and unruly, necessary only to attract tourist dollars. The authorities also appear ambivalent – concerned about the spread of 'social evils', but unwilling to take steps that might damage Sapa's tourism-based economy.

Rapid economic growth has had a huge impact. Families initially liked the extra income their daughters brought back from Sapa, but they did not foresee other consequences. Hmong society is very unforgiving to young women who break social rules, and at least one of the girls has been banished permanently from her village after being accused of sleeping with a foreigner.

Lowland communities remain largely ignorant of Hmong culture, and simple misunderstandings have exacerbated prejudices. One major misunderstanding surrounds the Hmong and Dao 'love markets', where young boys and girls traditionally court each other through music, songs, and games.

In the past, boys and girls dressed in their best clothes would form lines to play catch. Girls threw a ball to the boy of their choice, who, if they didn't catch the ball, would have to forfeit a small possession. This item would be reclaimed later, providing an opportunity for the young couple to meet again.

While traditional games like this are not often seen in Sapa anymore, the market place was always a location where Hmong and Dao youths met in the hope of finding a suitable partner. This was dubbed a 'love market' by the Vietnamese, who then sold the idea to tourists wanting to witness minority culture first-hand.

The result was too much attention from outsiders, and the youths went elsewhere. 'The love market was ruined because Vietnamese people and some tourists went looking for the girls, looking for sex, and the Hmong got scared,' says one American who worked for several months in Sapa town.

Ignorant of this fact, many tour companies and books still speak of Sapa's 'love market' and the innocent minority children who sing to each other. The reality is much less endearing, and those who have looked have found reference to Sapa's new 'love market' on paedophile websites.

Young girls have accompanied their mothers into Sapa for the weekend market – the normal kind – for many generations. When tourists began to arrive in the early 1990s, some Hmong women started selling handicrafts and small items of jewellery like bracelets. The women noticed that the tourists were enamoured with their young daughters – who were then used as bait to make more sales. The girls were initially very shy, but this changed when they received from tourists two things they were not accustomed to: emotional attention, and money.

In Sapa, Hmong girls found tourists who were only too willing to lather them with attention, and even better, buy things for them or give them a little money. It is not only their young minds that are vulnerable. On the streets late at night, or sitting in bars with groups of foreigners, the girls are exposed to situations they cannot control.

But the underlying problem, as it is in other countries, is poverty. Vietnam is poorer than many other countries in the region, and the highlands are the poorest areas of all. On top of poverty, the Hmong let their daughters run free at a young age. The problem is that, in Sapa today, this freedom is pulling Hmong girls away from their culture, towards a new identity they have no ability to shape.

Source: undp.org.vn

activity

SOCIO-CULTURAL IMPACTS

Read this case study about tourism in Sapa, Vietnam. In small groups, prepare and give a presentation that addresses the following questions:

1 **What are the main positive socio-cultural impacts of tourism in Sapa?**

2 **What are the negative socio-cultural impacts of tourism in Sapa?**

3 **Why do you think these negative impacts have occurred?**

4 **How could they have been avoided through responsible tourism development?**

The tourist area life cycle

Many of the examples in previous topics have shown destinations and facilities at different stages of development – from the newly emerging destinations to those that are well established. All tourism development goes through recognisable stages of development. In 1980, R. W. Butler, in his book, *The Concept of a Tourism Area Life Cycle of Evolution: Implications for Management of Resources*, suggested a model of development – the Tourist Area Life Cycle (TALC). In this topic we are going to explore Butler's TALC and its seven main stages:

- Exploration
- Involvement
- Development
- Consolidation
- Stagnation
- Decline *or*
- Rejuvenation.

Exploration

During the first stage, a small number of tourists visit a destination. The main attraction is that the resort is relatively 'unspoiled' by the tourism industry, so visitors can experience the true culture and environment of the destination. Because visitor numbers are small there are no major economic, environmental or socio-cultural impacts. At this stage the host community tend to be welcoming to the visitors, often seeing them as a small but valuable source of secondary income.

Involvement

The second stage sees the involvement of the host community and their acceptance of the increase in tourists. Visitor numbers are beginning to increase as people learn about the destination. Consequently, members of the host community become more involved by providing resources such as facilities, events and staffing. At this stage it is likely that accommodation provision and transport links will begin to improve to meet the needs of the tourists. The host community will become partly involved in the process of promoting their area as a tourist destination. The extract on the next page shows how the involvement stage of the TALC was witnessed in Transylvania (Romania).

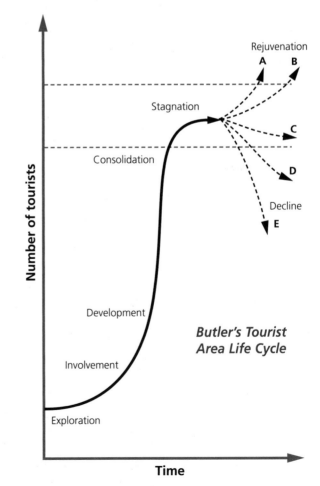

Butler's Tourist Area Life Cycle

Involvement: The Whole Village Project

This project, implemented by the Mihai Eminescu Trust, in Viscri, Transylvania, has helped turn a poor, remote village, deserted by young people, into a thriving cultural tourism attraction, without spoiling its traditional way of life and beautiful natural surroundings.

To date, more than twenty local women have registered as independent guesthouse operators; the Trust has installed bathrooms in five houses and is currently working on a project which will connect the whole village to an ecological waste system.

They have restored thirty old Saxon houses in the village, one of which has become the guesthouse, and have helped create a tourism centre and restore the beautiful fortified church – a UNESCO World Heritage site

To save the original village layout, the Trust have planted trees along the central stream and cobbled the road. They have also given local farmers small agricultural grants to support them in maintaining traditional farming methods.

Source: Online travel agency www.responsibletravel.com

Development

During the development stage, visitor numbers continue to increase. The main motivation for visiting continues to be the natural and cultural attractions, but purpose-built attractions are also beginning to develop. At this stage the host community will become more involved in promoting their area as a tourist destination and it is likely that the first package holidays will be offered. It is during the development stage that a destination will be recognised as a tourist destination.

Consolidation

When entering the consolidation stage, the local economy will have become heavily reliant on the income from tourism. Tourism-based facilities will have developed and expanded, resulting in potential strain on the local environment. Transport routes and access will also have improved, resulting in tourists being able to visit more easily. It is likely that agricultural land will have been sacrificed for tourism development, but that development will have brought with it an increase in employment opportunities and wealth. It is at this stage that some resentment might be voiced by some of the host community at the changes that tourism is bringing. The volume of tourists will continue to rise slowly, but not as fast as in the previous stage.

Stagnation

The destination is now moving into maturity, and the standard of facilities and services tends to decline. In addition, the negative impacts of development on the environment are becoming more apparent and visitor numbers begin to drop as the destination is perceived as having been spoilt. The host community are beginning to show increased hostility towards tourism.

Decline

During the decline stage, tourist numbers decline dramatically with the result that the local economy is severely affected. The image and reputation of the destination suffers as fewer and fewer visitors return.

Rejuvenation

Once in the decline stage, many destinations fail to recover. However, with effective planning, a destination can be successfully rebranded and regenerated. Frequently this will involve substantial investment to improve existing facilities and amenities. Some destinations regenerate by focusing on new markets and products – for example, the regeneration of British seaside resorts as conference venues. The rejuvenation stage results in an increase in visitor numbers, although these 'new tourists' may be different from the original visitors attracted to the area.

Butler's Tourism Area Life Cycle can be applied to any developing or developed resort. It is a useful tool for understanding the ways in which tourism development evolves and how future development can be planned. In addition, applying the TALC to existing destinations and evaluating their development provides valuable lessons on how tourism can be developed responsibly, so that negative impacts are minimised and positive impacts maximised.

Kenya and the Tourism Area Life Cycle

Kenya provides a good example of a less developed country which has embraced tourism as an important strategy for socio-economic development. At independence (1963), the Kenya government depended almost exclusively on a few export crops – mainly tea and coffee – for foreign exchange earnings and economic development. However, over the years, prices of agricultural products in the world market have fallen, and Kenya has experienced persistent shortfalls in foreign exchange earnings. In consequence, Kenya has increasingly turned to the development of tourism as an alternative source of foreign exchange earnings, job creation and economic growth.

Exploration stage 1880–1900

Prior to the establishment of British colonial rule in the late nineteenth century, Kenya and the rest of East Africa were little known to the outside world.

Furthermore, there was no basic transport infrastructure or conventional accommodation and hospitality facilities, except perhaps in a few locations along the East Africa coast, particularly in Mombasa, Zanzibar and Malindi. During this period the region was remote and exotic. Pioneer travellers mainly used on-foot caravan routes to trek into the East Africa interior, which was tiring and usually took several weeks.

Involvement stage 1900–1962

Kenyan Safari landscape

Colonial rule was formally established over the East Africa protectorate (the present Kenya) in 1895. The colonial government undertook to develop basic transport and communication infrastructures. Of particular significance was the construction of the Kenya–Uganda Railway, which became the main transportation artery into the East Africa hinterland.

In Kenya, the indigenous Africans had neither the expertise nor the capital to initiate and manage tourist facilities. In consequence, from the very beginning, the development of tourism, including the first conventional hotel and lodge facilities, was initiated by resident European developers and the colonial government. Africans were mainly hired to work in servile positions – as gardeners, cleaners, waiters, cooks and guards.

During this period, big-game safari hunting became a major recreational activity undertaken by the Westerners who ventured into the East Africa hinterland.

A distinctive characteristic during this period was the beginning of the organised and institutionalised development and promotion of tourism, involving both the public and private sector. The government, for instance, started to formulate various legislation aimed at the protection of Kenya's unique wildlife resources, and the promotion of organised recreational activities in protected wildlife parks and reserves . Thus it was realised that the diverse arrays of African savannah wildlife had great potential for tourism development. In consequence, the government created pioneer national parks in Kenya, including Nairobi in 1946.

Development stage 1963–1987

After independence in 1963, the young nation, eager to gain foreign exchange earnings, undertook specific initiatives to promote the rapid expansion of tourism. In 1965, the government established the Kenya Tourism Development Corporation to be in charge of tourism investment initiatives, and to monitor the establishment and operation of tourism facilities. It was envisaged that the country's pristine beach and wildlife attractions, coupled with improved tourism facilities, could attract an increasing number of international tourists, and their expenditure could earn the country much sought-after foreign receipts. During this stage, the structure and characteristics of tourism development in Kenya shifted from small-scale public and private enterprise to the establishment of large-scale tourism projects in Nairobi which were mainly financed by external multinational investors.

This phenomenon of rapid expansion was mainly caused by external factors in the major tourist-generating countries in the North. These included cheaper (and more frequent) flights which made it possible for an increasing number of people in the North to travel to far-off tourist destinations. Furthermore, the introduction by professional tour and travel companies of organised holiday packages helped reduce costs and minimised the risks and uncertainties associated with travelling to far-off destinations.

Consolidation stage 1988–1992

By 1988, Kenya's tourism and hospitality industry was relatively well developed, and tourism had became the leading economic sector. The number of international tourist arrivals had increased more than ten-fold, from 51,000 in 1960 to over 800,000 in the late 1980s – most of them in prearranged tour packages. A significant development during this period was the increased ownership and management of the country's tourism and hospitality facilities by foreign and multinational companies.

Nairobi

It has been estimated that over 50% of Kenya's tourism establishments in the major tourist centres (Mombasa, Nairobi, Malindi and the popular national parks and reserves) are under foreign ownership and management. Furthermore, It has been estimated that when visitors pay overseas tour companies for a complete travel package, leakages of receipts to the overseas companies may range between 40% and 70%.

Decline stage 1990s–present

There are increasing indications that Kenya's tourism industry is currently experiencing decline. The increase in room and hotel beds supply, particularly in the late 1980s, was not accompanied by an increased demand for the country's tourism product. Instead, the general trend has been towards low bed occupancy – less than 50%.

The coastal region (which usually receives over 60% of Kenya's international tourist arrivals) has been the worst hit. This has had a negative impact on other tourism-related sub-sectors, including handicraft, car rental, sports-fishing, boating, construction and retail. Consequently, thousands of workers in the tourism sector have been laid-off. Similar trends have also been observed in most of Kenya's major tourism centres, including Nairobi and the popular wildlife parks.

There are two main factors that can be said to be responsible for the premature decline of Kenya's tourism industry: the presumed reduction of the quality of the tourism product, and the recent perception of Kenya as an insecure tourist destination. The laissez-faire policy – particularly during the development stage – probably sowed the seeds of the premature decline. The rapid development of tourism was characterised by an unplanned and haphazard mushrooming of facilities, due to the lack of appropriate land-use policies and regulations.

In the fragile coastal and marine ecosystem, for instance, this resulted in severe problems of resource degradation. Hotels have been constructed without taking into consideration the environmental impacts on the delicate marine ecosystems (lagoons, fragile sandy beaches and coral reefs). High concentrations of tourists have led to overcrowding, trampling and over-exploitation of marine resources, such as coral reef and mollusc shells. In consequence, the quality of the coastal tourist product is increasingly being reduced, and the country is now experiencing severe problems of competition, as more tourists are switching to other countries in the region which offer similar tourist attractions.

Source (adapted): www.channelviewpublications.net

activity

KENYA: DECLINE OR REJUVENATION?

This case study outlines the development of tourism in Kenya, based on Butler's TALC model. Evaluate the stages at which it was becoming clear that Kenya was heading for a premature decline stage and how this could have been avoided. Suggest ways in which Kenya could move from the decline stage into a stage of rejuvenation.

Maximising positive impacts on destinations

As we have seen in previous topics, tourism development has the potential to have many economic, environmental and socio-economic impacts. In this topic we will explore some of the ways in which agents involved in such development can act responsibly to ensure that positive impacts are maximised, including:

- **Retention of visitor spending**
- **Widening access to facilities**
- **Staff training and development**
- **Investment of tourism income in community projects**
- **Training and employment of local people, and tourism education.**

Retention of visitor spending

Retaining visitor spending means that the money spent by visitors to a destination is kept within the area – first, by ensuring that all their needs are met locally, so that they don't need to look elsewhere, and secondly, by keeping 'leakage' to a minimum.

When tourists visit a particular destination they are likely to spend money on a wide range of products and services. These may include accommodation, food and drink, transport, entertainment, souvenirs, retail goods, etc. If some of the visitors' needs are not met in the destination it is likely that they will travel outside the area and buy the products or services elsewhere. For example, a tourist may go to a neighbouring city to the theatre if their chosen destination cannot provide the type of entertainment that they are looking for. Many tourism agents, such as local authorities and local tourism groups, are keen to ensure the retention of visitor spending so that visiting tourists spend their money at their destination rather than going elsewhere. This clearly benefits the whole area by increasing tourism revenue, employment and the quality of life.

Therefore, one of the ways in which the positive impacts of tourism development can be maximised is by ensuring that visitors spend money at the destination by meeting all of their needs. The development of purpose-built holiday resort centres is a good example of developers' attempts to maximise visitors' spending at the destination. Centres such as Disneyland Paris, Center Parcs and Warner have developed a wide range of facilities and services to ensure that visitors stay at the centre and spend money on more than simply accommodation and attractions. Such facilities frequently include shops, catering, entertainment, special events and leisure facilities.

We have already discussed the problem of leakage – where money passes from the visitor to organisations and providers outside the host community. Clearly when this happens there is little retention of visitor spending other than in the wages paid to staff in the destination. Retention is far higher where there is strong linkage in the local tourism industry. 'Linkage' means the extent to which the tourism industry uses goods and services from other providers within the same economy – i.e. within the same country or a specific geographical area. For example, if a tour operator uses locally owned hotels and restaurants rather than those provided by multinational companies the money paid will remain largely within the destination. In turn, if the hoteliers buy only locally produced goods and services, the retention of money will be even greater.

Widening access to facilities

Providing the opportunity for more people to have access to travel and tourism products and services is a key feature of much development. This may be through such amenities being more plentiful in a region or easier to get to. Alternatively, development agents may improve accessibility by making the product more affordable. For example, there has been a huge increase in visitor numbers to British national museums since the government made entrance free in 2001.

Whilst most tourism development is primarily designed to provide amenities and products for visitors, access to the facilities can be widened for specific sections of the local community. For example, the development of Merlin Entertainments' Sea Life Centres in the UK has provided considerable educational access for local schools and colleges. Specific learning packs linked to the National Curriculum have been produced by Merlin Entertainments, with discounted rates being offered to educational groups.

New rights to walk on the wild side

Sunday 19 September 2004 was an important date for the Peak District National Park and everyone who enjoys the countryside. On this day, around 250 sq km of private land was opened up for people to walk on – doubling the area of open-access land in the National Park.

Places such as Snailsden Moor, Bradfield Moor and Axe Edge Moor – great expanses of moorland that had been out of bounds for the outward bound for more than a hundred years – are now accessible to people on foot.

The new rights of access to open country are granted thanks to the Countryside and Rights of Way Act, passed in 2000. The new access is for anyone and everyone able to wander across the wilder, open spaces of Britain's mountains, moors, commons, heath and downland. Access land is opening up in stages throughout Britain and started in the Peak District.

As the 'Access Authority' for all open access land within the National Park boundary, we are working with landowners and farmers to lead the way on local arrangements for open access. New signs, stiles and gates are being installed, and new full- and part-time rangers have been appointed both to help landowners and farmers work with the new arrangements and to help the public enjoy the land safely and responsibly.

Source: www.peakdistrict.org

Public sector tourism development agents are also keen to maximise the access for both local communities and visitors. For example, the Peak District National Park Authority has developed a number of initiatives aimed at widening access (see below, left).

Staff training and development

One of the obvious consequences of tourism development is that employment opportunities will almost inevitably be created. However, there may also be a need for training and development of the local population, so that they can take advantage of these employment opportunities. For example, a new tourist attraction may need guides, receptionists, cashiers, catering assistants, and cleaning and maintenance staff. Whilst members of the local community may have the general skills and personal qualities required, it is likely that they will need additional training to meet the responsibilities of their new job. Training and development can take many forms. It may be provided by educational establishments such as universities and colleges, by individual tourism providers, by local authorities or by training organisations. The overall effect of maximising the level and quantity of training is to raise the general skills base of the local community. This can result in very positive social and economic benefits to the whole community by creating a more employable workforce. Where training is combined with the opportunity to gain recognisable qualifications, the benefits to the individual are even greater.

activity

RESEARCHING TRAINING AND EDUCATION

Investigate how a local tourism provider maximises the training and education of its workforce. For example, what internal training does the organisation provide? Do they arrange for external organisations to deliver training, such as the Tourist Board's Welcome Host programme? Are staff encouraged to study for further qualifications such as NVQs or part-time courses at local colleges?

Investment of tourism income in community projects

As we have already seen, tourism development can have significant benefits for the local community in terms of economic, environmental and socio-cultural impacts. One way of maximising these impacts is to invest some of the income generated from tourism in projects that benefit the community. Many tour operators are realising the importance and value of this aspect, and investing some of their profits in local community projects, as the case study below shows.

AITO Responsible Tourism Award for Pure Crete

Pure Crete has been awarded Star Status for Responsible Tourism. This reflects our commitment to responsible tourism. Pure Crete restores stone-built Cretan houses and villas, and helps to protect endangered species in Crete.

Houses are owned by local families so that the economic benefits go to local communities who engage in restoration and environmental work. We encourage recycling and the local production of organic foods. We sponsor a loggerhead-turtle hatchery, contribute to the protection of the bearded vulture, and subsidise the installation of solar energy in the houses we rent.

In all our locations we encourage the restoration of disused Cretan houses and the use of traditional building methods. We are not involved in modern building or ownership but instead work in friendship with local communities to protect and enhance the environment.

As conservation of the local culture and environment is central to Pure Crete we are pleased to have been a founder member of Green Flag International – now Green Globe – an organisation set up to promote environmentally responsible tourism within the travel industry.

Source: www.purecrete.com

COMMUNITY PROJECTS

Research some local and national newspapers and try to find examples of tourism organisations and providers who sponsor community projects.

Training and employment of local people, and tourism education

Responsible tourism development can often lead to increased employment opportunities for the host community (see below). This may be achieved by utilising local people's existing skills or retraining them to provide new services for visiting tourists.

Tourism can transform standards of living

Keeping tourists entertained, fed, watered, sheltered and moving involves a lot of people. Tourism provides millions of much-needed jobs and can transform standards of living. The World Travel and Tourism Council estimates that the industry, either directly or indirectly, creates 1 in 9 jobs in the world economy today. Its employment impact is forecast to grow by 46% by 2007, adding more than 100 million new jobs. Tourism can be the making of small-scale entrepreneurs and their families. In Vietnam, for instance, tourism was mainly government-owned 10 years ago, whereas now 58% is private. Even the most basic jobs in tourism often have high social status, especially where there are few alternative opportunities. For women, especially in Muslim communities, tourism can also provide a lifeline to the wider world and to an independent income.

Source: www.vso.org.uk

Many of the potential positive impacts of tourism can be maximised by effective tourism education. There are numerous groups involved in the tourism industry whose activities include educating visitors so that they bring positive benefits to host communities rather than harmful impacts. Tourism Concern, for example, provides the following six-point guide to better practice abroad:

1 Save natural resources – try not to waste water; switch off lights and air conditioning when you go out.

2 Support local trade and craftspeople – buy locally made souvenirs wherever possible, but avoid those made from ivory, fur, skins or other wildlife.

3 Ask before taking photos or videos of people – don't worry if you don't speak the language; a smile and a gesture will be understood and appreciated.

4 Don't give money or sweets to children – it encourages begging and demeans the child; a donation to a recognised project, health centre or school is a more constructive way to help.

5 Respect local etiquette – in many countries loose clothes are preferable to skimpy tops or revealing shorts; also, kissing in public is often inappropriate.

6 Learn about the country – knowing about its history and current affairs can help you appreciate many national idiosyncrasies and prevent misunderstandings.

(Code developed by Tourism Concern, in consultation with local tourism groups.)

MEDCs and LEDCs

Finally, it should be noted that the amount of importance attached to particular impacts of tourism development will vary according to the nature of the destination and the host community. There is often a marked difference between MEDCs and LEDCs (see definitions). Many of the countries of South and South East Asia, Latin America and Africa are classified as LEDCs.

LEDCs usually welcome tourism development since it represents wealth and investment. However, this can result in the too rapid expansion of tourism amenities and services without consideration of the long-term consequences. Much of the initial development of the Dominican Republic witnessed this – when there was insufficient infrastructure to support the growing all-inclusive package holiday market. In contrast, MEDCs are more economically stable and therefore consider any development more carefully. Their economies will be firmly established on a range of different industries, of which tourism will be just one.

A more economically developed country (MEDC) is one that has achieved a high standard of living, developing all sectors of its economy.

A less economically developed country (LEDC) means that there is a relatively low standard of living but that the country is trying to move towards greater prosperity through developing industry.

HELPING GAMBIAN PEOPLE BENEFIT FROM YOUR HOLIDAY

As well as their six-point guide, Tourism Concern also provide the following ranking exercise. Using the information in their six-point guide, as well as the information in this unit, rank the nine actions, giving reasons for your order.

You are intending to go on holiday to the Gambia and you know it is a very poor country. You also know that tourism can help a country develop economically. Below are nine actions you could take if you were asked to help Gambian people benefit from tourism (plus space for one more you may want to suggest yourself).

A) Take pens and sweets to give to children you meet

B) Agree to pay more for your accommodation

C) Decide to give money to a UK charity which supports development projects in the Gambia (e.g. providing clean water supplies in rural areas)

D) Make a point of using local shops, markets and restaurants

E) Agree to pay a higher departure tax at the airport

F) Give money or pens and notebooks to your tour operator to help a Gambian school

G) Employ a 'bomsa' (a local youth) to take you around the sights

H) Decide to do something to challenge global inequality on your return

I) *An action of your own choosing if you want to add one*

J) None of these – it's not your problem.

LEDCS AND MEDCS AND TOURISM

Use the internet to research LEDCs and MEDCs. Identify five examples of each, and explain the extent to which tourism contributes to the wealth of each country.

53

Topic 9 Maximising positive impacts on destinations

Maryanne Mills, Responsible Tourism Manager, Naturetrek

What does your job entail?

As Director, Operations Manager for Australia and New Zealand, and Responsible Tourism (RT) Manager, I have a broad spectrum of responsibilities, from company structure, through tour design, to implementation of RT policy. These responsibilities work effectively together, as the development of tours and working with ground operators is useful when implementing RT policy.

My job as RT manager includes the promotion and development of RT, both within and outside the company. This involves:

- the development of our company RT policy, which we post on request and publish on our website naturetrek.co.uk.
- development of tours (often in association with conservation groups) to wildlife parks and reserves, particularly those which do not benefit from mass tourism.
- ongoing development of projects with conservation and charity groups.
- providing information to our clients on RT issues in destinations.
- promoting the progress of our RT projects in our printed quarterly newsletters and bi-monthly e-newsletters.
- keeping up to date with RT issues within the industry.

Could you tell us a bit about Naturetrek?

Naturetrek, established in 1987, has tours worldwide focusing on birds, mammals, reptiles, insects and plants. In addition, we include historical, social and cultural aspects of the destinations we visit, and use local guides wherever possible.

All Naturetrek tours are led by expert guides with a concern for conservation of habitat and species, and the holidays appeal to wildlife enthusiasts. Together, they represent the 'raison d'etre' of the company, which is promotion of the need to protect wildlife and associated habitats for the present and future. Essentially, all Naturetrek founders, staff and tour leaders are naturalists and conservationists, turned 'tour operators' – not the other way around.

What are the main objectives and guiding principles that Naturetrek aim for?

The main objectives and guiding principles of our RT policy are:

- to provide information to our clients on the significant conservation and cultural value of the areas we visit.
- development of tours to lesser known wildlife parks and reserves, in order to raise awareness that tourism can benefit an area and consequently highlight the need to protect the habitat.
- development and promotion of tours with conservation groups and charities, to raise funds and awareness for wildlife and social projects in destinations.
- working with local ground operators to use local guides, local accommodation and local products.

- working with local ground operators, charities and conservation groups to ensure that the benefits of tourism are fairly distributed within local communities.
- liaising with our ground operators on training of local guides.
- committing our tours to an area on a long-term basis to encourage sustainability for the wildlife and local communities.

How does Naturetrek minimise the negative effects that their involvement in tourism has?

Our aim towards developing wildlife tourism is to do so in a positive way, and we do not feel that any negative impacts are created by our tours. However, to ensure minimum impact we:

- travel in small groups
- include walking on tour as much as possible
- provide a 'Traveller's Code' to our clients
- offer options to offset carbon emissions from flights (and alternative options to traveling by plane).

How do you maximise the positive effects?

We have a number of initiatives which maximise the positive effects. Wildlife tourism can bring recognition to areas otherwise overlooked, and by introducing tourism to an area we can initiate employment for local people and long-term conservation of the wildlife. The recognition by local people that preserving wildlife and associated habitats can provide income and a long-term future encourages local support. In turn, money raised from tours is donated to wildlife conservation groups and charities to further protect the environment.

How does Naturetrek involve itself in host communities?

- Most of our ground operators have their own RT policy or initiatives, which include working with local people so that they can benefit from tourism.
- We work with local people at Koshi Tappu, Nepal, for example, in establishing and promoting a tourism destination site managed by local people.
- We work with Birdlife International on projects in Madagascar and South America to protect threatened wildlife and habitats by employing and encouraging local people to help.
- We work with our ground operators in Nepal and India in training and employment of naturalist guides for our tours.

What other organisations does Naturetrek work with to ensure responsible tourism development?

We work with the RSPB, Birdlife International, Butterfly Conservation, the Environmental Investigation Agency (by donating funds from specific tiger and orang-utan tours) Friends of Conservation, and Climate Care.

I work with the Responsible Tourism Committee of AITO (Association of Independent Tour Operators), and with the Travel, Tourism and Conservation Group of Friends of Conservation (FOC). I also maintain a link with academic institutions which focus on RT issues, by helping with research and referring RT issues to researchers.

Minimising negative impacts on destinations

In the last topic we explored the ways in which responsible tourism development can maximise the positive impacts that it has on destinations. Of course, the reverse is also a prime objective of development agents – in terms of minimising the negative impacts that any development might have. In this topic we will explore some of the ways in which this can be achieved, including:

- **Visitor and traffic management**
- **Environmental impact assessments**
- **Environmental audits**
- **Planning control**
- **Sustainable development.**

Visitor and traffic management

Activities resulting from tourism development inevitably result in large increases in both visitor numbers and traffic. Road travel has risen by more than a third since 1996. Air travel has also risen considerably, with UK airports seeing a three-fold increase in passengers over the last twenty years. The impacts are usually concentrated in particular destinations at specific times of the year, and a growing concern for many agents involved in tourism development is visitor and traffic management. Increased traffic not only results in harmful environmental impacts, but also spoils the visual appeal and accessibility. For example, visitors to historic towns and cities are unlikely to enjoy their visit if the main streets are clogged with cars and pollution. For this reason, many local authorities have made specific areas of towns and cities pedestrianised zones. However, this raises the additional problem of how visitors in cars will actually get to the main tourist areas. There are many current initiatives designed to minimise the effect of excessive traffic in busy destinations. These include:

- Park-and-ride services, where visitors park on the outskirts of a destination and make the remainder of their journey by bus.
- Improved public transport.
- Designated drop-off points and parking for coaches (since 50 visitors on one coach is preferable to 25 couples arriving in 25 cars).

- Improved road systems, such as city ring roads, to keep through traffic away from the main tourist areas.

Managing the quantity of visitors in a destination is also a key issue. In an ideal world a destination would attract just the right number of visitors to fill all of the hotels and tourist facilities so that tourism revenue is maximised. In reality, many destinations experience too many visitors at certain peak times resulting in overcrowding and unsatisfied customers. In some destinations, such as Bermuda, authorities have taken dramatic action to manage visitor numbers. The Bermudan authorities have only authorised the building of an extra 464 hotel beds in the last 25 years, with a ceiling of 10,000 beds to be available on the island. In addition, the number of cruise ship passengers allowed on to the island is limited to 150,000 a year.

activity

TRAFFIC MANAGEMENT

Select a large town or city in your area and investigate how incoming road traffic is managed. For example, how are visitors informed about long- and short-stay parking facilities and park and ride services? Where is information displayed – only within the town or on approach roads as well? Are visitors given sufficient warning when car parks are full, and provided with suitable alternatives? How is pedestrianisation used to manage traffic?

Environmental impact assessments

Increasing concern about the potential negative effects that tourism development can have on the environment has resulted in many developers carrying out 'environmental impact assessments' (EIAs). This is a process whereby the developer evaluates the overall effect that the development will have and identifies any ways in which negative impacts could be minimised. Some of the issues that a developer will consider include:

- the costs of the development

- all of the possible benefits, and who specifically will benefit

- those who may be adversely affected by the development

- whether there is a different way of developing the initiative that would have fewer negative impacts

- how the negative impacts may be minimised.

Environmental audits

Environmental auditing is a process whereby an organisation identifies all of its key activities, the effects that these activities have on the environment and how the effects can be managed to minimise their negative impacts.

The total system, of which environmental auditing is a key feature, is often referred to as an environmental management system. ISO 14001 (previously known as BS 7750) was introduced in 1992 with the aim of encouraging organisations to look critically at the impact that they have on the environment and at how they can improve their performance while minimising negative environmental impacts. Organisations that have achieved this standard have demonstrated that they are able to control the effect that they have on the environment.

The Department for the Environment, Farming and Rural Affairs (DEFRA) suggests six steps to effective environmental management and auditing:

The six-step procedure opposite gives you an idea of some of the very complex activities undertaken by large organisations when implementing environmental management systems and environmental auditing. However, even the smaller tourism providers can use the concept of environmental auditing to ensure that they minimise the negative impact that their activities have on the environment. This can be achieved by organisations asking themselves three questions:

- What do we do?

- What possible effects could these activities have on the environment?

- How can we manage these effects to minimise their negative impacts?

It should be stressed that environment impact assessments and environmental audits are merely a form of analysis, and cannot, in themselves, minimise negative effects of tourism development. It is only when they are acted upon and implemented that impacts will be minimised.

Step 1
Define the activity, product and services
This requires the organisation to list all activities, products and services, irrespective of their impact on the environment.

Step 2
Identify all the aspects of an organisation's activity, product or service which can have a positive or negative impact on the environment.
These are split into 'inputs' and 'outputs'. Inputs are those things that are needed for an activity to take place – for example, energy, water, materials and services from suppliers. Outputs are the end effects that are produced by the activity – for example, waste, impacts on land, emissions, noise, dust, etc.

Step 3
Identify the associated environmental impact of each aspect
The environmental impact is the change that takes place in the environment as a result of the aspect – for example, contamination of soil or water, injury to wildlife, or conservation of energy.

Step 4
Determine the significance of the environmental impacts
This step involves evaluating the importance of and likely impact of each activity, product or service. For example, how probable is a negative impact likely to occur, and how severe would the impact be?

Step 5
Register of significant aspects
This involves the organisation listing the aspects of their operation (activities, products and services) that are likely to have a significant impact on the environment.

Step 6
Completion of the Register
Once the Register is complete, the organisation can begin to set specific objectives and targets for each significant aspect identified.

Planning control

One of the ways in which the negative impacts of tourism development can be minimised is by the careful control of planning permission. Factors that may be considered can include the overall effect on the character of the area, the number of similar facilities already available, the destruction of existing buildings and land, the effect of an increased number of visitors to the area, etc. Poor planning control may overlook some of these factors and allow tourism development to take place without realising the full impacts that it will have.

activity

LOCAL PLANNING APPLICATION

Research organisations that are seeking planning permission for a new development. Identify the factors that may affect the success of their application. For example, have local residents objected to the application and, if so, on what grounds? As a group, analyse how the negative impacts could be minimised and the positive impacts maximised for the proposed development.

Sustainable development

As we have already seen, the development of tourism can have both positive and negative impacts on an area and its environment, culture and economy. It is now generally accepted that tourism needs to be effectively managed to ensure that a destination's identity and natural resources are not damaged for future generations. The World Tourist Organisation defines sustainable tourism as 'tourism that meets the needs of present tourists and host regions while protecting and enhancing opportunity for the future'. Without an effective sustainable approach to tourism development the impacts can be devastating and permanent:

- local shops and facilities that have changed their identity to meet the needs of tourists rather than the local population

- the destruction of local heritage and historic buildings or areas to accommodate new buildings, car parks and other tourist facilities

- the spoiling of views and landscapes through uncontrolled development

- overcrowding and the range of problems that this can bring, such as air and water pollution, congested roads, damage to the infrastructure, etc.

- the loss of local culture and identity

- a change in the employment patterns as more of the local population move into tourism jobs at the expense of traditional local employment.

It is clear that ignoring the principles of sustainable tourism can have negative impacts. DEFRA outlines what the objectives of sustainability should be:

'The key sustainable development objectives are to maintain the quality of the environment in which leisure takes place, and which is an essential part of the UK's attractiveness to tourists, for future generations to enjoy; thus contributing to the quality of life of those taking part in leisure activities, and maximising the economic contribution of tourism, while protecting natural resources.'

The British Government recognised the need for sustainability and launched the 'A Better Quality Of Life' initiative in 1999. This states that sustainable development means 'meeting four objectives at the same time, in the UK and the world as a whole':

- social progress which recognises the needs of everyone

- effective protection of the environment

- prudent use of natural resources

- maintenance of high and stable levels of economic growth and employment.

Sustainability has also been considered on a more global scale. In 1992, more than 150 governments from around the world agreed to work together on an action plan for sustainability in the twenty-first century. The resulting action plan is known as 'Agenda 21', and within the UK all local authorities are expected to develop their own local Agenda 21.

activity

A TOURIST DEVELOPMENT AND SUSTAINABILITY

Try to find out the extent to which sustainable principles are considered in a tourist development of your choice. You might find useful articles in your local newspaper, from local councils or on the internet. Alternatively you could contact local environmental pressure groups and ask for their opinions. Can you identify any tourist development that does not comply with the World Tourist Organisation's definition of sustainable tourism as, 'tourism that meets the needs of present tourists and host regions while protecting and enhancing opportunity for the future'?

Responsible tourism: the 'Dream' and the 'Nightmare'

Throughout this unit we have looked at some of the key issues and impacts surrounding tourism development in the twenty-first century. All of the agents involved in tourism development have the opportunity to ensure that their activities result in the 'Dream' shown below, rather than the 'Nightmare'.

The Dream

'Sawadee Ka!' you say to your guide Khun Santara who meets you at the airport. You know that's 'hello' in Thai as you've heard it at the orientation meeting before the trip. You used to know nothing about your holiday destinations except the weather and exchange rate, but that's a little passé now.

And it's not just your attitude that's changed. The whole tourism industry has had an overhaul – and changes were made, luckily, before too much damage to local cultures and environments. You were one of the first to take the Fairtrade Holidays, but now they're pretty mainstream. When NGOs, working with Southern communities and entrepreneurs first suggested them, the big tour operators didn't like it. But when tourists started booking through Fairtrade operators, and communities complained about the impact of package holidays, the industry had to accept it.

Now, when you travel to the old 'Third World', poverty doesn't smack you in the face. When you were in Geneva in 2002 you saw a rally of people from all over the world, lobbying the United Nations. Santara tells you that now international regulations on community participation in tourism have been established, she gets a living wage and can send her children to school. That saves them from selling souvenirs, or working as child prostitutes in Bangkok. You've read that some communities decided they didn't want tourists at all. Others set up special tourist zones, such as the Tanzanian-owned hotel you went to last year which the local Muslim community has kept separate from the town for cultural reasons.

This time, you are staying in a lodge outside Chiang Mai owned by a hilltribe community. Instead of breeze blocks and concrete, the accommodation is built in traditional materials by local architects and builders. You walk out of your room and your solar-powered light turns off automatically, walk out past the reed beds, which naturally filter waste water from the accommodation in the area and divert it to nearby fields, and go to find Santara. You have an amazing walk through the forest and she points out native plants that they now cultivate and export for homeopathic remedies – luckily the forest was saved from logging and luxury eco-tourism in the early twenty-first century. Then you visit her village and buy some embroidered handicrafts from the hilltribe women.

Since they got small loans from a savings and credit scheme for small businesses, they look much healthier than the hilltribe community you visited in 1999. In those days the tour operators just brought the tourists and gave the Headman a small tip. Now the community manage the tours themselves and put profits into healthcare, education and sanitation.

Of course holidays with the Fairtrade accreditation are a bit more expensive. But the food is fantastic. An international tourism industry agreement means that hotels now buy local food instead of importing it. And these improvements are also due to political changes. Since 'Third World' countries were released from their foreign debt, they have used the money from tourism to improve living conditions instead of paying off loans. Also, international trading agreements organised by the World Trade Organisation were re-written after Southern governments and Northern campaigners joined forces to shame the politicians into reining-in multinationals.

You notice other local industries are flourishing too. Thailand is a world leader in environmental technology and has made a fortune from recycling plastic water bottles. This means that places aren't just slaves to tourism, which is a relief. As you say, you don't just want to see other tourists when you go on holiday do you?

How Unit 7 is assessed

Unit 7 is externally assessed. The format will be a $1\frac{1}{2}$-hour written exam, using a question-and-answer booklet.

The Edexcel website – edexcel.org.uk – has guidance on external assessment, including specimen papers and example answers, or you can get more information from your school or college.

The Nightmare

'Hi! My name is Lula – welcome to Utopia Thailand,' comes the greeting from the girl in the Hotel Utopia lobby. She wears a Max Factor smile and a plastic grass hula skirt, with an African-print bikini top. 'Please go over to Reception and they'll give you your Utopia Freedom Card.'

You've been here before, so you know that the Utopia Freedom Card is your all-in-one electronic ID card, room key, hotel tab to buy extras with (food and drink is 'all-inclusive' in the price of the holiday) and service request device. Actually, you haven't really been here before – you've been to Utopia Zimbabwe, but it's exactly the same.

Getting here was easy. You booked through your TV-Internet-Banking System, and flew Utopia Airways all the way, including Utopia Shuttle trains at either end – so no need for local transport. Utopia Airlines is part of the multinational Utopia Freedom Corporation which formed after the merger with Microsoft and now controls 40 per cent of the world's business in computers, logging, travel and the media. There was some controversy when it all happened, but it died down when Utopia bought out the international media tycoon, Rupert Murdoch.

Holidays have become more expensive recently, but that's OK – the strong euro means most places are still affordable. In fact, you and your friends avoid cheap holidays at 'twentieth-century resorts'. Full of dilapidated hotels, sewage slicks, very little in the way of a natural environment, and shops full of tacky souvenirs reflecting what was once the traditional culture, they're now far from fashionable.

No. You prefer going to a Utopia Resort, where you don't have to see anything uncomfortable – like poor people, or protesting locals. A few years ago you arrived at your hotel in Jamaica only to see a group of protesting farmers being pulled out of the swimming pool by the army. Apparently, the farmers said the hotel was using up their water and their crops were dying. This happened just around the time the world started experiencing freak weather conditions – happily not too much of a problem at Utopia Resorts, as you can relax in their artificially created tropical bubble zones, come rain or shine. Utopia also keep out desperate hawkers – much better than having to be accompanied everywhere by an armed guard which happened when you went to Kenya. One of the hawkers told you he used to be a fisherman, but couldn't fish anymore because the hotels had taken over the coastline.

At Utopia Resorts all that's a thing of the past. As you don't have to leave the hotel you're never disturbed by locals. Some, like Lula, serve you drinks, caddie for you on the golf course or serve you in the shopping mall. Sometimes they beg you in a whisper for euros or dollars. But of course you don't carry cash in Utopia, so they soon give up.

Utopia also tell you how dangerous it is to venture outside the resort (you take their word for it). But with spectacular trips inside the resort – like the Utopia Conservation Park – there's no need to go out. The American ecologists explain how they saved rare species of plants from extinction and now own the patents to thousands of species.

Exclusive food is mainly imported to keep customers happy. Actually, come to think of it, very little is produced in Thailand. What with lack of water and over-fertilised land, farming communities have been crushed. You saw the pictures of starving families on the news before you came. When you came here before Utopia took it over, the whole place used to be farmland in fact. No doubt the people were moved off to the city. That's progress you know.

Source (adapted): © Tourism Concern www.tourismconcern.org.uk

Topic 10 Minimising negative impacts on destinations

The world is a constantly changing place, and the 'issues' that affect travel and tourism vary from one place to the next, and from one day to the next. For the assessment of this unit you have to conduct a study of an issue that is currently affecting or has recently (within the last five years) affected the travel and tourism industry. You may choose an issue related to the subjects covered in the first seven topics of this unit, or any other area of interest to you. You will be developing your knowledge and understanding of this issue through research, using a variety of sources, and you will then collate your findings in a report. The final three topics will give you practical advice on selecting, planning, and carrying out your research project, and explain what your final report should look like. You will learn to determine the research requirements of the project and to undertake initial research to assess the potential availability of information. You will need to access and use a range of information and data from different sources and in different formats to complete the assignment.

An 'issue' is a topic for discussion and debate – something which is viewed differently by different people. Its effects spread far and wide and, although many people have their viewpoints, there seem to be no simple solutions or remedies. Many issues come to prominence through specific events. The 9/11 al-Qaeda attack in 2001, for example, was one such event, or the London bombings of July 2005. It is important that you distinguish between such events and the underlying issue – terrorism.

The factors affecting the travel and tourism industry may be political or they may be influenced by worldwide economic developments, or they may be climatic, or even tectonic, such as witnessed by the tsunami disaster in 2004, which claimed the lives of around 300,000 people. This disaster, along with climatic phenomena such as hurricanes will be discussed, together with the broader issue of global warming and how this will affect the industry now and in the future.

Advances in the ICT industry are having a profound effect on all our lives and some of these issues will be investigated, particularly the emergence of e-tourism which is leading to changes in the structure of the travel and tourism industry.

For some organisations in the industry, globalisation appears to be the most profitable solution, and we study the growth of the global conglomerates which are starting to appear, from hotel chains to tour operators.

The increasing number of acts of terrorism, such and those in New York, Bali, Madrid, Egypt and London – and the constant fear in many other areas – are investigated. But it is not just what humanity will do to itself that is a threat to travel and tourism – it is also the spread of diseases, such as SARS and avian flu, and how this threat affects people's attitudes to travel that we will cover in this unit.

It is clear that international relations can have a positive or negative effect on travel and tourism. Wars have an immediate adverse effect, and may limit tourism in an area for decades – as has happened in the Middle East. Political stability can only help the flow of tourists – as shown by the growing numbers of travellers who have chosen to holiday in America or Australia over the last few decades.

Many people in the world's less developed countries (LDCs) are often dependent on tourism for their livelihoods, so anything that affects the industry can have dramatic effect on them. Areas of Africa and South America, as well the Far East will be examined in this unit.

The Industry Focus is an interview with David Harris – a typical world traveller – who shares his opinions on many of the current issues in travel and tourism.

Unit 8

Current Issues in Travel and Tourism

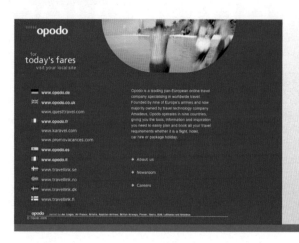

The first of the many and varied 'issues' that we will cover in this unit concerns advances in electronic technology. We will consider the considerable effects that recent advances have had on the travel and tourism industry, under the following headings:

■ E-tourism

■ E-retailing

■ Developments in Information Communication Technology (ICT).

E-tourism

E-tourism is the use of ICT to enable tourism providers and destinations to operate more efficiently, and to reach and serve consumers more effectively.

As one of the world's largest and most 'global' industries, the travel and tourism sector is as exposed as any other to the threats and opportunities brought about by all the developments in ICT.

The travel and tourism industry has, in fact, embraced ICT for at least the last 50 years – SABRE, the world's first airline computer system, for example, was developed by IBM and American Airlines in 1953. ICT has long been valuable in the area of air traffic control, automation and networking of distribution channels. Today, online booking systems, with their facilities to search, compare and buy tourism products, have revolutionised the way the industry conducts its day-to-day business.

The advent of the internet (see table) has had a profound impact on the travel and tourism industry. 'Travel' has become the single largest category of products/services sold over the internet, and the proportion of business being transacted through this medium is constantly growing. According to the Office of National Statistics (ONS) 48% of UK households had access to the internet in 2004 – up from just 9% in 1998.

Today there is a growing use of the internet by public tourism organisations such as National Tourism Organisations (NTOs) and Tourism Information Centres (TICs). Many of the travel and tourism suppliers, such as airlines, hotels, tour operators and rail companies are focusing more and more on the opportunities offered through the internet.

E-retailing

E-retailing is the selling of travel and tourism products via electronic means – over the internet. Over recent years, the internet has been a major issue in the travel and tourism industry – particularly among travel agents, who are concerned about the likelihood of business ebbing away from them. In this section we will look at the following:

• The popularity of e-retailing

• What is driving the growth?

The popularity of e-retailing

Travel is currently the largest e-commerce category on the internet, representing around one third of total online transactions. The sale of travel products is

The world's internet users

Region	Internet users (millions)	% of the region's population	% of total online population
Asia	302	8	34
Europe	260	36	29
North America	222	67	25
Latin America	56	10	6
Middle East	19	8	2
Oceania/Australia	16	49	2
Africa	14	2	2
World	**889**	**14**	**100**

Source: Internet World Stats, March 2005

ideally suited to the online channel, given the existence of a vast network of global travel suppliers (e.g. airlines, hotels and tour operators) and a widely dispersed customer pool. The order-fulfilment process is also simplified by the fact that there is no physical product to deliver to the customer, only instructions on where to catch your flight or how to reach your designated hotel.

E-retailing also helps organisations cope better with one of travel and tourism's key properties – the fact that its products are 'perishable'. Unlike most products, airline seats or hotel rooms cannot be stored and consumed at a later date – so every seat, room or holiday package needs to be sold beforehand in order to maximise profitability. Online selling and booking, with its instant two-way communication, can continue this process right up to the lastminute.com.

While tourism suppliers have traditionally used intermediaries such as travel agents and tour operators to facilitate the distribution process, advances in technology and growth of the internet as an e-commerce medium has led to the emergence of online travel intermediaries (or agencies). Over recent years, the increased popularity of these online travel agencies among consumers has led to a rapid migration of travel bookings from traditional means such as the high street travel agent to the online channel.

While the impact of this shift has been more widely felt in the US, with the success of online agencies such as Travelocity and Expedia, these companies are now targeting Europe for its high potential growth and are a source of increasing competition to existing players such as Ebookers and lastminute.com.

According to research carried out by PhoCusWright, it is estimated that Europeans spent $6bn on online leisure travel in 2001, compared with $13bn spent in the US. However, in time Europe could well overtake the US in the value of travel bookings made online – it has, after all, some 100 million more people than the US, and an average annual holiday entitlement of 33 days, compared with just 13 days in the US.

According to the latest Mintel report, the UK online travel market is expected to be worth £4.8bn by 2007 – up from £2.2bn in 2002. This growth can be attributed to the growing internet penetration, as well as the increased confidence amongst users, together with improved technology, products and content from online travel firms.

The Mintel research found that while some 44% of holidaymakers used the internet to research a holiday,

only 32% made an actual booking online. A study by MORI in 2002 supported this fact, as they discovered that although the internet is commonly used as a search engine to find out information about travel and holidays, relatively few people actually book their package holidays in this way. However, this trend looks set to change with 50% claiming (in a Mori survey) that they are likely to book a holiday on the internet over the next two years (see table).

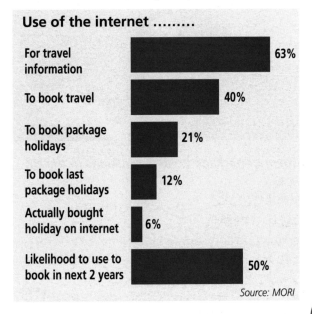

Use of the internet ....

For travel information	63%
To book travel	40%
To book package holidays	21%
To book last package holidays	12%
Actually bought holiday on internet	6%
Likelihood to use to book in next 2 years	50%

Source: MORI

The Mori survey showed that there were a number of reasons listed by those that did not use the internet to book their holiday. A reasonable proportion (11%) still preferred to deal with someone in person, and believed they could get a better deal this way.

The ONS figures on why people do not use the internet showed that around 10% had concerns about security on the web, and 6% said that they did not use the internet because they did not have the time.

What is driving the growth?

Travel suppliers (e.g. airlines, hotels and tour operators) are encouraging the consumer to book directly through their own websites in order to reduce distribution costs – by eliminating the commission paid to the high street agent. However, the lack of brand and/or product choice has limited the impact of these single-branded web sites.

In comparison, online agencies have grown in popularity by facilitating the search for the best travel deal, and offering independence and choice in terms of multiple brands and an extensive product range (e.g. flights, rooms and car hire).

While this intermediary role does not differ in many respects from that traditionally fulfilled by the high street travel agent, the online agency provides the convenience of 24-hour access, up-to-date content, capability of choosing from several brands and products and of course the promise of the lowest price, all with the comfort of being able to browse at leisure at home.

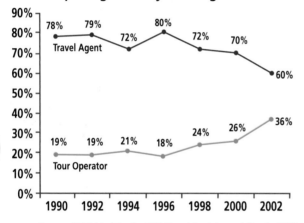

Share of package holiday bookings in the UK

Source: 2002 Mori Study, ABTA Travel Statistics and Trends, 2003

As the market grows, existing online agencies are adopting new business models in order to attract more customers. The two main models are 'dynamic holiday packaging' and the 'merchant pricing model'.

Dynamic holiday packaging is where online agencies create and sell their own packages from the selection of air, hotel and car-hire products that are available, at pre-negotiated rates. This 'dynamic' form of holiday packaging provides an opportunity for the online agencies to increase average spend as a result of cross-selling and generating higher profit margins. The established online agencies such as Ebookers, Travelocity, Lastminute and Expedia have already developed the technology to dynamically package, allowing customers to create their own tailored package holiday, in what to date has been the domain of the traditional tour operator.

A recent survey – which has surprised most industry observers and holidaymakers – showed that 80% of the time it was cheaper to disaggregate (separate out)

the components of the package and book them direct through individual supplier websites or via an online travel agency, rather than buy the same or similar package offered by a tour operator.

The merchant pricing model, which is being adopted by an increasing number of online agencies, is a flexible revenue model whereby they negotiate the bulk purchase of available rooms or seats from hotels, airlines and other travel suppliers at negotiated, discounted rates, and then resell them – at a margin – to travel consumers.

The merchant model effectively represents a 'win–win–win' outcome for all stakeholders: suppliers can get rid of excess capacity at low marginal cost, in a way that does not damage the integrity of published fares; online intermediaries achieve higher margins than under the traditional agency model, while the consumer pays a lower price than that often available from booking through the supplier direct. Hotels.com is an examples of a company successfully adopting this pricing approach.

As a result of several recent large transactions, the online travel sector is expected to remain highly concentrated – at the end of 2001 the top five global online travel companies controlled nearly 60% of the entire online travel market. However, while the online travel industry is likely to be characterised by ongoing consolidation in the years to come, there are a number of smaller players who are developing alternative online business models or serving niche markets to respond to these competitive pressures. Examples of some smaller UK travel companies who are achieving significant revenue growth include Active Hotels, an online provider of reservations to the UK hotel industry (and increasingly to the rest of Europe) and Iglu.com, an internet-based travel agency specialising in the sale of ski and snowboarding holidays.

Developments in ICT

Information and communication systems forming a global network are having a profound influence on the tourism industry. Reservation systems, distributed

Opodo CEO sees more consolidation in online travel

There will be further consolidation of the online travel industry said David Scowsill, Opodo.com CEO, in a keynote address at EyeforTravel's European Travel Distribution Summit (2004).

'Consolidation, for both the leisure and corporate travel players, has been the name of the game over the last 12 months, as we have seen a spate of acquisitions and mergers in the US,' he said, pointing out that in the US the three top online travel agencies (Orbitz, Expedia/Hotels.com and Travelocity) account for 84% of all sales.

'As predicted last year, the European airlines followed the trend set by the US carriers, and reduced commission fees (to travel agents) down to 1% in the UK,' he said. The cutting of fees to travel agents was started by British Airways and was quickly followed by more than a dozen other European carriers.

In the past year, there has been continued growth in the European online travel market as consumers move away from traditional travel agents in favour of buying online. 'Around 6% of total travel in Europe is now booked online,' Scowsill said, 'with the largest markets being the UK (34%), France (19%) and Germany (19%). The online sales mix is dominated by the low cost airlines who sell 95% of their tickets online.

The fastest growing travel sector in the past year has been hotels, and there is a bright future for online hotel sales in Europe. In the UK, online hotel bookings are forecast to grow from £2.2 billion in 2002 to £7.3 billion by 2007.

There will be further convergence of technical standards within the next 12 to 18 months, Scowsill said. 'What customers used to do on a PC, they can now do on a PDA (Personal Digital Assistant), or a mobile phone.'

Source: www.m-travel.com

One website: 80,000 brochure pages

surf2travel.com ('travel Google') has launched its online brochure service as a separate website on the back of buoyant demand. The website, www.onlinetravelbrochures.com, contains 80,000 brochure pages from operators including Airtours, First Choice, Somak, Kuoni, and Thomas Cook. It costs operators £50 to load each brochure on to the site.

Despite the increasing confidence for booking holidays online, consumers still want to view a 'tangible brochure page' according to Paul Green, managing director of onlinetravelbrochures.com.

The brochures can be viewed for free by consumers and agents who can search by operator, destination, category, resort or hotel. The site receives 300 unique visits per day according to its owners and the most popular brochures are mainstream offerings from companies such as First Choice, Thomson, Airtours and JMC. According to the company, travel agents are increasingly using the website to offer their customers access to brochure content.

Source: www.travelmole.com

supplementing PC internet usage with Smartphone and mobile device internet usage.

Much of the growth will come from populous countries such as China, India, Brazil, Russia and Indonesia. These countries will also see strong growth of wireless web usage, and for many new internet users the mobile phone will be their only internet-access device.

UK Consumer use of New Technology
Usage of New Technology by socio-economic group.

Personal digital assistants: a survey

According to the results of a My AvantGo Survey (2003), over 80% of personal digital assistants (PDA) users use their devices several times a day while they travel. The travel services its PDA users would most like to carry in their pockets while on the road are access to: driving directions (65%); weather (63%); flight schedules (60%); flight status (57%); airport maps (53%); air fares (43%); latest news (42%); email (40%); dining/hotel guides (39%); itinerary change facility (31%); exchange rates (22%); frequent flyers status (19%); frequent flyer offers (18%); frequent flyer partners (14%).

Source (adapted); www.m-travel.com

multi-media systems, mobile working places and electronics markets are notable results of this development.

The growth of internet users will continue in the developing countries for at least another decade. eTForecasts predicts that many internet users will be

LOST WITHOUT A PDA?

Read the article on the use of PDAs and explain the advantages and disadvantages to the business traveller of having a PDA.

Global warming

In this topic we look at global warming, which is an increasingly important issue for the world. Indeed, some people argue that it is the most important issue facing mankind today. There is still some disagreement among experts, however, about whether global warming is actually taking place, about what might be causing it, or about what its effects might be. We will look at this complex subject under the following headings:

- **What is global warming?**
- **The effects of global warming**
- **The Kyoto Agreement.**

What is global warming?

Global warming is the progressive gradual rise of the Earth's surface temperature, which may be responsible for changes in global climatic patterns. These changes could have serious effects on large parts of the world in the future. Global warming has occurred in the distant past as the result of natural influences, but the term is most often used to refer to the warming predicted to occur as a result of increased emissions of greenhouse gases. It is human activity – a significant part of it related to travel – that is producing these increased emissions.

Is the Earth getting hotter?

Scientists generally agree that the Earth's surface temperature increased by about 0.7°C during the twentieth century. It is predicted by some experts that it will rise a further 1°C by 2050, and by as much as 3°C, or even more, by 2100.

The first evidence of human-produced global warming in the oceans has been found, thanks to computer analysis of seven million temperature readings taken to depths of 700 metres, over 40 years.

What is the cause?

The Intergovernmental Panel on Climate Change (IPCC) recently concluded that increased concentrations of greenhouse gases are causing an increase in the Earth's surface temperature. Greenhouse gases are the components of the atmosphere that contribute to the greenhouse effect.

What is the greenhouse effect?

Greenhouse gases, like the glass roof of a greenhouse, let the sun's heat in, but don't let it all out again. They are transparent to certain wavelengths of the sun's radiant energy, allowing them to penetrate deep into the atmosphere or even all the way to the Earth's surface. But then the greenhouse gases and clouds prevent some of the infrared radiation from escaping. The heat is thus 'trapped' near the Earth's surface where it warms the lower atmosphere.

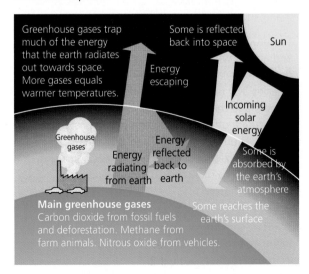

Greenhouse gases trap much of the energy that the earth radiates out towards space. More gases equals warmer temperatures.

Some is reflected back into space

Sun

Energy escaping

Incoming solar energy

Greenhouse gases

Energy radiating from earth

Energy reflected back to earth

Some is absorbed by the earth's atmosphere

Some reaches the earth's surface

Main greenhouse gases
Carbon dioxide from fossil fuels and deforestation. Methane from farm animals. Nitrous oxide from vehicles.

Over millions of years this process has been in a state of relative balance – it has kept the planet reasonably warm and allowed life to flourish. In the past, human activity has been so limited that it had no effect on the process. Now, however, it has been realised that today's human activity is so powerful that it is capable of altering the natural atmospheric barrier of greenhouse gases and so can raise (or lower) the mean global temperature of the Earth.

What are the greenhouse gases?

Greenhouse gases include:

- carbon dioxide (CO_2)
- methane
- nitrous oxide
- chlorofluorocarbons (CFCs)
- water vapour.

Carbon dioxide, methane, and nitrous oxide all have significant human sources, as well as natural sources, but CFCs are produced only by industries. Water vapour has the largest greenhouse effect, but its concentration in the lower parts of the atmosphere is determined within the climatic system. Global warming, in fact, will increase the concentration of water vapour, which in turn may further enhance global warming.

activity

EXPLAINING GLOBAL WARMING

Draw a diagram explaining what you understand by the term global warming.

The effects of global warming

A recently as 2000, the scientists on the United Nation's Intergovernmental Panel on Climate Change were confident that Antarctica was a 'slumbering giant' and its vast ice sheets so cold that they would not begin to melt for centuries, even if the climate changed elsewhere. Today we are told, 'the giant is awakening', and areas of the ice-bound continent melting, causing a faster rise in sea level than previously expected.

The 30-year time lag between man putting carbon dioxide into the atmosphere and the Earth responding by becoming warmer means that we are already committed to further climate change. Margaret Beckett, the environment secretary, said 'My understanding is that this level of temperature rise is already built in for the next 20 to 30 years from the climate change we have already instigated, so a significant impact is already inevitable'.

Collapse of the Gulf Stream

For western Europe and North America the most worrying finding revealed is the potential collapse of the sea current known popularly as the Gulf Stream. The melting of Greenland and Arctic ice and additional fresh water from rainfall is threatening to shut down the current completely.

Professor Schlesinger, from the Climate Research Group at the University of Illinois, said a 3°C rise in temperature this century, which is well within current predictions, would lead to a 45% chance of the Gulf Stream halting by the end of this century and a 70% chance by 2200.

The current, which carries one million billion watts of heat – a 'petawatt' – from the tropics past Scotland and northwards to the Arctic is known to be weakening slightly, but the chance of it being switched off completely by climate change was previously considered remote.

Figures from the Hadley Centre for Climate Change show that in some places in the North Atlantic the temperature might drop as much as 10°C, and over the UK Atlantic coast the drop would be around 5°C, causing a winter freeze up. The resulting climate in the UK for example would be substantially colder than that experienced during the 'Little Ice Age' of the seventeenth and eighteenth centuries. This was a period when ice fairs were held in winter on the frozen Thames.

Melting ice

According to Professor Chris Rapley, director of the British Antarctic Survey, the West Antarctic ice sheet is already slipping into the sea. This seemed to be following a pattern seen in the Antarctic Peninsula, where 13,500 sq km of ice shelf had been lost in 50 years. The loss of 'ice shelf' – which floats on the sea – did not itself raise sea levels, but when they disappeared, the glaciers behind them in the mountains then speeded up and slid into the sea. This raised sea levels around the world.

Currently most of the scientific research is looking at the melting of Greenland, the world's second-largest ice cap. This is already melting round the edges, and Dr Jason Lowe, from the Hadley Centre, said that 'quite modest warming' could pass a threshold that triggered more 'irreversible melting'.

He said the climate models varied in their results, but most showed that an increase of more than 2.7°C in Greenland triggered this melting.

One of the significant points about this was that the rise in temperature in Greenland was 1.5 times higher than in general, so the melting would be caused by a world rise of less than 2°C. It would take up to 1,000 years to melt, but would raise sea levels by 7 metres.

Effects everywhere

The climate shift that affected the oceans would have other consequences too. A dramatic acceleration of glacier melting in the Andes, and in western China, could leave millions of people without enough water each summer.

Climate warming would alter snow levels in the American mountains and could precipitate a water crisis in the western US within 20 years. In the past four decades, an extra 20,000 cubic kilometres of glacial ice has flowed into the sea, changing salt levels in the water and threatening to alter ocean flow patterns, with unpredictable consequences.

CO_2 emissions

The International Energy Agency, in its forecast for the next 25 years, predicted that the demand for electricity would double, and that the fossil fuels used to generate the electricity would supply most of the increase in CO_2 emissions. More efficient technologies and renewables will help, but in this period, emissions of CO_2 from all sectors are likely to increase by more than 60%. One of the main contributors of CO_2 is air travel (see below).

Fossil fuels contribute to CO_2 emissions.

activity

AIR TRAVEL AND GLOBAL WARMING

1) Analyse the effect of air travel on global warming. 2) Describe the actions that some companies/governments are discussing to combat the effect.

Assuming that after 2030 emissions remained stable, the world was committed to a 1 °C temperature rise by 2050, and 2 °C by the end of the century. But it is not just the rise in sea level that we need to be

Is travel the culprit?

A plane flying from Australia to London will use more than 200 tonnes of jet fuel, and pump out more than 500 tonnes of carbon dioxide. On a flight from London to Miami, one passenger will be responsible for climate change emissions equivalent to one car doing 12,000 miles. Multiply that by 350 people on the plane. Or, closer to home, travelling by plane from Scotland to Manchester produces up to nine times more CO_2 per passenger than travelling by train.

According to the Royal Commission on Environmental Pollution, if aviation grows as predicted, by 2050 it will contribute 75% of the total greenhouse gas emissions. Air travel has increased five-fold since 1970. Worldwide, passenger numbers are due to double to 7.4 billion a year by 2020 – and that's before Chinese and Indian people start using planes like we do. In Britain, numbers are expected to grow from 200m in 2003 to 470m in 2030.

Forty-five per cent of European flights are around 300 miles – barely long enough to reach maximum cruising height before coming down again. Many of these journeys could be made just as quickly on a high-speed rail network.

The world's number one climate killer

The no-frills travel boom, which has turned the world into an extraordinarily cheap adventure playground, has become the world's number one climate killer: It cannot go on. British Airways has launched a green donations scheme: their passengers are asked if they want to contribute something to compensate for the environmental impact of their flight. A £5 donation on the London to Paris route would be used for carbon off-setting – projects to help developing countries reduce emissions.

A similar initiative in Germany, Atmosfair, encourages passengers to contribute even more. But passengers on easyJet or Ryanair, criss-crossing Europe for fantastically tiny fares, are unlikely to be persuaded to cough up extra money in a voluntary green tax. Astonishingly, international aviation is specifically excluded from the Kyoto Protocol. Flight emissions were not included in the agreed targets, 'because of the difficulties that had arisen over the methodologies for allocating these emissions'.

Airlines and airports enjoy about £10bn of tax breaks and subsidies (unlike British motorists). Incredibly, no airline pays tax or VAT on fuel, an agreement which dates from the 1940s. If aviation fuel were taxed it would bring the Exchequer £6bn in extra revenue.

Source: 'The Hidden Risks of Flying', Melanie Reid, The Herald, 13 September, 2005 © The Herald 2005

worried about. The higher temperature and cooler waters will affect agriculture, fishing, increase the spread of disease and cause many other problems across the world. As the map below indicates, nearly everywhere in the world will be affected – and so, therefore, will travel and tourism.

The world in the 2050s

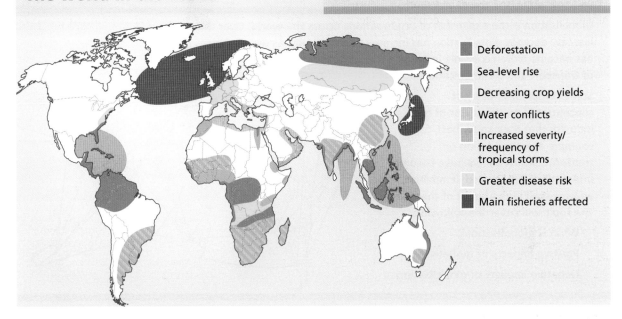

- Deforestation
- Sea-level rise
- Decreasing crop yields
- Water conflicts
- Increased severity/ frequency of tropical storms
- Greater disease risk
- Main fisheries affected

activity

GLOBAL IMPACT

Look at the map and identify a tourist resort in each of the affected areas. Research the impact that you think the predicted global warming effects will have on each of the resorts.

Spain warned of global warming threat to beaches

Global warming may cost Spain many of its famous beaches and could push summer temperatures over 50°C by the end of the century, according to research. The country is particularly vulnerable to hotter weather because of its economy and geographical situation, the environment ministry said. Spain already includes Europe's only desert, and tourism – much of it beach-based – accounts for more than 11% of the national economy.

'Over the last hundred years, Spain has warmed up 1.5°C, while the global average has been 0.6°C and the European average 0.95°C,' the ministry said in a statement. Temperatures have already soared to over 45°C in summer and could get up to seven degrees hotter by 2070–2100.

Many of the country's beaches may be swamped by the sea rising by 10–68 cm over the same period. 'With a general rise in the average sea-level, the most vulnerable zones are deltas and beaches. This could cause losses in an important number of beaches,' the ministry said. It will rain less overall, but the risk of extreme weather, including floods, heatwaves and fires, will increase.

The tourist-magnet Balearic and Canary Islands and the southern part of the Iberian peninsula could lose over a fifth of their water supplies by the end of the century. Higher temperatures will also alter natural ecosystems to the detriment of wildlife. Spain is home to rare species including lynx and bear as well as flocks of migrating birds.

Source: 'Spain Could Lose Beaches to Global Warming', Reuters, 15 February 2005 © Reuters 2005

activity

PROSPECTS FOR SPANISH TOURISM

Read the case study on Spain. If the global warming forecasts are right, what will be effect on the country's tourism industry? With the use of a map, identify five Spanish resorts that are likely to suffer the most, and explain how.

In this topic we consider the subject of globalisation, which is very much an issue within the travel and tourism industry.

Globalisation is the expansion of organisations across the world. Over the last few decades globalisation has increased dramatically, as everywhere has become more accessible in terms of transport and communication.

Some companies have just concentrated on the sector of the industry that they know best, for example accommodation or transport, whilst others have become international integrated companies, and we shall look at each of these. The topic will cover the following:

- **What is globalisation?**
- **Positive impacts of globalisation**
- **Negative impacts of globalisation**

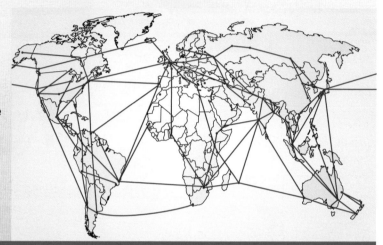

What is globalisation?

Globalisation has many definitions, but at its root it is about the planet 'getting smaller' because of the constantly increasing flow of people, goods, capital, power and ideas across national borders, across continental borders – across the whole world. Multinational companies now spread their services, their standards – and their cultures – all over the planet. There are Holiday Inn hotels, for example, in nearly 100 countries (and McDonald's in at least 120). Car-hire companies, banks, oil corporations, computer companies – all sorts of businesses are spreading their familiar branding into every country, where previously tourists found only local companies with unfamiliar, foreign, names.

The scale and influence of some of the global corporations is now so great as to challenge traditional notions of power only being in the hands of the world's sovereign nation-states.

The pace of globalisation has been increased by technology (computers, jets, satellites, etc.) and by the ever-growing affluence of most parts of the world. In 1980, about a million travellers and tourists crossed international borders each day. Today there are about three million a day. People around the globe are more connected to each other than ever before. Information and money flow more quickly than ever. Goods and services produced in one part of the world are increasingly available in all parts of the world. International travel is more frequent. International communication is commonplace.

Just as 'the Cold War era', or 'the Space Age' are used to describe particular periods of history, so 'the era of globalisation' is now used to describe the political, economic, and cultural atmosphere of today.

Positive impacts of globalisation

Today the world has become a global marketplace – with money flowing rapidly in and out of nations. This has had some positive impacts on the travel and tourism industry, examples of which are:

- lower costs
- familiarity of products and services
- ease of foreign travel.

Lower costs

Globalisation, with its economies of scale, has led to lower costs – especially in terms of air travel. Ticket prices have fallen dramatically over recent years, and this has led to mass tourism – 80% of passenger traffic is for leisure purposes. Lower costs have meant that more people than ever before have enjoyed travelling away on holiday, helping to lower costs still further, and this trend looks set to continue.

This huge surge in air transportation has been helped by subsidies and low tax regimes – airline fuel, for example, is tax-free. Within the EU, direct and indirect support to and subsidies to the air transport industry run at £45 billion per year.

Familiarity of products and services

Globalisation has been achieved by companies moving their existing technology, brands and experience to new markets, in order to profitably grow their business outside the home area. This means that people all across the world know and buy the same products. When they travel to new countries they see these familiar brands around them – and often spend money on them. For most people this makes travelling abroad easier and less risky – if the local food is strange, you can always go to the McDonald's. Indeed, globalisation has led to the birth of terms such as 'McDonaldisation' and 'Coca-Colonisation'– though these terms are usually used for some of the negative aspects of globalisation (see below).

When booking accommodation abroad, tourists often

The top ten global hotel chains

Rank (2005)	Hotels	Rooms
1 InterContinental Hotels	3,540	534,000
2 Cendant	6,396	521,000
3 Marriott International	2,600	478,000
4 Accor	3,973	463,000
5 Choice	4,977	404,000
6 Hilton Corp.	2,259	358,000
7 Best Western	4,114	309,000
8 Starwood	733	231,000
9 Carlson Hospitality	890	147,000
10 Global Hyatt	356	111,000

Source: MKG Consulting database, October 2005

The InterContinental Hotels Group is the largest hotel group in the world, with more than half a million rooms in nearly 100 countries. Every year more than 120 million people are their guests. Their brands include InterContinental Hotels, Crowne Plaza Resort Hotels, Holiday Inn Hotels, Holiday Inn Express, Staybridge Suites Hotels, and Candlewood Suites Hotels & Resorts.

choose familiar global hotel chains, such as Hilton or Holiday Inn, because they know they can be sure of their standards. Such companies establish 'global quality standards' and then train local people to implement them in their hotels around the world.

Ease of foreign travel

Foreign travel is no longer the headache that it once was. Today's global travel companies work hard to make the experience as pleasant and as comfortable as possible. From the luxury of booking their itinerary in their own home on the internet to fast flights and transfers, travellers can now reach their destination faster and more cheaply than ever before. Before you go, information is provided on everything from getting to the airport to which vaccinations you should have. On arrival most companies ensure that there is someone who speaks your language to meet you and that you are well looked after. International companies such as TUI make holidaying around the world easy by offering a full travel service from hotels, to airlines, to tour operators and distribution links (see the case study on the following page).

activity
TUI STRATEGY

Write a short report explaining the TUI strategy for moving into the tourism sector and how they have achieved their aim. What positive effects are there for TUI to be a global company? You may find their website, www.tui.com, useful.

Negative impacts of globalisation

'Aside from war, tourism is the single most destructive global force unleashed by man' (www.heureka.clara.net/gaia). Tour companies often claim to follow a 'code of conduct', but in reality they may only pay lip-service to it. Tourism is having a massive global impact, and not just on the global economy.

We have already considered the problem of 'leakage' (where most of the income generated does not stay in the local economy but boosts profits for the foreign multinational corporations). There are a number of other negative impacts that we will look at below:

- Economic domination of global organisations
- Loss of national and regional identity
- Loss of land or water.

Economic power of global organisations

We have already mentioned terms such as' McDonaldisation' and 'Coca-Colonisation'. Across the world today, nearly everyone is familiar with McDonald's and Coca-Cola. But at what cost? If people all over the world are choosing to spend their

TUI AG has expanded to become the world's leading tourism group within only a few years. The repositioning undergone by TUI AG, and its predecessor Preussag AG, is unprecedented in German corporate history. Within only a few years, the Group – with about 58,000 employees – underwent a degree of restructuring which normally takes decades. The former industrial conglomerate developed into a modern innovative tourism group – a European leader.

In 1997, a strong partner in the form of Hapag-Lloyd AG was acquired with its own travel agency chain, airline and global logistics services. With the complete acquisition of TUI Deutschland, the Group gained the leading quality brand for package holidays. And the tourism value chain was rounded off with the take-over of the FIRST travel agency chain and the shareholding in Magic Life: an integrated tourism group was born.

A crucial step in the European market came in 2000 with the complete take-over of the British Thomson Travel Group, and Fritidsresor in the Scandinavian market. In the same year, the Group acquired a stake in the French tourism group Nouvelles Frontières, which has now been completely taken over. The acquisition of additional shareholdings and the establishment of new companies in countries such as Belgium, Switzerland and Eastern Europe gained the Group major positions in all of the important European markets and made it the leading tourism group in the world.

More than 65 per cent of turnover was already generated by the tourism division in the 2003 financial year. By 2005, tourism will account for around 85 per cent of turnover.

The European tour operators within World of TUI reach over 80 per cent of European holidaymakers. In 2004, the Group had around 18 million customers. TUI now includes about 3,200 travel agencies, more than 100 aircraft, 37 incoming agencies and 290 hotels with 163,000 beds in 28 countries. Around 12,000 business travel professionals in over 80 countries also look after the Group's business customers. With a turnover of around £13 billion, the Group is the unchallenged market leader in Europe.

The opening up of new markets is a key part of the growth strategy. The establishment of the TUI China joint venture provides a new platform for all TUI Group companies, including the tourism and business travel segments, to open up the Chinese travel destination and the domestic Chinese holiday market. Additional growth potential is developing in Russia and Eastern Europe.

Source: www.tui-group.com

money on global brands, how many local companies have been squeezed out of the market? How many local, regional and even national companies in the travel and tourism industry have suffered at the hands of the big multinational players?

The domination by global organisations poses a big threat to the economic development of many countries, particularly those previously relatively sheltered from international trade such as India, China and in Africa.

A further issue for many people is that most of the global corporations are based in the USA, and it is American values and culture that they are spreading around the world.

Loss of national and regional identity

One of the major problems with globalisation is that the individual identity of a tourist region may comes under threat from the mass of tourists. In some cases, particularly where all the tourists are from the same country, the local identity can be swamped by the influx, and lost completely.

Tourists increasingly want to have their creature comforts on holiday – some even want exactly the same food, drink and entertainment as they are used to at home. To accommodate the tourists – and compete with the local outlets of the global corporations – local companies have to tone down their traditional services and provide 'foreign' products. In Tenerife, for example, local bars serve English beer and pander to English tourists. In Cyprus, local Cypriot bars make way for karaoke nights and English DJs. The result is that the local foods, customs and way of life gradually drain away from the tourist areas – though they may be preserved, often in a fake form, and put on show as a form of entertainment for the tourists. Many international hotel complexes, for example, use local dancers as after-dinner entertainment for their guests. For some people this may be as close as they come to experiencing anything to do with the local region – one of the main values of travel.

Loss of land or water

Globalisation, together with the travel and tourism industry, is using up large areas of land all over the world, that was previously used for local purposes. Airports, for example, are seizing vast tracts of land – and residents living nearby are having their lives made a misery by noise and pollutants. Some areas do not even want the airports – or the tourists that they bring – but are powerless to stop them being built.

Golf courses use up valuable land and water

Hotels and tourist resorts need land (and water). Golf courses, in particular, take up immense areas of land in destinations all over the world so that tourists – mostly from Europe and the USA – can still play their favourite game while on holiday. There are 350 new golf courses built every year. They demand large volumes of water for irrigation, and the pesticide, fertiliser, and herbicide run-off affects local water courses, bringing damage to fisheries and polluting drinking water. In Thailand the health of many local people has been damaged through eating fish poisoned by pesticide run-off from golf courses

It is in the Third World, however, that tourism is having the maximum impact (see examples right).

Examples of how tourism can use up local land and water

- In Malaysia, 29 local shops were destroyed to make way for a tourist development project, including its supporting infrastructure.

- The prime coastal sites that tourists like are often important fishery grounds, places where turtles come ashore to lay eggs.

- In Goa, water is piped through the village of Sinquerim to the nearby Taj Holiday Village and Fort Aguada complex. The villagers themselves, however, were denied piped water, and have to rely on a well.

- In Bali local people were forced from their land to make way for a golf course and hotel complex – by shutting off the water that irrigated their fields.

- In Zanzibar, villagers are being evicted from their coastal villages and placed in compounds, their beautiful coral cottages left to rack and ruin. All-inclusive tourist compounds surrounded by razor wire and protected by armed guards are built on the vacated land.

Source: www.heureka.clara.net © Keith Parkins 2005

activity

WEIGHING UP THE IMPACTS

Read the section on the negative impacts of globalisation and evaluate the key issues in relation to tourism. Analyse if the positive effects of globalisation outweigh the negative, and give examples of each.

Topic 3 Globalisation

Terrorism

This topic considers the subject of terrorism – a blight on the modern world, and something that has affected the industry significantly over the last few years. The threat of terrorism today is a worry to most travellers and has had devastating affects on some destinations. In this topic we will look at the following:

- **The threat of terrorism**
- **United States: 9/11**
- **Bali**
- **Madrid**
- **Egypt**

The threat of terrorism

Terrorism may be defined as 'the unlawful use or threatened use of force or violence against people or property to coerce or intimidate governments or societies, often to achieve political, religious, or ideological objectives'.

Today a more common definition is 'the use of extreme violence or the threat of violence by states, groups or individuals to generate fear in individuals and thus manipulate their behaviour'.

Terrorism is recognised as a global evil – and people's fear of travelling to other countries has certainly affected the travel and tourism industry. In the UK, the government issues advice – via the Foreign and Commonwealth Office (FCO) – designed to help travellers avoid trouble by providing information on threats to personal safety arising from terrorist activities, political unrest, lawlessness, and demonstrations.

It is designed to help travellers make informed decisions about whether or not to travel to a particular country. But they do not warn against travel to every country where there is a risk of terrorists operating, as it would cover a large proportion of the world, serving only to cause panic and disrupt normal life, which is precisely what many terrorists are striving to achieve. Since the mid-1990s, the al-Qaeda network and sympathetic groups have carried out attacks against

civilian targets: including the 11 September 2001 attacks in New York and Washington; the bombing of a nightclub in Bali in October 2002; the suicide bomb attacks in Istanbul in November 2003 (which were against British targets: the British Consulate General and the main HSBC office); and the attacks on the Madrid railway system in March 2004. Terrorism came to the UK capital in the London bombings of 7 July 2005 (see below).

Casualties: Hundreds were injured in bomb blasts

The series of terrorist blasts which rocked the capital on July 7 killed 56 people and injured up to 700 on London's tube and bus network.

The capital was thrown into chaos as three co-ordinated attacks tore through tube carriages, and a bus packed with commuters was ripped apart in a fourth explosion.

Source: Daily Mail

Despite an increase in anti-terrorism measures around the world, the threat from terrorism persists. Attacks may include suicide operations, hijackings, bombings, kidnappings, shootings and attacks on commercial aircraft and shipping. They may potentially involve the use of chemical, biological, radiological and nuclear materials.

LONDON BOMBINGS: IMPLICATIONS

Read the news story on the London bombings and explain the implications they have for visitors to London, both now and in the future. In particular explain the implications for the transport network in London. What are the knock-on effects for other areas of the industry, such as accommodation, historic monuments and cultural events?

Nonetheless, it is important to remember that the overall risk of being involved in a terrorist attack is still extremely low. Injury or death is far more likely through road accidents, swimming- or alcohol-related incidents, health problems or natural disasters and making the public aware of the comparative risks is important if the tourism industry is to overcome the downturn in trade from terrorism.

CURRENT ADVICE FROM THE FCO

Visit the Foreign and Commonwealth Office website (www.fco.gov.co.uk) and report on the latest information it is providing for travellers.

United States: 9/11

On 11 September 2001, terrorists hijacked four US commercial airliners crashing two of them into the World Trade Center in New York and one into the Pentagon, the US military headquarters in Washington, DC. The fourth plane crashed in a field in Pennsylvania. The World Trade Center's twin towers collapsed, one side of the Pentagon was decimated, and thousands of innocent lives were lost – all within one hour.

2,823 people were killed in the attack on New York – in the twin towers and in the aircraft that crashed into them. In the wake of the tragedy, the travel and tourism industry was reeling, largely due to the real-time media coverage that brought the event directly into people's homes. Airline travel and hotel bookings plummeted worldwide. Industry revenues, profits, and stock values were all down. Industry workers were being laid off in large numbers. Thousands of tours and hotel accommodations around the world from Egypt to Las Vegas to Australia were cancelled. Security measures at airports were increased dramatically. Francesco Frangialli, secretary general of the World Tourism Organization (WTO), called the attacks a 'terrible blow' to the tourism industry.

One year on, and the demand for travel and tourism fell by an estimated 7.4% worldwide in 2001 and 2002, compared with the growth that had been forecast for those years, as shown on the next page.

The fact that the 9/11 terrorist attacks occurred in the United States was particularly ominous for the global tourism industry. Americans are the world's biggest spending tourists. According to the WTO, Americans spent $60 bn on international travel in 1999. If Americans avoid travelling, and foreigners avoid visiting the United States, then the worldwide travel and tourism industry could face a truly dismal outlook in the years ahead.

However, according to the WTO's latest research (2004), the USA continues to lead the table of the world's top tourism earners ($74 bn) and has seen a strong comeback in 2004 on the losses of the three previous years as tourism earnings grew by nearly 16%.

Source: World Tourism Organisation 2004

Bombings fail to deter British travellers

The three-week reign of terror on London and popular overseas resorts is not deterring Brits from going on holiday.

Freedom Direct managing director, Martin Jones, said: 'I can't remember a time when we've had such a concentration of atrocities – yet people are still prepared to travel.

'The terror attacks have definitely had an effect – bookings are always down for 48 hours after an incident, which adds up to a lot of weak days when you take all four attacks into account. 'But people are still ringing up to book, and the market for July is only around 10% down. It's amazing.'

David Elstob, managing director of Future Travel, said: 'We've been inundated with people wanting special deals to Egypt since the Sharm el Sheikh bombing. 'It was the same after 9/11. We saw a couple of days of uncertainty and took our Egypt pages off Teletext at the weekend. But the market will recover. In fact, things picked up from Monday.

'The weather is the biggest dictator – and price. People are sitting at home waiting to book as soon as operators tweak prices down a bit.'

Source: Travel Trade Gazette, 29 July 2005

Life will never be the same again, some said as the twin towers fell. They were right. As the terror attacks continue, experts describe how the events of September 2001 still affect us all.

American tourists – the highest-spending in the world – have tended to stay closer to home. Airlines have been traumatised – especially the world's two largest carriers, American and United, each of which had two of their aircraft turned into guided missiles on that terrible day.

Both have lost hundreds of millions of dollars in the past three years. But the most extraordinary consequence of 9/11 has been the way that it has encouraged more travel – mainly because the cost of seeing the world has fallen.

After the attacks most airlines wondered by how much they could hike their fares to deal with the downturn in traffic and higher insurance costs. Michael O'Leary, chief executive of Ryanair, had a better idea: 'If you've got 10 quid, I'll fly you anywhere.' Within a week, the Irish no-frills airline's flights were full again, and Ryanair enjoyed a market capitalisation greater than that of both American Airlines and British Airways.

Soon, rival airlines found they could cut their fares from the punitive levels they previously charged, and removed restrictions designed to penalise business travellers. Hotels, too, started offering deep discounts to fill beds: with the cost of trips tumbling, people could again remember why they travelled.

As a result, people are travelling more extensively than ever before. In a world that needs to be brought closer, that must be a force for good.

Source: Simon Calder, The Independent, 12 September 2004 © 2005 Independent News and Media Ltd

activity

HOW DID 9/11 CHANGE THE WORLD?

Read the article about how 9/11 'changed the world for ever'. Explain and evaluate its view about the consequences of 9/11 on the airline industry.

Bali

The Indonesian island of Bali was once described as a 'high-density paradise theme park'. But, overnight, the bombings of 12 October 2002 exacted a tremendous toll on the lives of the Balinese people, the island's lucrative tourism industry and, most of all, its sense of security – the very factor which had led to it becoming one of the world's favourite tourist destinations.

An estimated 80% of its 3 million population rely on tourism for their livelihood, either directly or indirectly. For Indonesia, Bali is crucial since it generates 30% of the country's estimated $5bn in foreign exchange revenue from tourism each year.

Bali's image was badly damaged in the aftermath of the bombings, when it became glaringly clear that the push for tourism development had not been matched by development of the infrastructure. Photos of severely injured tourists receiving the most basic medical assistance in the island's hospitals did not instil a sense of confidence in prospective visitors. In the wake of the bombings:

- Almost two-thirds of hotels could not cover operational costs or debt repayment, with 54% of establishments reporting a drop in both international and domestic tourists.

- 30% of the island's villages reported people returning home because of lost jobs and insufficient income in the tourist centres.

Bearing the brunt was Kuta, the traditional hub for tourists – especially those from Australia – and the site of the bombings. Beach traders suffered average reductions of 78% in daily income.

Foreign tourists turned instead to Fiji, Vanuatu, Thailand, New Zealand or the Gold Coast in Australia as substitutes for the enchanted island.

Madrid

On 11 March 2004, back-pack bombs exploded on rush-hour trains in Madrid, killing 202, and injuring more than 1,400.

In a study undertaken by Exceltur, a lobby group of Spain's main tourist groups and companies, sector growth for the first three months after the bombings, was between 3% and 4%. Tourism would have been 'extraordinarily good' had the attacks not happened, said Jose Luis Zoreda, chief executive of Exceltur. Spain has compared well with other countries that suffered similar attacks.

'The effects were concentrated exclusively on the city of Madrid' the report said. In tourist areas of the Mediterranean coast the impact has been 'negligible'. In Madrid however, 82% of tourist operators suffered sales losses following the attacks, and 61% of Madrid hotel operators had not returned to normal sales three weeks later. The study noted that tourist business shares recovered on the Madrid stock exchange within days and some rose to levels even higher than before the attacks.

The tourism industry is important for Spain, accounting for 12% of the country's Gross Domestic Product and supporting over one and a half million jobs.

Egypt

Tourism is Egypt's second largest foreign exchange earner, and Egypt accounts for 50% of all tourist arrivals to Africa and the Middle East. But the country has suffered a string of atrocities targeting its vital tourist industry.

The first examples came in 1992–94 – sporadic ambushes and bombings carried out by a small hardline militant group called the Gamaa Islamiya (Islamic group). The attacks claimed few lives, but the bloodshed caused a significant drop in visitor numbers – down from 3.3 million per year before the attacks to 2.5 million afterwards.

But there was much worse to come. In 1996, gunmen attacked a group of Greek tourists waiting outside a Cairo hotel, apparently mistaking them for Israelis. Nineteen were killed and seventeen wounded. And a year later, a bomb exploded outside the Egyptian museum in Cairo, killing nine German tourists.

Then came the finishing stroke – gunmen systematically slaughtering 58 tourists and 3 policemen at the Hatshepsut temple in Luxor, at the heart of Upper Egypt's pharaonic archaeological treasures. The result was mass cancellations of holiday bookings to Egypt.

Visitor arrivals to Egypt declined by 14% from 1997 to 1998. International tourism receipts decreased by 45%. It took the country's tourist industry many years to recover from these blows. But, the recovery was helped by the fact that it seemed that the Gamaa Islamiya was beaten; its leaders were jailed, and the group, now fragmented, suspended its attacks on civilians.

Come the new millennium and, despite the global tourism downturn caused by the 9/11 attacks, Egypt was once again a popular tourist destination. More than 5 million visitors were coming to the country, about a quarter of them drawn to the newly developed resort of Sharm al-Sheikh. This is a modern holiday paradise: wonderful facilities, great watersports, amazing diving opportunities and a friendly atmosphere with welcoming locals.

Most of all Sharm – as it became known – seemed safe, despite the troubled times in surrounding areas. That was because it was located right at the tip of the Sinai peninsula, apparently insulated by mountains and desert from the teeming population centres that bred Islamic militancy, stoked by a repressive security regime.

Then came the October 2004 attacks that deliberately targeted Israeli tourists flocking to the Sinai for the Sukkot holiday. Unlike the 1990s attacks, these bombings were seen not so much as an attack on Egypt's tourist industry, but rather on the eastern Sinai resorts that had become a playground for Israeli tourists.

In other words, it seemed to be a response to the violence in the Israeli–Palestinian sphere. That said, the 34 dead included Egyptians, Italians and Russians, as well as at least 12 Israelis.

activity

TRAVEL, TOURISM AND TERRORISM

Terrorism is having an increasing impact on the travel and tourism industry both at home and abroad. Using at least three examples, write a short report analysing how each destination has been affected and how the industry has reacted. Conclude with your opinion on the implications for the future of the travel and tourism industry if terrorism cannot be contained.

Topic 5 World diseases

In this topic we look at how travel and tourism facilitates the spread of diseases around the world – and what it is doing about it, and how disease can affect tourism. As the barriers to travel come down across the world, people are moving across and between continents in their millions. As a result, diseases can now be spread right around the world in a matter of hours, sometimes with devastating effects. Recently, for example, SARS has affected South East Asia and, closer to home, foot-and-mouth disease damaged the tourism industry in many rural parts of the UK. In this topic we will look at the following:

- The increase in travel
- How travel encourages the spread of disease
- SARS
- Foot-and-mouth disease.

The increase in travel

Many of the barriers to travel have been removed over recent years, resulting in more and more people travelling further distances and more frequently. Some of the factors are:

- Lower costs in terms of air travel and staying abroad
- Increasing affluence, particularly amongst people in the developed world
- Easier access to the more remote areas of the world as modes of transport have improved and expanded
- More advertising, information and advice provided by the travel industry
- Greater media coverage of travel issues
- Computer booking has introduced efficiencies and cut costs for the industry
- The internet has helped consumers as a research tool and, more recently, as a booking vehicle
- The expansion of the European Union and the introduction of the euro have made movement around the continent easier
- Political changes have made access to areas such as Eastern Europe and China easier
- Advances in vaccination against some diseases.

World and regions: Inbound tourism

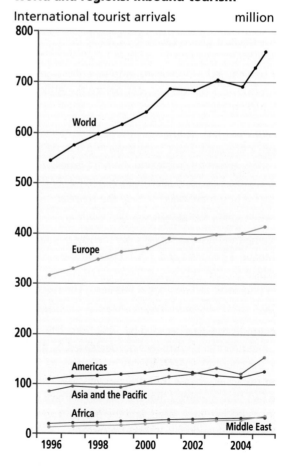

These factors, and others, have resulted in more people travelling from country to country than ever before. In 2004, international tourist arrivals reached an all-time record of 760 million (up 10% over 2003) according to WTO World Tourism Barometer (see graph).

Growth was common to all regions, but was predominantly strong in Asia and the Pacific (+29%) and in the Middle East (+20%). The Americas (+10%), Africa (+7%) and Europe (+4%) substantially improved their results of previous years. 2004 was marked by the strong rebound of Asia and the Pacific after the setbacks suffered in 2003 under the blow of SARS.

How travel encourages the spread of disease

Long-distance flights are the main facilitator for the spread of diseases, and these have greatly increased over recent years. The passenger capacity of long-distance aircraft is increasing, so that larger numbers of people travel aboard a single aircraft. Individuals who travel frequently and to several destinations may spread disease around the world more quickly.

The growing popularity of travel to the more isolated parts of the world has opened up a whole new arena of problems. Westerners are taking their diseases to previously isolated parts of the world, and closer to home, travellers are coming back to Europe with obscure African or Asian diseases.

Many countries require 'disinsection' (treatment for the removal of insects) of aircraft arriving from countries where vector-borne diseases such as malaria and yellow fever occur. This is to prevent the introduction of infection by insects inadvertently carried on board. There have been a number of outbreaks of malaria in the vicinity of airports in countries where malaria is not present, owing to the escape of transported mosquitoes. Some countries, for example, Australia and New Zealand, routinely carry out disinsection to prevent inadvertent introduction of species that may harm their agriculture.

SARS

SARS stands for Severe Acute Respiratory Syndrome. It is a new illness that emerged in the Far East early in 2003, first in southern China, then spreading to Hong Kong, Vietnam, Singapore, then Canada and more than 20 other countries. It is believed to be caused by a new strain of Corona virus – a family of viruses which has been linked to the common cold. By April 2003, it had killed more than 150 people worldwide, and infected more than 3,000.

The most obvious symptoms of SARs are breathing problems. Patients develop a high temperature (more than 38°C), dry cough, and severe respiratory symptoms follow swiftly. Some patients need to be put on a ventilator to keep them breathing while their bodies fight the infection. Four in every hundred people who develop SARS do not survive. Most of those who have died have been older, or had pre-existing health problems, which increased their vulnerability – but some younger, healthy people have died.

It appears to be passed on by 'close contact' with an infected person, perhaps carried in large droplets thrown out when the infected person sneezes or coughs. Patients suspected of having SARS are given a combination of antibiotics and antiviral drugs, which have produced an improvement in some patients, although their precise effectiveness is uncertain. A diagnostic test has been developed for the disease, but there is no vaccine for the virus that causes SARS.

Scientists believe the first case of the virus was in Guangdong in southern China. Guangdong is the gateway to Hong Kong, and the illness quickly spread to the territory. From there it spread to 23 countries via aeroplane travel.

There have been concerns about transmission within passenger aircraft. The latest advice suggests that those at risk of infection would need to be seated within a couple of rows of the infected person, with no evidence of risk to people sitting elsewhere on the plane.

People in the Far East have attempted to protect themselves by wearing face masks – but it is uncertain how much genuine protection these offer against the virus.

Because of the way it is transmitted, it is particularly virulent in very densely populated places such as Hong Kong, and in developing countries with poor levels of hygiene. In China, where there have been more than 2,000 cases, the government was recently forced to ban spitting in some cities for health reasons, but the legislation is largely ignored. This may help explain why the virus has spread so rapidly there.

The virus is being monitored by the World Health Organization, which issues daily advice to governments on how to respond. Individual countries are taking different measures according to the number of cases in their area and the level of risk.

The virus is mutating so rapidly that scientists fear as soon as they understand one version, it will have changed, making it almost impossible to develop effective drugs.

Experts are particularly worried that the virus will take

A SHORT PRESENTATION ON SARS

Check the websites of the World Health Organization, the Health Protection Agency or the Foreign and Commonwealth Office for the latest advice on SARS. Research the latest advice being currently issued to travellers about SARS and, in groups, prepare a short presentation which:

• Explains what SARS is, and the symptoms
• Explains whom it might affect and why
• Describes any actions being taken to prevent SARS
• Includes a map of the affected regions
• Includes advice to a traveller to one of the affected regions

root in Third World countries such as India, where there is a massive population and poor infrastructure. Most victims would be unable to obtain prompt medical help, and the virus could strike millions within days.

The outbreak of SARS in South-East Asia caused considerable problems for the local tourist industry. Richard Miller, of the World Travel and Tourism Council, said at the time: 'The SARS crisis in China, Hong Kong, Singapore and Vietnam is perhaps the most dramatic prolonged shutdown of the industry on record. Only the 9/11 events in the United States can serve as a point of reference and the SARS impact is five times greater. Although we do not expect the impact to be permanent, and in fact expect a return to normal levels of business by 2005, the short-term impact is unprecedented.' It was estimated that in 2003, 2.8 million travel and tourism jobs (20%) were lost in China, 62,000 in Vietnam, 17,500 in Singapore, and 27,000 in Hong Kong.

Foot-and-mouth disease

In February 2001 the UK government first confirmed the outbreak of foot-and-mouth disease in animals on a Northumberland farm. The disease, which quickly spread to other parts of the country, was to have devastating effects on agriculture – and on the whole travel and tourism industry.

In humans, foot-and-mouth disease is extremely rare (and relatively harmless) – in Great Britain there has been just one recorded case, in 1966. But humans can easily spread the disease from farm to farm, and from one part of the country to another. In 2001, therefore, alongside such drastic measures as killing more than 6 million animals, access to many rural

areas of the country was restricted.

It was these limits on access that hit the tourist industry most – the imposition of 'restricted areas' including many historic sites and attractions, closed countryside walking paths and waterways, and cancelled or postponed sports and public events.

There was also a more general impact on tourism across the United Kingdom as a result of the reduction in the number of overseas visitors. By the last quarter of 2001 the number of visitors to the UK had fallen 17% from 5.5 million in 2000 to 4.6 million in 2001, as shown below (though some of this fall must be attributed to the effect of 9/11).

Statistics from various parts of England give some illustration of the scale of the impact. By mid-April, the Cumbria Tourist Board estimated that there had already been 1,000 job losses. The Northumbria Tourist Board stated that visits to attractions in that region were down 71%, with 45% of accommodation bookings cancelled, and 18% of businesses having laid-off staff.

Topic 6 | Wars and tourism

In this topic, the final one concerned with individual issues, we consider the effects of war on travel and tourism. Generally, of course, war has had an adverse effect on tourism, and we will look at the subject under the following headings:

- **World wars**
- **Europe**
- **The Middle East: Iraq**
- **The effect of international relations.**

World wars

The two world wars in the last century made a significant impact on tourism. The movement of troops meant that people who had never been outside their own country – and for some outside their county – were travelling to places they had only ever seen in books. Many were sent to fight in mainland Europe but others were sent as far away as Africa and Asia. Those troops that were lucky enough to return told stories of the places that they had visited, and for many it stirred their interest in other areas of the world.

The advances in media technology, particularly television after the Second World War, also heightened people's interest in travelling to foreign destinations. But it was the advances in air transport innovation – much of it based on the accelerated development during wartime – that really made world destinations accessible to the masses.

Some of the historic sites of the great battles of the world wars have become tourist attractions in their own right. Visitors flock to the battlefields as a mark of respect and remembrance, as shown by those advertised by Leger Holidays below.

Battlefield holidays

Arnhem and the Rhine Crossings
Battle of the Bulge
Battlefields of Flanders
Battlefields of South Africa
Colditz, Dambusters and the 'Great Escape'
D-Day Beaches of Normandy
Dunkirk and Fortress Europe
Ypres and the World War 1 Battlefields

www.leger.co.uk

Europe

As we have seen in previous sections of this book (and particularly in Unit 3 Destination Europe in the AS book), the travel and tourism industry is very important to Europe. Since the two world wars, which clearly had an effect on tourism, the continent as a whole has been generally at peace but, unfortunately, in certain countries conflict has continued to influence the region. We will look at its effects on tourism in Turkey and Cyprus.

Turkey

Turkey attracts 13 million visitors a year. Tourism is vital to the country – it is now the second largest source of national revenue after foreign exports. More Turks work in tourism than in any other industry except construction. Tourism in Turkey has long been viewed as crucial to the country's future prosperity and growth, and its value to the economy has grown steadily since the 1980s.

The largest number of tourists are from major European nations, with more than three million Germans and over two millions Britons holidaying there each year. But significant numbers also come from Russia, the former Soviet states, and new EU members like the Czech Republic.

But the industry is blighted by the constant threat of conflict. In the past this resulted from sections of the Kurdish community rebelling against the Turkish government which had oppressed them and, it is claimed, murdered them in their thousands. These Kurds targeted tourist areas with bombs, because they saw tourism as providing the funds for the government's bloodshed. More recent bombings

(2005) are being attributed to the al-Qaida network of international terrorists. For whatever reason, Turkey is a place under constant threat.

Cyprus

Cyprus's location in the East of the Mediterranean has made it a key target for neighbouring empires for thousands of years. The Athenians, the Persians, the Egyptians, Alexander the Great, the Romans, the Venetians, the English – all had their own uses for Cyprus. Then, in the sixteenth century, stability came to the island with the Ottoman Turks, who ruled Cyprus for over three centuries – before ceding it to Britain in 1878. The rivalry between the island's Greek and Turkish communities became bitter and continued after Cyprus became independent in 1960, with Archbishop Makarios – head of the island's Greek Orthodox Church – installed as president. But in 1974 Makarios was deposed, in a coup orchestrated by Greece's military regime. It was the culmination of years of inter-communal strife on the island. Turkey quickly sent in their troops to the northern part of the island, with the aim of 'protecting' Turkish Cypriots – something the Greek Cypriot population saw as an illegal occupation. There are still many Greek Cypriots today who want the right to return to their homes in the north.

This division of the island into two separate halves is damaging for the tourist industry. Tourism is important to Cyprus – providing nearly 30% of the island's jobs and 23% of its GDP. But a divided country also means a divided tourism community and, to this day, the two halves of the island market themselves separately to visitors.

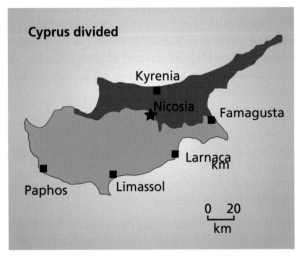

Cyprus divided

The Middle East: Iraq

The Middle East has had a long history of war and conflict – much of it in recent years provoked by the fact that the region produces 30% of the world's oil.

In this section we will look at the impact that war has had on tourism in Iraq.

Iraq has for centuries drawn people to its sites of ancient civilisations, such as Babylon and Ur, the Shia Muslim holy cities of Najaf and Kerbala. Tourists also visited Basra – regarded by some as the 'Venice of the East' with its lush gardens and lagoons, and the capital, Baghdad – packed with ancient bazaars, restaurants, museums, palaces, mosques and shrines.

Since 1990, however, as the world community imposed sanctions on Saddam Hussein's regime in Iraq, tourism declined and the country became more isolated.

In 2003, a US-led invasion ousted Saddam, occupied large parts of the country, and began the long and complex process of setting up a new democratic state.

This 'Second Gulf War' and the violence and insurgency that followed affected tourism in the Middle East most, but also had an impact on the global travel and tourism industry, just as 9/11 had done. Jobs throughout the industry were lost, as tourists, particularly Americans, decided to stay at home for a change.

Since the war, the few tourists visiting Iraq are mostly pilgrims from neighbouring Iran. But all may not be lost – if the country can start to stabilise. Efforts are being made to get the country's tourism industry back on its feet. The UK government, for example, pledged

Holiday in hell? Welcome to your flight to Baghdad

Tired of long waits at packed airline check-in counters? Looking for an exclusive holiday destination with guaranteed sunshine, unique historical sites and plenty of adventure? Iraqi Airways may have just the answer.

Beginning next month, Iraq's troubled national carrier is planning to resume direct scheduled flights from Baghdad International Airport (formerly Saddam International Airport) to London for the first time in 15 years, to lure visitors to one of the few countries in the world that has no tourists.

Certainly on paper Iraq has the potential to be an attractive destination for hardier souls interested in modern and ancient history. Awaiting them are some of the great sites of antiquity, such as Babylon and Ur, the biblical rivers of the Tigris and the Euphrates and natural wonders such as the marshes of southern Iraq. Those interested in more recent history can see the ruins of Saddam Hussein's palaces and the battle-scarred streets of Baghdad and Mosul.

But even before setting foot in Iraq a visitor faces real danger. There is the constant threat of a surface-to-air missile attack on all aircraft flying in Iraqi airspace. To avoid ground fire, flights into Baghdad perform an ear-popping corkscrew dive over the airport before hurtling down the runway for landing.

But getting from the airport into the city is probably the hairiest part of any trip. The drive down the airport motorway, considered the most dangerous stretch of road in Iraq, is littered with the debris of roadside bombs and destroyed vehicles.

Visitors can hire their own bullet-proof vehicle, medic and armed guards, for the half-hour drive into Baghdad. A British security company offers the most competitive rate at about £2,000 one way. Alternatively, there is the option of taking a humble Iraqi taxi for about £10, but with no guarantees of reaching your destination alive.

Iraqis realise that it will be a long time before their country will be safe enough for ordinary tourists to visit. But they hope that one day the violence will end and foreigners arriving at Baghdad airport will need to be armed only with a camera and guide book.

Source: The Times, 31 August 2005

£25,000 in 2005 to try and promote Iraq as a tourist destination. A big break-through that year was the opening up of flights into Iraq but, as the article below shows, there was a long way to go before Iraq would be ready for mass tourism.

The effect of international relations

International relations can have a positive and a negative effect on tourism. When a country is in conflict – for whatever reason – it has a negative effect on incoming tourism, because most tourists are looking for peace and tranquillity. The threat of conflict has a similar effect, or any dispute with the tourists' home country, because nobody wants to go where they may not be welcome.

Alternatively, good relations between countries helps promote tourism – in both directions. Britain has good relations with America and this has made Britain a popular choice of destination with American visitors. Other countries that have always experienced a close relationship with Britain are the Commonwealth countries, especially Canada, Australia, New Zealand and South Africa. In all these cases, Britain's past involvement included introducing the English language, which is a great benefit to both incoming and outgoing tourists.

activity

INTERNATIONAL RELATIONS AND TOURISM

From reading this topic you should now have a better understanding of how war can affect the travel and tourism industry. Using two of three examples, analyse the advantage and disadvantages of good international relations in encouraging the growth and development of tourism.

Closer to home, the friendship and stability of the European Union countries provide another example of good relations. In fact, the forerunner of the EU was founded on the basis of uniting the continent so as to prevent any more world wars starting in Europe. Now, its free movement of people and trade encourages a thriving tourist industry between all the member states. The introduction in many of the countries of the common currency – the euro – has helped tourism even further.

Topic 7 · Less economically developed countries

This topic looks at the effect of tourism development on the culture of less economically developed countries (LEDCs), under the following headings:

- **Definitions of LEDCs**
- **The cultural effects of tourism development**
- **The Sahara region**
- **The mountain areas of Asia.**

Definitions of LEDCs

There are a number of ways to define a less economically developed country. All definitions of economic development, however, are based on financial measures and, in particular, on the value of the goods and services produced by the country.

Narrow definitions of economic development might be based on:

- Gross Domestic Product (GDP) – the total value of goods and services produced by a country in a year, not including foreign investment.

- GDP per capita – the GDP divided by the number of people in the country.

- Gross National Product (GNP) – the total value of goods and services produced by a country in a year, *including* foreign investment.

- GNP per capita – the GNP divided by the number of people in the country.

Using these basic measures, countries with high GNP per capita are said to be 'more economically developed countries' (MEDCs), while countries with low GNP per capita are said to be' less economically developed countries' (LEDCs).

Study the table below and see which countries you would label as LEDC, and which as MEDC. The measure is often made in US$, as is the table.

Less economically developed countries is a term often used to describe countries in Africa, Latin America, and South and South East Asia. These LEDCs mostly correspond to what has long been referred to as the 'Third World'.

Selected countries: GNP per capita (US$) 2004

Nigeria	390
UK	33,940
USA	41,400
Brazil	3,090
Norway	52,030
Greece	16,610
Japan	37,180
India	620
China	1,290

Source: World Bank

Although some LEDCs are making great progress in trying to catch up with the MEDCs, the gap between the richest countries and the poorest is growing ever wider (see opposite).

The cultural effects of tourism development

Tourism is often offered as a model to LEDCs as a means of earning foreign currency and increasing their gross domestic product. But, like many other models offered to poorer countries, tourism keeps most of the power and the money with the rich countries.

LEDCs are encouraged to build their own tourist sector as a means of earning hard foreign currency, but the reality is often somewhat different. The holidays will be run by a foreign tour company, foreigners build, own and manage the tourist complexes, and food and capital equipment is imported. What little is paid to local people will be marginally higher than the local wage rate, thus ensuring

The growing gap between rich and poor

This graph shows how the world's twenty richest countries have been getter richer and richer, while the twenty poorest countries have just stayed poor. In fact, the figures for the poor countries are so small over the period (going up from $150 to $400 and then back down to $200) that their line on the graph hardly shows above the base line.

The twenty richest countries: Australia, Austria, Belgium, Canada, Hong Kong, Denmark, Finland, France, Germany, Iceland, Ireland, Japan, Luxembourg, Netherlands, Norway, Singapore, Sweden, Switzerland, United Kingdom, and United States.

The twenty poorest countries: Burkina Faso, Burundi, Central African Rep., Chad, Ethiopia, Ghana, Guinea-Bisau, Kenya, Madagascar, Malawi, Mali, Mozambique, Myanmar, Nepal, Niger, Nigeria, Rwanda, Sierra Leone, Tanzania, and Uganda.

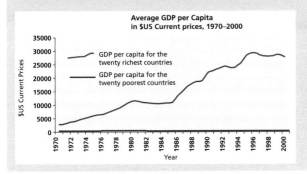

the destruction of the existing local industry. The few crumbs that trickle down to a handful of local people do not make up for the destruction of their environment and culture. There are many examples around the world, as shown below, of the exploitation of people by the tourism industry.

As we have seen, many LEDCs have appeal to the tourist as a holiday destination as many have hot climates attractive to the tourist all year round. However, the cost to the local communities can be great especially on island communities, as shown in the extract below on the effects tourism has had on St Lucia, an island in the West Indies.

activity

EVALUATING THE IMPACT

For each of the examples given below of exploitation, discuss the impact on the local people and culture.

Not all tourism development involves exploitation, however. Managed properly, it can provide less economically developed countries with a valuable income. Travel and tourism is now on the United Nations 'Agenda for Sustainability and Poverty Alleviation' as it is recognised that tourism can have a significant impact on countries and needs to be managed properly. The World Travel and Tourism Council (WTTC) says that this is a major breakthrough toward recognising the potential of the industry as an effective means to enable sustainable development and alleviate poverty in many parts of the world.

Places such as Kenya in East Africa, where tourists go on safari, or Bali in Indonesia, which people visit for the beautiful beaches, all benefit financially from tourism. However, tourism in LEDCs needs to be carefully managed to prevent harm to the environment or local communities.

The advantages and problems associated with tourism in an LEDC are shown on the following page.

activity

ST LUCIA EVALUATION

Evaluate the negative and positive effects of tourism on the culture of St Lucia.

UNESCO, part of the United Nations, plays a vital role in co-ordinating the development of tourism in LEDCs. Part of the organisation's stated mission is to help preserve the uniqueness and identity of countries: 'Every community has its cultural and spiritual affiliations reaching back symbolically to the dawn of time, and should be in a position to honour them. Cultural diversity has come under siege owing to the preponderance of a limited number of cultural and linguistic approaches and content disseminated via the new and old media. Indigenous peoples and cultures, as well as local knowledge, are most vulnerable'.

Africa, the developing countries, youth and women head the list of UNESCO's priority areas. The eradication of poverty and, in particular, extreme poverty, is the objective of a number of projects in the field of crafts and activities for developing sustainable tourism in remote areas such as the Sahara and the mountainous regions of Asia.

Examples of exploitation

- **Zanzibar** has a fragile eco- and social system, dependent upon agriculture and fishing. Villagers are being evicted from their coastal villages and placed in compounds, their beautiful coral cottages left to rack and ruin, so that all-inclusive tourist compounds surrounded by razor wire and protected by armed guards can be built on the vacated land. Fish bought from local fisherman for the tourist compounds drives up the price, reducing local people to a diet of boiled rice.

- In **Cuba**, dollar tourism is destroying the country, its people and its culture. Two internal markets are developing – the dollar market and the pesos market. The visitors bring the dollar market and the Cubans use the pesos market. The dollar market provides access to all the services that the visitor requires, such as hotel accommodation, good restaurants, etc. and the pesos market allows the local Cubans to buy the basics, such as food and clothing.

- **Antigua** and its 90,000 population was once an island of sugar cane growers, but since 1961 when the first planes full of tourists were flown in, the economy has changed significantly. Now the workers serve the tourism industry. Hotels, restaurants, bars, shops, taxis and many other amenities have sprung up to suit the needs of the tourist. It is not unusual to see three cruise liners at a time anchored off shore, with all 6,000 passengers descending into the busy streets for their day ashore.

- Tourists trample across sacred religious sites, showing no respect to the indigenous cultures. Native people are often expected to perform sacred rituals on demand. In **Peru**, Yagua Indians were forced from the remote Upper Amazon region to more accessible areas so that tourists – on specially built viewing stations – could see them perform their sacred rites.

- Tourism directly and indirectly supports and finances human rights violations and destroys the culture. **Burma** is one of the world's most repressive regimes. In scenes reminiscent of the Japanese occupation, forced labour is being used to prepare infrastructure and resort complexes. At Bassein 30,000 forced labourers helped to construct the new airport, and when cholera broke out they received no medical care. Hundreds of thousands of people have been forced from their homes and lands to make way for tourist projects.

Advantages	Problems
Foreign currency brought to the region by tourists can be invested in improving local education, health and other services.	Profits go to foreign companies, such as tour operators and hotel chains, rather than to the local community.
Jobs for local people are created, giving people the chance to learn new skills in tourism services.	Foreign companies may bring foreign workers to do the skilled jobs, so local people only do low-skilled, poorly paid work.
Construction of new houses and business premises creates jobs and develops skills for local people.	House prices are pushed up when foreign companies buy property for hotels and holiday homes. This often makes houses too expensive for local people.
The local infrastructure is improved as water and sanitation facilities, roads, buses, taxis and airports are provided for tourists.	Important projects for local communities might be side-lined because infrastructure developments are more focused on tourists.
Visitors will get an insight into local customs and traditions that don't exist in Western countries.	Activities that simply entertain, rather than educate tourists, may humiliate the local people.
Tourists can see beautiful landscapes, and interesting wildlife and plants, and be educated about the dangers to fragile ecosystems in the modern world.	Pollution and disruption to wildlife habitats and wildlife behaviour could occur if there are too many tourists.

The costs of package tourism in St Lucia

Package tourism has affected St Lucia in many ways. Tourists dress inappropriately – walking around in short skirts and short belly tops, which may be against the l

ocal people's culture or religion. The tourists do not try to understand St Lucia's culture – often looking down on the local people and treating them badly.

Flown in from the USA or UK, the tourists don't buy food from the local shops. Most of the hotels have private beaches in which local people are not allowed to come in to sell anything. The local economy does not get much foreign income from tourism because the tourists hardly ever leave their hotels.

On the other hand, tourism can also benefit the country because the infrastructure (airports, roads, water and electricity supplies) which has been improved for the tourists also benefits the local people. The local cultures and traditions may be preserved because of the tourists, and income from tourism may pay for management conservation and repairs for the environment.

The Sahara region

The UNESCO project 'The Sahara of cultures and people' aims at helping the relevant UN member states and tourism organisations to implement a strategy of cooperation in the Sahara, based on the promotion of sustainable tourism. The states concerned are: Algeria, Chad, Egypt, Libya, Mali, Mauritania, Morocco, Niger, Sudan and Tunisia. The issues addressed by the project are:

- What jobs and training opportunities will there be and for whom?
- What kind of trips should be promoted and what form should professional cooperation with local populations take?
- How can the participation of local populations be improved and poverty reduced?
- In the face of tourism, how can the cultural and natural heritage be better identified, protected and promoted?

The mountain areas of Asia

The relationship between tourism and local culture is a difficult issue everywhere, but it is at its most contentious in mountain areas – where the local communities have evolved their culture through centuries of isolation and survival strategies.

Historically, cultural change in these communities has been invariably slow. The fact that tourism can

accelerate an otherwise slow process of change in directions that may not be desirable is a matter of concern. The impact of tourism on culture, however, has both negative and positive sides to it, as shown below.

Perceived impact of tourism on culture in the Khumbu region, Nepal

Positive impacts

Promotion of the idea of the National Park

Increased sense of belongingness to the area

Increased popularity and revival of the Mani-Rimdu festival

Increased living standards of the Sherpas

Easy acceptance of new ideas.

Negative impacts

Agriculture decline

Decline in the number of lamas (Buddhist monks) in the monastery

Decline of traditional crafts

Commercialisation of art

Change in Sherpa demography, due to youth migration

Consequent decline in the quality of Sherpa village life, increased burden on women, family break-ups.

David Harris – a typical world traveller

Please can you explain your role?

I am the Director of Sales and Marketing for the Rochester Corporation, based in Culpepper, Virginia, USA. I have travelled extensively all over the world for over 20 years. I have been to many of the world's 'garden spots', and to many not so nice places. I go wherever the business opportunities are, because face-to-face contact is often the key to winning contracts.

The Rochester Corporation is a world leader in the design and manufacture of electro-optical cables intended for a vast array of applications – mining cables for mining and oil explorations, sonar tow cables for the US Navy, umbilical cables for remotely operated vehicles and underwater exploration, etc.

Please can you explain how you got to be in this position?

I went to a public school in Bedford, but did not go on to university. I joined Rochester Ropes straight from school and, working through management training schemes, I got where I am today through making use of the opportunities over the years – and hard work. I now live in the USA with my wife Daphne, and I run the company here in Culpepper and another office in Texas.

How has the internet affected the way you travel?

Internet travel booking and ticketless travel are the way forward in the future. Travel agents and company travel services are a thing of the past. As far as email is concerned – it is now our company's way of life. At least 80% of our business is now done via email.

Are you affected by global warming?

Much of our business is related to energy – oil and gas exploration and production – so environmental issues, including global warming, are very much part of our daily lives. For example, I have just had to return to America from the UK because the hurricanes have caused so much damage to the oil rigs that we are now having to run flat out to provide cabling for reconstruction.

How has your company been affected by globalisation?

The oil industry is a global industry. As far as the western world is concerned, however, much of the oil and gas in the world today is basically in the wrong place, and it is not easily accessible. Asia and the former Soviet Union will play a major part in all our lives in the future. Despite the world being a smaller place these days, oil and gas transportation issues will soon be very much to the fore, and fuel prices are likely to remain high for the foreseeable future.

How has your travel been affected by terrorism?

Terrorism has made business travel harder, more stressful and less appealing. Business travel, with all the extra security delays and restrictions, is no longer glamorous. It has become a necessary burden. Flights into Washington and New York, for example, provoke extra security – and they have now introduced the cameras that take the snapshot of the retina for anyone entering the USA over the age of 14.

How have world diseases affected your travel?

Diseases around the world are not something I have ever worried about or been frightened of. I am always very careful when I travel with regard to food and drink, and I often eat what the locals eat – it's likely to be fresh and better! Whenever I travel overseas I always check on the recommended injections etc. needed for the specific countries to be visited.

Can you give examples of any changes you have witnessed in the less economically developed countries that you travel to?

I have travelled to quite a few 'underdeveloped' regions in the world – in China, Eastern Europe and Asia. The biggest differences in these areas, compared to the western world, are the level of poverty, the uneven distribution of wealth, the infrastructure and the level of corruption.

What influence do wars and terrorism have on your travel?

Wars and terrorism always lead to heightened levels of security. About 15% of our company's business is, in fact, military-based, so when any wars are going on we often get an increased level of business. In many ways, this is really business that we could do without!

Selecting and planning a research project

In the last seven topics we have been looking at issues that can affect and influence the travel and tourism industry. The final three topics of this unit are going to look at how to complete a research project so that you are able to conduct your own research on a particular issue that interests you.

For the assessment of this unit you have to conduct a study of an issue that is currently affecting or has recently (within the last 5 years) affected the travel and tourism industry. You may choose an issue related to one of the subjects covered in the last seven topics, or any other area of interest to you. You will be developing your knowledge and understanding of this issue through research, using a variety of sources, and you will then collate your findings in a report.

You will learn how to plan, then carry out, and finally present a project in an acceptable format. These final three topics will therefore show you how to:

produce a research proposal; use research methodology, and evaluate it; and present your project in an appropriate format. This first topic covers producing a research proposal, under the following headings:

- ▪ Thinking of an idea for a research proposal
- ▪ The structure of your research proposal.

Thinking of an idea for a research proposal

A research proposal is a rationale – including a summary of the research project, its aims and parameters of study – stating the 'what', 'why' and 'how' of the project. In the academic world, a research proposal is the basis of the study, and is produced first – often in order to get funding or permission for the project to continue. Your research proposal – which will be included in your final project – will help you (and your tutor) ensure that your research project is appropriate and practical, and uses a range of research techniques. Remember that 'independent research' is encouraged for this project.

Before you can write a research proposal, however, you first have to chose a subject or issue to study. The choice of issue will be influenced by one or more of the following factors:

- personal interest in the issue
- the fact that there is so much literature available about the issue
- political importance of the issue
- social significance of the issue
- current popularity of the issue.

Examples of these factors are shown below.

Examples of research issues related to different influencing factors

Influencing factor	Examples
Personal interest	An issue relating to a personal holiday experience Tourism issues in your local area
Literature available	SARS World terrorism The tsunami debate
Political importance	Unrest in Zimbabwe The American Dream The Chinese Revolution
Social significance	The impact of tourism on the social environment The role of tourism in LEDCS
Current popularity	Are tourists safe after 9/11? Global warming – fact or fiction? Hurricanes and tourism

CHOOSING THE ISSUE

1 Think of three issues that are of interest to you – perhaps you can get some ideas from the table of examples.

2 Create a mind map (spider diagram) for each issue by writing down the key words in the centre of a page and then writing down all the other related issues around it – remembering all the time that the project is about travel and tourism.

3 Compare your mind map with a friend's. Are there any common themes? How relevant are they to travel and tourism?

4 Investigate how easy it would be to find out information about each of the issues. Remember to consider books, magazines, newspapers, the internet and talking to people.

5 Decide which of your issues would be most appropriate for your research project, and which would be least appropriate.

6 Present your findings back to the group.

Personal interest can range from personal holiday experiences – or experiences of friends and family – to an issue that is affecting the area you live in and may have an impact on your life. The advantage of choosing a personal issue is that it will be a subject that you care about and know something about. The disadvantage is that others may not be so interested in it – or think it not worth researching – and there may not be much literature available for you to work with.

Literature is the most common source of material for research and can take a variety of forms, from books, magazines and journals and other written research reports, to the internet. Newspapers, magazines and journals are often a good source of ideas because they are current. The more literature there is available on an issue, the easier it will be for you to find information that is relevant, up to date and at the right level for your project. However much you may be interested in a particular issue, if you can't access enough appropriate information, you will struggle.

Political issues – which may be linked to personal interest – are ones that are generally recognised as important in relation to the development of tourism around the world. Social issues might concern deprived or neglected social groups, such as those in the less developed world, and how tourism will impact on their lives.

Finally 'currently popular issues' are those portrayed in the media, which tend to focus a lot on the threat of terrorism and national safety. In a way, all of these factors may affect your final decision on the issue you to choose to study.

The structure of your research proposal

Your research proposal is essentially a summary of the research project, its aim and the parameters of the study, and stating the 'why', 'what' and 'how' of the project. So, the proposal should include the following elements:

1. Title
2. The issue (the 'why')
3. The plan
   (a) Aim, objectives and parameters (the 'what')
   (b) Methodology (the 'how')
   (c) References.

Title

The title should be a concise statement of the nature and topic of the research study. It should convey, in just a few words, what the project is about, so that the reader knows what to expect when they read the rest of the proposal. There is no need to cram all the detail into the title. The precise research question, how you intend to tackle it, and the limitations of your study will all be explained in the two main sections of the proposal – the issue and the plan (see below).

The issue

Issues may be political, economic, environmental, social, cultural or technological – but they will affect a travel and tourism organisation, sector or the industry as a whole. This opening section is your justification for your proposed research. It should take the form of a description of the issue, which answers the questions: Why is the research needed? Why is it important to tourism? How much research has been conducted before? Is this research only a specific part of a much larger area of research?

For example, if you have chosen to study a local issue about too many tourists to an area, then your proposal should include a description of the local area and the associated impacts of the tourism. This may mean that you have to access local books and newspapers, and even talk to local people, to see if the issue is significant enough to research.

The plan: (a) Aim, objectives and parameters

The aim is a statement setting out the intention and purpose of the work. For example, the aim is 'to analyse the impact of terrorism on air travel'. Or, the aim is 'to investigate the impact of global warming on UK tourism'.

The aim may be written as a research question or as a hypothesis (though hypotheses tend to be used more in science). For example, a research question might be expressed in the form 'What is the relationship between holiday-taking and income?' A hypothesis dealing with the same topic might be expressed as 'There is a positive relationship between income and taking holidays'. The purpose of the research would be slightly different in each case.

Once the aim is established, a number of objectives should be created – all contributing to that main aim. Objectives should be: specific, clearly expressed, measurable (where appropriate), achievable, result-oriented, and time-bound. For example, if the aim of the study is 'to discover the effects of e-tourism on the industry' the objectives might be:

1. To show that there has been an increase in use over the past two years.

2. To identify people using e-tourism regularly and establish whether their use is increasing and, if so, why.

3. To identify people changing to e-tourism and discover what made them change.

4. To rank people's motivations for change (time/cost/ease/etc.) and the barriers to change (access/security fears/etc.).

The parameters are the limits or restrictions on the study and often include factors such as:

- the physical area to be considered in the research (e.g. 'within the Peak District National Park').

- the physical area within which the research will be conducted.

- the timescale to be considered (e.g. 'over the last four years') or how long the research will take (e.g. 'interviewed over a three-week period').

- the budget limitations (e.g. 'using no more than 10 postal questionnaires').

- the human resources to be used.

activity

AIMS, OBJECTIVES, PARAMETERS

Think of a tourism issue that interests you. Think of an aim for your intended research. Now write the aim as a question and then as a hypothesis. Write at least three objectives linked to the aim that you wish to research. Now describe the parameters that may influence your research.

The plan: (b) Methodology

This section will include information answering the following questions:

- What sort of research design will be used?

- What methods will be used to collect the data?

- What type of data will be collected?

- If using a questionnaire or conducting interviews, what questions will be asked?

- How will the data be analysed?

- How appropriate is the analytical technique to be used?

- What is the justification for the methodology to be used?

This section will state if you will be using primary or secondary research, or a combination of both. Primary research is your own original research, using methods such as surveys, one-to-one interviews, group interviews or focus groups. Secondary research is finding and using other people's research which has already been reported in, for example, articles, official statistics or written reports.

The extent of data collection needs to be stated in the proposal, along with where the process will take place – by going into the field or by using the local library, for example. Generally speaking, the more extensive and wide ranging your research, the better the results will be.

The plan: (c) References

These are the planned sources of reference to support the study. They should be listed at the back of the research proposal, in a consistent/established format.

How to present your research proposal

1. Typed, with reasonable margins on all sides

2. Space and a half or double line spacing is best

3. Internally consistent – no contradictions in it

4. Free of spelling errors and grammatically correct

5. Neatly presented.

Topic 9 Research methodology

In the last topic we looked at how to produce a research proposal – a summary of the project. Now we will go on to look at the different research techniques that could be employed when undertaking the project.

Methods of collecting primary data fall into two main categories – **qualitative research** and **quantitative research** (see below). Qualitative research is usually undertaken using in-depth interviews or discussion groups (focus groups) among a relatively small number of people. Its purpose is to provide exploratory, explanatory and diagnostic information – the how and the why – in depth. Such interviewing needs to be conducted by experts, preferably face-to-face, although telephone and online methods are also used.

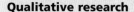

Quantitative research incorporates the statistical (how many?) element, designed to quantify the extent to which a target group are aware of something, think this, believe that or are inclined to behave in a certain way.

Qualitative research	Quantitative research
looks at feelings, attitudes, desires and perceptions	provides more structured information that is statistically measurable
provides detailed in-depth explanations	enables researchers to draw specific and measurable conclusions from the results
is often difficult to present statistically	
does not usually lead to clear conclusions	does not explain in-depth reasons
generally includes questions that start with 'explain', 'why' or 'describe'	generally includes questions that start with 'when', 'how many' or 'which'
involves gathering large amounts of information about relatively few subjects.	involves gathering relatively small amounts of data on large numbers of subjects.

Primary research

Primary research is where the information is collected first-hand, and this may be done in a number of ways:

- Interviews
- Questionnaires
- Focus groups and panels
- Observation (including participant observation).

Interviews

An interview is defined as 'a session of formal or informal questioning'. This method ranges from one-

Plan and conduct a formal interview on a one-to-one basis to discover what an interviewee thinks about some of the issues that affect the travel and tourism industry. Identify some key questions on issues you wish to discuss, but do not create a questionnaire. How much information did you discover? Write up your results, and then analyse how you could have improved the interview.

to-one, in-depth discussions, to telephone or online interviews. Interviews tend to provide qualitative information. Because they take time to set up and conduct, they usually involve only small numbers of individuals, although the use of the telephone or internet can make it possible to interview greater numbers of people, across a wide range of locations. In fact, the internet provides the opportunity for worldwide interview research.

The informal interview may just occur as part of a conversation, and is often the way that research issues are first discovered. For example, a conversation with a local tour guide could provide the initial idea for researching a local tourism issue, such as erosion of local woodland. Unlike informal interviews, which tend not to be planned and have no defined direction, the formal interview will probably have a defined direction around key topics. It may not have set questions but the interviewer will aim to discover key points during the conversation. A formal interview may even have an established time limit and take place in a formal setting.

Questionnaires

A questionnaire is a set of printed questions, devised for a survey or statistical study. This may be sent to a person's home, a postal questionnaire, or used as the template for a face-to-face interview conducted in the home or on the street as an 'oral questionnaire'. In addition, telephone questionnaires may be conducted over the telephone or online, as shown in the example overleaf.

The questions may be 'open' or 'closed'. Open questions invite the interviewee to give any answer they

activity

ANALYSING THE QUESTIONNAIRE

Look at the eco-tourism questionnaire overleaf.

1 Explain the type of data that it would collect.

2 Why do you think this questionnaire uses a lot of closed questions?

3 Can you suggest any open questions that could be included?

4 Think of a current issue that interests you and create a questionnaire that you could use in your research.

choose. 'What is your favourite resort?', for example, is an open question. With closed questions, the interviewee must choose an answer from given options. The most common choice of answer is 'Yes' or 'No', but those with a fixed range of options, such as 'strongly like', 'like', 'dislike', etc. are also closed questions.

Choosing a sample

It is not normally possible to survey the views of large numbers of people – it would be too expensive, too time-consuming and too much trouble to carry out. Researchers therefore choose a representative 'sample' of the people they are interested in and just survey their views. It is important, however, that the people they choose are truly representative of the whole group. If they just chose their friends, or their colleagues, it would make their life easier – but the results wouldn't be representative. There are several

Eco-tourism internet questionnaire

Please indicate your answers with an X or a number, as appropriate.

1. How many times per year do you go holiday?
   ☐ 1 ☐ 2 ☐ 3 ☐ 4 ☐ 5 ☐ More than 5

2. How many of the holidays you have stated above, are eco-tourism holidays?
   ☐ 1 ☐ 2 ☐ 3 ☐ 4 ☐ 5 ☐ More than 5

3. How are your holidays organised? Please choose one.
   ☐ Independently   ☐ Independently with organised tours
   ☐ Non-profit group organised tours   ☐ Tour operator/travel agent

4. Please list the activities below in order of importance to you when choosing an eco-tourism holiday. Use numbers from 1–15 (1 = most important, 15 = least important).
   ☐ Nature   ☐ Local people   ☐ Wildlife   ☐ Bird watching
   ☐ Landscape   ☐ Hiking   ☐ Quietness   ☐ Diving
   ☐ Culture   ☐ Kayaking   ☐ Historical monuments ☐ Photography
   ☐ Conservation ☐ Mountaineering   ☐ Rare animals/plants

5. What do you consider to be the most important factors when choosing your holiday? Please list in order of importance, using numbers 1–5 (1 = most important, 5 = least important).
   ☐ Destination ☐ Price ☐ Referrals ☐ Popularity ☐ Conservation interest

6. What proportion of your holiday is spent on contact with nature?
   ☐ All of it ☐ Most of it ☐ Some of it ☐ Not a lot of it ☐ Almost none

7. What benefits do you seek the most when on holiday? Please list in order of importance using numbers 1–7.
   ☐ Visiting uncrowded destinations   ☐ Experiencing remote and unspoiled nature
   ☐ Increasing knowledge of wildlife   ☐ Interacting with native people
   ☐ Supporting economic benefits to local communities ☐ See unusual plants and animals
   ☐ Increasing confidence through challenging activities

8. To what degree do you consider yourself to behave in an environmentally conscious way?
   ☐ Very responsible   ☐ Responsible   ☐ Not always responsible
   ☐ Not responsible   ☐ Irresponsible

9. How long do you go on holiday for?
   ☐ 1–2 weeks ☐ 2–3 weeks ☐ 3–4weeks ☐ 4 weeks +

10. What recreational activity do you engage in most often when on holiday? Please choose one.
    ☐ Hiking ☐ Rafting   ☐ Canoeing   ☐ Cycling   ☐ Kayaking
    ☐ Skiing ☐ Wildlife viewing   ☐ Cultural activities ☐ Horseback riding

11. Gender: ☐ Male ☐ Female

12. Age: ☐ 18–25 ☐ 26–35 ☐ 36–45 ☐ 46–55 ☐ 56–65 ☐ 66–75 ☐ 75+

13. Education. Please mark all that apply.
    ☐ A levels ☐ HND ☐ Undergraduate ☐ Post-graduate ☐ PhD

14. Income. Please choose one category only.
    ☐ £10,000–£20,000   ☐ £20,001–£30,000   ☐ £30,001–£40,000
    ☐ £40,001–£50,000   ☐ £50,001–£60,000   ☐ £60,001 +

15. How much do you spend on an eco-tourism holiday?
    ☐ £0–£500   ☐ £500–£1,000   ☐ £1,000–£1,500
    ☐ £1,500–£2,000   ☐ £2,500 +

16. Do you belong to a conservation-oriented organisation? ☐ Yes ☐ No

methods of choosing samples, each designed for a slightly different purpose (see below).

Focus groups and panels

Focus group research involves organised discussion with a carefully selected group of individuals to gain information about their experiences of, and views on, an issue or topic. Focus group interviewing is particularly useful for obtaining several perspectives about the same topic.

The role of the moderator/interviewer is very significant in focus groups. Good interpersonal and group leadership skills are required to moderate a

group successfully to ensure that any one person does not dictate the opinions of the group.

The recommended number of people per group is usually six to ten, and sessions usually last from one to two hours. Neutral locations can be helpful for avoiding either negative or positive associations with a particular site or building.

activity

ANALYSING FOCUS GROUP RESEARCH

Identify and discuss the advantages and disadvantages of using focus group research.

Observation

Human beings spend much of their life observing the world in which they live. But observation does not just include vision – it includes other senses too, and when we are observing something our brain is still working, so perception also comes into play. For example, our observation of holidaymakers' activities will be affected by not just what they are doing, but perhaps also by our perception of how much they are enjoying it.

A participant observer is someone who is also

Sampling methods

Simple random sampling

The researcher decides the size of the sample needed and then picks them from the whole group on a random basis – by drawing names from hat, for example, or sticking a pin in a list of all the names. The method used must ensure that every name has an equal chance of being selected. Computer-generated random selection uses this method.

Systematic sampling

This involves selecting names from a list at regular intervals, after choosing a random starting point. So, if you needed 20 names from a numbered list of 1000, you could select every 50th name, starting at, say, number 18. The sample would therefore be the names numbered 18, 68, 118, 168, 218, etc.

Stratified random sampling

This method weights the sample on the basis of the importance of each group. For example, if an organisation has 500 small users accounting for £1million of their sales, but 100 big users accounting for £2million of their sales, then they need to make sure that they interview twice as many big users as small users to represent their total sales.

Cluster sampling

In this method the whole group is divided into small subgroups, but instead of choosing a random sample, you select those subgroups typical of the market. So you may break an area like London into 200 sections, but only chose to survey those that have the large tourist attractions.

Quota sampling

In this method, interviewers are given instructions to select a certain number of people according to their characteristics – sex, age, or socio-economic group. For example, a travel company interested in marketing a holiday to 18 to 30 year olds would only select people in that age group.

Convenience sampling

This method involves gathering information from anybody available for the interviewer to survey – no matter what their background.

Judgement sampling

This method involves selection of the respondents by the interviewer based on his or her judgement that they seem to be and look representative of the group being researched.

taking part in the activity themselves, for example being a visitor on a trip whilst observing others. A non-participant observer is someone who is observing from the outside and is not part of the activity they are observing. These two types of observation can obviously produce quite different results, because being a member of a group can provide a different perspective on the findings.

Observation may be used as an initial exploratory form of research. For example, looking for evidence of environmental damage, or of the effects of tourism in less developed countries. Other forms of more quantitative research may follow from initial observation work.

Observation is often thought of as one of the cheaper options, but it is often a very restricted form of research. One observer in one location, witnessing one string of events is not a very scientific form of research, nor does it provide any great breadth of detail. Observation is not a suitable form of research to undertake for long periods of time and that is why technological equipment is often used now for this role. For example, the Meteorological Office has observational equipment all over the world for measuring temperature, wind speed, etc. and this helps produce more accurate weather forecasts.

Secondary research

Secondary research is sometimes called desk research because it is an activity that mainly takes place at a desk. There are a variety of sources of information that can be used in this type of research:

- Books
- Journals
- Newspapers
- Television
- Statistics
- The internet.

Books

There are a wide variety of books that you can use in your research. These range from books that relate to specific issues, such as conservation, to more general textbooks (like this one) covering travel and tourism in general. You could select a textbook, other than this one, that is most relevant to your study and use the bibliography as a guide for your further reading.

Ensure that any book you use is relatively current – published in the last five years, say – so that its information is reasonably up to date . Also make sure

that you can understand the level of writing. If you end up copying great chunks of text that you do not comprehend, it will be glaringly obvious to the examiner. Copying is called plagiarism and is taken very seriously by exam boards.

Journals

Industry-specific journals or magazines provide current information, and may be a good starting point for your research as they have thought-provoking articles that may give you an initial idea. Journals that may be useful to your research include: *Travel Trade Gazette*; *National Geographic*; *Condé Nast Traveller*; *Wanderlust*; *Gap Year*; *Business Travel World*; *Heritage*; *InBritain*.

Newspapers

Newspapers provide current information on a daily or weekly basis. They often provide stimulation for ideas, particularly as each of the nationals often decides to cover news issues from a slightly different angle. Many of the newspapers have good travel sections. The weekend newspapers in particular often provide an overview of the week and have more detailed travel information. *The Times*, *The Independent*, the *Guardian*, the *Daily Telegraph* and the *Daily Mail* are good sources of information, and they have good supporting website too.

activity

COMPARING NEWSPAPERS

In a group, select a current travel and tourism issue that is in the news. Allocate a different newspaper to each member of the group and then compare the information they provide on the issue. What is the main focus of each newspaper?

Ian Wright, TV presenter of Lonely Planet travel programme on the Discovery channel

Television

Television is good for researching ideas as long as you chose the programmes to watch that are relevant. The news programmes are always good for providing information on relevant issues, such as wars, terrorism and natural disasters.

Less economically developed countries are sometimes featured as extended news items or as documentaries, as are issues such as global warming and examples of globalisation. But you have to find out when the programmes are to be run on a regular basis to get the most from television research.

Statistics

Statistics are useful to show changes over time and to show evidence of trends. Most of the evidence for global warming, for example, is statistical. Tables of statistics will often give you the opportunity to analyse the data to support your argument and so add credibility to your work. Statistics are collected and published by a whole range of sources, such as the International Passenger Survey, the Department of Culture Media and Sport, ABTA and worldwide organisations such as the World Travel and Tourism Council.

activity

SELECTING SOURCES OF STATISTICS

Sources of statistics related to travel and tourism may be found on the www.altis.ac.uk website. Select the Travel and Tourism section, then tourism statistics, and you will find over 90 sources listed. Select ten that you may find useful for your research project.

The internet

The internet provides access to a huge amount of information, and is fast becoming one of the most commonly used research tools. In fact, one of the main drawbacks of using the internet for research is the sheer quantity of information that is accessible. For example, if you use a search engine such as Google and type in the simple phrase 'Trends in Travel' it comes up with nearly half a million matches. Obviously, the more refined the search, the fewer and more relevant will be the matches, but they can still run into several thousand, only some of which will be of use in your research.

When the relevant sites have been found, you still have to distinguish between reliable sites and unreliable ones. Reliable sites will:

- provide information from a recognised source – a newspaper, for example

- provide current information – check that it isn't referring to documents written years ago

- not represent a personal point of view on a subject, as in a personal account

- not consist of biased information from a single, perhaps campaigning, source.

In conclusion, you can see that there is a vast array of research methods for you to choose from, and you have to decide which best fits the issue that you have chosen to study. There are advantages and disadvantages to each of the methods (see table overleaf), and your own personal circumstances will probably decide which you choose to use.

activity

INTERNET PRACTICE

Using the websites listed below, assess the usefulness of the information that you can find on an issue of your choice.

Websites: www.altis.ac.uk; www.tutor2U.net; www.marketingteacher.com; www.bized.ac.uk; www.dailymail.co.uk.

Undertaking your research

Now that you have chosen an issue, prepared your research proposal – and had it approved – and learnt about all about research methodology, you can carry out your actual research. The next topic will deal with how this unit is assessed and explain what your final research project should look like.

97

Topic 9 Research methodology

The advantages and disadvantages of different research methods

PRIMARY RESEARCH

Interviews

- Good for obtaining individual attitudes, beliefs and feelings
- Easier for the researcher to control
- Good for gaining qualitative information

but

- Can be time consuming
- Depends on the skill of the interviewer

Questionnaires

- Good way to obtain quantitative data
- Use of the same questions makes analysis easier
- Can cover a large target audience over a wide area

but

- Can be time consuming to collate

Focus groups

- Good for testing out new ideas or products
- Compared to observation, a focus group enables the researcher to gain a larger amount of information in a shorter period of time

but

- Depends on the skill of the researcher
- Not necessarily representative of the whole population

Observation

- Relatively cheap

but

- Tends to depend on waiting for things to happen
- Often limited to one person in one location

SECONDARY RESEARCH

Books

- Useful to refer back to on a regular basis

but

- Can be expensive if you have not got access to a good library

Journals

- Useful for current issues and information

Newspapers

- Useful for current issues of the day
- May provide food for thought

Television

- Strong pictorial images that can stimulate ideas for study

but

- Difficult to refer back to (unless the programme has been recorded)

Statistics

- Useful for qualitative analysis of data
- Can provide more factual evidence
- Can help to provide evidence of trends

The internet

- Worldwide information at the press of a button

but

- Usually too much information
- Not always up to date or reliable

Topic 10 How this unit is assessed: what your research project should look like

In the last topic we looked at the different research techniques that could be employed when undertaking your project. This topic looks at how to present your research project in an appropriate format. Having spent so much time planning your project, conducting your research and analysing your findings, it would be a shame if all this hard work was let down by the writing-up process. However, for many students, not taking enough time in the presentation can result in an inaccurate, incomplete or sloppily presented report that achieves a lower mark than anticipated.

The assessment evidence for this unit is a completed research project that focuses on a current travel and tourism issue. (An issue is regarded as current if it has arisen within the last 5 years, or is ongoing.) The project must have used a range of research methods.

Your project will include written commentary, and may also be supported by witness testimonies and observation statements if some of the tasks are presented orally. Written notes should be presented in support of any oral presentations.

The project could be presented in four distinct sections:

1. The research proposal

2. The research plan

3. The research and the analysis

4. An evaluation of the project and research methodology

A bibliography should also be included, plus appendices of supporting material, if necessary.

1. The research proposal

The proposal has been fully covered in Topic 8. Remember it should have the following elements:

1. Title
2. The issue (the 'why')

3. The plan
   (a) Aim, objectives and parameters (the 'what')
   (b) Methodology (the 'how')
   (c) References.

2. The research plan

This section should show how you have followed your original research plan (set out in the proposal) to meet the project's aims and timescales and, where relevant, how you have dealt with changes to your plan. It should also show how you have worked independently. Your section on methodology should be sufficiently detailed so that the reader knows exactly how the research was carried out. It is important that you explain why you took the approach that you did. For example, if you chose the questionnaire method, explain why this method was a better choice that any of the others. In other words justify your selected method.

3. The research and the analysis

This section should include all the evidence of the research undertaken as indicated in the plan you set out in the proposal. This will take the form of a description of the results of the research, analysis, discussion and interpretation of the findings, and your conclusions – a summary of key findings, referring back to aims of the research. It should also include an analysis of the issue and its effect on the travel and tourism industry or one of its component sectors.

The research is often called the 'results' section in a report because it deals with the findings. The results should be presented clearly and concisely. Tables and graphs can be useful tools as a means of summarising data (see below).

'Analysis' refers to the examination and interpretation of your findings. Your research will have identified key facts but the facts do not speak for themselves and need to be interpreted in the report, especially as some of the facts may need to be linked together.

It may be tempting to just list your findings – your questionnaire responses, for example – but this is to be avoided. You should analyse your findings and group them around your stated research aims. It may not be necessary to include all the responses collected during the research, but a sample or the collated results should be included in the appendix.

The golden rule for your conclusions section is not to introduce any new material – the conclusions must focus on your findings and not stray into other areas. You may, however, wish to compare your findings with those of other researchers. Have you confirmed what others have found?

Tables, graphs and diagrams

You should always use the most appropriate method to show your findings. For example, a bar chart is not an appropriate way of showing a 'yes' and 'no' answer but may be suitable when there were a number of answers to chose from.

All tables and diagrams must be numbered and given a title. They should also acknowledge their source – although, of course, it is not necessary to provide a source if it is your own primary research. Lengthy tables may be better presented in the appendix, but this depends on their significance to your findings. Again, appropriateness is the key to presentation.

---

4. An evaluation of the project

This section should contain an evaluation of the project and the research methodology, together with recommendations for approaches to be adopted for future projects. Sometimes it is useful to ask yourself a series of questions:

- Did I choose the correct aims and objectives? How would I have changed them?

- Did I select the right method of research? Could I have selected an alternative method ,and what would have been the effect on my findings?

- Was the research conducted effectively? How could it have been improved?

- Did I select the correct sample and sample size? How could it have been improved?

- If I were to do this project again, what would I do differently?

Bibliography

The bibliography should include all the sources of information that you have used to complete the assessment for this unit. You must always cite the sources of your information for three good reasons:

- It gives your work credibility.

- It avoids the charge of plagiarism (copying someone else's work).

- It allows your reader to trace and check material.

There are a number of methods of referencing, but the easiest and most widely used is the Harvard system (see opposite).

The best advice is to collect all references and bibliography details as you go along. Leaving this task to the end can waste hours whilst you try and re-trace your steps and find the resources again. Get into the habit of systematically recording your resources as you do your work.

The Harvard system

In your main text – where you have quoted someone's work – you just put, in brackets, the author's surname and the year of publication.

Example: (Hamilton, 1995).

In the Bibliography, you must put all the details needed by the reader to find the source, if they want to. All the entries are arranged alphabetically, in one list. This means that the reader, who won't know from the main text whether a reference is to a book, an article or a website, can always find the details. These details are laid out in a standard way, which varies for books, articles and internet sites:

Books

Author's surname, followed by their initials
Year of publication in brackets
Title of publication – in italics
Place of publication
Publisher

Example: Hamilton, F. (1995) Tourism and Crime, London: Collinson.

Articles in journals, magazines or newspapers

Author's surname, followed by their initials
Year of publication in brackets
Title of article – in quotation marks
Name of the journal, magazine or newspaper – in italics
Day and month of publication
Page number (abbreviated to p.)

Example: Selvey, S. (1999) 'Caught in a pitch and toss', Guardian, 13 June, Travel p.10.

Internet sites

Author's surname, followed by their initials (If no name is given, use the name of the organisation.)
Year in brackets (If no publication date is given, put 'no date'.)
Title in italics, followed by 'online' in brackets
'Available from:' website address (the URL – Universal Resource Locator – or at least the website homepage address)
The date when you accessed it – in brackets.

Example: Rough Guides (no date), Australia (on-line). Available from: http:// www.hotwired.com/rough/australia (accessed 10 April 2000).

For more information on this method of referencing you may visit your local library or see the website www.libweb.apu.ac.uk.

activity

USING THE HARVARD SYSTEM

Select three of each of the following, and reference them in a bibliography using the Harvard system: a book, a newspaper, an internet site. Remember to list them alphabetically.

Appendices

Relevant supporting information should be included in the appendices – examples of marketing materials, policies and procedures, etc. The appendices should not just be padding but should add something to the report. They should be numbered and referenced in the text. (e.g. 'see Appendix A'). All important information should be included in the main body of the project, of course, but sample copies of questionnaires or any other evidence supporting the report should be in an appendix. Complex tables or diagrams may also be best in an appendix, including any lengthy tables of the questionnaire or survey results

Presentation of your project

- Your title page should have the title on your proposal, plus your name, the date, the name of your institution, and the name of the unit: 'Unit 8 Current Issues in Travel and Tourism'. The title page must be well laid out, with appropriate use of colour and fonts.

- The Contents page should list all the sections included in the project, using the same wording, with their page numbers. It is probably best left as the last task – after all the changes have been made.

- The Acknowledgements (optional) should thank – as a matter or courtesy – all the people who have helped you with the project: organisations, individuals, your supervisor, your friends and family.

- Numbering of sections and subsections. In lengthy documents, it helps if there is a consistent numbering system for the various elements. The subsections within Section 2, for example, would be numbered 2.1, 2.2, etc.
  Appendices are normally called Appendix A, Appendix B, etc.

- The wording of the text – the language level – should always be appropriate to the audience.

- You should carefully read and edit your work more than once before submitting it.

Travel and tourism is, by many estimates, the largest global industry of all. It is certainly one of the most exciting and dynamic industries to work in, providing a wide range of varied and challenging job opportunities. For those who yearn to travel there are jobs in transport – with airlines and cruise companies – or jobs in resort operations or visitor attractions. Closer to home, opportunities exist in all areas of the country in the public, private and voluntary sectors. Further opportunities are available for those who want to specialise in a specific area of business or management, such as human resources, marketing, finance or event management.

In this unit we are going to look at the range and nature of employment opportunities and the type of skills that you are likely to need for a successful career in travel and tourism.

Working in travel and tourism is very much focused on being able to work well with colleagues, so that together you can provide products and services that meet your customers' needs and expectations. Therefore we will explore the ways in which teams operate effectively and the skills that you need to contribute to effective teamwork.

Finally we will look at the specific skills that you already possess and further skills that you could acquire to enable you to follow your chosen career. This will involve undertaking a 'personal skills audit' and creating a 'personal development plan' for a chosen employment opportunity within the travel and tourism industry.

There are two Industry Focus interviews in this unit to help your understanding of working within the industry. The first is with the manager of an employment agency, and provides general advice on how to present yourself successfully to potential employers. The second interview is with a resort rep and explains the types of skills that are needed for this very popular area of employment.

Unit 9

Working in Travel and Tourism

Topic 1 The range of employment opportunities

The travel and tourism industry provides a wide range of exciting career opportunities. In the first four topics of this unit we are going to look at the range, nature and skills required for such careers. Let's start by examining the range of opportunities, under the following headings:

- **Employment opportunities**
- **Advertising of employment opportunities**
- **General skills required for jobs**
- **Entry requirements.**

Just some of the jobs in travel and tourism

Travel agency clerk/travel consultant – is responsible for advising customers and selling travel services. Personal experience of independent travel is particularly relevant to companies specialising in tailor-made itineraries.

Holiday representative – employed in resorts to look after holidaymakers. Includes children's reps and administrators. Work is hard and demanding, usually working on rota systems.

Tour manager/courier – travels with groups of holidaymakers on package tours at home and overseas. Couriers are usually employed on a freelance basis and work may be seasonal.

Tourist information centre adviser – provides information to visitors to the area and sells guidebooks, maps and products. Advisors also operate booking services for accommodation, local events, sightseeing tours and theatres.

Heritage officer/interpreter – responsible for making historical resources such as buildings, sites, landscapes and monuments available to the public whilst ensuring their preservation for future generations.

Historic property manager – responsible for the management of historic properties including maintenance and income. Liaises with specialist staff over conservation of grounds and repair of building, with owners and with organisations such as the National Trust.

Hotel manager – manages hotel, restaurant, etc whilst promoting facilities and services, organising special events and recruiting staff.

Event/conference organiser – A conference organiser arranges the programme, obtains delegates and books the venue. Event organisers: liaise with exhibitors, caterers, contractors, as well as newspapers and other publications to gain maximum advertising coverage; write press releases, organise tickets, posters, catalogues and sales brochures; ensure that health and safety regulations are adhered to.

Public relations officer – writes press releases, produces publicity brochures and promotional literature (may work in conjunction with marketing dept), produces customer/staff newspapers and magazines.

Arts administrator – responsible for managing the theatre/gallery etc, managing financial resources, marketing, and attracting sponsorship to support the arts.

Employment opportunities

Job opportunities within the travel and tourism industry are probably more varied and diverse than in any other industry. They exist at all levels of responsibility – from the part-time seasonal jobs, such as bar staff and theme park attendants, to permanent roles in travel agencies and at airports, to supervisory and managerial jobs, such as Tourist Information Centre Manager or Head Resort Representative. Those with ambitions to progress within travel and tourism will find numerous openings that allow them to achieve their goals. It would be impossible to list all of the job opportunities within the industry, but the careers service 'Prospects' lists some of the roles open to aspiring travel and tourism professionals (see previous page).

The jobs listed represent many different sectors of the travel and tourism industry. However, even within a specific sector there are usually a wide range of different opportunities. For example, the cruise industry is experiencing a dramatic increase in popularity, particularly following the introduction of new forms of cruising such as easyCruise and Ocean Village. This buoyancy has lead to an increase in the number and range of employment opportunities in cruising – many of which would not be immediately obvious as part of the travel industry, such as hairdressers and beauticians. Most cruise ships represent small floating towns and therefore have all of the facilities that you expect to find in a town, as shown below.

Advertising of employment opportunities

As with any career, finding the right job within travel and tourism can be difficult unless you know where to look – in other words, where employers advertise their vacancies. Finding suitable advertisements really depends on the type of job that you are seeking. For local jobs, the best sources are usually local papers, the Job Centre or local employment agencies. National and international jobs are more likely to be found in:

- The national press and trade journals

Forty different jobs in the cruising industry

Deck Department	Casino Staff	Cruise Directors	Cruise Staff
Disc Jockeys	Entertainers	Expedition Leaders	Gentleman Host
Hosts and Hostesses	Lecturers	Naturalists	Production Managers
Shore Excursion Managers	Lifeguards		Shore Excursion Staff
Water Sports Instructors			Beauticians
Youth Counsellors			Cosmetologists
Massage Therapists			Fitness Directors
Fitness Instructors			Medical Staff
Personal Trainers			Air/Sea Reservation Agents
Bar Stewards			Bartenders
Bedroom Stewards			Gift Shop Positions
Hospitality or Hotel Managers	Photographers		Deckhands
Junior Assistant Pursers	Pursers		IT Staff
Dance Instructors	Administration Assistants		Booking Agents
Customer Service Representatives		Sales and Marketing Positions	

- Employment agencies
- The internet.

The national press and trade journals

Newspapers such as the *Guardian*, *The Times*, *Daily Telegraph* and *Daily Mail* and journals such as *Travel Weekly* and *The Caterer* are a good source of job information. Most newspapers have a specific day when they publish job vacancies. The *Daily Telegraph*, for example, carries most advertisements on a Thursday. In addition, a large number of journals and newspapers have a jobs section on their website that has a facility to search for opportunities within a particular industry. Many also provide a free service of emailing new job opportunities to subscribers.

Employment agencies

Using an employment agency, whether local, national or international, can provide information on openings into the travel and tourism industry. The services offered are usually free to the job seeker, as the agency makes its money from charging the employer. Some of the most useful agencies for people seeking opportunities in travel and tourism are shown below.

Examples of employment agencies

Reed
General graduate site often advertising travel-related and language-related vacancies
www.reed.co.uk/graduates

C&M Travel Recruitment
Travel jobs agency, including airline and cruises
www.candm.co.uk

T&T Training Solutions
Travel and tour company recruitment agency, including hotels and HR sections
www.tandtrecruitment.co.uk

Lister Charles
Mainly bar and restaurant jobs
www.lister-charles.co.uk

Berkeley Scott
Agency handling hospitality, leisure and retail jobs and advice
www.berkeley-scott.co.uk

Portfolio International
Hotel, catering and leisure recruitment agency
www.portfoliointl.com

AA Appointments
Travel, tourism and hospitality jobs in UK, Ireland and Australia
www.aaappointments.com

Action Recruitment Europe
Specialist hospitality recruiters
www.actionrecruitment.co.uk

The internet

Searching for jobs and career advice on the web is often an efficient way of finding what opportunities are available and making direct applications. Some examples of the better recruitment sites are shown below. Do not forget that many travel and tourism organisations advertise vacancies on their own websites. If you have a clear idea of what you would like to do – or who you would like to work for – it is useful to visit some of these corporate websites to see what is available.

Examples of recruitment websites

www.flightinternational.com
www.traveljobsearch.com
www.travelindustryjobs.co.uk
www.jobsin.co.uk/travelandtourism
www.hcareers.co.uk
www.hotelandcaterer.com
www.hotel-jobs.co.uk
www.jobsin.co.uk/catering
www.recruit4leisure.co.uk
www.leisuretourism.com
www.cruisejobfinder.com

activity

FIND SIX DIFFERENT JOBS EACH

Visit three of the websites listed above. Select two different travel and tourism jobs from each, and write brief descriptions, comparing and contrasting the skills required. Display the findings from the whole group on a display board.

General skills required for jobs

We will explore the skills needed for specific travel and tourism jobs in Topic 2. Here, we consider some of the general skills that all travel and tourism employers may be looking for.

Travel and tourism is, first and foremost, a service industry that focuses strongly on the customer experience, so its staff need to have excellent customer service and personal skills to meet the demands of customers. In addition, one of the characteristics (and attractions) of working in the industry is the unpredictability and the challenges that arise in dealing with different situations and customers. This requires staff who can use their initiative and make effective and quick decisions as to the best course of action. Being able to work effectively as a member of a team is a further skill that most employers will be looking for. We look at the importance of teamwork In Topics 5, 6 and 7.

Your skills: a personal audit

In the final two topics of this unit you are going to look at how you can evaluate your own potential and then assess the appropriate career opportunities. A strong awareness of where your true strengths lie is an important aspect of selecting and aiming for a suitable career. This topic deals with the first stage – identifying your personal skills and then carrying out an audit, under the following headings:

- Your personal skills and qualities
- Your values and attitudes
- Your knowledge and experience
- Personal skills audit.

Your personal skills and qualities

Personal skills and qualities are the specific strengths of your character or personality that make you particularly employable. Some of these skills are inherent (i.e. you were born that way) such as being friendly and outgoing. Others may be learnt through experience, such as how to communicate effectively with different groups of people or deal with difficult situations. Broadly speaking, personal skills and qualities can be categorised in the following four ways:

Examples of different types of personal skills

Personality: a sense of humour, maturity, tactfulness, friendliness, hard working
People skills: communication skills, being able to work in a team, being customer-focused, interpersonal skills
Self-management: ability to work on one's own, self-discipline, willingness to learn, time management
General: flexibility, ability to solve problems, personal efficiency, ability to make decisions.

activity

SKILLS AND QUALITIES NEEDED?

Select one of these jobs in travel and tourism: travel agency adviser, resort rep, cabin crew member, tour guide, customer services adviser for a rail company, host on a cruise ship. Write a 200-word report on the personal skills and qualities that someone would need to carry out the role.

Your values and attitudes

We talked in depth about the importance of attitude and values in Unit 2 The Travel and Tourism Customer. It is vital that this area is seen as part of your overall skills development. Having an appropriate attitude (see below) towards your job, your employer and your customers will often be a key factor in your career progression.

Attitude skills

- Caring about your customers and wanting to meet their needs
- Always maintaining professional behaviour
- Respecting and supporting authority and colleagues
- Willingness and enthusiasm for your job responsibilities
- Understanding the basic rules of good manners when dealing with customers and colleagues
- A desire to 'do a bit extra' to ensure the job is done well
- Understanding the importance of complying with work procedures such as good timekeeping and wearing the correct uniform
- Taking responsibility for your actions
- Taking pride in the work that you do and the organisation that you work for.

By 'values' we mean the issues that we rate as important – in other words, our own moral code. Many of these values overlap with some of the attitude skills that we looked at above. For example, anyone aspiring to do well in the travel and tourism industry will have personal values that include pride in

MATCHING CAREER AND VALUES

Tom has just completed a BA Hons degree in Environmental Tourism. As part of his final year he spent three months working in an eco-tourism project in the Gambia. The project involved regenerating rundown, remote villages with the view to creating destinations that tourists could visit to experience a realistic insight into the Gambian village culture and way of life. Whilst he was there he lived with the villagers and was humbled by their simple way of life and sense of pride in their culture. At the end of his stay he visited some of the nearby large, overdeveloped resorts where he was shocked to see the ways in which the Gambian way of life had been destroyed to provide the services that rich tourists demanded. He decided, as he was leaving, that the only career in tourism that he wanted to have was one that had the core values of responsible tourism at its heart.

In pairs, identify six possible career options – three in the UK and three international (not in the UK) – that Tom might find rewarding, given his strong personal values.

Identify three other career options that you think Tom would find difficult to succeed at, given his values.

their work and ensuring that they satisfy their customers' needs. Additional values might include issues such as inclusivity. For example, recognising that everyone, regardless of race, age, gender or disability, has the same rights in terms of the ways in which they are treated. Sometimes personal values might affect someone's choice of career path. For example, if you have already studied Unit 7 Responsible Tourism, you will appreciate that there are a range of ethical issues within tourism that many people hold as strong values, as the activity above shows.

Your knowledge and experience

Knowledge includes all of the qualifications that you have gained to date and areas that you are familiar with. This will include GCSEs, further education and part-time qualifications that you may have achieved, such as Pool Life Guarding, Basic Food Hygiene or First Aid qualifications. There are a vast range of short courses that you can undertake to supplement your main knowledge-based skills – customer care, fitness

instructors, specific IT courses, etc. At the very least you would be wise to ensure that you have the 'big three' qualifications at level 2 (GCSE grade C or above, or a comparable vocational qualification). These are:

- English (or Communications key skills)
- Maths (or Application of Number key skills)
- IT (or IT key skills).

Many travel and tourism jobs demand the first two and, with the increase in the use of information technology, IT is rapidly becoming an essential part of any applicant's CV.

It should also be stressed that fluency in a second language helps to give any CV an edge over other applicants for many jobs. Those who struggled with French, German or Spanish at school might like to consider taking a qualification in Sign Language – recognised by many travel and tourism organisations as a 'second' language.

Employers are not just interested in your formal qualifications and knowledge. In recent years, an increasing amount of emphasis has been placed on what are known as 'transferable skills'. These are the skills that you have acquired from part-time jobs, hobbies or student life in general. Many are invaluable when it comes to assessing your suitability for a particular job. For example, a part-time job in any customer-oriented role will demonstrate that you have acquired experience of working and dealing with customers, working as a member of a team, solving problems, dealing with complaints, etc. – all skills that employers rank highly. So rather than dismissing a part-time job as '*I worked Saturdays in a café for 8 months to earn some extra money,*' learn to present it as a positive aspect of your work-experience skills: '*I had a part-time job in the hospitality industry that enabled me to develop skills in working and dealing with customers, working as a member of a team, solving problems and dealing with complaints.*'

Likewise, any activities that you are involved in through student life or hobbies can provide sound evidence of skills development – although be careful that the areas that you choose to highlight really do support the acquisition of valuable skills. The increasingly common inclusion of 'socialising and going out' on CVs as an example of a' hobby' is a good example of what is better left out. Most people do this as part of their leisure time so it really does not tell potential employers anything new! However, the following hobbies and interests suggest acquisition of skills that an employer might be interested in:

- Officer on the student union
- Organiser of a Rag Week event
- Voluntary work
- Student representative
- Student Governor
- Member of an amateur dramatics group
- Member of a local environmental group
- Member of a sporting team
- Member of the local Territorial Army
- Participation in a Duke of Edinburgh award scheme.

activity

MAKING THE MOST OF YOUR TRANSFERABLE SKILLS

The following identifies and explains one of the transferable skills that could be achieved from playing football.

Transferable skill: Teamwork – being able to work as a member of a team was an important part of my interest in football. As well as playing an active part in matches, I also helped to organise social events and helped to coach younger members of the team – enabling me to develop good communication skills when working with different people.

As a group, discuss the transferable skills that might be achieved from the following hobbies and interests:

- Member of the Student Council at school
- Voluntary visitor at a local old people's home
- Playing lead guitar in a local amateur band
- German exchange visit for the last two years with school.

Personal skills audit

In the final section, you are going to carry out a personal skills audit. This means identifying all of the skills that you already possess and what strengths these provide you with for future employment.

activity

LIST ALL YOUR SKILLS

Make a copy of the table below. It would be useful to set it up as a spreadsheet or a table in a Word document so that you can add further information and details later.

Based on the examples that we have looked at in this topic and your own ideas, complete the table, listing all of the skills that you currently possess and what evidence there is that you possess them.

SKILLS	EVIDENCE
Personal skills and qualities	
Values and attitudes	
Knowledge and experience	

Once you have completed the table, select three careers that you are interested in pursuing in the travel and tourism industry. Evaluate which of the skills that you have included in your skills audit are particularly valuable for each career.

Potential opportunities and your career plan

In the last topic you explored and evaluated your personal skills by carrying out a personal skills audit. In this final topic we are going on to identify potential career aspirations and plan how you could achieve them. Whilst many people change their mind about their future career at some point, having some sort of overall plan about where you are headed and how you intend to get there is a sound foundation for a successful career – regardless of where you might eventually end up! We will examine the process under the following headings:

- **Identifying your career goal**
- **The types of job involved in achieving your career goal**
- **How you will develop the skills, qualities, knowledge and experience required**
- **How you will adapt attitudes and values to be successful in the career identified**
- **The timescales involved**
- **The sources of support that will be needed**
- **Formulating a career development plan.**

Identifying your career goal

The first stage in formulating a career development plan is to identify your career goal. You may already have a clear goal in mind or simply a rough idea of what you appeals to you. It is always a good idea to focus on a long-term career goal rather than simply what you are hoping to do in the next few months or years. In this way you can plan your skills development over an extended period of time – ideally five years at least.

Of course, there is nothing to stop you from changing the plan if a different career opportunity presents itself in the future and, in fact, this is usually a productive step to take. A career development plan should always be flexible enough to allow you to seize opportunities as they arise – since no one knows exactly how their career is going to eventually work out, as the example on the right shows.

---

activity

CHARACTERISTICS OF YOUR CAREER GOAL

Write a list of the ten characteristics that you hope your future career in travel and tourism will have. They might be about some (or all) of the following aspects:

- The extent to which you deal with people
- Who you work with
- Level of responsibility
- Anticipated salary and benefits
- Qualifications and skills required
- Training provided

- Promotional opportunities
- Location
- Working hours
- Variety versus routine
- Challenge
- Excitement
- Long-term opportunities.

Once you have completed your list, explain to the rest of the group what your overall career goal is.

Liz graduated with a degree in travel and tourism management. She originally started the course with the intention of working for a tour operator. However, she had particularly enjoyed the management modules on the course so she applied to a number of hotel chains to undertake their graduate management training course. Having worked as a duty manager in a large city centre hotel, she decided that she was particularly interested in the role of personnel and training within hotels so applied for and got a job within the company as a regional Human Resources Manager. During this time she gained further qualifications in HRM. After two years, she noticed a job advertisement for a Training Manager with a regional tourist board and her application was successful. She continued studying by taking a part-time teaching course and a range of IT qualifications. Three years later, Liz decided that she had sufficient skills to set up her own business and started a consultancy firm offering in-house training courses to travel and tourism organisations. The consultancy proved highly successful and she is currently looking to expand the services into marketing and internet website design.

Her original career development plan when she left school outlined how she would achieve her degree and then apply to tour operators. Clearly it has been radically revised during her career!

activity

THREE POSSIBLE CAREER OPPORTUNITIES

Having identified your general career goal in the last activity, now identify three possible career opportunities in different sectors of the travel and tourism industry that appeal to you ,and explain to the rest of the group why you think that each might help in achieving your career goal.

The types of job involved in achieving your career goal

Having identified the main characteristics that you hope your future career will have, let's move on to evaluate potential careers. If you are still unsure about which direction you would like your career to take, you might like to consider some of the areas listed below.

How you will develop the skills, qualities, knowledge and experience required

In the last topic we looked at the general skills, qualities, knowledge and experience needed for a successful career in the travel and tourism industry, and you completed a personal skills audit. The next section will help you to see how you can further develop your strengths to enhance your future career potential. One of the simplest ways of identifying where you may have some skills gaps is to look at job advertisements or job descriptions and match your current skills against those that are demanded in a particular job.

Possible career directions

Travel services – tour operating, resort operations or travel agencies

Tourist attractions – museums, art galleries, theme parks, historic houses and cathedrals, or natural attractions such as National Parks

Tourism support services – National or Regional Tourist Boards, Tourist Information Centres, local council tourism departments or tourism agencies

Transportation – airlines, rail companies, ferry, cruising or coach companies, or in termini (e.g. airports, train stations and ports)

Accommodations – hotels, holiday centres or corporate events

Generic areas – marketing, HRM, training, finance or IT.

WHAT'S NEEDED? HAVE YOU GOT IT?

Select one of the following job advertisements from the *Travel Weekly* website (www.travelweekly.co.uk) or choose another advertisement that appeals to you. Identify the skills, qualities, knowledge and experience that the job requires and evaluate which criteria you meet. Evaluate what evidence you have of the criteria that you meet.

Airline reservations

A great opportunity has arisen to join this established airline and tour operator on a 6-month contract, based in London, as an airline reservations agent. You will be booking flights using the Sabre reservations system, dealing with amendments and any customer service issues. The successful candidate must have a minimum of a year's travel industry experience using a CRS (preferably Sabre), have an excellent telephone manner and like working in a fast-paced environment.

Conference consultant

This role will involve sourcing venues and making reservations to meet clients needs – this could be booking a meeting room for two people, to arranging a full conference for 200 delegates!! It is all UK-based, therefore knowledge of airfares is not required!! An excellent telephone manner is essential as 90% of the role will be telephone-based; you must be well organised, pay attention to detail and work to tight deadline. You will be based within a large vibrant office, working for a company with many career opportunities.

Hotel consultant

An opening has arisen within a busy business travel office for a hotel consultant to join their team. You will possess excellent geographical knowledge, together with experience of hotel reservations and preferably knowledge of CRS. A background in retail travel may be considered. This could be your step into business travel.

Having evaluated the job advertisement in the last activity, you will have identified some skills gaps. The next stage, if you were keen to secure a similar job in the future, is to identify how you are going to 'plug' the skills gap. In other words, what could you do in the coming years to gain the skills, qualities, knowledge and experience that would enable you to achieve your career aspirations. Depending on the nature of the skills gap there are a number of ways in which you could enhance your career potential. The table on the opposite page shows some of the common skills that are required, and how you might acquire them if you do not already have the necessary evidence.

Skill, quality, knowledge or experience	How to acquire
GCSE English and Maths, grade C or above	Local colleges and sixth forms usually offer both qualifications on a part-time basis.
IT literacy	Recognised part-time courses are available at colleges, training providers and via the internet. Even if you are already IT literate it is worth considering updating your skills with specialised qualifications such as website design, spreadsheets, databases, etc.
Second language	Available at evening part-time courses across the country. Self-study packs are also available. Do not forget that Sign Language often counts as a second language.
NVQs (Many jobs require NVQ qualifications, particularly jobs in travel agencies.)	One of the easiest ways of achieving this is to secure employment with an organisation that allows you to gain the relevant NVQ whilst also working.
Specialised qualifications, such as First Aid, Basic Food Hygiene, Pool Life Guarding, etc.	Offered both at colleges and by private training organisations. If you are in part-time work, your employer might offer you the opportunity of gaining some of these qualifications at their expense – take it! The same applies to any other 'free' training that an employer offers you – even if it means undertaking it in your own time.
Telephone/CRS experience	There are plenty of part-time jobs in this area, and they give valuable experience. Consider work in call centres or on telephone information lines.
Selling skills	Working in any area of retail will provide substantial evidence of this, and you will probably receive some free training in selling skills.
Customer service skills	Any situation that involves working with the public provides evidence of customer service. Ideally the experience should expose you to a wide range of different types of customers and situations. You will need to be able to evaluate and explain how you identified and dealt with different customers and situations.
Working as a team member, communication skills and problem solving	Evidence for this might be gained from part-time work or hobbies and interests. If you lack such evidence, consider joining clubs or societies or doing some voluntary work. Fundraising activities or membership of a committee are also good sources of experience.
Further formal qualifications	You may decide that your career cannot progress in the way that you would like without a further period of study. This might involve a higher education qualification or studying for a professional qualification such as HRM or marketing. UCAS and professional awarding bodies will provide information of study at this level.

How you will adapt attitudes and values to be successful in the career identified

As we discussed in the last topic, attitudes and values are a very personal issue. Yours may be so strong that you do not want to adapt them to fit into a career, but would prefer to find a career that matches your attitudes and values – as the activity in the last topic showed. However, general positive attitudes and values are required for all jobs and need to be developed and often adapted. The initial stage in developing new attitudes and values, or adapting existing ones, is to identify what is appropriate to any given job role and the extent to which you meet the criteria. Having done this, you have the opportunity to decide whether or not you think that you could adapt your attitude, where necessary, for the new job. You need to be realistic, because many personal attitudes and values are so entrenched that it is almost impossible to change them. Alternatively, you might feel personally compromised by having to adapt to attitudes or values that you are not comfortable with. In such a situation it is probably best to admit that the job is not suited to you, rather than try to 'fit in' and risk failing.

PEOPLE WITH ATTITUDE NEED NOT APPLY

Look at the following, somewhat negative, statements from some people hoping to work in the travel and tourism industry. In pairs, discuss what jobs in travel and tourism their attitudes and values would make them unsuitable for. Evaluate which, if any, of the attitudes and values could be adapted, and how.

'I hate formality. All this calling people "sir" and "madam" just makes me sound stupid. Why should I anyway? They're no better than me.'

'Old people really annoy me. I used to get loads of elderly customers in my last job and they were so demanding, always wanting me to stop and chat to them.'

'I'd like to be a manager one day. It seems a really easy job – just telling other people what to do rather than having to do it yourself. Must be great.'

'I want a well paid interesting job, but I don't fancy working evenings or weekends because I'd miss my social life. Nine to five, Monday to Friday would suit me fine.'

'I worked in a travel agency for a while and was disgusted by the amount of money that people spent on holidays. Half the world is starving, but the customers would just go on about the poor standard of in-flight meals.'

'I'm much better working on my own. Can't see the point of working as a team as it just involves arguments, and takes far longer.'

'Paperwork bores me stiff. I cannot see the point of it – you're much better off being with the customers and making sure they are happy.'

'The customer is always right? I don't think so! Most of them are just after a refund or compensation.'

'I've not learnt to use a computer or the internet, on purpose. I'm sure that it's all just a passing phase and everyone will lose interest soon.'

The timescales involved

Because the travel and tourism industry is changing so rapidly, it is wise to identify timescales for career development that are long-term, yet flexible. As already stated, the minimum length of time for such a plan is ideally five years – although there is certainly nothing wrong in having a longer-term plan. It is usually a good idea to plan at least the next three stages.

Therefore, if you are currently studying for your A2 in Travel and Tourism (and possibly additional qualifications) you should try to identify the next stage (which may be Higher Education), your first job, and the direction that you hope to progress in from that job.

Be realistic about timescales. For example, a gap year adds a further twelve months to your plan but, if well thought out, can add a huge amount to your employability. In addition, do not overlook the smaller issues in your plan. For example, if you do not already have GCSE English or Maths (at grade C or above) make sure that achieving them is in the early part of your plan. It is worrying how many aspiring travel and tourism professionals get all the way to achieve an Honours Degree, or higher, only to find that they are not eligible for a particular job because they have overlooked their GCSEs.

Finally, make sure that you maximise the times when you could quite easily gain further skills. For example, you might plan to take a gap year that involves six months of working to raise the necessary money and a further six months travelling abroad or doing voluntary work. Use the first six months wisely – choose a job that provides you with new skills rather than one that simply pays well. In addition, consider taking at least one part-time qualification during this time. If you do not already have a driving licence this would be a good goal to focus on, as many jobs in travel and tourism expect their employees to be able to drive.

The sources of support that will be needed

An important part of developing appropriate skills for a career in travel and tourism is understanding and identifying what support is available to enable you to achieve your goals. The table, above right, outlines some of the support that you might consider using.

Source of support	Use
Colleges, universities, training providers	If you want to study for further full-time or part-time courses, educational organisations offer a wide range of opportunities.
Teachers/lecturers	Staff who currently teach you will almost certainly have a broad knowledge of the travel and tourism industry as well as contacts in the various sectors. Discuss your career options with them and ask for advice and guidance.
Careers Service/ adviser	The careers service 'Connexions' and school or college careers advisers have a vast amount of information on potential careers in travel and tourism and the skills required, and they offer advice on how you can achieve these skills.
Employers	Most travel and tourism organisations are keen to provide advice to people aspiring to work for them. Many will also offer work placements or work shadowing to allow you to evaluate whether or not it is the right career for you.
Recruitment agencies	Recruitment agencies usually offer a free service to job hunters. Many include advice on developing skills, interview techniques and compiling CVs as part of this service.
Job advertisements	Getting into the habit of reading job advertisements in the press is a good way of keeping up to date with what employers are looking for.
Internet	Searching on the internet for advice on jobs in travel and tourism results in literally thousands of sites. Researching effectively by being specific in your search can be very useful. For example, rather than searching by 'jobs in travel and tourism', try 'jobs with UK tour operators'.
Careers fairs and exhibitions	General and job-specific careers fairs are held both nationally and regionally. Details are usually found in the press or by searching on the internet. The advantage of a careers fair is that you have the opportunity to evaluate a wide range of jobs and organisations at one go, as well as being able to ask specific questions.
In-house training	Many initial jobs in travel and tourism are offered as a trainee's position. Whilst the salary may be reduced, the job supports the development of valuable skills whilst also allowing the employee to earn.

Formulating a career development plan

We have now got to the stage where you are going to formulate your own personal career development plan. By now you should have completed much of the work that is required.

Look at the plan below and complete the columns and rows. (Some examples are included to show you the idea.) You will need the information that you have accumulated in this and the previous topic. As with the skills audit, it is suggested that you set the plan up as a spreadsheet or a table in a Word document so that you can make changes to the content.

Career Development Plan
General career goal:

Stage in career	Skills, qualities, knowledge, experience, attitudes or values that will be developed	How they can be achieved	Sources of support that will be required	To be achieved by (specify the date)
Complete 2 years of further education	• A level T&T • Pass driving test • First Aid certificate • Customer service	Complete all coursework to deadlines Driving lessons Part-time course at local college Part-time job	Course leader/ tutors Driving school College Job centre/ local press adverts	

How Unit 9 is assessed

The assessment evidence for this unit is in three distinct parts. It is suggested that they are presented in three sections within a portfolio. The sections should be titled:

(a) Participation in a team
(b) Employment opportunities, and the skills and qualities required
(c) A career development plan.

In addition, you should include a Bibliography and any relevant Appendices.

Your assessment evidence could be in many different forms, to allow for your learning preferences and strengths to be accommodated. These could include written reports, or witness testimonies of oral presentations with supporting notes. Task (a) would be evidenced through witness testimonies.

The following guidance outlines how you can achieve the assessment criteria for each of the three parts.

Task (a) Participation in a team

This section should show evidence of your participation in a team, working towards completion of a significant travel and tourism-related task. This could be as a result of work completed on another unit in the qualification or a specific task designed for this unit.

(a.0) Introduction

Give a detailed overview of the travel and tourism-related task that your team organised.

(a.1) Team roles

Describe the nature of the team that was formed and the range of individual roles that were identified and implemented for the team task.

(a.2) Personal team role

Explain in detail your role within the team and how it related to the role of others within the team.

(a.3) Participation in team task

Describe, in detail, the ways in which you participated in the team task and contributed towards the achievement of the team's goals. You should include details of any conflicts that arose and how they were dealt with.

(a.4) The contribution of others within the team

Describe the contributions of other team members and how this affected your personal participation.

(a.5) Evaluation of achievement of the team's goals

Evaluate the extent to which the team were successful in achieving their goals.

(a.6) Evaluation of personal contribution to team

Evaluate your personal contribution to the team's task and the extent to which you helped the team achieve its goals.

(a.7) Recommendations for improvement

Recommend and justify ways in which your personal contribution and the team's work as a whole could have been improved.

Task (b) Employment opportunities, and the skills and qualities required

This section should show evidence of an analysis of the range of employment opportunities and the skills and qualities required for a successful career in the travel and tourism industry.

(b.0) Introduction

A detailed overview of the range of job opportunities within the travel and tourism industry.

(b.1) Sources of information on job opportunities

Describe the range of sources of information that can be used to find out about job opportunities within the travel and tourism industry.

(b.3) The contractual requirements for jobs

Describe the various contractual terms that might be offered for travel and tourism jobs, and what each one means.

(b.4) The rates of pay for travel and tourism jobs

Explain the different rates of pay that might be offered, including current details of the national minimum wage.

(b.5) *The working hours for different jobs*

Explain the different working hours that are required in travel and tourism jobs. Include details of rest breaks, holiday entitlement, maternity/paternity/adoption rights, sick pay and time of for specific situations.

(b.6) *The location of different jobs*

Explain the various locations that might be used for travel and tourism jobs, giving examples.

(b.7) *Seasonality of jobs*

Explain what is meant by seasonality and describe examples of specific jobs that are seasonal.

(b.8) *Entry requirements of different jobs*

Describe in general terms what entry requirements might be needed for jobs within travel and tourism. Explain the entry requirements for a range of specific jobs.

Task (c) A career development plan

This section should show evidence of a detailed career development plan based upon a personal skills audit, produced using information from a range of sources.

(c.0) *Introduction*

Explain what is meant by a personal skills audit and career development plan and why they are useful tools when considering a career in travel and tourism.

(c.1) *Personal skills audit*

Complete a skills audit that contains an analysis of the following areas:
• Personal skills   • Attitudes   • Qualities
• Knowledge and experience.

(c.2) *Career development plan*

Complete a career development plan that includes the following:
• Your career goal and the skills, qualities, knowledge, experience and attitudes required
• The types of jobs that might help you achieve your career goal
• How you will develop the skills, qualities, knowledge, experience and attitudes required to be successful in the career that you have identified as your career goal.
• The timescales involved
• The sources of support that you intend to use to help you achieve your career goal.

Bibliography

List all of the sources of information that you have used to complete the assessment for this unit. This should include books and journals, websites, direct contact with tour operators, etc.

Appendices

Include any relevant supporting information in the appendices, such as examples of materials that you produced for the team task, witness statements, peer appraisals, examples of job advertisements, etc.

General guidelines on presentation of assignments (for Units 8, 9, 11 and 12)

Whilst the way in which you present your assessment evidence will not directly affect your grade, it is important that you strive to present it in a professional and well-structured way. The following are a few tips on achieving good presentation.

1. All assignments should be word processed, using a suitable font, such as Arial. Try to avoid 'casual' fonts, such as Comic Sans.

2. You can use a different font for titles if you wish, but do not use more than two fonts in your work.

3. Be consistent in your font size. Generally, 14 or 16 is suitable for titles, and 12 for the main text.

4. Only use bold for titles – not the whole report.

5. Use italics and 'quotation marks' to show when you have copied text from another source, and indicate the source in brackets after the quote.

6. If you choose to use more than one colour in your work, limit this to two, e.g. blue for titles and black for the main text.

7. Avoid using 'Wordart' for titles!

8. Use 1.5 line spacing throughout your work.

9. Do not cut and paste cartoon-style clipart into your work.

10. If you use photographs in your work, label each image underneath.

11. Insert page numbers into your finished work.

Regardless of the type of organisation or the products and services that it offers, promotion and sales play a key role in the success of any travel and tourism organisation. All staff who work within the industry need to understand why promotion and sales are important and the ways in which they contribute to the whole process.

In this unit you will gain an understanding and appreciation of how marketing, sales and promotion are a continuous process that includes everything that an organisation does to attract and keep customers, identify and satisfy their needs, and continue to grow and develop as a successful and effective organisation. In particular we will explore:

• The sales process and buyer behaviour
• The role of promotion in the marketing process
• The promotion mix.

Promotion and sales are part of the wider function of **marketing**. Marketing is particularly important in travel and tourism because the industry is fiercely competitive, with different providers often aiming their products and services at the same customers. For example, the visitor-attractions market is highly competitive, with providers constantly trying to develop new products that will be seen as more attractive than those offered by competitors.

Frequently, the effectiveness of an individual provider's marketing, promotion and sales activities will determine whether or not they are successful in attracting customers, rather than seeing their potential customers choosing the products and services of a competitor.

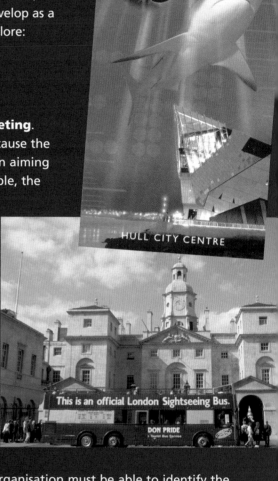

So what is marketing? The Institute of Marketing describes marketing as:

> 'The management process of identifying, anticipating and satisfying customer requirements profitably'.

This means that those responsible for marketing within an organisation must be able to identify the needs of both existing and potential customers in order to develop and provide products and services that satisfy those needs. In more general terms marketing means:

> 'Getting the right **product** to the right **people**, in the right **place**, at the right **time**, at the right **price**, using the right **promotion**'.

There are numerous examples of travel and tourism providers' ability to get it 'right' when it comes to marketing activities, and we will be looking at many of these in this chapter – from the slick brochures produced by tour operators such as Thomson, to highly successful promotional campaigns by tourist attractions such as The Deep.

But before you go on to the first topic, consider the following – whilst we are going to look at the whole marketing process within this unit, the actual unit title focuses on 'promotion and sales'. To what extent do you think this focus might be explained by the opinion of Management Consultant, Richard Walton who stated that:

Promotion and Sales in Travel and Tourism

The sales process and buyer behaviour

Understanding why customers buy products – and the ways in which the sales process can be used to ensure that customers buy the most appropriate products – is an important part of promotion and sales. **Selling skills** are a vital part of customer service and an integral part of marketing. They provide numerous benefits for the organisation, including: increasing sales and profitability, gaining an edge over the competitors, and ensuring that customers' needs and expectations are met.

In this topic we are going to look at the ways in which selling skills contribute towards the successful marketing of an organisation's products. In particular we will focus on:

- **The skills and qualities required to effectively sell a product**
- **The sales process**

The skills and qualities required to effectively sell a product

Skills refer to personal abilities that are learnt, whereas qualities refer to positive aspects of someone's personality or character. Many of the skills and qualities that you will need to sell successfully are similar to those needed in customer service, which you studied in Unit 2. In general, you should be able to demonstrate all of the following:

- Good product knowledge • Enthusiasm
- Honesty • Initiative • Friendliness • Judgement
- Consistency.

The skills and qualities required will vary according to the situation and the specific customer's needs and expectations. For example, a travel agency adviser would need tactfulness if dealing with a customer with a very limited budget who was expecting to book a luxury cruise. Alternatively, if the customer was elderly and not used to travelling abroad, the adviser would need to display skills including patience, understanding and encouragement. In other situations, speed, accuracy and efficiency might be the main skills and qualities required, such as with an airport check-in clerk, airline reservations staff or ferry port customs staff. When selling excursions and additional services, resort reps need a range of skills and qualities, such as persuasiveness and enthusiasm.

The sales process

The sales process refers to the stages involved – from initial contact with the customer through to and beyond the actual sale of a product. In general, these include:

Establishing rapport with the customer

⮟

Determining customer needs and expectations

⮟

Outlining the features and benefits of a product

⮟

Overcoming objections

⮟

Closing the sale

⮟

Delivering after-sales service

Establishing rapport with the customer

Establishing rapport with the customer involves establishing contact and developing a conversation with the customer in which you are both communicating on the same level. This requires good judgement for, while no customer likes to be ignored, people do not like to feel that they are being pressured or rushed by over-enthusiastic sales staff. The eager member of staff who pounces on you as you walk through the door with 'Can I help you?' can be as irritating as the one who totally ignores you and carries on chatting to a colleague. It is usually possible to read from a customer's body language and behaviour whether they feel comfortable talking to you and want to pursue the conversation. Essentially, establishing rapport involves making initial contact with the customer by introducing yourself and obtaining their name. It is then important to identify the best communication approach, based on the way that they speak to you. If they are formal, for example, your attitude and manner should mirror this. Finally, it is vital that the sales person establishes a feeling of two-way communication where the customer feels confident in responding to, and asking, questions.

Determining customer needs and expectations

Initially, the easiest way of determining customer needs and expectations is to ask 'How may I help you?'. The reply will indicate what further questions you need to ask to establish the customer's specific needs. For example, if a customer expresses an interest in booking a holiday in a European city you might ask about preferences for countries, accommodation, transport or time of year. It is vital not to rush the customer or interrupt them as you may well miss vital information. Imagine how much time a travel consultant could waste trying to find a suitable holiday for the following customer if she cut him off after the first sentence in her eagerness to sell a product?

'My wife and I would like to go on a two-week Caribbean cruise, first-class, in July. We cannot afford more than £400 each and really want to see the Pyramids.'

Not only is she unlikely to be able to provide a first-class Caribbean cruise at this price, she would also have to tactfully explain that Egypt was not included in Caribbean itineraries. However, if she had listened and fully identified the customer's requirements she may be able to find a Nile cruise for him.

Outlining the features and benefits

In a selling situation, the member of staff and the customer will discuss and hopefully agree what products or services can meet the customer's needs. 'Product features' are the main characteristics of a product, including what is included in the price and the level of quality of the product. 'Product benefits' are what the customer would gain from buying the product. So, for example, the features of a package holiday might be flights, accommodation, meals and resort services. The benefits of the holiday to the customer might be relaxation, excitement, status or adventure. Staff need to be able to outline the main features and benefits of suitable products in a way that satisfies the customer's needs. This process usually involves considering the available options and possibly suggesting compromises. The customer will often expect to see examples of the product or service that they are considering buying. For example, a travel consultant might show the customer package holiday brochures or give them videos to watch at home. Whilst the main objective must never be to sell as much as possible – regardless of whether the customer wants it – it is realistic to expect staff to **maximise a sale**. This means outlining additional products to the customer that you feel meet their needs and would increase their overall enjoyment. There are four main ways of maximising a sale:

Sales technique	Situation	How it is done
Suggestive selling	The customer has not decided what particular product they want.	'Can I suggest a Greek island in May, as the Spring is one of the best times to go there.'
Alternative selling	The product that the customer wants is not available.	'I'm afraid that tonight's performance of Les Miserables is fully booked, but we have a number of seats available on Tuesday and Wednesday.'
Related selling	The customer has bought something and there are other, related products that can go with it.	'Would you be interested in a private taxi transfer to your hotel rather than the coach, so that you can begin enjoying your holiday straight away?'
Up-selling	The customer has decided to buy a particular product, but a better quality version is available.	'For only £10 extra I could offer you an upgraded room with sea view and balcony.'

Overcoming objections

In some selling situations a customer may raise some objections to the products and services being offered. If such objections are realistic and suggest that the product does not fully meet the customer's needs, then there is little point in trying to persuade them to buy it. However, if the member of staff feels that the objections are not realistic, it is helpful to try to reassure the customer and explain the features and benefits more fully. For example, a customer might state that they are tempted to go on a foreign package holiday but do not like the heat and mosquitoes. A travel adviser might suggest a holiday in the Greek islands in May when the weather is milder and the mosquito invasion has yet to begin.

Closing the sale

Closing the sale means actually getting the customer to buy the selected product. Not all sales can be closed straight away. Often the customer may want to go away and think about it or discuss it with someone else. However, it is always preferable to close a sale as quickly as possible. A number of techniques can be used to achieve this. One of the most frequently used is to stress that the product may not be available if the decision is deferred – for example, a suitable holiday may not be available in a few days time. Another approach often used is to put a time limit on special offers, such as flights or accommodation.

Delivering after-sales service

Good service and selling skills do not end when a customer hands over his or her money. The service should continue after the sale has been made to show that you care about the customer. Sometimes the after-sales service will be immediate, such as asking customers if they have enjoyed their visit to a museum and listening to the comments that they make. In other situations there may be a need for service a long time after the sale has been made. For example, a customer buying a time-share apartment may have a need for after-sales service for many years.

It is important to remember the maxim: 'Once a customer, always a customer'. In other words, once you have established a relationship with a customer, he or she is entitled to receive good service from you in the future, even if you are not in the position of being able to sell them something.

activity

EXPLAINING EFFECTIVE SELLING SKILLS

Design a two-page section for a staff training handbook explaining how they can use effective selling skills. Produce your handbook for the staff in one of the following organisations:

1 A travel agency
2 A theme park
3 A theatre
4 A rail terminal
5 A hotel.

Remember who your audience are and keep the language simple yet instructive. The effectiveness of the handbook will be greatly improved if you use diagrams, pictures and bullet points – don't overwhelm the staff with lots of text!

activity

SELLING EXTRA SERVICES

The information below, taken from Thomas Cook's Finesse brochure, outlines some of the extra products and services available to their customers for an additional charge. In pairs, role-play a travel consultant with a customer, and see how many of the extra services you can sell by outlining their features and benefits to the customer. If you are playing the role of the customer, you should outline your main needs prior to the role play. Remember your main objective is to ensure that you meet the customer's needs and not just to sell as much as you can! So you need to explain the benefits of each additional service to the customer.

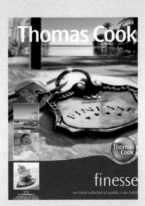

Premium seats: Enjoy the extra room and seat comfort in a separate spacious quieter cabin with Thomas Cook Plus on long-haul flights.

Pre-bookable seats: Upgrade to Thomas Cook Extra, and pre-bookable seating is included in your package.

Golf: Pre-book your tee-off time through overseas golf booking specialist Tee Times Abroad.

Room upgrades: Make your stay extra special by staying in a Superior room, junior suite or suite.

Flowers and champagne: Get your holiday off to a special start with flowers or champagne on arrival at your hotel.

Late checkout: Ease the inconvenience of night flights by pre-booking a late check-out room.

Buyer behaviour

An essential part of sales and promotion is understanding buyer behaviour. This means the process that a customer goes through when deciding whether or not to buy a particular product, as well as the factors that influence their decision. If an organisation has an accurate idea of the buying behaviour of their customers they can react effectively by providing appropriate products. In addition they are able to use promotional techniques effectively to persuade customers to buy the organisation's products and services. Understanding this behaviour involves asking a series of questions such as:

- **Who** buys our products and services?
- **Who** do they buy them **for**?
- **Why** do they buy them?
- **When** do they buy them?
- **Where** do they buy them?
- **How** do they buy them?

There are many different models that seek to explain buyer behaviour. We will look at the five stages of one such model, shown below.

Need recognition and problem awareness

At this stage, the consumer recognises the need for a particular product. For example, a customer might recognise that they need to book a summer package holiday for themselves and their family.

Information search

Having recognised the need for a product, the consumer will search for information on possible products that could fulfil their need. For example, the customer wishing to buy a package holiday may obtain brochures, look at advertising materials, talk to friends, read the travel sections in newspapers and magazines, or consult a travel agent for advice.

Evaluation of alternatives

Having collected information, the consumer will then move on to evaluating all of the potential alternatives and decide which ones meet their needs best. Any number of factors can influence the consumer at this stage. For example, they may have consulted with a travel agent and read through brochures before deciding that Portugal seems the best option. However, if a friend says that they had a terrible holiday in Portugal, the consumer is likely to re-evaluate the options and select a different product.

Purchase

Once all options have been evaluated the consumer will move on to purchase the most suitable product.

Post-purchase evaluation

Finally, following the purchase and use of the product, the consumer will evaluate the extent to which it met their needs and expectations. This post-purchase evaluation will influence their future buying behaviour. For example, the customer who has enjoyed a particular holiday is more likely to select the same tour operator, destination or travel agency in future.

Whilst most customers will go through each of the five stages in the order in which they are presented, sometimes the order may be altered. This makes the understanding of buying decisions far more complicated. For example, a customer may not have even considered going on a summer holiday ('need recognition and problem awareness') so therefore not have started an information search. However, they may see a television programme about various activity holidays and decide to go on one of the holidays featured. In this case, they are entering the buying process at the 'evaluation of alternatives' stage.

Before undertaking any promotional or sales activity it is important to clearly focus on what it is hoped will be achieved. This involves setting marketing **objectives** from the outset, and then continually reviewing and monitoring them to measure progress. In this topic we will look at:

- The type of objectives that organisations set
- SMART objectives
- Differences in objectives between sectors of the travel and tourism industry.

Unit 10 Promotion and Sales in Travel & Tourism

The type of objectives that organisations set

Organisations may have several key promotional and sales objectives. They may include some, or all, of these:

- maximising income
- generating profit
- satisfying customer requirements
- managing the effects of competition
- managing the effects of change
- co-ordinating a range of activities
- generating community benefit
- optimising customers' perception of the product.

In general, the nature of the objectives will largely determine the type of promotional and sales activities used. For example, if a tour operator's objective was to increase national sales they are more likely to select promotional media such as television and national papers rather than local press or radio. The case study opposite outlines the marketing objectives set by the National Maritime Museum and some of the promotional methods that they aim to use to achieve them.

SMART objectives

In order to achieve its overall goals, an organisation sets itself a series of short-term, medium-term and long-term **marketing objectives**. These are vital to the success of the operation and must be 'SMART':

- **S**pecific – be clearly linked to a particular area of operation
- **M**easurable – have a method of measurement to gauge success and effectiveness
- **A**chievable – be feasible and realistic, so that staff can work towards set objectives
- **R**ealistic – be compatible with the organisation's mission statement
- **T**imed – have deadlines for review – weekly, monthly, annually.

Such objectives may cover financial, social and environmental issues. Some examples of SMART objectives are:

- Increase income for the next month by 10 per cent
- Generate 50 per cent of all bookings from existing customers and repeat bookings
- Achieve 10,000 paying visitors per month during next 12-month period
- Give local youth organisations and disabled groups priority usage of the facility between June and September
- Generate 25 per cent of all bookings from registered unemployed or those receiving income support
- Give pensioners free use of the facility during off-peak periods
- Reduce the number of customer complaints by 25 per cent in July and August
- Increase use of park-and-ride scheme to 30 per cent of visitors to city centre.

The National Maritime Museum

The National Maritime Museum must focus clearly on what it aims to achieve before carrying out any marketing activity. This involves setting marketing objectives right from the outset, and continually reviewing and monitoring them to measure progress. These objectives are defined in the context of the Museum's 5-year business plan.

The Museum has several overall marketing objectives, including:

- predicting and satisfying customer needs
- analysing market trends
- monitoring competition
- anticipating change and overcoming its effects
- increasing positive perception among its customers.

The Museum has commercial objectives like any profit-making organisation in the travel and tourism industry. However, like other publicly funded organisations, the Museum has additional objectives set by the Government.

Objectives for the following year

In order to achieve its overall mission, the Museum, like all other organisations, must set itself a series of short-term, medium-term and long-term marketing objectives.

For the following year, the marketing objectives include:

1. To co-operate with other local attractions to promote Greenwich as a tourist destination (especially those within the Maritime Greenwich World Heritage Site)

2. To achieve 930,000 visitors from the following markets:
   - individuals and families 75%
   - school groups 20%
   - tour groups/societies 5%

3. To meet the social inclusion target set by the Government (through the funding agreement with the Department for Culture, Media and Sport) – to attract more visitors from disabled, ethnic and lower-income groups.

Source: www.nmm.ac.uk

Differences in objectives between sectors of the travel and tourism industry

The objectives of sales and promotional activities are largely determined by the overall business objectives of an organisation. There is frequently a marked difference between the objectives of private sector organisations and those in the public or voluntary sectors. This will determine, to a large degree, the range of promotional and sales techniques that they use.

Private sector objectives

Private sector operators in travel and tourism must gear their marketing towards achieving profit for their owners or shareholders. Consequently their sales and promotion objectives usually include a combination of the following:

- achieving a target level of sales
- expanding sales revenue to a specified level
- increasing market share
- entering new markets
- achieving an overall specified level of profit.

Due to the competitive nature of the travel and tourism industry, it is very difficult to get details of

marketing objectives from private sector organisations – they would, in fact, be telling their competitors about their plans and run the risk that their strategy would be copied. However, in the public and voluntary sector such information is freely available. A simple search of 'promotional objectives' on the internet results in thousands of website listings – but they are almost exclusively from the public and voluntary sector.

Public and voluntary sector objectives

Public and voluntary sector organisations that operate on a non-profit basis may also have some of the objectives listed above. However, these organisations usually have other objectives, such as:

- generating community benefit
- targeting under-represented and disadvantaged groups in the community
- promoting a cause – such as more active, healthy lifestyles
- increasing participation.

Frequently, public and voluntary sector organisations will be working for the benefit of a specific region or country and their objectives will reflect this, as the case study on Bulgaria, overleaf, shows.

SETTING OBJECTIVES

Imagine that you are a candidate for the position of marketing manager at Creative Travel. The selection process includes the following short written test. What would your answer be?

Candidate Selection Test (30 minutes)

The background: Creative Travel is a privately owned tour operator, catering for the European package holiday market. We operate four distinct brands of holiday:

1 'Hotspots' which targets the family market by offering year-round package holidays to beach locations in European resorts.
2 'Summer-sizzlers' which caters for the 18–30 market, offering budget holidays to popular resorts in Spain, Greece and Turkey.
3 'Snowscene' which focuses on the winter sports market by providing skiing and snowboarding package holidays in France, Switzerland, Austria and Bulgaria.
4 'City Sights' which offers short breaks throughout the year to five European cities.

The issues: Our current trading figures show:

- Demand for 'Hotspots' packages has gradually declined over the last three years but this brand still generates most of our profits. The main reason for the decline is thought to be the cheaper prices offered by the larger tour operators. We are unable to reduce our prices any further, but feel that we offer better value for money because we provide the 'personal touch'.
- Demand for 'Summer-sizzlers' has shown the largest increase out of the four brands. During peak season (June–September) demand exceeds the number of holidays available. Off-season (April–June and October–November) only 35% of holidays available are sold.
- Demand for 'Snowscene' has remained the same for the last three years, with 66% of customers having been on a 'Snowscene' holiday before.
- Demand for 'City Sights' has shown an increase each year for the last three years. We are considering offering a further three European cities in the future.

The question: If you were appointed as Creative Travel's marketing manager, explain what your first five marketing objectives would be.

Bulgaria: a new marketing strategy

Varna, Bulgeria

A new marketing strategy for Bulgarian tourism will form the basis for the future marketing programmes of the newly set up Tourism Agency and the Ministry of Economy. The previous overall marketing objective used to identify the number of arrivals rather than the tourism earnings – a priority for development and marketing. To achieve the new overall marketing objective the following strategies have been defined:

- Reposition Bulgaria as a tourist destination offering a varied product mix of culture, nature and activities in addition to the traditional sun, beach and ski products. Shift a greater percentage of its tourist trade away from low-revenue package tours into more luxurious and upscale projects.
- Select and concentrate on the most promising and profitable markets that fit in with the positioning strategy.
- Renovate and diversify the product, and stimulate alternative types of tourism.
- Maintain traditional markets and segments, and open new market segments gradually.
- Develop the activity-holiday market (particularly golf), the city-break market in the largest towns, as well as health tourism at luxury leisure centres
- Expand the internal tourist market by offering more favourable package terms and prices to Bulgarians and encourage them to take part in tourism activities.

Source: www.strategis.gc.ca

OBJECTIVES FOR VISITBRITAIN

Read the information below on the ways in which VisitBritain aims to promote England to domestic (UK) tourists. In pairs, write four SMART promotional and sales objectives that would support the strategy, and explain why you think they are appropriate.

VisitBritain, the organisation created from the merger of the British Tourist Authority and the English Tourism Council, markets England to the British (and Britain to the rest of the world). This is a summary of some of the characteristics of the market, and its short-term and long-term plans for marketing England to the British.

Marketing England – some insights into the market

1 Changing work and leisure patterns mean that many people are taking shorter but more frequent holidays.
2 Consumers' choice is less influenced by affordability than by what is desirable and good value.
3 The English tourism product has improved almost beyond recognition in the past decade, offering better attractions, better value and better infrastructure.
4 A large number of British residents already regularly take – and hugely enjoy – holidays and short breaks in England.
5 Many British residents consider it easier to get information about and book overseas holidays than holidays at home.
6 One-third of British holidaymakers use the internet to research and plan their holidays.

Marketing England – the core objectives of the long-term strategy

- Grow the value of the total domestic tourism market by encouraging key audiences to take additional and/or longer breaks in England.
- Add value to the many initiatives and resources already in place at a regional, sub-regional and destination level by creating national initiatives that motivate people to travel at home and the means to make purchase easier.
- Coordinate and lead key national campaigns with partners from public and private sectors.

Marketing England – the planned activities

- Leading a programme to establish a robust foundation of market insights about the domestic market.
- Developing a brand architecture for England that builds on consumers' perceptions of England and works effectively at local, regional, national and international levels.
- Defining the most compelling product sectors, niches, promotions and themes which will make England stand out from the competition.
- Creating campaigns to increase understanding, awareness and appreciation of the English tourism offering.
- Identifying, developing and nurturing long-term strategic alliances with key national partners in both tourism and non-tourism sectors.
- Developing the VisitEngland website to make it easier for the visitor to source England information and make bookings, and pave the way for the launch of EnglandNet.

Marketing England – the campaign so far

- A £4 million campaign – the biggest domestic marketing initiative for England for several years
- A unique partnership between VisitBritain, the RDAs, the RTBs and the private sector
- Marketing mix includes TV and press advertising, PR, national newspaper supplements and promotions, and print, with fulfilment via call centre and internet
- PR agency: leading agencies pitching 27th March
- Campaign aimed at presenting people in their 30s and upwards with a positive, contemporary and refreshing view of their own country
- Launch on 23 April (St George's Day), to stimulate bookings between then and the start of the high-season (mid-July)
- Partners offered a range of benefits, including inclusion in the brochure, website and newspaper supplements, according to the level of buy-in.

Source: www.visitbritain.com

In this topic and the following one, we are going to look at the ways in which the needs and expectations of customers are identified and analysed through the use of market segmentation and market research. Market segmentation involves dividing the overall market into segments or groups of customers who are sufficiently alike to suggest that they will have similar needs for products or services. These similarities in turn affect the specific types of promotion that are likely to be effective with particular segments. There are many ways in which markets can be segmented such as:

- **Demographics**
- **Family circumstances**
- **Lifestyle.**

Demographics

Demographics deals with factors relating to the population, such as socio-economic groupings, age and gender. It is a popular method of market segmentation as it is relatively easy to identify specific groups. For example, a tour operator will have information on its database that allows them to identify the gender of customers booking holidays as well as an approximation of age in terms of children, adults, senior citizens, etc. Let's look at some of the ways in which travel and tourism organisations use demographic segmentation.

Socio-economic grouping

- Class A   Senior managers and professionals, such as managing directors of large firms, doctors and lawyers.

- Class B   Intermediate or middle-level managers and professionals, such as managers of leisure centres, teachers and accountants.

- Class C1   Supervisory or junior management, administrative or clerical positions, including office managers, receptionists, computer operators and qualified fitness advisers.

- Class C2   Skilled manual workers, such as electricians and carpenters.

- Class D   Semi-skilled and unskilled manual workers, such as cleaners and construction workers.

- Class E   Others in low incomes, including casual workers and those dependent on state benefits and pensions.

In marketing, social class (or 'socio-economic grouping') is often used to differentiate groups according to income and occupational status. One of the most widely used classifications based on social economic class is that developed by the Institute of Practitioners in Advertising.

In broad terms, people in these groups tend to have similar tastes, preferences and lifestyles; for example, As and Bs generally buy papers like the *Telegraph* or *The Times*, whereas C1s and C2s prefer the *Daily Mail* and the *Daily Express*, while Ds and Es prefer the *Sun* or similar tabloid papers. Many travel and tourism products are seen to be attractive to a particular group. Holidays to Florida are increasingly popular with high-earning people in group C2. Butlins is seen as a holiday product that appeals to C2s and Ds, for example, while Center Parcs tends to appeal to As and Bs. However, in recent years, many traditional preferences have become blurred, in part due to changing income patterns. Some manual workers have high earnings and can afford luxury holidays, whereas public sector professionals including teachers and nurses may have to take more modest holidays and pursue cheaper pastimes.

Age

Many products and services are aimed at people in a particular age group. SAGA Holidays, for example, caters mainly for the over 50s while Escapades aims to attract the youth market. Carrying out market research into the age segments using particular products and services can help an organisation develop products and services to meet their customers' needs. Frequently this will mean adapting existing products or developing new ones to meet the needs of new and different age groups of target customers. In recent years there has been an increasing focus on the older market as people live longer, retire earlier with increased capital and spend more on travel and tourism products. These segments are referred to in marketing by a number of titles including 'aging greys', 'goldies' and 'skiers' (spending our kids inheritance!)

'Goldies' are a key target market segment for many tour operators.

Read this extract from the TUI website which explains this important market segment in more detail:

> The travel and tourism industry is increasingly realising that the future belongs to the 50+ age group. This realisation has less to do with clairvoyance than with demographic factors, as the United Nations expects that by 2010 there will be an increase of nearly 14% in the age group of 45 to 65 year-olds and of more than 14% in the number of people over 65 years of age. The age of the seniors and therefore of the generation designated as the 'Goldies' because of their financial strength is therefore just about to start.
>
> People in the older age bracket not only like to travel a lot but when on holiday they are also very generous on the spending front. The cliché-ridden day trip with a sing-a-long in the evenings no longer fits the bill. According to information provided by the World Tourism Organisation the new elderly prefer holiday destinations such as Germany, Austria or Spain.

Accurate market segmentation not only allows organisations to develop products to meet the needs of specific segments but also to target their promotions at

activity

IDENTIFYING THE SEGMENTS

Look at the figures below which show two demographic characteristics of visitors to the National Parks – age and socio-economic group. Identify which segments comprise the main visitors, and explain why you think this product would particularly appeal to them.

Socio-economic group		Age	
AB	40%	16–34	20%
C1	23%	35–54	38%
C2	22%	55+	42%
DE	15%		

Source: Great Britain Day Visitor Survey 2002/3

these segments. For example, young adult holidays are not advertised in the broadsheet papers because the target market is unlikely to be the main readership.

Gender

Some travel and tourism products are targeted at specific genders. For example, sports tourism, such as trips to European venues to watch football matches tend to attract a higher percentage of men, whereas shopping weekends in New York are more popular with women. Many organisations develop specific features or differentiate their product to appeal to a particular gender. For example, the increase in the number of female businesswomen (often referred to as LFT – 'lone, female travellers) has led to some hotels developing their service for this market, as the extract below shows.

> London's Hilton on Park Lane is launching a floor just for women guests. The 22nd floor will offer enhanced security including private check-in, double locks on bedroom doors, security cameras and extra discretion when room keys are issued. Elsewhere, bedrooms are getting additional toiletries, more powerful hairdryers and improvements to make-up mirrors and lighting. A range of magazines will replace conventional reading material.
>
> As some female guests prefer to eat in their rooms, the hotel is adding a number of healthy options to its room service menu.
>
> *Source: Leisure Management magazine, Vol. 23, No. 4*

Family circumstances

Customers frequently experience travel and tourism products and services with friends, partners or family members rather than on their own. This means that the market segment for many travel and tourism products is not an individual but a group of customers each with a range of individual needs. Market segmentation by family circumstances classifies customers according to their stage in the family life cycle. These stages can vary, but generally include most of the following for the majority of people, at some stage in their life:

- child
- young adult
- young couple
- young couple with baby/young children
- couple with growing family (aged 5–18 years)
- empty nesters, i.e. couple whose children have recently left home
- elderly couple
- single elderly person.

Travel and tourism organisations may find through market research that their customers are from specific life-cycle segments and therefore tailor their products and services to meet these segment needs. For example, over the last 10–15 years there has been a large increase in the number of young couples with babies and couples with growing families using travel and tourism products as a family group. This has led to many tourist attractions introducing special family-priced entrance tickets and the development of specific children's areas and facilities in pubs and hotels.

Family circumstances are further complicated by recent changes in family composition. For example, the traditional family consisting of two (married) parents with 2.4 children that was common 40 years ago is no longer the norm:

- A quarter of all families are single-parent families, most of them headed by a woman.
- 40% of children are born outside marriage.
- Couples heading families are not married in one in eight families.
- 40% of all marriages are re-marriages.
- 10% of children live with a stepfamily.

Source: Social Trends, *2003*

DIFFERENT FAMILY CIRCUMSTANCES

Brian and Sonia Gregory have two daughters aged 12 and 17. Because Brian and Sonia run their own business they are able to take a number of holidays each year. In the last 12 months they have taken the following holidays:

- A mid-week break at Center Parcs with their daughters in the October half-term. Brian and the younger daughter enjoyed the sporting activities whilst Sonia and the elder daughter took advantage of the Spa facilities.

- A New Year's, 3-day package in a 4-star hotel in the Lake District. The Gregory family were joined by Brian's sister, her husband and their three children. The package included a New Year's Eve dinner dance as well as discos and entertainment for younger guests.

- A week in a rented cottage in Northumberland at Easter. The Gregory family took Sonia's mother on the holiday to celebrate her 70th birthday. Most of the week was spent touring around local castles and stately homes.

- Two weeks at an all-inclusive resort in Turkey in July for the Gregory family and Brian's 20 year-old daughter from his first marriage. The daughters enjoyed the non-stop entertainment and freedom, but Sonia and Brian found the resort over-developed.

- A three-day city break in Salzburg for Brian and Sonia to celebrate their 20th wedding anniversary. The daughters stayed with their grandmother.

- A one-night stay at the Alton Towers hotel (with two-day pass into the theme park) for the Gregorys in September – mainly to thank the daughters for agreeing to stay with their grandmother whilst their parents went to Salzburg!

1 List all of the different 'family circumstances' that are mentioned in the holidays above.

2 Imagine that you are responsible for selling the holidays listed. What specific product features and benefits would you highlight?

Lifestyle

A more complicated method of market segmentation is to identify how customers' lifestyles influence the types of products that they buy. This is particularly useful when looking at travel and tourism products because they often form an integral part of the customer's lifestyle. For example, in recent years there has been an increasing tendency for people to take second, third or even more holidays. This has created a huge market for short-break holidays and out-of-season holidays.

The concept of lifestyle segmentation has given rise to many organisations giving titles to their main segments that describe the general way in which they work, spend their money and use their leisure time. You have probably heard of one of the first, generally used lifestyle segments to be identified – the yuppie. The term 'yuppie' arose in the 1980s and described a young (25–35-year-old), single, successful, professional person who earned a high salary and spent their money on expensive products including extensive travel.

APPEALING TO THE MONEY-RICH/TIME-POOR

A recent development in lifestyle segmentation has been the 'money-rich/time-poor' trend. This refers to people in high-earning jobs who have to work long hours to maintain their earnings – consequently they have limited time left for leisure. So, for example they are unlikely to go on a six-week cruise. But this segment tends to spend a lot on high quality travel and tourism products that are of a limited duration. As a group, identify two products in each of the following categories that you think people in this lifestyle segment might buy, and explain why.

1 public transport
2 holiday
3 restaurant
4 entertainment
5 visitor attraction
6 destination
7 hotel.

It is important to remember that identifying market segments is only an approximate way of targeting customers – it would be very risky to assume that everyone within a specific segment such as age or socio-economic group enjoyed the same products. However, increasingly sophisticated market research is allowing the identification of market segments to become more and more precise.

SPECIAL EVENTS AT CHATSWORTH

Chatsworth House in Derbyshire is well established as one of the UK's most popular historical houses. In recent years the organisers have expanded their product range by introducing special events that rely heavily on the skills of the staff involved. Look at some of the events outlined below and discuss what type of market segment you think each event is aimed at.

Trailer rides Our 28-seat trailer, fully accessible for visitors using wheelchairs, offers rides in the woods and/or the park on most days, with a full commentary. The rides take approx 1 hour; tickets are sold on the day.

Garden talks Free talks every Tuesday and Thursday through the season; a gardener offers a short, free, introductory talk about the garden.

Sewing schools Our sewing schools started four years ago, and more than 200 people have since attended our courses to learn from the Chatsworth seamstresses, in the glorious surroundings of Chatsworth's 19th-century theatre, which is used for textile conservation and is not seen by other visitors. We now run a number of full-day practical courses, as well as shorter afternoon demonstrations.

Behind the scenes days offer visitors a new view of Chatsworth. You have an opportunity to meet the people who look after the house, garden and park, and to learn about its history and the diverse skills that are needed to maintain Chatsworth today. We try to add to the programmes each year, so that they appeal to regular visitors and those of you who may never have booked one of these days before.

Travel and tourism organisations need to know who their customers are and the type of products and services that they want. In addition, organisations seek to evaluate the effectiveness of their promotional activities to ensure that future promotions are appropriate. To achieve this it is crucial that effective market research is one of their key marketing activities. **Market research** is the planned process of collecting, analysing and evaluating information and data about customers and markets. Effective market research helps organisations to make decisions about the types of products their customers want, the price they are prepared to pay, where they prefer to buy the product and how it should be promoted. The market research process is therefore closely linked to the development of an effective marketing mix and underpins an organisation's **marketing strategy**.

In this topic we are going to look at:

- **The objectives of marketing research**
- **Primary marketing research**
- **Secondary marketing research.**

Objectives of market research

Market research can be used to obtain a wide range of information. The objectives of undertaking market research commonly involve identifying:

- customer needs
- new and existing markets
- trends and fashions
- changes in markets
- opportunities for market and product development
- competitors
- effectiveness of promotional activities.

Conducting market research is a systematic and highly skilled process. There are two basic types of market research:

- Primary (field) research
- Secondary (desk) research.

Primary market research

Primary market research is also known as field research. It refers to any research that involves contact with past, existing or potential customers. Primary market research is what most people think of as market research and includes methods such as:

- surveys
- observation
- focus groups.

Before looking at each of these in further detail it is important that you understand the difference between qualitative and quantitative research.

Qualitative research

- looks at consumers' feelings, attitudes, desires and perceptions
- provides detailed in-depth explanations
- is often difficult to present statistically
- does not usually lead to clear conclusions
- generally includes questions that start with 'explain', 'why' or 'describe'

Quantitative research

- provides more structured information that is statistically measurable
- enables researchers to draw specific and measurable conclusions from the results
- does not explain in-depth reasons
- generally includes questions that start with 'when', 'how many' or 'which'

Let's compare how quantitative and qualitative research may differ in use. If you (qualitatively) asked 2000 people how the brochures provided by a tour operator could be improved you could receive 2000 different answers. Using all of this information could be difficult. Alternatively, if you (quantitatively) asked 2000 customers if they were satisfied with the brochures provided, it might lead you to find that, of those surveyed, 43% were satisfied with them and 57% were dissatisfied. As useful as these figures might be to give an overall idea of customer satisfaction with the brochures, quantitative research does not give any detailed information that explains the results – why were those 57% dissatisfied with the brochures? Sometimes research needs to ask 'Why?'.

In practice, many organisations use a combination of both quantitative and qualitative research. They may ask the original 2000 customers if they were satisfied with the brochures and then select a smaller group to find out some of the reasons for the percentages.

Surveys

Surveys are usually conducted as a quantitative research method based on a questionnaire given to a large sample of people. Questionnaires are one of the most widely used research methods in the travel and tourism industry because they are relatively quick and easy to administer and analyse.

The success of a survey depends to a large extent upon the quality of the questionnaire used. A well-designed questionnaire, including structured questions with answers classified into predetermined categories, is quick to administer and the resulting data easy to process.

Compiling a questionnaire is a skilled process that needs careful consideration. One of the most difficult aspects of compiling an effective questionnaire is writing questions that are easily understood and interpreted in the same way by all respondents. If you really want to ensure that your questionnaire is effective you need to carry out a pilot survey. This means testing the questionnaire on a small group of respondents to make sure that all of the questions are easily understood and cannot be misinterpreted. Once you have carried out the pilot you will probably find that some of the questions will need re-wording to make them more effective.

There are three main ways (contact methods) in which survey information can be gathered:

- by mail
- by telephone
- by personal contact.

Many organisations send questionnaires through the post. The advantage of this method of research is that it is quick to administer and that a large sample can be reached relatively cheaply. The drawback is that the reply rate can be very poor – as low as three per cent in many cases. Some organisations carry out surveys by asking respondents questions over the telephone. This is more expensive and time-consuming than using the mail but usually has a higher response rate. However, because so many organisations use the phone as a sales tool, respondents are often suspicious, thinking that the purpose is to sell them something. A further method is through personal contact between the researcher and the respondent. Face-to-face contact is clearly more time-consuming and therefore expensive, but the response rate is usually higher than responses to mail and telephone surveys. The contact method used depends largely on the type of research being conducted and the amount of time and money available.

Observation

Observation is a research method in which information is obtained by observing customers' behaviour or events taking place. For example, much research into visitor traffic is conducted by local tourism departments by counting the number of cars that pass different points at various times. In travel and tourism there are many situations in which observation methods can be used to provide valuable information. For example, observational research has shown that up to 90% of customers automatically go to the right when entering a souvenir shop. This is valuable information for providers in terms of what they decide to display at the first point of customer contact.

Focus groups

Focus group research is when a group of people is encouraged to discuss their opinions and feelings about a particular organisation, product or service, or a topic that affects the organisation's marketing activities. It has the great advantage that the information collected is qualitative and therefore very detailed. However, it is extremely expensive and the information collected is based on a very small selection of respondents. You should also appreciate that focus group research is a highly skilled research technique that is often carried out by qualified psychologists. This is because the researcher must be able to encourage the respondents to talk freely about the topics that are of interest without leading them to say something that they do not really mean.

VISITOR QUESTIONNAIRE

SEA·LIFE

VISITOR SURVEY

TODAY'S DATE: [_____] (112-119) For office use only

Q1 How did you hear about Sea Life before your visit today?
Please tick as many boxes as apply.

Web site	☐ 3 (471)	Recommendation from friend/relative	☐ 7
Holiday guide	☐ 2	Radio	☐ 9
Sea Life leaflet	☐ 8	National newspaper	☐ 10
Road sign	☐ 4	Local newspaper	☐ 11
Saw the Sea Life tram	☐ 5	Promotional offer	☐ 12
Television news	☐ 6	Posters	☐ 13

Q2 How satisfied overall are you with your visit?
Very satisfied ☐ 1 Satisfied ☐ 2 Neither satisfied nor dissatisfied ☐ 3 (477)
Dissatisfied ☐ 4 Very dissatisfied ☐ 5

Q3 Would you recommend a visit to your friends or family? Yes ☐ 1 No ☐ 2 (130)

Q4 How would you rate the value for money from your visit?
Excellent ☐ 1 Good ☐ 2 Average ☐ 3 Poor ☐ 4 Very Poor ☐ 5 (138)

Q5 How satisfied were your children with their visit today?
Very satisfied ☐ 1 Satisfied ☐ 2 Neither satisfied nor dissatisfied ☐ 3 (201)
Dissatisfied ☐ 4 Very dissatisfied ☐ 5 Don't have children ☐ 6

Q6 How much time did you spend at Sea Life today?
0-½ hour ☐ 1 ½-1 hour ☐ 2 1-1½ hours ☐ 3 1½-2hours ☐ 4 2-2½ hours ☐ 5 Over 2½ hours ☐ 6 (125)

Q7 We aim to do things well at Sea Life.
For each option, please rate it by ticking the box which shows how you feel about it.

	Excellent	Good	Average	Poor	Very Poor	Didn't Visit/Use	
Staff efficiency	☐1	☐2	☐3	☐4	☐5	☐6	
Cleanliness	☐1	☐2	☐3	☐4	☐5	☐6	(140)
Restaurant/Catering	☐1	☐2	☐3	☐4	☐5	☐6	(141)
Gift Shop	☐1	☐2	☐3	☐4	☐5	☐6	(142)
							(143)

PLEASE TURN OVER

Look at the questionnaire above, which Sea Life Centres give to their visitors, and consider the following:

1 Are the questions quantitative or qualitative?

2 What might they do with the responses from each question?

3 This is only the first page of the questionnaire. What further questions do you think might be on the second page?

Secondary market research

Secondary market research is also known as desk research and refers to getting information from sources that are already published or easily accessible. Secondary research is economical and comparatively quick to undertake. It has the advantage that it can be conducted with complete confidentiality – in other words, without competitors finding out! On the other hand, because the information yielded by secondary research is not generated for the particular purposes of an organisation, it may not be sufficiently relevant and more specific (primary) research may be required. There are two main sources of secondary research:

- internal
- external.

Internal sources of information

An internal source of information refers to information that an organisation already has. Most organisations can avoid much of the need for expensive marketing research if they use internal sources of information wisely. For example, a conference centre might look at their customer database to identify which regions the majority of their customers come from and promote heavily in these areas. Some of the most commonly used sources of internal market research include:

Sales records	Provide information on the quantity and frequency of products sold over a given period and can often be used to provide a comparison between current and past performance. Information is available from a number of sources, such as customer bills and cash till records.	**Financial information and customer databases**	Provide information on customers' accounts, methods of payment and credit arrangements. Many organisations have their own computerised databases that include a range of information on past and present customers. Much of this information is obtained when customers fill in booking forms or registration forms.
Usage figures	Provide information about the number of people using a facility.		
		Customer compliment and complaint letters	Provide information on aspects of the products and service provided that customers value or are dissatisfied with.

External sources of information

An external source of information refers to information that has been gathered by a third party, and includes:

Government publications	Both central and local government carry out research and publish the results. The Office for National Statistics (ONS) publishes several very useful volumes of statistics, trends, demographic and census-related data. In all, the government publishes 400 sets of statistics, and many publications have specific sections on travel and tourism.	**Professional associations**	Professional associations are organisations that perform a coordinating, informing or leadership role. Within the travel and tourism industry they include the Association of British Travel Agents (ABTA), the Institute of Travel and Tourism (ITT), and the Tourism Society.
Press reports	National, regional and local newspapers are often a good source of information on current trends, issues and competitors' activities.		Members of these associations pay a subscription charge in return for a range of services, which frequently includes marketing research information.
Trade journals	A trade journal is a publication produced for a particular occupation or industry. Many, such as Caterer & Hotelkeeper, Travel Weekly, and Travel Trade Gazette, carry out research and publish the results.	**Commercial marketing research organisations**	Extensive research is carried out by marketing research organisations, such as Mintel and Gallup, which specialise in collecting market data in a particular business sector. The information can then be purchased by travel and tourism organisations.

USING EXISTING INFORMATION

Arcadia Travel is a small independent tour operator offering European city breaks to Paris, Rome, Athens, Prague and Barcelona. They are currently considering extending their product range to include Milan. They have maintained an extensive customer database that includes details of frequency of bookings, destinations and personal details of customers. They also have sales figures for the last ten years as well as a file of all letters received from customers. In pairs discuss what information Arcadia might have that would support the development of Milan as their next European city break destination.

Comparing research techniques

Clearly, there are many primary and secondary techniques available to collect market research information. Travel and tourism organisations need to identify which techniques are the most suitable for their particular research needs. A number of factors need to be considered when selecting a research method but the general advantages are shown in the table below.

CHOOSING THE RIGHT METHOD

A national tour operator is concerned that their sales of young adult package holidays to European beach resorts fell by 23% this year. They are keen to carry out research to identify the reasons, and hence formulate their future promotions strategy for the product. Propose and justify two primary and two secondary methods of research that they could use.

RESEARCH TECHNIQUE	COST	TIME	ACCESS TO MARKET	VALIDITY AND RELIABILITY	FITNESS FOR PURPOSE
SURVEY	Cost depends on the extent of survey and sample size. Can be low if questionnaires are produced in-house.	Can be very quick to implement, e.g. telephone surveys and self-completion questionnaires.	Postal and telephone surveys can access a wide geographical area. Face-to-face surveys have a more limited accessibility.	Good if survey questions are well constructed.	Especially good for quantitative research
OBSERVATION	Cost can be very low for quantitative research but rises if qualitative information is required.	As with cost, time-consuming for qualitative research but relatively quick for quantitative research.	Usually fairly limited accessibility, to localised area only.	Good if well-controlled.	Can be used for both qualitative and quantitative research.
FOCUS GROUP	Very high in terms of time, small sample size and the need for highly experienced researchers.	Very time consuming.	Usually fairly limited accessibility, to localised area only.	Good if well controlled, but requires highly skilled researchers to be effective.	Usually only used for qualitative research.
INTERNAL SECONDARY	Minimal since data is usually readily available.	Can be very quick if accurate internal records are kept, especially if computerised.	Good access to existing market.	If records are accurate and relevant they will be highly valid and reliable.	Especially good for quantitative research. Documents such as complaints letters may provide more qualitative data.
EXTERNAL SECONDARY	Much data is freely available, but commercial data can be expensive.	Can be very quick. Purchasing commercial data is instant.	Wide access to regional, national and international data is available.	Dependent on source.	Can provide both qualitative and quantitative data.

Analysing the business environment

As we have already discussed, marketing involves 'getting the right product to the right people, in the right place, at the right time, using the right promotion'. To achieve this requires a systematic approach that is usually based on a clearly defined **marketing strategy** that outlines what is to be achieved, by when and by what methods. The strategy will often be presented in stages, such as those shown below:

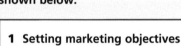

1 Setting marketing objectives

2 Analysing key factors of the business environment

3 Identifying and analysing the needs and expectations of customers

4 Developing a 'marketing mix'

5 Continually evaluating progress to determine if the marketing mix meets customer needs and expectations

Stages in a marketing strategy

We have already looked (in Topic 2) at how objectives are set. In this topic we are going to look at the ways in which travel and tourism organisations analyse factors of the business environment likely to affect promotional activities. Analysing the business environment involves looking at factors that are outside the control of an organisation which influence customers' decisions to buy products. Understanding these factors helps an organisation to plan its development of products and other marketing activities such as sales and promotion. The factors can be divided into different types:

- Legal
- Environmental
- Profitability
- Competition
- Economic
- Technological.

Legal factors

When formulating promotional activities it is important to remember that there are certain legal restrictions on what can and cannot be included. The four main relevant acts and regulations are outlined in the box below.

Trades Description Act 1968

This act states that any description of a product or service must be truthful at the time that it was written, and that if circumstances change the organisation must inform customers of the changes. Therefore it would be a contravention of the act to describe a holiday destination as 'quiet and tranquil' if the tour operator was aware that there was a lot on ongoing construction work taking place in the resort.

Package Travel Regulations 1992

These are European Union regulations (full title: Package Travel, Package Holidays and Package Tours Directive) which give consumers increased protection and compensation when something goes wrong with a travel product or service. The regulations cover tour operators, hotels, conference organisers, tourist information centres, coach operators and local resort offices and require them to provide accurate information in brochures and leaflets.

Consumer Protection Act 1987

This act requires organisations to accurately show prices for products and services. Therefore activities such as sales promotions for special offers which are in fact more expensive than advertised would contravene this act. It also gives consumers who 'buy at a distance' (that is, not face to face) the right to cancel their purchase if they are not given sufficient information about the product that they are buying.

Data Protection Act 1984

In terms of marketing communications this act has particular implications for direct marketing. The act affects all organisations that hold personal details on customers. In particular an organisation is only allowed to keep relevant information on customers for the purpose for which it was collected and not longer than is necessary. So, for example, a tour operator who collects names and addresses of customers when they enter a competition cannot keep the data and use it for other promotional activities unless the customer has given permission.

When designing and using promotional materials, travel and tourism organisations also need to conform to regulations set down by bodies such as Ofcom and the Advertising Standards Authority (ASA).

Ofcom

The regulatory role of the ITC (Independent Television Commission) was taken over by Ofcom, the Office of Communications, in 2003. Ofcom regulates the whole communications sector and is responsible for television, radio, telecommunications and wireless communications services. One of its many principles is:

'Advertising should not mislead, cause deep or widespread offence, or lead to harm, particularly to children or other vulnerable people. Viewers should know when they are watching a programme and when they are receiving a commercial message.'

A full explanation of Ofcom's role and principles can be found on www.ofcom.org.uk.

The ASA

The Advertising Standards Authority (**ASA**) is responsible for ensuring that advertising conforms to the British Code of Advertising Conduct which requires all advertising to be *legal, decent, honest and truthful*. If an advertisement is found to contravene the code it has to be withdrawn. Below are three examples of ASA adjudications where the complaint was upheld.

1. Objection to a magazine advertisement. The text stated 'Flying Economy with Virgin Atlantic, you enjoy … 31" of legroom'. The complainant, who experienced discomfort travelling in economy and believed the legroom was smaller than claimed, challenged the claim '31" of legroom'.

2. Objection to a Ryanair newspaper advertisement which stated 'SUMMER 2005 FLIGHTS NOW ON SALE!'. Text at the bottom of the advertisement stated 'Travel from 07.03.05 until 26.05.05.' The complainant objected that the advertisement was misleading, because the period when flights were available was not in 'Summer'.

3. Heatherlea (Scotland) Ltd objected to a magazine advertisement and a brochure, for wildlife holidays, headlined 'Speyside Wildlife No 1 in Scotland, Leaders Worldwide'. The complainants, who believed that they sold more holidays in Scotland than the advertisers, challenged the claim 'No 1 in Scotland'.

Source: www.asa.org.uk

Environmental factors

Increasing public awareness of the environment has resulted in travel and tourism organisations needing to consider environmental factors when planning promotional activities. The more environmentally aware customer will want reassurances that any travel or tourism product that they buy will have a minimal negative impact on the environment. There are many operators which specialise in environmentally friendly products – as we explore in depth in Unit 7. Such operators devote a substantial part of their promotional content to highlighting this aspect, as the extract from one such tour operator below shows.

What makes this holiday different?

- We actively encourage our clients to be environmentally aware of all their actions and act in a proper, responsible manner at all times.
- Information, tips and recommendations on the life and customs of the local people are given to all clients.
- As much as we can, our office recycles waste and we use recycled products whenever possible.
- All possible steps are taken to ensure that we operate all our tours in an environmentally responsible manner, by, for example, using local guides whenever possible.
- We always use local services and accommodation, as well as visiting rural restaurants and local shops selling local products.
- We are aware that travel in any country has some effect on the area and, with this in mind, we strive to lessen the impact, promote local employment through use and at all times show a positive attitude towards the environment and encourage others to appreciate its importance.
- We also pay our guides, local services and accommodation the market price for their services.

Source: Online travel agency www.responsibletravel.com

Profitability

Private sector organisations strive to maximise profitability. Public and voluntary bodies aim to at least cover their operating costs, and may aim for profits. This means that the need for profitability frequently affects the type and volume of promotional activities. All promotion has some cost attached to it, but some methods are considerably more expensive than others. Whilst a large organisation such as an international tour operator may be able to afford extensive television advertising, this form of

The success of Center Parcs may be partly due to an increased appreciation of the environment

Source: Center Parcs brochure

promotion will be beyond the budgets of smaller operators. We look at promotional budgeting in depth in Topic 10 of this unit.

Competition

The amount and nature of competition that exists is also a factor that will affect an organisation's promotional strategy. Where competition is fierce, such as in the package holiday and visitor attractions markets, organisations will be eager to communicate to customers the ways in which their products and services are better than the competitors. Often this may be in the form of offering a price promise, such as the example below.

Economic factors

The overall size and value of markets in the travel and tourism industries are largely determined by income levels and the cost of goods. Consumer spending may be influenced by a range of national and international economic factors such as unemployment, income levels, inflation, taxes, exchange rates and mortgage rates.

It is simplistic to assume that the more money people have, the more they will spend on travel and tourism products. Whilst it may well be true that in times of economic boom more will be spent on luxury products such as long-haul holidays, other tourism products may benefit from economic recession when people have less disposable income. For example, a family where the main breadwinner has recently been made redundant may not take their usual foreign package holiday but take a series of day trips to local tourist attractions instead. Therefore a decrease in disposable income may benefit some travel and tourism organisations. Travel and tourism organisations will be aware of economic factors when using different promotional techniques. For example, if their products and services are aimed at the economy end of the market, such as 'no-frills' airlines, the value for money aspect will be a strong part of the promotional message. Alternatively, at the other end of the scale, luxury travel and tourism products such as world cruises may be promoted with the message that the higher cost guarantees a high degree of luxury and exclusivity.

EFFECTS OF COMPETITION

Amalfi (Italy) is a typical Phoenix Travel destination.

Phoenix Travel is an independent travel agency specialising in quality, tailor-made holidays to Europe and America. Their main customer base is local, affluent, 45–70-year-olds. Approximately 70% of their customers have used the agency before, and 61% book two or more holidays a year. Feedback from surveys indicates that customers value the high level of personalised service received and the guaranteed quality of the transport and accommodation provided.

Phoenix have used the local paper for advertising their services but had little response from new customers. They have four main competitors in the area – three national tour operators with travel agency outlets, and a new independent operator who is offering similar products to Phoenix plus packages to less developed destinations.

Analyse the effects that competition is likely to have on the type of promotional activities that Phoenix Travel use.

Technological factors

Developments in technology give rise to a range of promotional techniques. The rapidly growing use of information technology, for example, allows customers to select and purchase products such as package holidays more quickly and easily via the internet

Advances in computer and audio-visual technology have had a profound effect on the range of promotional techniques that are now available to organisations. The smaller travel and tourism organisations, in particular, have reaped the benefits of this. Many now operate their own websites to promote and take bookings for their products. In addition, digital cameras and basic desktop publishing programmes allow organisations to produce leaflets, brochures, posters and flyers easily and at minimal cost. Larger organisations, with more resources, have developed complex websites that often allow customers to take virtual tours of facilities, or they produce CD-ROMs for customers to browse through at home.

activity

PROMOTION AND THE BUSINESS ENVIRONMENT

In pairs, select one of the following holiday products and analyse how some or all of the factors discussed in this topic might affect the promotional activities:

1 Long-haul package holidays to the Far East
2 Weekly packages to traditional holiday camps, such as Butlins
3 European city breaks
4 Short breaks at holiday villages such as Center Parcs
5 Two-week all-inclusive packages to European beach destinations
6 Stag and hen parties to Dublin.

Topic 5 Analysing the business environment

The marketing mix refers to the factors that need to be combined ('mixed') to enable an organisation to achieve its marketing objectives. These factors are often known as the four Ps:

- Product
- Price
- Place
- Promotion.

Using the four Ps effectively involves developing products that meet the needs of the customers, identifying a price that customers will consider appropriate for the product or service offered, deciding where and how it should be made available, and promoting it effectively to the target market. In this topic we will explore the first three 'P's' – product, price and place. Promotion will be discussed in depth in Topics 7–10.

Product

In marketing, product refers to both goods and services. Goods are physical objects, such as food and drink or tourist souvenirs. Services involve the combination of skills, information or entertainment to provide an experience such as a package holiday, theatre production or guided tour.

When developing and offering new products, organisations need to be aware of the specific product characteristics that encourage customers to buy a specific product. Product characteristics are the specific features of a product that the customer sees as being important – the features that attract them to buy it or use it. Different customers may value different characteristics as being important to them. For example, separate members of a family going on a package holiday may have different expectations of what they hope it will be like. Whilst the parents may anticipate lazy days relaxing on the beach in the sun, their children may have quite different expectations, as the advertisement below demonstrates.

Travel and tourism organisations must constantly review their product characteristics to ensure that they continue to meet customers' needs, and they must identify any gaps in the market where new products might be developed. This is particularly true in the visitor-attractions industry where a vast range of attractions compete to attract visitors to their product. Recent trends have seen attractions based on nature and ecology, science, food and drink and technology. So called 'Dark Tourism' has created attractions that present scenes, settings or memorabilia commemorating wars or disasters such as the example from the Imperial War Museum above, right.

THE HOLOCAUST EXHIBITION
Imperial War Museum

Tireless searching for artefacts, relics and film has given us something which takes at least two hours to examine properly and, I suspect, will stay in the memory for ever

David Robson, *Sunday Express*

Branding

Branding is the process in marketing of giving a product a distinct identity that creates a unique image that will make it easily identifiable and separate from its competitors. A product's brand image can be created and reinforced by its name, logo, advertising, packaging, price, use of specific colours, etc.

activity

BRAND CHARACTERISTICS

Clearly a product's brand image is closely related to its brand characteristics. Look at the two lists of brand characteristics that describe two separate travel and tourism products below. Can you suggest what each product might be?

Product 1	Product 2
• Fun for all the family	• Relaxing
• Exciting	• Tranquil
• Different	• Scenic
• Heart-stoppingly thrilling	• For older people
• Young	• Educational
• Colourful	• Healthy

Four useful branding terms are:

Brand awareness means that a customer is able to identify a particular brand and its characteristics as opposed to others.

Brand leader refers to the brand with the highest share of the market in its category. For example McDonald's is the brand leader in fast food restaurants.

Brand extension is when an existing strong brand is used to create other products that carry the same brand title and image. For example, Cadbury World in Birmingham is an extension of the Cadbury confectionery organisation.

Brand loyalty which means that a customer is loyal to a particular brand and will buy it on a regular basis.

Branding is a very powerful marketing tool, and has a strong influence over the products and services that we buy. Branding is used both to establish customer awareness and loyalty, and to target specific segments of the market in order to achieve a higher market share. For example, tour operators have well-established brands for particular market segments. Look at the range of product descriptions for companies within the First Choice group, and see how a tour operator establishes distinct branded products.

The success of the confectionery led to the development of Cadbury World.

First Choice

First Choice offers a wide range of holidays across the world. Accommodation meets our high quality standards and the majority of our flights are with the award-winning First Choice Airways. First Choice can look after your kids in our Looney Tunes clubs.

Unijet

At Unijet we have years of experience in providing quality holidays at excellent value for money. Unijet offers a wide selection of high quality self-catering apartments, villas and hotels throughout the Mediterranean and the Caribbean. Our properties have been chosen to provide a feeling of space, giving you room to relax and unwind.

Sunstart

Sunquest offers low-cost holidays to low-cost destinations. We concentrate on '2-sun-rated and 3-sun-rated' properties, enabling us to keep our costs to a minimum. Sunquest has something for everyone – so go further for your money.

2wentys

Choose 2wentys for the best bunch of people to party with, the most up-for-it resorts and some totally off-your-trolley events. Alongside all the partying you can expect a first-rate service and a decent place to rest your bones.

Please note: You must be 17 years or over to book a 2wentys holiday. These holidays are not suitable for families.

Falcon

Falcon Holidays offer a wide range of holidays across the world. Accommodation meets our high quality standards and the majority of our flights are with the award-winning First Choice Airways. Falcon can look after your kids in our Looney Tunes clubs, and our representatives in resort will ensure your holiday is everything you're looking forward to.

JWT HOLIDAYS

JWT Holidays offer holidays for adults of all ages. Alongside your favourite sun destinations such as the Canary and Balearic islands, mainland Spain and Portugal, we also cater for the more independent traveller with holiday choices in Italy, Croatia, Slovenia, Malta and many other destinations.

Place

Place describes the location and availability of the product or service and the method by which it is distributed to customers. There are two distinct elements to 'place' – location, and channels of distribution.

Location

When Charles Ritz, founder of the famous Ritz hotels, was asked what was important when opening a new hotel he replied that there were only three things that needed to be remembered: 'Location, location and location!'.

The Ritz hotel in London is situated at the heart of the capital's shopping and theatre district.

While it is obviously an exaggeration to state that location is the only factor that is important, it is clearly something that travel and tourism providers need to give a lot of thought to. If a product or service is not accessible to potential customers, then no matter how well it has been developed, or how attractively it has been priced and promoted, it will not be successful. For example, most travel agencies are usually located in a main shopping area because they realise that their customers will often visit them as part of a general shopping trip rather than a special visit.

There are many factors that could be considered important when deciding on location such as:

- Space available
- Image of the area
- Other facilities nearby (such as hotels, restaurants and other tourist attractions)
- Competition in the area
- Parking
- Public transport/road links
- Cost
- Availability of staff and supplies
- Weather
- Local and visiting population
- Local planning regulations
- Future plans for the area.

The relative importance of each of these factors depends on the nature of the product being offered and the targeted customers. For example, a small tea shop would probably rate factors such as being in a busy area near to other attractions, with good parking or public transport as very important. This is because they may gain a lot of their business from passing trade who are staying locally or live in the area. Conversely a provider who attracts customers from a wide geographical range may have different priorities. For example, a major theme park is clearly not going to locate in the centre of a town as there would be insufficient space. They would, however, be concerned that their chosen location had good motorway access and room for future expansion as well as a local population who could be employed to work at the park. The distance that a customer is willing to travel to get to a specific travel or tourism facility is often crucial when considering 'place' – for example how far would you travel to get to a concert, and how far would you travel to rent a video of a concert?

Many travel and tourism organisations use the 'place' element of the marketing mix in their promotional materials by advising customers about the various ways in which they can travel to them.

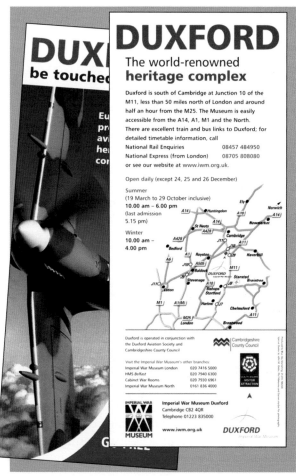

The Imperial War Museum Duxford provides advice on how customers can reach them by road, rail or coach excursion in their leaflet.

It should be remembered that many travel and tourism providers have no control over where they are placed. Tourist destinations, natural tourist attractions and most historical/heritage attractions exist because of where they are – they cannot be moved to a more suitable location in order to attract more visitors! Whilst the operators of these destinations and attractions can campaign for improved transport links and services, their location is fixed. Hadrian's Wall might well attract more visitors if it were moved to the South East of England where most overseas visitors go – but then it would not be Hadrian's Wall, would it?

Channels of distribution

Another important aspect of 'place' in the marketing mix is the channels of distribution that an organisation uses to bring its products and services to the market. For some small providers this may be a single channel. For example, a privately owned art gallery may only sell admission tickets at the entrance to the gallery. However, many larger organisations have a number of channels of distribution that allow customers to buy their products. Consider the ways in which you might buy a package holiday from a leading tour operator. You could:

- Book at a local travel agency
- Access the tour operator's website (and probably get a discount for online booking)
- Access through Ceefax/Teletext or a Satellite TV Travel station
- Make a booking by phone.

All of the above are channels of distribution in that they allow you, the customer, to buy the product. Many travel and tourism organisations seek to maximise the number of channels of distribution that they have in order to increase their sales.

---

activity

THE TWO PARTS OF THE 'PLACE' ELEMENT

Select one travel or tourism agency within your area. Evaluate the location part of the 'place' element in their marketing mix, based on any of the factors that are relevant in the list on page 00. Then, explain how the location of the travel agency might affect any promotion that they use. For example, how do they promote specific products at the premises?

Price

Once an organisation has identified a product or service, it must decide on the price at which it is going to be offered to customers. Decisions on price need to take into consideration a number of factors:

- What are the costs of producing the product?
- What are the customers willing to pay?
- What are competitors charging?
- How will the price help to reinforce the product's brand image?
- What will be the overall pricing strategy of the range of products offered?

Price determination

Price determination involves ensuring that the price selected appears to customers to be the right price – in other words, the customers should feel the price reflects the quality of the product and is therefore good value for money.

It is important to remember that lower prices are not always more attractive to customers. This is because the price charged will often help to reinforce a product's brand image and the customer's perception of what they will get. For example, customers may be suspicious if a price seems to be too low and assume that the product will be of a poor standard – imagine the impression of the engaged couple wanting to book a luxury Caribbean wedding who are told that one is available with an unknown tour operator for £250 per person!

Conversely, some travel and tourism operators have been very successful in selling products at the economy end of the market where customers realise and appreciate that the low price reflects the fact that there will be minimal service included. Budget hotels and airlines have proved a huge success, simply because they have been clear about the fact that the low prices charged are possible because of the basic product that is offered.

The process of communicating prices to customers in a way that the customer can easily understand is an important part of the marketing mix. Customers need to be able to identify what is included, and what is not included, in the price charged. In addition, there are numerous legal requirements about the ways in which prices are presented, as we discussed on page 164. Tour operators face a number of difficulties when determining and communicating prices for their package holidays. This is because package holidays are complex products, comprising a number of elements which will often vary in price according to the customer's needs. Differences in prices may result from the time of year, the number of people sharing accommodation, meal requirements, flight time, departure airport and any number of selected extras such as upgraded rooms, sea views, cots, etc. Tour operators try to make this as easy as possible for customers by using clear pricing panels in their brochures, such as in this Thomson's pricing panel below.

	Rialto			Dalmatas								
Board basis	Full Board			Full Board								
Flights	Tue,Sat			Tue,Sat								
Accom code	RIA			DBE								
Prices based on	Bathroom, wc, bl			Bathroom, wc, balcony								
Adults sharing	2			2								
Number of nights	7	14	All	3	4	7	10	11	14	21	28	All
Adult/child	Adult	Adult	1st Ch	Adult	Adult	Adult	Adult	Adult	Adult	Adult	Adult	1st
20 Oct - 31 Oct*	335	489	209	329	329	375	439	439	505	635	719	20
01 Nov - 06 Nov	325	479	199	319	319	365	429	429	495	625	709	19
07 Nov - 13 Nov	315	455	179	299	299	349	405	405	469	595	709	17
14 Nov - 23 Nov	295	445	149	285	285	335	399	399	459	559	705	14
24 Nov - 30 Nov	275	415	149	269	269	315	365	365	429	569	775	14
01 Dec - 12 Dec	265	395	139	235	235	305	339	339	405	685	805	13
13 Dec - 17 Dec	245	535	289	225	225	285	465	385	555	799	989	28
18 Dec - 24 Dec	615	845	379	495	345	655	819	819	889	1079	1195	37
25 Dec - 28 Dec	529	669	309	–	415	569	–	605	699	809	875	30
29 Dec - 30 Dec	509	649	309	–	–	545	–	–	679	829	865	30
31 Dec - 31 Dec	489	599	299	475	–	525	579	–	625	805	835	29
01 Jan - 04 Jan	275	419	139	–	265	315	–	355	429	659	745	13
05 Jan - 26 Jan	275	429	139	255	255	315	345	345	439	649	735	13
27 Jan - 08 Feb	325	459	189	285	285	365	415	415	475	589	709	18
09 Feb - 12 Feb	425	509	229	375	–	465	485	–	529	615	689	22
13 Feb - 20 Feb	385	469	199	335	335	419	475	475	485	635	745	19
21 Feb - 15 Mar	329	435	179	305	305	369	435	435	449	659	775	17
16 Mar - 30 Mar	339	445	199	315	315	379	445	445	459	669	785	19
31 Mar - 02 Apr	395	555	319	349	–	435	535	–	535	789	885	31
03 Apr - 09 Apr	439	515	319	425	425	475	549	549	579	789	–	31
10 Apr - 16 Apr	429	515	289	415	415	465	549	549	579	–	–	28
17 Apr - 30 Apr	385	–	279	355	355	425	–	475	–	–	–	27
Supplements per person per night	Single room £10			Single room £3								
Reductions per person per night	3rd Adult only sharing £3			3rd Adult only sharing £5								
2nd Child pays 1st Child price plus £30 per week												

Source © 2005 TUI UK

Because of the high level of competition within the travel and tourism industry, the determination of price is often based on what competitors are charging. For tourist attractions the comparison of admissions charges is looked at in relation to how long a visitor stays at the attraction – a concept known as dwell time. So, for example, a theme park may charge £12.00 admission with the average length of visitor stay being 7 hours, whereas a museum may charge £4.50 with the average visitor stay being 1.5 hours. In terms of dwell time the theme park works out at £1.71 an hour and the museum is £3.00 per hour. Dwell time is an important issue in terms of the customer's perception of a travel and tourism product and many providers try to think of ways in which they can extend dwell time so that customers view their visit as better value for money.

DWELL TIME

Consider a small farming visitor attraction in a rural area, comprising a children's 'petting' farm (i.e. where children can hold or feed small animals such as lambs, rabbits, chickens, etc), farming displays and exhibitions, and a tea shop. Current dwell time is 2 hours. There is ample space on the farm to develop additional attractions for the visitor. Suggest three ways in which the attraction could increase dwell time.

Pricing policies

Getting the pricing policy right will determine both the financial success of a particular product and, in part, the long-term success of the organisation. In addition, pricing policies are usually an integral part of an organisation's promotions. For example, a series of special offers and discounts might be part of a tour operator's promotion to sell more holidays at off-peak times. The type of organisation and the sector it operates in have a direct impact on the choice of pricing policies, such as the need to make a profit, break even or operate at a loss. There are several different pricing policies which can be implemented by travel and tourism organisations when bringing products to the market:

- **Market-penetration pricing** This is usually used by organisations wanting to get into a market new to them, in order to establish a product. It might involve setting a lower price to attract new business or to undercut competitors.

- **Competitive pricing** Often the prices charged by competitors will dictate what price an organisation can set for a particular product. For example, guest houses in a seaside resort will frequently charge very similar prices since they know that to charge more than the competitors would result in a loss of business.

- **Discount pricing** This involves offering a reduced price for certain products. Discount pricing is widely used in the travel and tourism industries and includes numerous sales promotions and special offers such as 'two for the price of one', ten per cent off, free holiday insurance and free child places.

173

Topic 6 Developing a marketing mix

Discount pricing may be a planned part of the overall pricing strategy or in response to low sales. If there is insufficient demand at their anticipated peak periods, then providers may have to discount heavily in order to fill their capacity – a situation that many tour operators face.

- **Variable pricing** Organisations can vary price by customer types, levels and quality of service, times, days, season, and so on. For example, an art gallery may set lower prices for certain groups, such as the unemployed, students and pensioners. Similarly, prices may vary according to peak and off-peak times during the day, week or year. Within the travel and tourism industry variable pricing is often used to maximise the profits at peak times (by charging more) and encourage customers at off-peak times (by charging less). For example, look at the prices shown below for a UK holiday village and note how the cost varies. Can you explain the differences in price at different times?

07–28 Jan	■	341	209	389	239	505	299
04 Feb	■	341	229	389	259	505	329
11 Feb		544	608	620	693	805	881
18 Feb	■	431	372	492	425	638	540
25 Feb	■	409	249	466	289	605	369
04–11 Mar	■	394	249	449	289	583	369
18 Mar		469	490	535	559	694	710
25 Mar		529	561	603	639	782	813
01 Apr		510	537	582	612	755	779
08 Apr		469	439	535	500	694	637
15 Apr	■	383	353	436	402	566	512
22 Apr	■	386	363	440	414	571	526
29 Apr		510	363	581	414	754	526
06–13 May	■	394	363	449	414	582	526
20 May		394	383	449	437	582	555
27 May		579	641	660	731	856	930
03–10 Jun	■	409	411	467	469	605	596
17 Jun	■	429	443	489	506	634	643
24 Jun	■	436	492	497	561	645	713
01 Jul	■	436	512	497	584	645	742
08 Jul	■	456	581	519	662	674	842
15 Jul		456	581	519	662	674	842
22 Jul–19 Aug		506	706	577	804	748	1023
26 Aug		560	544	638	620	828	789
02 Sep		425	443	484	506	628	643
09–16 Sep	■	386	403	440	460	571	585
23–30 Sep	■	386	367	440	418	571	532
07 Oct	■	386	367	440	418	571	532
14 Oct	■	432	452	493	515	639	655
21 Oct		548	657	625	749	811	953

Center Parcs variable pricing

- **Market-skimming strategy** With some travel and tourism products, customers may be prepared to pay high prices for the quality and status associated with using them. Upmarket long-haul package holiday companies often adopt a high price strategy to retain their exclusivity, status and quality image.

PRICE DETERMINATION

Look at this pricing panel for Windsor Castle.

ADMISSION PRICES 2004

	Individual
Adult	£12.00
Over 60/Student	£10.00
Under 17	£6.00
Under 5	Free
Family Ticket	£30.00
(2 adults, 3 under 17s)	

	Group (15+)
Adult	£11.00
Over 60/Student	£ 9.00
Under 17	£ 5.50

Half-price admission applies when the State Apartments are closed. Visitors can see the Castle Precincts, Queen Mary's Dolls' House, the Drawings Gallery and St George's Chapel.

As a group, discuss the following:

1 What does an entrance fee of £12 for adults imply about the quality of the product that they are buying? – What level of dwell time would you expect for this?

2 Why do you think that under-17 year olds are charged £4 less than over 60's and students?

3 Why are under-5-year-olds free?

4 Why would the attraction offer a family ticket that is £12 less than if each of the family had bought a separate ticket?

5 Can you suggest any additional pricing that might be added to this pricing panel – if so justify your answers.

WINDSOR CASTLE
OFFICIAL RESIDENCE OF HER MAJESTY THE QUEEN

Source: The Royal Collection © Her Majesty Queen Elizabeth II

Each year the marketing department will put a marketing plan together which covers the following areas:

Product Although, almost without exception, a new attraction is launched each year, and the main launch communication will focus on that, general communication about the rest of the Park is required. Theme Parks provide a whole day out for the family and it is not just about the rides. The other attractions, places to eat, games, photography, the atmosphere – all play an important part in delivering a great day out.

Pricing There is a complex pricing structure for the Park which looks to maximise the revenue the Park can achieve with its targeted number of visitors. Marketing will review the pricing each year and, along with the finance department, look at how the budgeted targets can be achieved through the pricing matrix. Advance bookings help to reduce the queues at admissions as visitors already have their tickets and can go straight into the Park. This year advance booking comes with added benefits. On certain days, full-paying adults receive 4 fast-track tickets, for the most popular rides, and an early rider, which allows entry into the Park half an hour before the official opening time to enjoy Quantum and Zodiac. The fast-track tickets are for Colossus, Nemesis Inferno, Logger's Leap and Tidal Wave.

Promotion of the Park happens via a number of different communication channels:

- Advertising is generally broken down into two areas; the creative production of the advert and then the choice of where to place that advert – TV, radio, press, etc. [This year] adverts will feature Colossus, Nemesis Inferno and Samurai, targeting a youth market. No new adverts will be created for TV but a message about Samurai will be made for radio use.
- Promotions are very important in incentivising visitors to come to the Park. Promotions offering discounts and conditional free tickets will be run with Nectar and Tesco. This year there are no 'buy one get one free' promotions, only discounts.
- Public relations is all about getting positive exposure in the media, TV, radio and press. This is generally achieved through issuing Press Releases and hosting events for the media. The aim is to develop the 'Twisted Pleasure' image of the Park. 'Twisted Pleasure' is the *strapline* that appears on TV adverts and any messages about the Park.

Measuring the success

Throughout the year, how the Park is doing against its financial targets is constantly reviewed, but in addition Marketing conducts ongoing research in to how the Park is performing on a daily basis. Questionnaires are handed out to visitors as they leave asking them to rank the rides, experiences, eating places, how friendly and helpful the staff were, etc. This provides information on where things may be going wrong and how to put them right.

New media is a crucial area for involvement now and in the future. In addition to maintaining its own site, www.thorpepark.com, the Marketing department looks to exploit other opportunities for advertising, promotions and PR on other sites.

Use of agencies Thorpe Park uses a wide variety of agencies as they bring different areas of expertise and experience to the Park. We use an advertising agency to create the TV, radio ads, etc. and also for all the design work for the Gate Map. The space for the TV, radio slots, etc. is purchased by a media-buying agency. We also use a sales promotion agency, a PR agency and an internet design agency. Some of these are different agencies to those used for Chessington World of Adventures.

Corporate hospitality makes it possible for businesses to entertain their guests at Thorpe Park. Thousands of corporate guests can be catered for at any one time, or businesses can even hire the whole Park for an evening.

Education An establishment like Thorpe Park offers the opportunity for students studying the leisure industry, business or animals to visit the Park and find out more about their subject. For this reason, it is possible for groups to incorporate an educational talk into their visit.

Most often asked marketing questions

Are ticket prices changed when a new ride is introduced?

Ticket prices are reviewed annually. Any adjustments will consider the new attractions in the Park and other attractions in the Tussauds group, and competition in the market place.

How often do you introduce a new ride?

It is our intention to introduce a new and exciting attraction every year. The nature of this attraction is dependent on a number of contributing factors based upon research results.

Are there any discounts or special offers?

Yes, and these vary throughout the season. Discounts are available all season on those tickets that are booked in advance. Promotional offers/discounts vary throughout the year and are generally conducted with third-party partners.

Source: Thorpe Park's 'Student Pack'

In the last topic we looked at the first three 'P's of the marketing mix – product, price and place. In this and the following three topics we are going to explore the final 'P' – promotion. Let's start by looking at some of the common terms used in promotion and what they mean within the marketing environment:

- **Marketing communications**
- **Communication channels**
- **Promotional techniques**
- **Promotional materials**
- **Promotions mix.**

Marketing communications

Marketing communications refers to the processes that organisations use to communicate with existing or potential customers. The purpose of the communication can be for a range of reasons, including:

- To create brand awareness of specific products or services

- To make customers understand and appreciate the characteristics of the product or service

- To describe how particular products and services could meet the needs and expectations of customers

- To persuade customers to buy the product or use the service

- To encourage customers to develop brand loyalty and therefore prefer it to alternatives provided by competitors

- To encourage customers to continue to buy the product and to recommend it to others

- To raise awareness of the organisation or improve the organisation's public image.

The precise purpose of any marketing communications will be firmly based on the organisation's strategic objectives, and, more specifically, its marketing and promotional objectives.

Communication channels

Communication channels are the range of ways in which marketing and promotional information is relayed to customers. Such channels can include:

Television
Radio
Cinema
Newspapers and magazines
Internet
Posters
Direct (face-to-face).

Promotional techniques

Promotional techniques describe the methods used by organisations to promote their products and services, and include:

Advertising	Holiday brochures
Displays	Direct marketing
Public relations	Sponsorship
Sales promotions	Personal selling.

Travel and tourism organisations may use any or all of these techniques, depending on the nature of their products and services, the markets that they aim to target and attract, and their promotional budget. (In the next two topics we will look at these techniques in detail and the ways in which they are used in the travel and tourism industry.)

Cheddar Caves is one of Britain's oldest and most popular tourist attractions; a honey-pot operating within a fragile and scientifically important natural environment. Tourism is the fastest growing employment sector in Britain, and, with the decline in agricultural employment, more people in this rural area are now employed in tourism than in farming. The scale of Cheddar Caves' operations significantly affects the local economy, and the high profile and easy visibility of our policies and activities make our sites textbook examples of many aspects of tourism management.

Marketing

There are many different kinds of products, and each needs to be marketed in a different way. A person buying a ticket at Cheddar Caves is making a particular type of purchase: considered (not impulse); comparison (not convenience); one-off (not repeat). A promotional campaign which would work for baked beans at your local supermarket would not sell Cheddar Caves tickets to families in Newcastle. Because of this we use particular kinds of publicity and not others. In the past we have tried, and have now rejected, television advertising, newspaper advertising (except for events and special promotions), local radio advertising, adverts in trade magazines and specialised guide books. We no longer employ an advertising agency; our promotions material is produced by a designer working closely with our own Marketing Department. We do a limited amount of

promotion with consortium leaflets, door-to-door deliveries, open-topped buses painted to look like our leaflets, and out-of-season events. The bulk of our effort goes into producing a single promotional leaflet and then distributing 1.5 million copies per year in all the shops, pubs and cafés within a fifty-mile radius. Almost all our visitors either live, or are staying, within this 'core area'. Producing a leaflet, which potential customers select, carry round, read closely and then pass on to someone else, is the best way of encouraging a 'considered purchase' of this type. Our visitors need to master quite a lot of information, which is all set down in the leaflet for easy reference. Spending on marketing and publicity in the tourist industry tends to be between 5% and 15% of gross turnover, and our own spending is 10%. As all income is derived from publicity, this is another way of saying that a marketing strategy has to generate at least ten times more income that it costs if it is to be regarded as cost-effective.

Source: Cheddar Caves and Gorge 'Discovery Pack' www.cheddarcaves.co.uk

Promotional materials

Promotional materials are the actual printed materials that support the various forms of promotional techniques, and can include:

Brochures and leaflets	Posters
Advertisements	Display materials
Mailshot letters	Merchandise
Press releases.	

Any particular promotional technique may require a range of different materials to support it. For example, a travel agency wanting to promote late-availability holiday deals might put up posters in the shop window, write an advertisement for the local press and send mailshots to existing customers.

Promotions mix

'Promotions mix' refers to the blend of promotional techniques and materials that an organisation uses to achieve its overall marketing and promotional objectives. It is unusual for an organisation to use only one type of promotional technique. This is because different techniques will be effective in attracting different markets. For example, a large tour operator

that offers several distinct holiday package brands will use different techniques for each target market.

> **activity**
>
> ## CHEDDAR CAVES & GORGE
>
> Read the case study on the Cheddar Caves and discuss the following:
>
> 1 Why do you think that 'a promotional campaign that would work for baked beans at your local supermarket would not sell Cheddar Caves tickets to families in Newcastle'?
> 2 Consider the reasons why Cheddar Caves have tried and rejected using television advertising, newspaper advertising, local radio advertising and adverts in trade magazines and specialised guide books as promotional techniques.
> 3 Evaluate the reasons why distributing a promotional leaflet to shops, pubs and cafés within a 50-mile radius has been the most effective promotional technique.
> 4 Explain why the nature of the buying behaviour at Cheddar ('considered', 'comparison' and 'one-off') has affected the choice of promotional techniques and materials used.

Susan Hornby
Marketing Director, The Deep, Hull

How did you get to where you are now?

I studied hotel and catering at Huddersfield University, working first for Crest Hotels and then Thistle Hotels. My first position was as a junior manager running hotels, but within two years I'd moved into a sales function – where the hours were better and the job satisfaction greater. In 1988 I joined a luxury hotel company with properties in the UK and Caribbean, where I did sales and marketing. At this point, I studied part-time to gain the post-graduate diploma in marketing which ultimately allowed me to cross from the hotel industry into other business sectors.

After a year undertaking freelance projects, I joined the University of London as Sales and Marketing Manager, based at Royal Holloway, where I stayed for 5 years. I then undertook a 'year out' as a volunteer in Ethiopia.

After a brief spell as Marketing Manager at a regional university, I moved to The Deep in 2000 as Marketing Director.

This job has to be the ultimate in jobs ... a combination of a commercial role, working for the benefit of educational and conservation causes, and yet in the private sector. I joined as part of a management team of six, and we are all still here four years later! We planned The Deep, opened it, and are now running it. I believe passionately in the project, and can be a bit of a bore about it sometimes!

What were the main objectives of The Deep when it opened?

When we opened in March 2002 we expected about 350,000 visitors in our first year, dropping off to 250,000 each subsequent year. We had received a market research report from KPMG which had provided us with these expected visitor numbers but they, and we, had underestimated the power of the media and the interest the public have in most things 'new'. In our first year we welcomed 852,000 visitors, which fell to just under 600,000 in year 2.

The millennium commission awarded us a further £3m in 2003 which, together with our own profits, has allowed us to build Phase 2 – an extension which improves reception facilities, increases the size of the shop, provides an internal queuing area, improves the Learning Centre space and, most importantly, provides a huge exhibition space about the Twilight Zone – an area of the ocean where animals live between 200m and 1000m below the surface. This area, where light struggles to penetrate, is virtually undiscovered – indeed more is known about the moon that the deep waters of the ocean.

Who did you see as your main target audience and what promotional techniques do you use to communicate to them?

Our predictions for this were right – families with children aged 4–14, those aged over 55, coach groups and school groups. We had however expected people to travel from just over an hour away, whereas in fact they come from up to two-hours drive away. This means our catchment area goes down to Grantham and Sheffield in the south, to Huddersfield and Halifax in the west and to Bridlington and Harrogate in the north.

We use different methods to communicate to different target markets. To attract school groups we produce a brochure about the different learning sessions available, and this is sent to local authorities, schools and libraries. Those travelling by coach find out about The Deep from the coach company.

What about the national and international markets?

Having undertaken market research we know that our audience is unlikely to travel to us from further than three hours away, so to promote ourselves nationally or internationally doesn't provide value for money. However a good quality and ever-changing website ensures that potential customers from all over the world can learn about The Deep.

What has been your most successful promotional technique?

PR – without doubt! We have an experienced PR Manager on our marketing team and she worked with the millennium commission in London, together with a number of other partners, to ensure that The Deep opened with a blaze of publicity. We appeared in all national newspapers on the day we opened, including being on the front page of *The Independent*

and *Guardian*. In the following year we had film crews on site most weeks, and continued to appear in regional papers and specialist magazines. We were featured on *Blue Peter*, *Tomorrow's World*, *Would-Like-To-Meet*, *Tikabilla*, *Newsround*, *Look North*, *Calendar* and *GMTV*, to name but a few.

We produce about 500,000 leaflets each year, and these are taken from distribution sites all across the north of England. We also sell around 10,000 tickets via Jacksons Supermarkets, who have over 100 shops throughout the midlands and north, and this ensures that people coming from afar could buy their tickets locally before travelling to Hull. Other promotional methods include displays about The Deep in Tourist Information Centres, banners on site facing the passing traffic, and occasional 48-sheet adverts in major northern towns and cities.

Promotional techniques (1)

Promotion is a vital component of the marketing mix. It includes all those activities used to communicate with existing and potential customers. For promotion to be effective, an organisation must be talking to the right people about the right product and convincing them that the price is right. The ultimate aim of promotion is to encourage consumers to buy or use a product or service.

In this and the next topic we are going to explore the various **promotional techniques** that can be used by organisations. There is a wide range of different techniques, including:

- advertising
- holiday brochures
- displays
- direct marketing
- public relations
- sponsorship
- sales promotions
- personal selling.

We will explore the first four in this topic and the other four in Topic 9.

Advertising

Advertising is the paid-for space or time in a medium such as a publication or on television which usually aims to persuade consumers to buy a product or service. Advertising is one of the most common promotional techniques used by travel and tourism organisations, and ranges from national television advertisements costing many thousands of pounds to small classified ads in local newspapers costing just a few pounds.

Practically all travel and tourism organisations undertake some form of advertising which might be in any or all of the following media:

- newspapers and magazines
- radio
- posters.
- television
- internet

Newspapers and magazines

- There are 21 national dailies and Sunday papers in the UK, and approximately 1,330 local and regional newspapers.

- Over 27 million people read at least one national daily newspaper.

- 30 million read a national Sunday paper.

National press advertisements are cheaper than many other forms of mass media, such as television advertising, and large national audiences can be reached. Alternatively, press advertisers can reach audiences in individual localities or regions by using local and regional paid-for or free newspapers.

Advertising in newspapers is very flexible. Advertisements can be placed or changed at relatively short notice, while the advertising message can be read at leisure, re-read, or even cut out and kept for future use. There are a few disadvantages to press advertising, however. The advertisements are static – they lack movement and therefore can't show products or services working. With many travel and tourism products this is an important consideration because they are intangible experiences. For example, advertising a product such as a holiday in America will have greater visual impact on colour television than in a black and white newspaper.

Advertisements in magazines have similar advantages and disadvantages to newspapers since they are also a printed medium. Print quality varies but in nearly all cases it is vastly superior to newspapers, with the use of better paper producing clearer reproduction of colour photographs.

The magazine advertisement for British Airways Holidays is made more effective by the strong colours made possible through this medium.

Television

The greatest advantage of television advertising is that it can show products working. Added to this, the use of music, dialogue, personalities, colour, special effects and animation can help to create a stunning visual impact on a mass audience. However, unlike printed advertising, the exposure is very short, usually just 10–60 seconds at a time. This means that the amount of information given is limited and can be missed altogether if the advertisement fails to attract the attention of the viewer. A further problem for advertisers is the use of remote control devices that allow viewers to 'zap' between channels when advertisements appear. Television advertising is often backed up by Teletext services that direct viewers to sources of further information. Tour operators and travel agents make very effective use of the Teletext system, providing details of special offers, late availability offers and so on.

For many travel and tourism providers, the single greatest disadvantage of television advertising is the expense. Many smaller providers, such as privately owned tourist attractions and council-owned tourism facilities, therefore cannot afford to consider any form of television advertising.

Radio

Some travel and tourism providers use local or national commercial radio stations to promote products to the local population. It is a lot cheaper than television and still has the advantage over print advertising that music, dialogue and sound effects can be used. However, relying totally on sound to deliver the advertiser's message is often a drawback because of the tendency of listeners to use radio simply as 'sound wallpaper'. Nevertheless, radio advertising is often an effective means of promoting specific products and local events, particularly when it can be linked to public relations activities such as live radio coverage of an event.

Internet

The rapid increase in the use of the internet has meant that many travel and tourism organisations have realised the benefits of using it as an advertising channel.

Source: www.airtours.co.uk

The internet combines many of the advantages of both printed and visual advertising media. Customers have the opportunity to browse through a large amount of information at their own speed and print out specific pieces of information that they are interested in. Unlike other forms of advertising, the information is completely up to date – it can accurately show current availability, for example. A further advantage is that customers are frequently offered the opportunity to buy products online. Of course, the internet is not without its disadvantages as an advertising media. Many people do not have access to the Internet or are simply reluctant to give the personal details required to make an online purchase or reservation.

Poster advertising

Posters

The use of posters is the oldest form of advertising, and is still used extensively by travel and tourism organisations. Posters can be displayed on billboards, bus shelters, on transport such as underground trains, at sports stadiums or simply on the wall of the provider's own premises. One of the main considerations with poster advertising is that its effectiveness depends largely on where it is located. For example, a poster advertisement on the London Underground will be seen by a lot of people and they will probably have time to read it properly during their journey. However, it will be a very broad audience. A poster outside a tourist attraction such as a museum will have a limited audience but the targeted market may stop to read it fully.

Holiday brochures

Holiday brochures and leaflets are one of the most widely used promotions for travel and tourism organisations. Brochures are used extensively to promote package holidays, travel services, hotels and many tourist attractions. Despite their size, holiday brochures are actually relatively cheap to produce in comparison to many other forms of promotion, costing around £2–5 each. However, you need to remember that many customers may take a brochure but not actually buy any of the holidays that they see in it. Therefore, organisations who use brochures as promotions usually calculate the cost of producing a brochure based on the number of sales it generates.

The obvious advantage of brochures is that a great deal of specific information can be included that potential customers can read at their leisure. However, this can sometimes be one of their disadvantages, since they may appear too complicated to the customer unless they are laid out effectively.

Most of the tour operator's brochures contain similar key sections.

1. A contents list
2. Sections on each country with introductory general descriptions (weather, food, etc.) and
3. Sub-sections on each resort with resort descriptions (e.g. location, landscape, attractions, etc.) and
4. Accommodation descriptions (hotels, apartments, etc.)
5. Pricing panels
6. Details of excursions
7. Flight information
8. Travel insurance details
9. Car hire
10. Extra services and facilities such as special discounts, children's clubs, etc.

Leaflets have similar advantages to brochures and provide effective promotion for travel and tourism organisations such as individual tourist attractions, entertainment venues and special events. Rather than

the 'book' format of brochures, a leaflet is usually a single folded A4 page.

Leaflets are used to promote many special events such as the Royal Norfolk Show.

The increasing use of computers has also meant that many travel and tourism organisations are now able to produce their own leaflets using simple desktop publishing software.

Displays

Many organisations use displays to promote their products and services. Such displays may include brochures and leaflets, posters, examples of products, free gifts and demonstrations. Such displays are often provided at the 'point of sale'. The term point of sale refers to the place that the customer actually buys a product, such as a ticket or reservation desk, a shop counter or a travel agency.

Displays at the point of sale have the advantage that they are targeted at customers who are clearly interested in the product. Its main disadvantage is that it rarely reaches new markets. It is often used when the marketing objective is to develop existing markets or products. For example, a point-of-sale promotion might be used in a travel agency to inform customers about special holiday deals.

Not all displays are at the point of sale. Many travel and tourism organisations use displays at local, national or international exhibitions to promote their products and services. Whilst some of these events are generalised travel and tourism exhibitions, most focus on specific sectors of the industry. For example Reed

Travel Exhibitions (one of the largest exhibition organisers) arrange the following exhibitions:

- The World Travel Market
- The Arabian Travel Market
- British Travel Trade Fair
- Asia Pacific Incentives and Meetings Expo (AIME)
- International Golf Travel Market
- Mediterranean Travel Fair
- International Luxury Travel Market
- City Break.

Direct marketing

Direct marketing is one of the fastest growing promotional techniques. It is so called because it directs the promotion to specific customers. One of its main benefits is that it enables organisations to target products at specific markets, as when a tourist attraction sends a list of its forthcoming events to past customers, for example. There are a number of ways in which direct marketing can be carried out, such as:

- direct mail
- telemarketing
- door-to-door distribution.

Direct mail

The process of posting promotional material to a potential or existing customer is known as direct mail or a mailshot. One of the misconceptions about direct mail is that everyone throws it into the bin without reading it. In fact, research shows that this is not true. However, it is not enough for the customer to simply open a direct mail letter and read it. The promoter also wants the customer to buy the product as a result of reading the mailshot. It is common practice to include a letter in the mailshot explaining the contents of the sales literature. The letter may include some form of sales promotion, perhaps offering a discount or prize if an order is placed within a certain period.

Mailshots are also more effective if they appear to have been written to an individual rather than to dozens of customers. Using the word 'you' is effective, as is addressing the recipient by name rather than as Sir or Madam.

Customer ref: AN4WILLIAMS41

KUONI

Kuoni Travel Ltd
Kuoni House
Dorking
Surrey RH5 4AZ, UK

Mrs K M Williams
41 Main Street
Anytown
Anyshire
AN4 8SG

Telephone: 01306 747010
Email: holidays@kuoni.co.uk
Website: www.kuoni.co.uk

DWM0905   18712

September 2005

Dear Mrs Williams,

Welcome to your Autumn 2005 issue of Kuoni World magazine, packed with holiday ideas and inspiration, travel news and competitions.

Read on and discover the diversity of holidays available to the Maldives, from medium class value to deluxe indulgence, specialist activities to relaxing getaways, and save over £1000 per couple at a selection of enchanting island-resorts! Or for a shorthaul break, visit the breathtakingly picturesque country of Switzerland, Kuoni's home for almost a century. We highlight four of the most spectacular regions and railway journeys.

There are also fascinating features on the colour and culture of Indochina (including 14-night Thailand holidays for only £575 per person!), our top five shopping cities for Christmas bargains, Caribbean honeymoon ideas and two of the world's most extraordinary, extravagant and exotic places – flowers of the desert, Dubai and Oman.

And have a go at solving the new travel crossword for your chance to win a 7-night holiday to the luxurious Evason Phuket Resort!

I hope you enjoy reading World magazine, and we look forward to welcoming you on a Kuoni holiday soon.

Yours sincerely,

Sue Biggs
Managing Director

PS – Special offer just in! Five superb Sandals resorts are offering a $150 voucher for all new bookings made by 31 October 2005, which may be redeemed at the sumptuous Red Lane Spa centres, resort shops and towards room upgrades! If you are looking to book a romantic holiday for two, don't delay! Call our Caribbean team on 01306 747010 for full details.

We respect your privacy so you can be assured your information is safe with Kuoni. We do not share your personal information with other companies or third parties. If your address details have changed, or you do not want to receive holiday news and offers from Kuoni Travel, please visit www.kuoni.co.uk/changes or call 01306 747010.

00039916/NM

Registered Office: Kuoni House, Dorking, Surrey, RH5 4AZ. Registered in England No. 395623

Mailshots, like the one shown below left are often very successful because they are sent to past customers who, the organisation knows, have bought products before and are therefore likely to be interested in similar ones in the future. But how does an organisation know to whom to send mailshots? Most organisations achieve this by the use of a mailing list. Mailing lists are compiled by using information already held on people who have either bought or enquired about a product, or by targeting specific groups of people, for example, by using the postcode system. Mailing lists are usually held on a computer database so it is a very efficient way for many organisations to communicate with existing or potential customers.

Telemarketing

Like direct mail, telemarketing – in which customers are contacted by telephone with the aim of promoting a particular product – is an increasingly common marketing technique. It suffers from a number of drawbacks – many potential customers are suspicious of unsolicited sales calls and therefore unwilling to engage in a conversation, or they are simply too busy. However telemarketing can be successful if properly conducted and targeted.

Door-to-door distribution

Rather than mail materials to customers or contact them by telephone, many organisations deliver direct marketing materials to the customers' home in person (door-to-door distribution). This can work out a lot cheaper than mail or telephone. It also provides the opportunity for personal face-to-face contact with potential customers – which can encourage customers to try a product or service. For example, a restaurant may send staff out to local houses, with discount vouchers, who make contact with residents and ask them if they would be interested in using the restaurant.

SUCCESSFUL USE OF DIRECT MARKETING

Direct marketing is frequently an essential part of what is known as 'relationship marketing'. This means using promotional techniques that build a personal relationship between the organisation and specific customers. Read the account of the British Airways Executive Club below. Analyse why you think direct mail is particularly effective with this market segment.

British Airways is one of the UK's most pre-eminent brands and a recognisable name around the world. Like many businesses in the service sector, attracting new customers and building relationships with existing customers is vitally important. It's not surprising then that British Airways started using direct marketing as a major communications tool many years ago.

The British Airways Executive Club is regarded as being one of the most successfully established loyalty schemes, which has been copied by many companies both within and outside of the airline sector. It provides a vehicle for regular communication with frequent travellers, ensuring that they remain as loyal as possible to the brand.

Beyond this, direct marketing is also used in a variety of other ways. For example, when the airline launches new routes or enhances its cabin brands, direct marketing is a natural choice to drive highly targeted messages to the appropriate audiences. In spite of the tough economic climate that the airline currently faces, it continues to invest heavily in direct marketing and this may prove to be its saviour until the good times come back again.

Source: www.think-direct.com.

Promotional techniques (2)

In the last topic we looked at four different types of promotional techniques. In this topic we will go on to explore a further four techniques:

- **Public relations**
- **Sponsorship**
- **Sales promotions**
- **Personal selling.**

Public relations

The Institute of Public Relations (IPR) defines public relations as:

'The planned and sustained effort to establish and maintain goodwill and mutual understanding between an organisation and its public.'

In this definition 'public' means the whole range of people who come into contact with the organisation – not just its customers and employees. These may include trade unions, suppliers, press, shareholders or councillors, for example. In 1999 the IPR extended its original definition to include:

'PR is about reputation, which is the result of all you say, all you do and what others say about you'.

In other words, an organisation is continually communicating messages to the public – whether it wants to or not. Let's look at some of the ways in which this is done. Public relations includes activities such as:

- Media inclusion
- Community relations
- Corporate communications.

Media inclusion

Media inclusion refers to the inclusion of a travel or tourism product in a cinema or TV film or programme or in a printed medium such as a newspaper. An obvious example is the featuring of a particular resort, tour operator, tourist attraction, etc. in one of the many holiday programmes. Of course, sometimes this can have a negative PR result such as many of the travel and tourism items featured in consumer and 'fly on the wall' programmes, such as *Holidays from Hell*.

More often, media inclusion is welcomed by travel and tourism providers and used as part of their marketing communications. This is a growing trend as tourism organisations realise the great PR benefits of film crews using their towns, cities or companies as the backdrop for their productions. For example, the National Trust estimates that media coverage of their properties generates approximately £30 million a year. Similarly Alnwick Castle in Northumberland has seen a 500% increase in child visitors since part of the castle was used as Hogwarts in the Harry Potter films.

---

activity

SUCCESSFUL MEDIA INCLUSION

In pairs, identify one example of media inclusion (i.e. a film or television programme) that has benefited the following travel and tourism organisations or destinations:

1 a hotel
2 an airline
3 a Greek island
4 the Yorkshire Dales
5 a stately home
6 a tour operator.

A further example of media inclusion is the use of press releases. A press release is a statement written by an organisation describing a particular event, occasion or piece of interesting news which is sent to the media in the hope that editors will consider it of interest and therefore publish or air it. In many newspapers, particularly local ones, a large proportion of the editorial (articles) is in fact made up of stories based on press releases rather than articles written by reporters. The decision as to whether or not to use a press release depends not only on its content but also on the relationship that the organisation has with the paper. Therefore part of PR requires maintaining a good relationship with media staff to ensure that they look favourably on news items submitted. Apart from the fact that it is free, the main advantage of getting editorial coverage based on a press release rather than, say, advertising is that people are likely to read it properly without thinking that it is trying to sell them something.

Community relations

Maintaining a good relationship with the local community (community relations) is an important part of PR. This is often achieved by providing support to various groups or participating in events. For example, entering a float in a local parade, offering free guided tours to school groups or becoming involved in community action groups.

Corporate communications

Many organisations establish much of their corporate image through their communications. Corporate communications use consistent and recognisable formats and images such as logos, colours and typefaces on their leaflets, bills, faxes and advertising.

Sponsorship

Sponsorship is when an organisation provides financial support to another organisation, individual or event in order to gain prestige and status from their association with them. It is often included in an organisation's public relations activities since it indirectly enhances the customer's perception of the organisation or its products and services.

There are many examples of sponsorship in the travel and tourism industry where organisations provide financial support for an event, service or product in return for their name being prominently linked to it. For example, First Choice holidays achieved a high profile due to their sponsorship, as described below.

First Choice banks on reality TV show

First Choice says it hopes to get maximum exposure out of its sponsorship of the television show, *I'm A Celebrity! Get Me Out Of Here!*, which will air in the UK in the first half of next year.

The company will use the coverage to inform the public about the recent unification of its businesses under the First Choice brand.

The campaign is embracing all areas of the business including themed January sale brochures, released this week. The brochures will offer deals like free child places on holidays from regional airports and lead-in prices of £99 on Mediterranean holidays.

The First Choice campaign will also include jungle-themed shops. Both First Choice Travel Shops and First Choice Holiday Hypermarkets will feature special window displays and some will have 'jungle noises'. Television screens in-store will run trailers for the programme.

The sponsorship deal means First Choice gets a mention either side of the advertising breaks and in the opening and closing credits of the show.

Source: www.travelmole.com

Sales promotions

A sales promotion is a short-term activity aimed at generating sales or improving public perception. Sales promotions are often undertaken in response to the activities of competitors so that an organisation can keep its market share. An example is the sales promotions offered by tour operators, such as the Butlins offer shown here.

Sales promotions can include any or all of the following activities:

- Price reductions (discounting). Discounts are offered to increase sales or usage, often at periods of low demand. For example, look in the window of any high-street travel agency and you will find discounted late availability holidays on offer.

- Free gifts and incentives. These are used to encourage consumers to purchase products or services.

- Special offers. This is another form of discounting. Special offers are often run in conjunction with some form of advertising campaign in which consumers have to produce the advertisement (or coupons) to qualify for the offer. For example, Little Chef advertisements frequently feature 'buy-one-get-one-free (BOGOF) coupons.

- Competitions. Many travel and tourism organisations run free competitions to encourage consumers to buy their products and services. Prizes include a wide range of products, services, memberships, activities, holidays and cars, such as the one shown below.

- Extra products. This is another form of special offer. Customers are provided with extra products or services at no extra charge. A free bottle of wine with your meal, or three weeks holiday for the price of two, are just two examples of extra products being used as incentives to persuade consumers to purchase products. Many tour operators are keen to persuade customers to purchase excursions from them as this generates a large amount of revenue for the company. Companies such as Thomson frequently offer extra products as part of their sales promotions

Personal selling

In Topic 1 we explored the sales process and personal selling skills. Personal selling is just as important as the other types of promotional technique that we have looked at in this and the previous topic. In fact, in many cases it will be the one technique that helps to influence the customer's final buying decision. For example, a potential customer may have seen the destination that they like on a travel programme (PR), considered tour operators from reading newspapers (advertising) and looked at possible resorts and holidays from brochures. However, the final decision may well be based on their visit to a travel agency where the consultant outlines and suggests products that will meet their needs and expectations.

activity

SUGGESTING PROMOTIONAL TECHNIQUES

You are on a work placement at a privately owned small stately home. The owners have decided that they would like to target the schools market, as they feel that they could provide a valuable visit linked to the history curriculum. They plan to hire performing arts students as guides who will dress in costume and play historical characters. You have been asked to suggest and justify at least one promotion under each of the following headings:

- advertising
- brochures
- displays
- direct marketing
- public relations
- sponsorship
- sales promotions
- personal selling.

Topic 10 Promotional campaigns and budgeting

This topic explores the ways in which promotional techniques can be effectively used in promotional campaigns, including a consideration of budgeting. In particular we will look at:

- Designing effective promotional materials
- Timing and targeting of promotional activities
- The promotions mix
- Budgeting
- Promotional campaigns
- Evaluating the effectiveness of promotional campaigns.

Designing effective promotional materials

To be successful, all promotional materials need to be well designed so that they appeal to the target markets and persuade them to buy the product. Most advertisers use a model known as AIDA, which stands for:

Attention
Interest
Desire
Action

The AIDA approach to promotion is designed to first attract the customer's attention, and then to create enough interest in order to produce such a desire for the product that the customer takes action and actually buys it. Advertisers applying AIDA to the design of advertising material frequently attract attention through the use of slogans, bold headlines, well-known personalities or celebrities, vivid use of colour, and eye-catching graphics. Often a humorous headline, such as the one below, is used to make the reader stop and read the rest of the advertisement.

Interest is created by highlighting the benefits and

product characteristics which in turn create desire for the product. With many travel and tourism products this involves describing what the experience is going to be like. For example, look at the extracts below from a leaflet used to promote the National Football Museum. Notice how they create interest and desire by telling the customer about some of the activities that they will be able to do if they visit the museum.

Prompt action is encouraged by providing instructions on how to purchase or use the product, providing booking information or directions and opening times.

AIDA IN ACTION

Competition between the budget airlines is fierce, and most of the organisations rely heavily on national press advertising. The one feature that these advertisements seem to have in common is that they are simple and contain limited information – perhaps to underline the fact that there are 'no-frills'! Look at four advertisements and compare them in terms of their success in using AIDA.

Timing and targeting of promotional activities

The more precise the timing and targeting of marketing communications, the greater the chance of the target audience seeing the promotion and therefore buying the product. Advertisers need to bear in mind that all promotion needs to be timed for when the consumer actually decides to buy the product, not necessarily when they will actually experience it – in other words at the 'action' stage of AIDA. So for example, many summer package holiday customers decide on their summer holiday in the preceding November to February. Therefore most tour operators spend a large amount of their promotional budget at this time, issuing the next year's brochures and launching extensive press and TV campaigns. A further promotional campaign is usually set from May through the summer, featuring special offers to enable tour operators to sell the remaining package holidays.

activity
TIMING YOUR PROMOTION

You work in the conference and banqueting department of a large hotel that secures a lot of business from wedding receptions. As part of the future promotion of such receptions you are arranging a 'Wedding Fair' that will be open to the general public. Whilst the main objective is to sell your facilities to potential brides and grooms you are also including displays from local suppliers such as florists, photographers, car hire firms and wedding gowns/suits suppliers. Your manager has informed you that you can use the promotional methods listed below and asked you to suggest when each should be used.

1 The actual Wedding Fair. (Which month and day of the week would you suggest and why?)

2 Point of sales promotion in the hotel foyer. (This can only be for two weeks as the space will be needed for other promotions – but which two weeks?)

3 Direct mail shot to couples announcing their engagement in the local newspaper. (When would you send this out?)

4 Three advertisements in the local press. (How soon before the Fair, and on what days of the week?)

5 A five-minute interview on the local radio station. (How close to the event and on what day/time of day would be best, and why?)

With other travel and tourism products the decision to buy may be much nearer the time of actually experiencing the product or service and therefore the timing of promotions needs to reflect this. For example, the decision to go to a particular film may be made during the week before the visit by reading a local paper and seeing what films are being shown.

A further consideration in timing when using media such as television, radio and cinema is the effect that the time of day and type of programme being aired will have on the nature of people listening or watching. For example, you would expect different types of people to be watching television at 6.30 a.m., 2.00 p.m., 4.30 p.m., 8.00 p.m. and 11.30 p.m. Likewise, there will be a different audience for programmes such as *Coronation Street*, *Big Brother*, *ITV News* and *Who Wants To Be A Millionaire?* Advertisers will time their promotions to target particular types of customers who they believe will be interested in their products.

Targeting of specific customers can also be achieved through the selection of different newspapers and magazines, since each attracts a different readership.

activity
TARGETING BY NEWSPAPER

Discuss which of the publications in the left-hand column would be most suitable for an advertisement for the products in the right-hand column.

The Independent	A traction engine rally
The *Mail on Sunday*	Budget European city breaks
The *Sun*	
A local daily newspaper	Caribbean cruises
A regional weekly newspaper	A guided 'Ghost Walk' in an historic town
	A holiday camp

A further method of targeting is to produce separate promotional materials for different types of customers. For example, a mass-market tour operator such as Thomson publishes separate brochures for different markets such as Summer Sun, Young at Heart, Small & Friendly, Villas with Pools, Gold, and so on. The information in each is clearly focused on the needs and expectations of the specific target markets.

The promotions mix

Whilst each type of promotional technique and communication channel has its individual benefits and uses, most organisations use a range of different approaches to achieve their marketing objectives. This is because different types of communication and techniques will influence different customers. Likewise, different products and services will benefit from different types of marketing communications.

For example, a tour operator may use:

- brochures to target customers who go to a travel agency or book directly when selecting a holiday
- press advertisements to attract new customers
- TV advertisements to raise general consumer awareness of the products that are offered
- point-of-sale posters for sales promotions
- direct marketing to past customers, etc.

The effective use of promotion at British Airways

British Airways wanted to profitably launch a competitive, low-cost European airline – using newspapers not only to 'hit the ground running', but to get off the ground altogether!

Campaign objectives

Go positioned itself uniquely, breaching the gap between the expensive, quality national carriers and the cheap and cheerful budget operators. Go was born as the 'low-cost airline from British Airways', thereby offering something new – 'smart value ' – which meant it could compete in both sectors.

Go was started from scratch, so it was important to establish the brand quickly. The launch campaign had to build awareness of the Go brand and its value as 'the low-cost airline from British Airways' as well as drive sales by publishing destinations and prices. There was a need to communicate a wide variety of messages to as many potential passengers as possible.

The primary target audience was people who could be stimulated to fly by the very low fares (growing the market); the secondary target was people already looking for low-cost flights (growing market share).

The campaign

The famous 'Go circles' were used across all external and internal communications, providing an instantly recognisable branding device. It also offered an eye-catching way of conveying the brand personality – forward thinking, optimistic and confident.

The integrated communication plan included newspapers (national and regional), posters, TV, cinema and local radio. Every single piece of communication that was produced in the first year of advertising carried both the phone number and web address to drive consumers toward booking.

Impact of the campaign

Go was launched into a highly competitive and fast-paced business. Consumers recognised the advertising and quickly understood the brand's values, which resulted in outstanding business growth, as shown by these results:

- In a tracking research study, Go scored the highest spontaneous awareness for its advertising amongst 'airlines flying to European cities', beating BA, easyJet and Ryanair.
- In its first year, Go's brand awareness reached the same level as its key rivals easyJet and Ryanair and it became the preferred choice of low-cost flyers.
- The Go fleet grew from 2 planes at launch to 26, and went on to transport over 6 million passengers each year, to 24 destinations.
- Built from an initial investment by BA of just £25m, Go was eventually purchased by easyJet for £375m, and now operates under the easyJet brand name.

Testimonial

Go was voted Campaign Magazine's Multimedia campaign of the Year in 1999.

Go won New Brand of the Year at the first Marketing Society Awards in June 2000.

Source: www.nmauk.co.uk

Budgeting

As we have already seen, promotion and marketing can present a great expense to travel and tourism organisations. Because of this it is vital that organisations are aware of the costs involved and able to evaluate whether or not the costs are justified. This is because the costs of promotional and marketing activities are deducted directly from the profits. Of course it is hoped that such activities will help to increase profits – but organisations must have mechanisms in place to ensure that this is, indeed, the case.

Organisations such as Thomson Holidays spend large amounts on television advertising – so need to be sure that it is money well spent.

A marketing budget sets out in realistic terms all of the costs involved in conducting marketing and promotional activities. Most organisations will plan their marketing budget for the forthcoming year (or years) as part of their overall budgeting process. This usually involves allocating a set amount of money to marketing and identifying how this money will be spent. Frequently the amount is specified as a percentage of anticipated turnover or sales.

The key to successfully managing a marketing budget is being able to identify and anticipate all of the costs involved. This may seem straightforward, but in reality any number of unforeseen costs can arise. The example on the right shows one of the many ways in which a marketing budget can go wrong.

So what are all of the costs involved in marketing and promotion? The following list, though by no means exhaustive, gives you some idea of what needs to be considered:

- Staff costs (the amount of time multiplied by the salary of the staff carrying out the activity)
- Advertising media (such as press, TV, poster sites, etc.)
- Printing and production costs
- Entertaining (particularly with public relations)
- Photography (relatively cheap if an organisation takes its own photographs, but increasingly expensive if it hires professional photographers or buys pictures from agencies)
- Mailing and telephone costs (for direct marketing)
- Travel time and accommodation (such as staff getting to exhibitions and staying in hotels during the exhibition)
- Buying secondary research information
- Hiring advertising and PR agencies to create media campaigns
- Stationery
- Products that are offered as part of a promotion (remember the Gemini's wine offer!)
- Primary research methods.

Two buzz terms in marketing costs

Above-the-line advertising

Refers to promotions where a fee is paid to an agency such as the press, television, etc.

Below-the-line advertising

Is advertising when a fee is not paid to an agency, such as direct mail, demonstrations, etc.

Costly marketing mistake

The Gemini restaurant decided to boost their low level of trade during January and February by printing a voucher in the local paper offering a free bottle of wine for every couple having a three-course dinner. They budgeted for this costing £2.45 per couple, based on the wholesale price of their house wine. As the average spend for dinner was £22.43 per person, this represented a very small percentage of their profits, and they were confident that the offer would be cost-effective. Unfortunately they had failed to state on the voucher that the offer only applied to house wine. The first couple ordered their meal and a £65 bottle of vintage wine from the wine list and produced the voucher when their bill was presented. The restaurant had no option but to not charge them for the wine. Worse was to follow when the couple wrote to the local newspaper to tell readers of the excellent deal that they had received at the Gemini. Gemini was inundated with customers during January and February, all of whom were clutching a voucher and asking 'What's the most expensive wine you have?'

ADDING UP ALL THE COSTS

Broadacres Farm is a visitor attraction that includes a children's petting farm, farming demonstrations and exhibits, cafeteria and gift shop. They plan to launch the summer season by holding a free 'Open Day' for local schools and companies. Their objective is to show locals what they have to offer and encourage them to return with friends and family. As part of the promotion for the open day they are going to:

• Mailshot all local schools and 200 companies with a letter and leaflet outlining the event

• Advertise once a week in the month before the Open Day in the local paper

• Submit a press release to the local paper

• Display posters at the entrance to the attraction and at the point of sales

• Provide free drinks and light refreshments at the Open Day

• Try to persuade the local radio station to broadcast from Broadacres on the day

• Keep a record of the name and address of everyone who attends the Open Day and send them a follow-up offer of a discount if they return.

In pairs, identify all of the types of costs involved in the promotion of Broadacres Open Day.

Of course, many smaller organisations will use relatively simple forms of promotion where the costs may be small and easy to calculate, such as a weekly advertisement in the local press, and mailshots. But these are often the type of organisation with the least appreciation of just how much their marketing activities are costing them. For example, a privately owned historic property may decide to mailshot five thousand locals with details of their forthcoming events. Relatively economical, you might think – perhaps 3 pence to produce each letter and then the cost of second-class postage. However, what happens to the predicted budget if there is no member of staff

to actually do the 'envelope-stuffing' – in other words putting the mailshot into envelopes and sending them off? Perhaps the manager (who earns, say, £26,000 a year) decides to do it himself. Suddenly the cost of the mailshot has rocketed when his costs have been taken into account.

As we have already discussed, there is a huge difference between the amounts spent on promotions by different organisations. Multinational companies often spend considerable sums on television advertising that would be way beyond the budgets of smaller organisations. It is interesting to note that

Marketing Canterbury Cathedral

Running a cathedral is a balancing act in every respect, perhaps most significantly, financially. What is more urgent: to repair the leaking roof, ensure the music sung at services is the best, or to increase the 'Visits' marketing budget? Although it is recognised that Canterbury Cathedral needs to be marketed as a high quality visitor destination, funds to do this are not readily available. The current marketing budget is £25,000, which, compared to the budgets of £500,000+ of other major attractions in the region, is very low.

Miracles have taken place before in Canterbury, but it is unlikely that marketing budgets will increase sufficiently for extensive consumer advertising campaigns in all the key markets.

Source: Insights, March 2004

MAKING THE MOST OF A BUDGET

The article below left goes on to explain how the marketing team at Canterbury Cathedral have managed to promote the cathedral on such a limited budget. Using your knowledge of promotional techniques, suggest how you think they might have achieved this.

none of the major travel and tourism organisations feature in lists of companies that spend the most on advertising. The main players tend to be multi-national organisations that supply fast moving consumable goods (FMCGs). Food brands feature heavily in the lists, including McDonald's (who spent £42m on advertising in 2002, according to A. C. Neilson), Coca Cola (£16m) and KFC (£15m) – who all contribute to the provision of travel and tourism services.

Smaller travel and tourism organisations, and particularly those in the public sector, cannot afford advertising on this scale. For example, look at the extract on the opposite page focusing on some of the financial problems that a public sector attraction faces when it comes to marketing. As with many public sector attractions it performs a tight balancing act between allocating funds to improve the attraction whilst also letting potential customers know about it through marketing activities.

Limited advertising is not only restricted to the public sector – some private organisations choose to minimise the amount that they spend in this way in order to reduce the price that they charge for products. Remember that every time you buy a travel or tourism product that is advertised on television or the press – you are paying for that advertising! Some organisations such as easyJet promote themselves through the fact that their lack of expensive advertising allows them to sell products so cheaply (see above, right).

Cutting down on advertising expenditure is not always the road to financial success for organisations competing in the budget market. The no-frills airline, Duo, folded in 2004 – largely due to a lack of advertising (see right).

The costs of operating a typical easyJet flight are broken down as follows:

Airport charges: £817
Plane: £676
Crew costs: £643
Fuel: £614
Maintenance: £584
Ground-handling: £542
Navigation: £420
Tax: £252
Advertising: £215
Credit card fees: £101

The fact that advertising is the second smallest expense is a very rare situation within the private sector of the travel and tourism industry – but one that has certainly paid off for easyJet.

'The carrier collapsed because it failed to embrace the travel trade and did not allocate sufficient funds to advertising. Interim Sales and Marketing Manager Rob Rees blamed Duo's downfall on a lack of marketing funds. The company spent about £1 million on advertising, but it was not enough to compete with other carriers.'

Source: Travel Weekly, 10 May 2004

195

Topic 10 Promotional campaigns and budgeting

Promotional campaigns

An organisation's promotional activities are usually expressed in the form of a 'promotional campaign'. This is a plan with a clearly defined timescale that sets out what the objectives are, how they are going to be achieved (i.e. through which promotional techniques and materials), who is responsible, and how much each activity will cost. Below is an example of the promotional plan launched by the Lake District National Park Authority.

The Lake District National Park's promotional campaign for its redeveloped Visitor Centre

Objectives

- To position the Centre as the Lake District all-weather visitor attraction, offering a unique combination of location, activities and facilities.
- To raise awareness of the Lake District and of the work of the National Park Authority and partner organisations, in an entertaining and enjoyable way.
- To gain awareness, identity and impact for the Centre amongst target markets.
- To generate demand for repeat visits to the Centre amongst target markets.
- To help achieve the Centre's business plan targets.
- To communicate the Centre's purpose.

Target markets

- Travel trade
- Internal, e.g. NPA staff
- Families
- Group visits
- Schools
- Independent adults
- Special interest, e.g. gardens
- Local residents.

Market research and analysis

- Leisure trends
- Competitor analysis
- Quantitative and qualitative research.

Product development

- Evaluate new developments to ensure they meet visitor expectations
- Review other elements, e.g. shop, restaurant, gardens, interpretation, events, periods of opening, and implement any changes required to meet visitor expectations.

Pricing

- Review pricing policy to ensure that it is in line with targets, visitor expectations, competition.

Advertising

- Increase awareness, profile and understanding of the Centre amongst visitors through a planned programme of advertising in local, specialist, education, tourist and trade press.

Public relations

- Increase awareness, profile and understanding of the Centre amongst travel trade, visitors, partner organisations, staff and local communities through a planned public relations campaign in the relevant media and with familiarisation visits.

Promotion

- Translate awareness of the Centre into action (trial and repeat visit) through a programme of promotional activity, including joint activity with other relevant companies.
- Develop appropriate direct mail communications for schools, groups, travel trade.

Sponsorship

- Extend marketing budget through sponsorship/ partnership funding of marketing activity with appropriate organisations.

Events

- Continue to provide a range of relevant events at the Centre to enhance the visitor experience.

Printed material and signs

- Review the current range of material and signs and ensure that all future material produced is consistent in terms of image/identity for the Centre.

Marketing activities

Marketing is primarily regionally based, but does include national promotions to the travel trade.

April–June: independent adults

May–July: school groups

July–September: families, overseas visitors

September–October: independent adults

All year: local residents, other organised groups.

Promotional mix

Advertising: National Park Authority publications, including annual 48-page events booklet and Parklife; a local community newspaper, local newspapers, magazines and journals, including *Westmorland Gazette, Cumberland Herald, Cumbria Life, Cumbria Magazine, Lakeland Walker, What's On* and *leisure guides*.

Local radio: Bay Radio

Evaluating the effectiveness of promotional campaigns

A marketing budget is part of the process in which an organisation evaluates the success of their promotional and marketing activities. By analysing the impact of each promotional activity an organisation can identify whether or not it was cost-effective. In simple terms, cost-effective means that the activity generated more profit than it cost. The effectiveness of promotions can be measured in a number of ways but two of the most common are:

- Cost per response – this means dividing the total cost of the promotional activity by the number of customers who responded to it.
- Cost per conversion – this refers to dividing the total cost of the promotional activity by the number of customers who went on to buy the product advertised as the result of the promotion.

For example, a newspaper advertisement might cost £1,000 and produce 500 enquiries from interested customers – cost per response is £2. However, of these enquiries only 100 go on to buy the product – so cost per conversion is £10.00. Clearly, most organisations are going to be more interested in the cost per conversion than the cost per response.

One of the vital elements of being able to evaluate whether or not a promotion has been cost-effective is the inclusion of some way of measuring which promotions have influenced a customer to buy a product. Large multi-national companies often achieve this by commissioning expensive independent research asking respondents to identify promotions that they have seen. For smaller operators, less complex methods need to be used.

Posters

Brochure: 200,000 brochures are produced annually and distributed to all Lake District Information Centres and to all holiday accommodation in the Lake District.

'Group visits' leaflet

Trade exhibitions: British Travel Trade Fair; World Travel Market; North West Tourist Board Great Days Out; local attractions previews.

Other activities

- Familiarisation visits for local hotels, tourism operators, travel writers, journalists, teachers and group leaders
- The National Park's ten information centres and the other 25 tourist information centres throughout Cumbria.
- The annual 'Welcome to Lakeland' folder; 34000 copies are produced annually and are available in all Lake District hotels and self catering accommodation.
- Joint ticketing with other local attractions
- Joint marketing with Windermere Lake Cruises (1 million passengers)
- Direct mail to tour guides and travel companies
- Promotion of the Mawson Gardens as part of British Gardens Open Days
- Secondary promotion, as a result of British Trust for Conservation Volunteers and Cumbria Wildlife Trust having offices on the site.

Evaluation

In order to ensure the success of the marketing strategy, evaluation is part of the ongoing process. Monitoring and review of targets, budget, pricing strategies, promotion, advertising, and public relations will indicate its effectiveness. Market research in the form of visitor surveys will be undertaken to evaluate how far the 'product' is meeting visitor needs and expectations, and to determine future development areas. This information, together with an awareness of competitors and leisure trends, will enable us to develop The Lake District Visitor Centre marketing strategy for the future.

Source: *Lake District National Park Authority, Education Service, Brockhole, Windermere, Cumbria LA23 1LJ*
Website: *www.lake-district.gov.uk*

activity

MEASURING RESPONSE RATES

The Rio Grande theme park is planning to advertise in all of the local and regional newspapers within a 50-mile radius of the park. This is the first time that they have conducted such extensive (and expensive) advertising and the manager is keen to know which newspapers produce the best cost-per-conversion rate. Explain three ways in which the theme park could evaluate the success of the promotional campaign.

How Unit 10 is assessed

Advertising: Unit 10 is externally assessed. The format will be a 1.5 hour written exam, using a question-and-answer booklet. The Edexcel website – www.edexcel.org.uk – has guidance on external assessment, including specimen papers and example answers, or you can get more information from your school or college.

Special interest holidays are designed for people who want to pursue their interest in a particular activity or subject whilst on holiday. In this unit you will learn about special interest holidays in worldwide destinations, from trekking in the Himalayas to cruising in the Caribbean. The special interest holiday market is growing, so this sector is important to the travel and tourism industry.

Although the main reason Britons choose a holiday is still to relax in a sunny environment, an increasing number of people are buying activity packages and adventure holidays.

According to a MORI 2002 survey, 8% of people going on holiday from the UK had participated in an activity holiday, i.e. water sports, cycling, skiing, etc. over the previous twelve months, and 7% had been on discovery holidays to a new/unusual or third world destination. One of the largest growth areas has been the cruise market, with 6% of travellers enjoying a cruise holiday. Although these figures are small compared with the summer sun package holiday figure (71%) they reflect the growth in 'niche marketing' or more specialist holidays in the tourism industry.

There is now a variety of special interest holidays that people can enjoy across the world, from game hunting in Africa, to skiing in the Alps, to helicopter rides over the Grand Canyon. In this unit we will look at the following:

• The features of special interest holidays
• Who provides them
• Their itineraries and how to put them together
• Their appeal and popularity
• Factors influencing their appeal.

We will look at the features of special interest holidays from cultural holidays in the European cities to horseback riding at the Taj Mahal. Some special interest holidays are based in one place whilst other cross countries and even borders. We will look at the organisations that provide these holidays from the mass-market tour operators to the small, tailor-made package holiday companies that cater for a select market.

An itinerary for a special interest holiday can become very complex, especially if it covers several countries over a long period of time. You will learn to how to plan an itinerary for a holiday of your choice, and you will have the opportunity to recommend itineraries designed to meet the needs of different types of tourists.

Finally, we will consider the factors affecting the popularity of special interest holidays, such as accessibility and the shift in holiday patterns. Changes in people's attitudes and expectations, and their health and wealth, have also influenced what tourists expect and wish to experience.

The industry focus in this unit looks at the work of a Yorkshire man who has made his life in La Rosière, in France, providing special interest holidays. In winter he runs the ski school and during the summer he is in charge of the golf course that is on the same slopes.

Unit 11

Special Interest Holidays

Single-destination holidays

In this first topic you will learn about special interest holidays that take place in one destination, focusing on the following types:

- **Cultural, such as attending a music festival**
- **Religious, such as a pilgrimage or retreat**
- **Heritage, which could be industrial or historical**
- **Sporting, which could be participating in an activity, such as scuba diving, or attending an event, such as the Olympics, as a spectator.**
- **Specialist activity, such as dancing or cooking**
- **Health and fitness, such as staying at a health spa**
- **Weddings and honeymoons**
- **Working, such as on a kibbutz or at a summer camp**
- **Conservation, such as restoring natural habitats.**

What's special about special interest holidays?

Special interest holidays are designed for people – whether alone or in a group – who want to pursue their interest in a particular activity or subject whilst on holiday. This can range from whale watching to wine tasting, from cruising to safari – the list is endless, as people have so many varied interests and activity pursuits. The focus of the holiday is that it revolves around one particular interest so that the majority of the time is taken up being involved in the activity or interest.

The vast range and variety of special interest holidays makes this sector quite different from traditional mass-market holidays, which all tend to be similar in nature, wherever they are located. As most of the special interest holidays are not aimed at the mass market they can be expensive. They can range in time from a short break – a weekend's cookery course, for example – to a lengthy trek in the wilderness, which may take a number of weeks or months. The location of these types of holiday will obviously depend on the interest, but they can take people to many more parts of the world than traditional holidays would.

Cultural holidays

Cultural holidays are those that provide access to view music, art or literature. Usually these holidays are based in major cities, where the museums, theatres, galleries, opera houses, etc. are located, but sometimes they are in locations established especially to host a specific event or festival. Glastonbury Festival, for example, originally started in 1970 in a farmer's field in Somerset and now hosts an international three-day music festival for over 100,000 people every year.

Europe plays host to many cultural holidays based around one or more cultural cities. For example, Florence is known as the 'Renaissance Crown', and is home to some of the most famous art galleries and museums in the world.

Prague, the capital city and the economic and cultural centre of the Czech Republic is one of Europe's newly emerging cities of culture. It includes a number of theatres, museums, galleries and exhibition halls. Prague also contains an extremely large number of significant architectural buildings dating from all periods. The large historic town centre has been included in the UNESCO World Cultural and Scientific

Heritage list since 1992. Prague is also one of the nine cities which were awarded the title of 'European capital of culture' in 2000 by the European Union. See the other Capitals of Culture listed below:

The Capitals of Culture 2000–2004

2000: Avignon, Bergen, Bologna, Brussels, Cracow, Helsinki, Prague, Reykjavik and Santiago de Compostela (Spain).

2001: Porto (Portugal) and Rotterdam (Netherlands). In the same year, European Cultural Months were organised by the cities of Basle and Riga.

2002: Bruges (Belgium) and Salamanque (Spain).

2003: Graz (Austria).

2004: Genova (Italy) and Lille (France).

---

activity

CULTURAL CAPITALS

Locate the capitals of culture on a map. Research any one of the cities of culture named above, and analyse the factors that you think contributed to them gaining the award.

You could do this exercise as a group activity, each selecting a different city and presenting your findings to the rest of the group.

As you have seen, many cultural holidays revolve around cities. Some cities stage annual events – such as an arts festival – which makes them more popular at certain times of the year. For example, the timing of visits to St Petersburg (Russia), may be influenced by when the world-renowned Kirov Ballet are at home and performing in the historic Mariinsky Theatre.

Some holiday destinations take on a cultural role for a brief period each year. Aspen, (Colorado), for example, is more famous for skiing than its culture, but each summer the world's most accomplished and promising musicians have made a pilgrimage to Aspen (see the case study below).

Religious holidays

Religious special interest holidays range from pilgrimages to retreats. Religious pilgrimages are based on making a trip to a certain place because of its religious importance. The pilgrims are the visitors. The world's largest religion is Christianity, followed by Islam and then Hinduism. Each religion has special places that are significant to them – Mecca, Medina, Jerusalem and Karbala for Muslims, for example, or the river Ganges for Hindus. The river is the site of many religious rituals. Every 12 years, for example, up to 10 million Hindus take part in ritual bathing at the Kumbh Mela festival at Allahabad in India, where the waters of the Ganges and the Jumna meet.

Aspen Music Festival

Founded in 1949, the Aspen Music Festival and School is an internationally renowned classical music festival that presents world-class music in an intimate, small-town setting. It is also one of the world's premier training grounds for pre-professional musicians.

The nine-week festival comprises more than 200 events, including orchestral concerts, chamber music, opera, contemporary music, master classes, lectures, and kids' programmes. Concerts take place daily at the 2050-seat Benedict Music Tent, an acoustically superior and award-winning permanent structure that made its debut in 2000, the beautifully restored Victorian Wheeler Opera House, the jewel-like Harris

Concert Hall, and in churches and smaller halls around town. Many events are free, lawn seating outside the tent is always free, and other tickets range up to $57.

Aspen is also where the world's brightest young musicians come to study with the world's foremost instructors. Year after year, the Music School has inspired young musicians to mature into some of the most brilliant and creative classical artists in the world, from New York to Paris, from Tokyo to Rome. Generation after generation, masters of the craft pass along their knowledge and passion for music to students.

Source: www.aspenmusicalfestival.com

In addition to Hinduism, India also has holy places associated with Islam, Sikhism, Buddhism and Jainism. Buddhists from all over the world come to Bodhgaya to see the place where Lord Buddha gained enlightenment. Pawapuri in Bihar (where Lord Mahavira attained salvation) is a holy shrine of the Jain faith. Amritsar is the holiest shrine of the Sikh religion and is visited by Sikhs from all over the world.

Christian pilgrimages vary from a visit to Vatican City and the home of the Pope, to a visit to Lourdes or the Holy Land. Lourdes is a small town in the Hautes Pyrenees region of south-west France. In 1858 'Our Blessed Lady' appeared to a young peasant girl, Bernadette Soubirous, at the Grotto of Massabielle in this town. Bernadette related 'Our Lady's' wish for people to come on pilgrimage to Lourdes, and so established the tradition of Lourdes as a holy place.

Since then, many millions of pilgrims have travelled to pray in Lourdes, requesting Our Lady intercede on their behalf to her Son, Jesus Christ.

The Holy Land, Israel, is one of the most renowned and religiously important regions of the world, and the setting into which Jesus was born. People visit to walk in the footsteps of Jesus and visit places associated with Him and His Holy Family.

Every ten years, thousands of people travel to Oberammergau in Bavaria (Germany) to attend a large-scale dramatic interpretation of Jesus's life which has been performed in the town since the seventeenth century (see below, left).

At the other side of the world, in the Himalayas, Bhutan, one of the homes of Tibetan Buddhism, hosts the annual Paro Festival (see below).

The Oberammergau Passion Play

'A Play of Life and Death, promised in a moment of mortal threat' – so began the history of the Oberammergau Passion Play. In 1633, in the middle of the Thirty Years War, after months of suffering and death from the plague, the Oberammergauers swore an oath that every ten years they would perform the 'Play of the Suffering, Death and Resurrection of Our Lord Jesus Christ'. At Pentecost 1634, they fulfilled their pledge for the first time, on a stage they put up in the cemetery above the fresh graves of the plague victims.

In the year 2000, more than 2000 Oberammergauers, actors, singers, instrumentalists and stage technicians, in approximately six hours of playing time, brought to the stage those events that Christianity regards as its central source of life and hope.

The next Passion Play takes place in 2010. Ticket sales start in 2008, and before that a reservation is not possible!

Source: www.oberammergau.de

The Paro Festival in Bhutan

Bhutan, the 'Land of the Dragon', is almost completely unaffected by Western influences. The landscape is awesome, with steep forested hills and misty mountains rising from fast-flowing rivers. But it is the culture that makes Bhutan unique, where a traditional way of life continues, little changed by the passage of time. At the Paro Festival, hundreds gather to see the monks, dressed in brightly coloured brocade robes, perform ritual dances. For several days there are masked dances, prayer meetings and a general carnival atmosphere, as many villagers arrive to meet old friends and catch up with the mountain gossip. The festival culminates with the unfurling of a giant Thanka (painting), three stories high, which has to be carefully folded away before the rays of the morning sun catch it.

Source: www.exodus.co.uk

Traditionally, a retreat has meant an extended time of silent prayer and reflection, away from everyday life. Usually such retreats have been made in a religious setting such as a monastery or retreat house, and consist of a chain of closely connected religious exercises: prayer, silence, reflection, meditation, and spiritual reading. Religious retreats have become more and more popular, as shown below.

Escape from the hectic life

According to a *Time* magazine article, 'Get Thee to a Monastery', there is a startling increase in the number of people looking for the solace and escape offered by traditional religious abbeys, convents and monasteries. 'Across the country, Catholic monasteries and convents, usually regarded as strange or the stuff of medieval myth, are besieged with would-be retreatants and booked months in advance.'

While the Christian monastic tradition is in decline all over the Western world, retreat facilities of every spiritual denomination are full – weeks, even months, in advance. People are looking for places to escape the noises, pressures and anxieties of their busy daily life. In North America there are over 1,000 monasteries, abbeys and spiritual retreat centres where one can reorient oneself from the hectic life to a place of spiritual, mental and physical refreshment.

The *Time* article states 'while organized church retreats are not new, what is startling is that much of the increase is in individual retreatants, including many Protestants and even non-Christians, who say the Catholic monasteries, with their ancient chants, beautiful grounds, and prices at a pittance, offer the most refreshing vacation going. Now, say the monks, if only they could keep the growing horde down to the true spiritual seekers, not just vacationers at Club God.'

Source: www.findthedivine.com

Americans seem to be particularly keen on holiday retreats, but this pattern is reflected across the world. Many religions have long established retreats that provide many of their followers the chance to escape for a break. Some of these are single-sex holidays, while others cater for whole families.

activity

RELIGIOUS CENTRES

Research a number of religious centres (like Oberammergau) or retreats, and locate them on a map. Then research and identify some holiday providers for these locations.

Heritage holidays

Heritage destinations are popular because of their historical or industrial appeal. Historical holidays vary from visiting ancient ruins to getting involved with history itself on archaeological digs. The world's great historical sites range from the pyramids and temples of Egypt to the Great Wall of China and the Taj Mahal (see below).

The two stories of the Taj Mahal

The Taj Mahal, near Agra in India, is one of the world's greatest architectural treasures. But there are two stories of how the Taj came to be.

The love story

The Taj Mahal is a real monument of one man's love for a woman. In 1631, when his wife, Queen Mumtaz Mahal, died in childbirth, the emperor Shah Jahan brought to Agra the most skilled craftsmen from all over Asia and even from Europe, to build the white marble mausoleum that is the Taj Mahal. (He intended to go on and build a black marble mausoleum for himself, and the link between the two was to be a silver bridge, but this fantastic plan suffered a dramatic and permanent setback when the Shah himself died.) This romantic story of the Taj Mahal's origin is all part of its appeal to the millions of visitors each year.

The other story

Professor P.N. Oak, author of *Taj Mahal: The True Story*, believes that the whole world has been duped. He claims that the Taj Mahal is not a queen's tomb, but an ancient Hindu temple palace of Lord Shiva (who was then known as Tejo Mahalaya). The temple palace had been taken over by Shah Jahan and remodelled into his wife's 'memorial'.

Oak also says that the love story of Mumtaz and Shah Jahan is a fairy tale created by court sycophants, blundering historians and sloppy archaeologists. Fearing a political backlash, the Indian government tried to have Oak's book withdrawn. Perhaps the only way to really find the truth is to open the sealed rooms of the Taj Mahal, and allow international experts to investigate.

Industrial heritage holidays are those that are based around an area of industrial history. According to the *Which Holiday* magazine (summer 2005), 'Ironbridge Gorge in Shropshire sets the standard for the industrial sites as there is more that enough to do in a day'. The gorge is where the Industrial Revolution started, and it has the world's first iron bridge as a spectacular example of technological innovation. As well as the bridge, there are plenty of museums showing the development of the industry of the area. There is a recreated Victorian town at Blists Hill, the Darby Furnace, and museums on tile making and china production, and a pipe works.

The world's first iron bridge, built in 1779.

Any area that has been a significant part of the industrialisation of a country is a potential tourist attraction. Obviously some of the areas are more developed as tourist attractions than others. Saga Holidays, which organises trips for the over 50's, recognise the attraction of historical sights and offer holidays based on archaeology and visits to historic houses. For example, Saga are currently offering trips to the Roman landmarks of Northumbria, and to Crete – to the archaeological treasures of Heraklion or to the Minoan ruins.

Sporting holidays

There are two types of sporting holidays – attending an event, such as the Olympics or the World Cup, as a spectator, or participating in an activity, such as golfing or scuba diving. Any great sporting occasion means that the host location becomes the focus of the world for that brief period of time. Below is a list of the more common sporting events.

Spectator sporting events

- The Olympics (summer and winter events)
- World Cup (football)
- Euro finals (football)
- World Cup (rugby)
- World Cup (cricket)
- Davis Cup (tennis)
- Ryder Cup (golf)
- Formula 1 Grand Prix (motor racing).

activity

RESEARCH A SPORTING EVENT

Select a sporting event from the list above and research its location over the last 10 years. Show the locations on a map and analyse the features that affect the choice of location for the event.

Participating sporting holidays

- Skiing
- Golf
- Deep sea diving
- Sailing
- Tennis
- Cycling
- Walking
- Horse riding.

Golfing holidays are a popular special interest holiday. Many centre on a collection of courses in one location, such as the 24 courses located at 'The Villages' complex, just north of Orlando (Florida). In this resort, holiday homes are located around the golf course to buy or to let – mainly targeted at the large market of retired golfing enthusiasts.

Golf has always been popular in the UK, with Spain being the number one destination for golfers travelling abroad. The La Manga Club, situated in an unspoilt corner of southern Spain, east of the Costa del Sol, has been voted Europe's top golf resort twice in the past five years. It covers 1,400 acres and offers 3 championship golf courses and a golf academy. The resort has hosted five Spanish Opens, as well as numerous national, charity and corporate golfing events. But the La Manga Club also offers tennis, swimming, diving, equestrian and a host of other sports in a year-round Mediterranean climate.

Diving holidays are also becoming increasingly popular and are estimated to be worth £75 million a year. According to the BSAC director and Travel Club coordinator David Dixon, 'More people are travelling, and the dive market is no exception, with divers visiting more remote places and the popular destinations getting busier. Indications are that diving is expanding faster than other markets.' The Red Sea remains the most popular spot for British dive holidaymakers, but the long-haul options appeal too. For example, in the Far East, Malaysian Borneo, Vietnam, the Andaman Islands and even Cambodia are growing in appeal. 'Cuba is developing its diving product too,' he added.

Specialist activity holidays

Specialist activity holidays vary enormously, but all tend to focus on a particular skill, from dancing or cooking to pottery and wine tasting. Gastronomic holidays, combining the art of cooking local cuisine and tasting the local wines, are particularly popular. France and Italy top the destination lists for this type of holiday (see the case study below on the famous La Varenne School in France), but there are also more and more long-haul gastronomic holidays available.

activity

CHOOSE A SPORTING HOLIDAY

The following groups of people would like to try a sporting holiday. Research a number of holidays that you think would suit each group, justifying your findings.

1 Jake and Elizabeth are in their thirties and enjoy walking at weekends. They are relatively fit and would like to take a two-week walking holiday somewhere in the world. They enjoy experiencing different cultures.

2 The Johnson family are all sport mad. Tom used to be a semi-professional footballer and his wife, Susan, is a PE teacher. They have two boys, aged eight and ten, who are also very active. They would like a sporty family holiday that they can all enjoy together.

3 George and Rose are retired, but enjoy sailing and have an active social life. They would like a holiday that would allow them to sail and socialise.

Present your findings to the rest of the group, including a map of the holiday destinations that you recommend and a list of the relevant holiday providers.

Specialist holidays in India, for example – cooking traditional Indian cuisine using the local fruit and vegetables, with guidance on using natural spices – are many a foodie's dream.

La Varenne

Anne Willan founded La Varenne, the famous French cooking school, in 1975 and directs its culinary programs. She is well known on both sides of the Atlantic as a leading authority on cooking, with over 35 years' experience as a teacher, cookbook author and food columnist. Visitors to La Varenne enjoy the special experience of staying in the historic Château du Feÿ, with its swimming pool and tennis court, in a beautiful setting 95 miles south of Paris.

The school offers 3-day and 5-day programmes, limited to just twelve people, and run by Franco-American staff. The atmosphere is serious, and the schedule quite full, as they like you to learn as much as possible about French cooking techniques and ingredients, as well as something about the local wines (notably Chablis).

Visitors can also savour the outstanding restaurants in the area and enjoy guided excursions as well as special tastings of fine wines and cheeses.

Source: www.lavarenne.com

Dancing holidays are popular all over the world. Club Dance Holidays is the market leader, running dance trips all over the world – from Buenos Aires to New York and Greece to Cuba. Their holidays cover numerous dance styles: flamenco, salsa, ceroc, lindy hop, modern, Latin, ballroom, line dancing, Brazilian, African, etc.

A specialist activity holiday can focus on any activity that appeals to the tourist. Other examples include painting, bridge, sewing and needlecraft or pottery holidays. Obviously it is the more popular pursuits that will provide the widest choice for the tourist, but this is a growth area and as people's interests change so the provision for this type of holiday expands.

activity

DANCE, DANCE, DANCE

Using a variety of sources investigate three different types of dance holiday in three different destinations around the world. For each holiday, locate its destination on a map and identify the holiday providers. Present your findings to the rest of the group.

Health and fitness holidays

Health and fitness holidays appeal to the growing number of people who want a break from the pressures of life and particularly their office-bound jobs. Their break can range from relaxing and being pampered at a health spa (see right), to a rigorous physical work-out at a sporting complex. Between these two extremes, yoga holidays are particularly popular with a variety of age groups (see below).

Health Spa: Ragdale Hall

Ragdale Hall, in Leicestershire, is a top spa resort for health and beauty advice, relaxation, pampering and beauty treatments, and has been voted 'Health Spa of the Year' for six years running. We combine state-of-the-art facilities with the charm of traditional Victorian architecture to create one of the most luxurious and relaxing health spas in the country.

Whether you are looking for total relaxation, some pampering, and an unrivalled range of treatments or to kick-start a healthier lifestyle, our luxury spa resort is the perfect retreat for a holiday or weekend break. We offer holistic therapy, health advice and beauty treatments from leading skincare companies Clarins, Elemis and Decleor. A spa break is a great way to get health and beauty treatments to make you feel good about yourself.

Source: www.ragdalehall.co.uk

Gentle yoga for health and wellbeing

This week-long course is about using yoga as a way of helping you to feel good about yourself, to help you live in the moment and to manage your energy levels more effectively. This is gentle yoga and it's suitable for everyone from complete beginners to experienced practitioners. There will be a yoga session before breakfast, starting at around 8:30 and finishing around

9:30. This will include a short meditation exercise. 'Start the day with yoga and the whole day will flow in a different way!' promises Jenny, our course leader. Later on each morning there will be another hour session, which will include working with the breath, visualisation work and ideas about how to put into practice what we have learned. The intention is to bring together the mind, body and breath in a harmonious way and so remove blocks in our energy flow, leading to improved health and a greater sense of wellbeing.

There will also be short workshop sessions later on each afternoon on related topics. Individual Reiki, Indian head massage and cranio-sacral therapies will also be available for anyone who wishes to use these techniques to assist in promoting their own energy flow.

Source: Spanish Reflections Holistic Holidays
www.spanish-reflections.co.uk

TWO HEALTHY HOLIDAYS

Read the two extracts on the two very different types of healthy holiday and explain why they are different. Is location important to these holidays? Explain why. Analyse the locations of three or four more examples of each type of holiday around the world, explaining which features of the locations are important to the holiday.

Weddings and honeymoons

As the cost of weddings and honeymoons mount, so more and more people are choosing to travel abroad – not just for their honeymoon but also for the wedding itself.

Many people who wed overseas choose to marry in a beautiful outdoor setting – in the hotel gardens with an ocean view, for example – but those who choose the Mediterranean usually exchange vows in the local town hall.

Accommodation can vary from spending two relaxing weeks on a beach, to the more active holiday. Some of the more adventurous couples have even tied the knot whilst skydiving or snorkelling.

Many companies offer a vast array of locations for the wedding, with the most popular locations being in the Caribbean or the Mediterranean – for example, Antigua, Barbados, Jamaica, Cyprus, Halkidiki and Rhodes.

WEDDING CHOICES

Read the extract on the Moon Palace Hotel and explain why you think couples might chose to have their wedding at this destination. Describe the features that give this hotel and its location their appeal. Research at least six other worldwide destinations that are popular for weddings, and locate them on a map. Identify some of the holiday companies that provide for these destinations and describe any differences in the holidays you have selected. Analyse the features that affect this type of holiday.

Moon Palace Hotel, Cancun, Mexico

This hotel is very popular with couples wanting their 'Wedding in Paradise', in one of Cancun's best resorts. Scattered throughout 55 acres of well-kept gardens, accommodation is in three-storey buildings. Guests have full use of the facilities at the adjoining Moon Palace Sunrise, including a disco and gourmet Italian and Oriental restaurants.

This hotel is also home to: • the fabulous Moon Palace Jack Nicklaus golf course. • 1.5km of white, sandy beach in front of the hotel (any seaweed on the shore is constantly removed by the hotel) • the largest pool in Cancun • two swim-up palapa bars with daytime snacks • Ballroom with 6 show nights a week • Weekly casino night • Disco (over 18 yrs only) • 2 floodlit tennis courts • Minigolf • Health club • Gym, sauna and steam room • Basketball, bicycles and roller blades • Pedalos and small sailing boats • Windsurfing, kayaks and snorkelling.

Other Facilities

• Green fees and club/equipment hire • Beauty parlour • Shop • Scuba-diving • Motorised waterspouts • Laundry • Spa facilities at the Golf Club house. These facilities do not form part of your all-inclusive package.

Honeymoons

Honeymooners will receive a welcome call, 'Just Married' banner in room on arrival (or later, if the wedding takes place in the hotel). Other services include a turn-down service (on request), special room decoration, a fruit basket and a bottle of sparkling wine on arrival. Room will be cleaned after 11.00 (on request). They also receive a candle-lit dinner with special menu and decoration and two complimentary T-shirts.

Working holidays

In contrast to most holidays, the majority of the time on a working holiday will be taken up with some form of work. This may be work that the person has never done before, but is prepared to learn and do, or it may be familiar work which they want to do in a

YOUR WORKING HOLIDAY

Research a working holiday that you may be interested in taking either now or when you are older. Research the destination and the type of activities you would be involved in. Present your findings to the rest of the group.

GAP-YEAR OPPORTUNITIES

Read about the gap-year opportunities shown below. Gap-year opportunities clearly vary. Research at least six different types of gap-year holiday and explain the geographical distribution of each. Present your findings to the rest of the group. You may find the following website useful: http://www.yearoutgroup.org/organisations.htm

different context. For example, someone with a skill, such as a builder or plumber, may want to help build homes and schools in the less economically developed areas of the world. Some working holidays are unique projects in their own right, whilst others are organised and ongoing – such as working on a kibbutz in Israel or in summer camp in the USA.

Working on a kibbutz in Israel can be a very rewarding experience. The work is for 5 or 6 days a week, for 6–8 hours a day. Although Israel is a Jewish state, only about 15% of the volunteers are Jewish. The kibbutz life is varied, from working outside in the fields to picking fruit or milking cows. The accommodation is free and so is the food, but the wages are little more than pocket money.

BUNAC is an organisation that runs summer camps for children throughout the USA. Most of the staff looking after the children at the camps are young people (18–35) on working holidays. Being able to deal with children is essential for this type of holiday. They work for at least nine weeks from June to mid-

August. This leaves a few weeks of summer for them to travel around the States if they want to.

Other types of working holiday include working as a volunteer in one of the less developed countries – perhaps helping to build homes or dig water supplies. These types of working holiday are usually conducted by charities or other support organisations, and are ideal for students taking a 'gap year' before continuing their studies or getting a job. More travel companies are offering travel deals specifically aimed at 'gappers'. The Year Out Group is an association of organisations formed to promote the concept and benefits of well-structured year-out programmes and to help people select suitable and worthwhile projects. The Group's member organisations provide a wide range of year-out placements in the UK and overseas, including structured work placements (see examples below).

Examples of Year Out Group organisations

Frontier conservation

Join a Frontier expedition and help protect endangered species and threatened tropical environments while gaining a qualification in your gap year. (We offer BTEC qualifications in Tropical Habitat Conservation or Expedition Management.)

www.frontier.ac.uk

GAP Activity Projects

GAP Activity Projects (GAP) Ltd, founded in 1972, organises voluntary work overseas in 24 countries. Currently 2,000 young people are involved annually in GAP schemes. GAP volunteers work alongside staff in such areas as foreign language assistants, assisting with general activities in schools, caring for the disadvantaged, outdoor education and conservation work.

www.gap.org.uk

World Challenge Expeditions

World Challenge Expeditions offer gap year safety training for students aged 16 and over. The TravelSafe course is packed with workshops seminars and scenarios.

www.world-challenge.co.uk

Madventurer

Madventurer are leaders in 'development travel', providing anyone taking time out the opportunity to combine voluntary work on community projects with adventurous overland expeditions. Projects and expeditions run from 2 weeks to 6 months, across four continents. Coach and play rugby in Tonga, barter for silver in Timbuktu, teach English on the slopes of Kilimanjaro, dive with Manta Rays in Tobago, or build schools in the Andes.

www.madventurer.com

Conservation holidays

Conservation holidays are for people who are interested in the issues of conservation, whether this is saving the whale or researching the ecosystem. Like working holidays, these are often based around doing some form of work, but not necessarily strenuous work. It may just be observing the environment and collecting statistical information as part of an ongoing research project. These types of holiday are often conducted by large environmental organisations, such as the Kenya Project, which is run by the Friends of Conservation. They are currently supporting the Masai Mara area in Kenya. At the request of the local people, a tree nursery has been established and there are plans for a building project at the local school. This project is to help develop the tree nursery and aid the reforestation of the local area, as well as improve the standards at the school.

Earthwatch is another organisation that runs education and research holidays, as shown in the case study below.

activity

CONSERVATION HOLIDAY ORGANISATIONS

Investigate an organisation like the Earthwatch Institute, and research the number of different projects that they are involved in. Create a map showing the location of the projects and describe their special features.

Earthwatch Institute

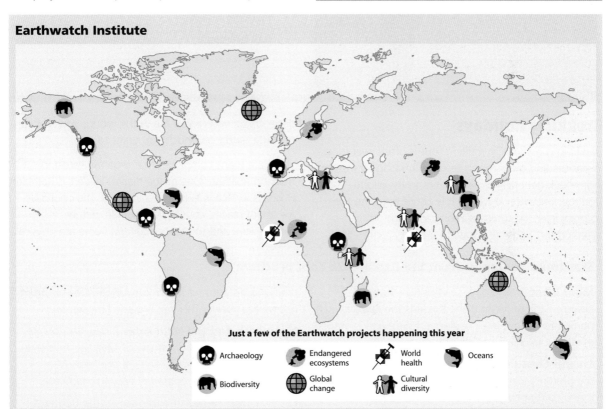

Just a few of the Earthwatch projects happening this year

- Archaeology
- Biodiversity
- Endangered ecosystems
- Global change
- World health
- Cultural diversity
- Oceans

The Earthwatch Institute is a worldwide organisation that provides work experiences for individuals who want more from their holiday that to just lie on a beach. Its mission is to engage people worldwide in scientific field research and education to promote the understanding and action necessary for a sustainable environment. Most projects are 10–14 days long, but there are also shorter opportunities available.

In 2004, the Earthwatch Institute sponsored over 130 projects in 44 countries and 18 US states. Topics span a wide range of scientific study, including ecology, zoology, and archaeology.

Earthwatch expeditions are not tours. They live and work and eat as scientists do in the field – that means working long hours. Expeditions range from saving the life of a butterfly in a rainforest to discovering a new species of dinosaur or bringing clean water to an African village.

Volunteers are diverse in age, experience and nationality, and expedition teams are extraordinarily intergenerational. The minimum age is 16, and there is no maximum! Sixty per cent are female.

Source: www.earthwatch.org

Transport-based travelling holidays

In the last topic we looked at special interest holidays that take place in one location. In the next two we look at those special interest holidays that involve tourists moving around. In this topic we focus on holidays where the means of moving around is the main point of the holiday:

- Trekking holidays (for example, walking or horse-riding)
- Cycling holidays
- Cruising holidays
- Rail holidays.

Trekking holidays

Trekking is essentially walking, but is often over long distances and quite rough terrain. Trekking by foot or horseback generally appeals more to the slightly younger and fitter traveller. It is about enjoying the journey itself. Accommodation can range from sleeping out under the stars to a luxury room – it depends on where you are in the world, your choice of route, and how much you want to pay.

There are many companies that organise escorted trekking holidays. One of the market leaders is Ramblers Holidays, which was founded in 1946. Their holidays are about places, countryside, people, nature, camaraderie and sometimes culture. Some are physically

Star treks: examples from the *Explore On Foot* brochure

Mont Blanc Trek 8 days of walking – from the eastern flank of Mont Blanc towards the Swiss/French border. Each day's walk averages 13km, and is graded as strenuous, hiking at an altitude of up to 2500m.

Chianti Classico 8 days of hiking through some of the prettiest scenery in Europe. The holiday is centre-based so that participants are free to join group walks or relax at the hotel.

Greenland Trek 15 days circumnavigating Ammassalik Island, enjoying breathtaking glacial scenery. Graded as strenuous, walking 6–8 hours a day at up to 900m.

Mountains of Macedonia 8 days rambling in Macedonia, where 80% of the country is mountainous. Graded as easy to moderate walking.

On foot in Northern Cyprus 8-day, centre-based trip exploring one of the most unspoilt parts of the Mediterranean. Graded as easy to moderate walking.

The Lycian Way 8-day hike through history on Turkey's only long-distance walking route, which stretches from Fethiye to Antalya. This trek is graded moderate.

Marrakesh and the High Atlas 8-day, two-centre trip to discover the vibrant city of Marrakesh before heading for the Berber villages of the High Atlas Mountains. This trek is graded easy to moderate.

Ladakh Trek 16-day trek to discover the Buddhist Pilgrimage Trail linking Kashmir and Tibet through the Himalaya. Graded as strenuous, and for experienced hill walkers only.

Rockies Escape Twin-centre, 9-day trip to the Rocky Mountains visiting icefields, glaciers, lakes and forests teeming with wildlife. The walking is graded as easy, and there is also the chance to go horse riding.

Trek New Zealand 23-day trip, hiking among some of the most picturesque scenery on earth, witnessing first-hand the amazing backdrop to *The Lord of the Rings*. The trekking is graded as moderate to strenuous.

Source: www.explore.co.uk

TREKKING TRIPS

1 Locate each of the 'Explore' trips on a map.

2 Choose a trip for each of the following groups and explain you reasoning:
   (a) Two fit young Swedish men who wish to test their stamina and enjoy experiencing a very different culture. They have up to one month to travel.
   (b) Three fit, but elderly, women looking for a healthy holiday lasting no more than ten days.

3 A mixed family group of walkers (of varying abilities) who enjoy each other's company and are looking to spend a week away.

challenging but the over-riding philosophy is to provide an active and stimulating holiday with fellow travellers who share the same interests and feel that the best way to see the world is on foot – to experience the sights, sounds, tastes and smells of the real country. Every holiday is graded to suit the individual's level of fitness and walking ability and people are grouped accordingly. These types of holidays often involve covering a lot of miles but include breathtaking scenery and wildlife. The accommodation is often in tents or Alpine huts.

Trekking holidays are popular throughout the world. Explore is an adventure holiday company organising small-group walking tours and challenging treks in no fewer than 52 countries. Their favourites are the trek to Kilimanjaro, the Inca Trail, the Himalaya trek and the High Atlas trek.

The trips are graded according to ability and fitness, and on most of the holidays the group walks from hotel to hotel, but there are also some centre-based trips for those who prefer more flexibility (see examples on the previous page).

The Inca Trail is a classic Andean trek combining some of the world's most breathtaking mountain scenery with fine archaeological sites. It was an Inca highway that connected Cuzco with the ancient city of Machu Picchu. Although it is now a simple matter to visit Machu Picchu by train from Cuzco in one day, the approach along the Inca Trail, apart from being a most beautiful walk, puts the whole area into perspective, and shows what an extraordinary feat Machu Picchu's construction must have been.

Other types of trek are focused on wildlife. Gorilla trekking in Uganda, for example, involves a strenuous trek through primal rainforest. Virunga National Park, with its mist-covered hillsides, dormant volcanoes and bamboo forest, provides a fitting and evocative backdrop for the experience. This holiday is one of many trekking holidays offered by Exodus (www.exodus.co.uk).

Cycling holidays

Cycling has become increasingly popular over the years, and a number of holiday companies offer a whole new range of trips designed around this environmentally friendly mode of transport. Almost everywhere in the world that is physically accessible on a bike can be part of a tour (see examples below). Most organised tours stick to tarmac roads (but not all) and use small hotels or hostels for accommodation, moving the riders' luggage on each day.

Examples of cycling tours

Petra and Wadi Rum by bike (9 days) A week on two wheels, exploring the spectacular sites and scenery of Jordan – Petra, Wadi Rum and the Red and Dead Seas.

Trail to the Taj Mahal (16 days) Taj, tigers and temples on a two-wheeled adventure through India's colourful desert state.

Classic cols of the Tour de France (8 days) Pull on your polka-dot jersey, enjoy the views, and ride some of the famous mountain passes of the Tour de France.

Saigon to Hanoi (17 days) A fascinating journey, using a combination of bikes, boats and trains to see the best of this unique country.

Cycling the Great Wall (14 days) Emperors' tombs,

rural villages, bustling Beijing and a ride in the shadow of China's greatest monument.

Lhasa to Kathmandu ride (20 days) An epic ride across the 'forbidden land', taking in the fascinating cities of Kathmandu and Lhasa, the north face of Everest, five 5000m+ passes, and an unrivalled 4000m descent into Nepal!

Source: www.exodus.co.uk

Exodus is an adventure company with 30 years' experience of organising cycling tours. Some of their tours are shown on the previous page. Visit the exodus website – www.exodus.co.uk. Locate on a map at least three of their tours in different parts of the world. Identify three other companies that organise cycling tours and, for each, locate three of their tours on your map, using colour coding to differentiate the different organisations.

Cruising holidays

Cruising holidays are now available to almost anywhere in the world. Popular cruises still include the Mediterranean, the Caribbean and the traditional transatlantic cruise from the UK to America, but now cruises have expanded around the world.

One of the best-known cruise companies is Cunard, whose liners have sailed the high seas more than 160 years. In 2004 they launched the largest ocean liner ever built – the *Queen Mary 2*. Cunard offer cruises to the Mediterranean, Scandinavia, the Caribbean, the Americas, and Africa. Their 'Around The World' cruise explores 39 ports of call in 24 nations. The trip includes 102 days aboard the *QE2*, plus 6 days aboard

the *Queen Mary 2*. Alternatively, holidaymakers can choose a shorter itinerary, ranging from 14 to 80 days, and join the ship at any one of its ports of call.

It is not just ocean cruising that is popular – river cruising is also growing in demand. For example, the Yangtze river valley boasts some of the world's most spectacular landscapes of misty mountains, breathtaking gorges and serene lagoons. Some say that no visit to China is complete without a cruise on this great river, visiting the ancient cities along its

activity

JUST CRUISING

Using brochures and the internet, research the different types of cruise holiday – round the world, regional (e.g., Caribbean), and river cruises. For each type, locate the routes on a map and analyse their different features. Explain any differences in provision between at least three companies.

www.cruiseline.co.uk has a large list of all the available cruises available, or you can visit the individual sites such as:
www.cunard.co.uk
www.fredolsencruises.co.uk
www.pocruises.com
www.crystalcruises.co.uk

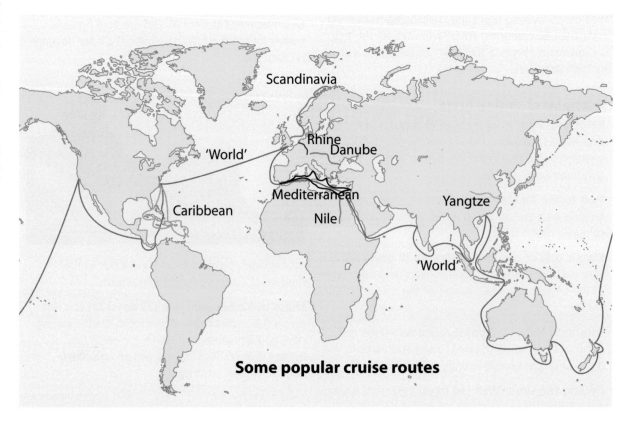

Some popular cruise routes

route and the spectacular Three Gorges Dam.

The Rhine has always been popular for cruising, as it threads its 900-mile journey down from the Alps, through Switzerland, France, Germany and Holland to the North Sea. With its medieval castles and quaint villages, the Rhine offers the river-cruise passenger a kaleidoscopic mix of awe-inspiring scenery, history, art and culture.

Similarly, a cruise down the Danube takes the traveller to cities such as Imperial Vienna and Budapest, as it winds its way from Germany's Black Forest through Austria, Slovakia, Hungary, Bulgaria and Romania before reaching the Black Sea.

Rail holidays

Travelling by train is a relaxing and enjoyable way to absorb changing landscapes over long distances, in comfort and without effort – letting the train take the strain of the journey. There are many popular rail holidays, from the InterRail holidays that many students take as they travel around Europe, to the more extravagant train holidays involving special trains such as the Orient Express.

The Orient Express Company, in fact, owns five tourist trains, including the legendary Venice Simplon Orient Express in Europe, the Eastern & Oriental Express in Asia, and the Great South Pacific Express in Australia. The company also part-owns and manages PeruRail, which operates the Cuzco–Machu Picchu train service used by nearly every tourist to Peru (the alternative route to the famous Inca ruins is a four-day hike – there are no roads).

Another luxury train ride is found on the Blue Train that runs through South Africa's spectacular landscapes and visits interesting tourist attractions along the way. The Blue Train is unique as it combines the luxury of the world's leading hotels with train travel. The scheduled routes are:

Pretoria–Cape Town (1 day and 1 night) and Cape Town–Port Elizabeth (1 day and 2 nights).

The Trans-Siberian Railway, connecting Moscow with the Far East, is the world's longest train route, and the most legendary of all. A real working railway, carrying huge amounts of freight and passenger traffic, it's effectively the backbone of Russia. The 'Red Express' classic trip takes 10 days.

activity

PUT THEM ON THE RIGHT TRACKS

Ben and Jo, both in their 20s, want to take a month-long rail holiday – but they are unsure where to go. They live in London, and want to see as many different European capitals as possible. Fortunately, money is no object, because they have saved hard for this trip. What would you suggest?

213

Topic 2 Transport-based travelling holidays

The Venice Simplon Orient Express runs a number of different trips:

- London–Paris–Venice (plus on to Rome)
- Venice–Budapest–London
- Venice–Vienna–London
- Venice–Prague–Paris–London
- Paris–Budapest–Bucharest–Istanbul

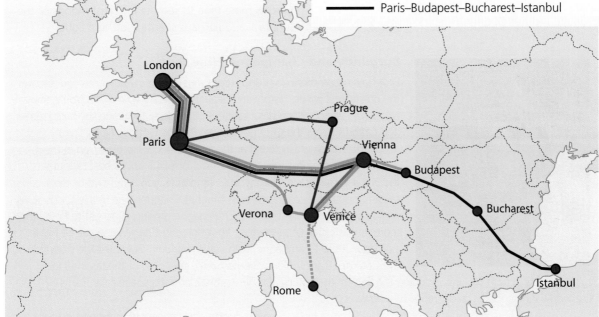

Theme-based travelling holidays

This topic continues our look at special interest holidays that involve tourists moving around. Unlike the last topic, however, where the means of moving around was the main point of the holiday, this topic looks at holidays based on various themes:

- **Specialised tours, such as wine tasting**
- **Overland adventure**
- **Safaris**
- **Independent travel, such as backpacking.**

Specialised tours

Specialised tours are designed to attract tourists with particular hobbies, pastimes and interests. Wine-tasting holidays are particularly popular. Vineyards across the world have realised that they can profitably sell their image, their branding (and their products) directly to the public by making their vineyards accessible to tourists. Wine drinkers are often interested in seeing how the grapes are grown, and how the wine-making process can vary – and then tasting the finished product. Wine-tasting holidays are popular in the traditional European wine-growing areas, such as France (see below), Italy and Germany, and further afield in California, Australia and New Zealand.

Other types of specialised tour include nature holidays. Naturetrek offers Britain's largest selection of organised natural history holidays. A leading ornithologist or botanist with a good knowledge of the area expertly guides the tour. Although seeing (and photographing) birds, mammals and plants is the main focus of these holidays, there is also time to take an interest in a region's people, culture, history and architecture. Naturetrek offers treks throughout Europe, America, Africa, Asia and Australia. See page 54 for an Industry Focus interview with Naturetrek.

Another example of a nature watch tour is the Polar Bear Tour on Hudson Bay (Canada). Accommodation is in the Tundra Lodge, a movable lodge that is positioned in the best locations for the buggy rides that seek out the bears as they shift around the tundra. Staying at the Tundra Lodge allows the tourists more time to see the different moods of the tundra – and perhaps see the northern lights.

Burgundy and Champagne Wine Tour

First-class accommodations and sumptuous dining await you as you discover the prestigious wines, history and beauty of these two regions. You'll enjoy extensive tastings at top wine estates in Burgundy, including the best Premier and Grand Crus in the Côte de Beaune and the Côte de Nuits. Luxury accommodations are included at the elegant 4-star Hotel Le Cep in the delightful town of Beaune, as is dinner at one of France's best restaurants, the 3-star Lameloise in Chagny. In Champagne, you'll visit two of the world's most famous Champagne houses, Moet et Chandon and Veuve Clicquot, as well as some of the best smaller Champagne producers, to get to know the more intimate side of this region. Your home in Champagne will be the 4-star Hotel Royal Champagne, with a commanding view over the vineyards of the Côte des Blancs. Along the way, we'll see some of the fascinating cultural sights in both regions, including the thirteenth-century Clos de Vougeot, and the spectacular Reims Cathedral, where the kings of France were crowned.

Source: French Wine Explorers www.wine-tours-france.com

Overland adventure

The term 'overland adventure' describes trips by foot, animal or vehicle, often lasting several weeks, that involve tourists experiencing all aspects of an area – the great sites, historic monuments, natural beauty and wildlife – and meeting the local people and seeing their customs first-hand.

This type of holiday appeals to those people who are fairly active and prepared to cope with the unusual and the unpredictable. The holiday provides a basic level of comfort rather than luxury, and the focus is on responsible tourism with minimum disruption to the area and the culture visited. Unit 7 provides more detailed explanation of the range of responsible tourism holidays and activities. Adventure travel doesn't always go exactly as planned, but that's part of the attraction, and many people who go on these types of holiday choose them again, time after time.

Today there are companies that specialise in providing a whole range of overland adventure holidays that involve crossing countries or even continents. iExplore, for example, claims to be the world's leading adventure travel specialist. It has pioneered and led tours to over 100 countries, for the last twenty years (see below, left).

Dragoman has been one of the world's leading adventure travel companies for over 20 years. They take groups of travellers on overland holidays (2–6 weeks) or on an overland expedition (7–42 weeks) around the world. The trips don't just stick to the main roads, but try to get off the beaten track to visit the places usually missed by the tourist. Trips can range from rafting down the mighty Zambezi, to exploring the Amazon, to hiking up Mt Kilimanjaro. There are some examples shown below.

Top ten world travel destinations

(List based on iExplore's adventure and experiential travellers)

2005	(position in 2004)
1. Egypt	(2)
2. Peru	(1)
3. China	(5)
4. Galapagos	(9)
5. India	(10)
6. France	(7)
7. Alaska	(3)
8. South Africa	(14)
9. New Zealand	(18)
10. Morocco	(35)

iExplore CEO, George Deeb, said '2005 has seen continued growth in faraway travel destinations, particularly in the Middle East, which has Egypt displacing perennial best-selling Peru as our number one seller and Morocco entering our top ten.'

In addition to the Galapagos Islands, India, South Africa, New Zealand and Morocco, who have seen strong growth in the top ten, other destinations seeing notable growth over last year include Jordan (#13) and Venezuela (#15), neither of which had any sales for iExplore in 2004.

Dropping out of last year's top ten were Italy, Costa Rica and Canada, who are now ranked numbers 12, 22 and 26 respectively. Other destinations seeing notable declines from last year include Vietnam and Japan.

Source: www.traveldailynews.com

Examples of Dragoman holidays

The Vaquero is one of the most popular trips in South America. Lasting $6\frac{1}{2}$ weeks, it includes horse riding, glacial treks, mountain walks, climbing volcanoes, white-water rafting and mountain biking. However, you do not have to be Indiana Jones to enjoy it. Whether you are active or not, the stunning scenery of Chile's Lake District, Patagonia and Tierra del Fuego are magnificent. Add in Buenos Aires, Iguassu Falls, the Brazilian beaches and the delights of Rio and you have a very well balanced journey. 75% of accommodation is in tents, and the rest in hotels. There is no cook on this trip so you need to be prepared to help out.

The Silk Route to Xi'an follows the most famous trade route in the world, the Silk Route. Leaving the mountains of Kyrgyzstan we cross high passes to take us on to the vast desert plateaus of Xinjiang, China's Turkestan, where we travel from oasis to oasis. After our first contact with the Great Wall, we move east, and the world becomes more Chinese, but we detour to get a flavour of Tibet in the seldom-visited mountainous region around Xiahe. The trip finishes at the historic city of Xi'an, home of the fabled terracotta warriors.

Source: www.dragoman.co.uk

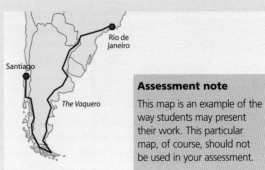

Assessment note

This map is an example of the way students may present their work. This particular map, of course, should not be used in your assessment.

Overland adventure holidays often appeal to those taking a gap year or a year's holiday from work. In the past it was mostly young university leavers who enjoyed such adventures but today more and more people are leaving their jobs, cashing in on their property, seeking new careers and filling the gap with some form of far away adventure travel.

Overland trips make it possible for individuals to visit remote parts of the world, as shown in the case study below, and offer individuals the opportunity to embark on adventurous excursions, such as white-water rafting, trekking, climbing, bungee jumping, etc.

activity

PROMOTING YOUR OVERLAND ADVENTURE

Research an overland adventure holiday that would appeal to you. Create a promotional brochure showing all the aspects of the trip and explaining to whom it would appeal, and why. Try to include a number of illustrations showing the nature of the holiday and the route.

Desert holidays

Desert holidays provide the inquisitive traveller with a slice of another world that was previously unknown to them. Camel safaris and oasis resorts have made desert travel both available and affordable in recent years. Tour companies command fleets of camel owners to charter tourists across some of the most beautiful desert scenery known to man.

Accommodation is often in tents and occasionally in the 'luxury' of former shikar camps that provide a slice of a bygone era. These camps have all kinds of modern facilities including fresh water – and occasionally hot water. Entertainment in the evenings usually takes the form of juggling, puppet shows, traditional music, dancing and special camel parades. Modern resort complexes provide even more luxury in the form of air-conditioned rooms and all the usual benefits that are associated with staying in five-star accommodation.

Safaris

Safari holidays are traditionally based in Africa, though they are becoming more popular in unusual destinations, such as tiger watching in India, whale watching in Iceland, and searching for the fauna in the Amazon.

The great plains of the Masai Mara and the Serengeti in East Africa, however, still provide the world's most popular safari spectacle, with their great migrations of

Some safari destinations

animals an outstanding sight (see map). To the south, safaris in Botswana, Namibia, Zambia and South Africa are all very different, from the deserts of the Etosha Pan, to the great elephant herds of Botswana, to the tarmac roads of the enormous Kruger National Park.

Kenya safari

Kenya has no fewer than 40 national parks and game reserves, supporting a wide range of unique habitats – from the great wilderness of Tsavo National Park to African Safari Club's exclusive Kimana game reserve situated at the foot of Mount Kilimanjaro, and the dense rainforests of Mount Kenya National Park to the vast plains of the Masai Mara. Here bird and beast roam free in their natural habitat. For years adventurers, travellers and photographers alike have been drawn to Kenya's natural beauty to sample what to many is the 'real Africa'.

African Safari Club offers a superb range of safaris in Kenya, from one-night 'tasters' to a fabulous six-night expedition. Each day extensive game drives are arranged, sometimes at daybreak when many of the animals are at their most active. Travel is in four-wheel-drive Toyota Land Cruisers, Land Rovers, Unimogs (open-back lorries) or specially adapted minibuses, and led by experienced drivers/guides, all with a vast knowledge of the game reserves and when and where to find the animals.

Source: www.africansafariclub.com

Animals are generally much less shy of vehicles than they are of people on foot, and in many of the parks they all but ignore vehicles altogether. Safaris can really only be successful for small groups of people, because of scaring the animals and other conservation issues. However, walking safaris are one of the most rewarding ways to see the animals. Though there are many places where walking may be strenuous, a walking safari in Africa is often quite the opposite. As a basic rule, the more game there is, the slower you go and, equally, the slower you go the more you are likely to see.

Independent travel

Independent travel has always been popular with those people who like the idea of arranging their own itinerary – or who feel they can get a better deal if they plan and pay for everything separately. Travel, accommodation, food and entertainment are some of the main components of a holiday, and many people like the flexibility of deciding their own combination. For example, if they want to eat in expensive restaurants and stay in basic accommodation, or visa versa, then that is up to the individual. Package holidays tend to clump everything into standard packages with all the components at the same level, whether it's basic or luxury or somewhere in between.

Independent travel has always had some followers but today, with online booking and budget flights, it is becoming increasingly popular.

Backpackers were the traditional independent travellers – often students taking a gap year or long vacation. This type of holiday appeals to people who like the feeling of freedom. Travel can be pre-planned, or the traveller can decide what to do on a daily or even hourly basis. Many backpackers use the versatile InterRail card, or other such open-ended ticket, to travel around Europe.

There are a number of sources of information that support the independent traveller. Travelmag, for example, is an interactive website that provides a collection of features written by independent travellers, and reflects the huge variety of individual travel experiences – often well beyond the guidebook routes in little-known corners of the globe.

Independent travel is not just for the young. Many older (and in particular more affluent) people prefer to make their own travel arrangements. This gives them the flexibility to go exactly where they want, when they want and how they want.

Imagine you are planning an independent holiday for the groups described below. Research and recommend an itinerary for each group. Plan the route on a map and identify the key tourist attractions that they would see on the trip. You may find these websites of interest:

www.packback.com
www.attitudetravel.com
www.travelindependent.info

1 Jane and Ally are taking a gap year between their studies, and are to buy a round-the-world ticket that allows them to stop six times between leaving and returning to Heathrow. They have a limited budget, and know they will have to work some time during the trip.

2 Edward, who lives alone, is retiring from full-time work as a bank manager. He would like to see as much of the world as possible before he comes back after six months to work part-time in the bank. He is very keen on historical and cultural destinations. Money is no object, and he is fit and walks regularly.

3 Dick and Margaret are in their thirties and are keen to take an independent holiday that includes some form of conservation work, as they feel they have not done enough in contributing to the welfare of the planet. They can take up to a year out from their jobs. Neither of them is particularly fit, and Margaret has an artificial leg.

4 The Hamilton family, consisting of John, Judy and their two teenage daughters, want to visit as many European cities as they can in a month. They feel that this will help the girls with their studies, and see this as an educational trip. John and Judy speak a little French and German between them, and they want to experience some of Eastern Europe too.

In the last topic we finished looking at the different types of special interest holidays, and now we go on to look at the features of destinations that are significant for special interest holidays. The features we will look at are:

- Climate
- Landscape
- Transport routes and accessibility
- Accommodation
- Local services
- Natural and built attractions
- Events and entertainment
- Local culture and heritage
- Activities and facilities.

Climate

While the mass of holidaymakers are just looking for a week or two of sunny weather, many people's special interests are located in particular climatic zones around the world – and not always in the most obvious places for holidays. Some people, for example, would prefer the searing heat of the desert landscapes, or the cold clear air of a high-altitude skiing resort.

Polar climates

Tourists who really want to get away from it all – and are prepared to endure very low temperatures – can now experience the magnificent icy terrain and the hardy wildlife of the polar regions. The Arctic and the Antarctic are both very inaccessible, which tends to make visits expensive, and they are both very delicate ecologically, which limits opportunities for tourist development or too much activity. But trips to the polar climate zones can be very rewarding (see the case study, right, about a South Seas cruise to the Antarctic Circle, run by Exodus).

Cold climates

Holidays to destinations in the 'cold climate' zones have a long history, and are still growing in popularity. Visits to Iceland, Norway and Sweden are popular with specialist tour

South Seas Cruise

One of the most popular and exciting cruises in the South Seas, going south of the Antarctic Circle and beyond – into waters untouched by all but the very lucky few.

The aim on this voyage is to head as far south as the ice and weather permit. The adventure begins in earnest when we approach the Antarctic Circle. Our ice-rated ship enables us to navigate through some of the world's most scenic waterways – many littered with brash ice, 'growlers' and colossal, stunning icebergs. We'll attempt to land on the Antarctic continent south of the Circle and perhaps visit a scientific research station. After a few days exploring the 'deep south', we'll make further shore excursions on our northerly route along the Antarctic Peninsula. Our boat is small enough to navigate through the narrow Lemaire Channel, with glacial walls towering high on both sides, leading to a jigsaw of jewel-like islands that are home to penguin rookeries, whales, elephant seals and countless seabirds. If you can spare the extra time, the rewards on such a unique icy pilgrimage are immeasurable.

Source: www.exodus.co.uk

operators. Much of the tourist activity takes place in the short summer with its long days (June to August in the Northern hemisphere). People are usually attracted to these cold areas by the glacial scenery (the Norwegian fjords, for example) and the wildlife viewing (whale-watching especially). More active tourists may go for the snow- and ice-based activities, such as skidooing. For the less adventurous tourists there are cruises to Alaska.

Warm temperate climates

The warm temperate climate zones provide the best conditions for human comfort, and can therefore support tourism all year round. Destinations such as Spain and Florida have become popular places for extended stays in the winter, as well as in the summer months. There is a wide range of specialist holidays supported in this region from trekking to honeymooning. Cruising has always been popular in this zone, because warm weather can be assured all year round.

Hot climates

The rainy tropical climates near the Equator produce the thick rainforests of the Amazon, the African Congo and Malaysia. Although much of the rainforest is inaccessible, there are numerous wildlife-viewing trips along the rivers. Further south from the Equator, the drier sub-tropical forest and the temperate grasslands are much more accessible. In Africa, these are the safari areas, in countries such as Kenya, Zambia and South Africa, where a thriving tourism business is based on people's special interest in wildlife.

Desert climates

Arid and semi-arid areas have a distinctive climate, with very little rain, which, over millions of years has allowed the development of unique and often beautiful landscapes. Holidaymakers with an interest in these landscapes are prepared to endure the inhospitable conditions to see such sites as Monument Valley in Arizona, or Uluru (Ayer's Rock) in Australia. Nearer home, specialist travel companies offer desert holidays in the Sahara.

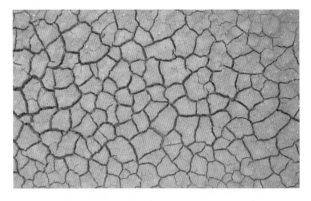

Mountain climates

Mountainous areas have their own climates. Unlike other climatic zones, which are mostly the result of latitude, in mountainous areas it is the altitude which is the major factor, reducing temperatures considerably. This is why the Alps can be covered in snow when the Mediterranean coast is basking in warm sunshine. It is the snow and the slopes of mountainous areas, of course, that have allowed the development of one of the most popular special interest holidays – skiing. There is no need for Europeans to go all the way north to the Arctic Circle to find snow – there is always snow in the Alps every winter, usually for several months. In the USA, there are ski resorts in Colorado and in the mountainous parts of Utah and Arizona – states usually considered part of the hot arid southwest.

Landscape

The term landscape refers to features such as lakes, mountains and coastlines. Some special interest holidays can only exist in particular landscapes – skiing in the mountains, for example, or water sports along a coastline or on a lake.

Apart from being popular for water sports, such as sailing and surfing, some coastlines are popular because of the wildlife that the (underwater) landscape attracts. The Great Barrier Reef, for example, on the North East coast of Australia, is the world's largest coral ecosystem. The attraction of the coral and the brightly coloured fish that live in it attract people from all over the world. This unique environment boasts over 200 varieties of coral and over 1,000 species of fish. Tourists can access the coral reef by snorkeling and diving, in glass-bottomed boats, or by viewing it from the air.

Mountainous areas of the world provide for many special interest pursuits, such as walking and climbing. The more rugged terrain provides the opportunity for trekking and for grueling cycling tours such as those cycling the Tour de France route.

Transport routes and accessibility

Transport routes may be the sole reason for the holiday – cruising down the Danube, for example or traveling on the Orient Express is the heart of the holiday experience. Many of these holidays are based on the pioneering development in earlier centuries of transport routes across vast areas of the world. Travelling from the east coast to the west coast of America by train, bus or independently in a camper van provide examples of different types of special interest holiday based on the access to transport routes.

Ultimately, it is the transport gateways – airports, railway stations, sea ports or roads – that provide access to any area or region, and are therefore significant features for most special interest holidays.

The lack of accessibility, however, may explain the appeal for some special interest holidays. For example, mountain trekking the more remote areas of the world or climbing Everest or Kilimanjaro appeal to some because there are only a few people who can actually do it.

Accommodation

Special interest holidays have a variety of accommodation ranging from tents to luxury hotels. The choice of accommodation may be the main feature of the special interest holiday. For example, a camping or caravanning holiday is based on the accommodation and the features of the holiday that this provides, such as the experience of the outdoor life and basic accommodation, with the flexibility of moving around from site to site if desired.

Local services

Local services may influence the special interest holiday market more perhaps than one would think. For example, in Las Vegas the local services of casinos, entertainment and even wedding chapels have created the resort's great appeal. Recently, there has been a growth in the number of weddings abroad because some destinations, such as the Caribbean Islands, provide local church services to meet the needs of this type of special interest holiday.

Natural and built attractions

There are many natural and built attractions that are significant for the special interest holiday market. Natural attractions are those created by nature, such as the Himalayas, the Florida Keys or the Sahara Desert. Built attractions are those created and built by man, such as the Pyramids, Stonehenge or the Great Wall of China.

Seeing the attraction may be the main purpose of the

holiday, or just part of the holiday experience. For example, many people visit Egypt because they just want to see the Pyramids and the Sphinx, but for others these are just part of their cultural exploration of an ancient civilisation.

Events and entertainment

Special interest holidays include those in which people go to a destination solely to watch a sporting event, such as international football, rugby, cricket or golf. If the sporting event involves a whole series of matches then the holiday may last several weeks as the supporters follow the matches around the host country. This clearly is of benefit to the local travel and tourism industry.

Cultural and religious festivals are often a focus of special interest holidays, too. One of the largest is the Rio de Janeiro carnival – the world's largest street party – which attracts over 300,000 foreign visitors every February. For four days, the already vibrant city hosts a raucous knees-up, with street dancing, fantastic outfits, and partying until dawn in the tropical climate.

Local culture and heritage

For some people, discovering and living – however briefly – in the culture of a different country, with all the different experiences it provides, is the key feature of their holiday. On a city or cultural tour, the extent of the tourists' involvement with the local culture may only be experiencing the local customs, cuisine, dance and rituals whilst staying as a visitor in a hotel. On the other hand, tourists on a long conservation holiday – in the tropical rainforest, perhaps – will become much more involved in the daily life and work of the local population.

A special interest in heritage – the physical remains of the past – is the focus of many people's holidays. They are interested in seeing surviving religious buildings, monuments, shrines, burial grounds, castles, stately homes – even whole towns and cities, such as York or Venice. In addition, towns throughout the world have collected together historical evidence and artefacts, and put them on display in museums for tourists to see. In many of the bigger centres, such as Florence and London (British Museum) these museums themselves are major tourist attractions.

Activities and facilities

Many special interest holidays are dependent on certain activities and facilities being provided. The activities often revolve around the skills and knowledge of the local people, and the facilities depend on the availability of certain equipment. In mountainous areas, for example, the existence of suitable slopes and adequate snow is not enough to generate a skiing industry – there must also be ski lifts, equipment hire, food outlets, instruction, first aid provision, etc.

activity

ACTIVITIES AND FACILITIES

Analyse and compare the activities and facilities you would expect on the following types of special interest holiday: wedding in the Caribbean; trekking in the Himalayas; flying over the Grand Canyon; safari in Kenya; surfing in Newquay; whale watching in Alaska.

Simon Atkinson

Head of tourism in La Rosière, France

Can you give me a brief introduction about yourself and your roles?

I'm 38, and I live in a small village in the Savoie region of the French Alps. In winter I run the ski school at La Rosière (I'm Deputy Director) and in summer I run the 9-hole golf course on the same slopes (I'm the Director). I'm also a DJ for RFM Radio La Rosière, and Vice-President of the Tourist Office.

I'm originally from West Yorkshire. I went to South Craven Comprehensive in Keighley and passed nine O levels and four A levels. Then I trained as an estimator in the printing industry, working in Keighley for 4 years, before deciding to come to live in France in 1989.

During the first two winter seasons, I worked for Ski Olympic in La Rosière and passed my British Association of Ski Instructors (BASI 3) and Artificial Ski Slope Instructors (ASSI) licences. In France, this didn't suffice to teach legally, so for 3 years I trained for the Brévet d'Etat d'Educateur Sportif, and began work with the ski school – the Ecole du Ski Français (ESF), including teaching English to French instructors (and examining them). As the ESF is an association, each instructor is self-employed and has a vote. Over the years I became a committee member – and eventually Deputy Director.

Can you tell me about the resort of La Rosière?

La Rosière is a medium-sized resort, situated at an altitude of 1850 metres, just 8 km from the Italian border on the Petit St. Bernard Pass. Most of the resort faces south, and it has one of the best snow records in France. The permanent population of about 300 rises to approximately 10,000 during the winter holidays, mainly accommodated in apartments and chalets – there are only four hotels.

What type of special interest holidays do you provide at the resort?

The holidays in La Rosière can be broken down into two categories – winter and summer. In winter, of course, skiing is the biggest activity – skiing including all types of equipment, snowboard, telemark, etc. However, over the last few years the number of hours per person on the slopes has diminished, and other activities such as snowshoe walks, cultural walks, and dog-sled rides have become popular.

In summer, there's mountain biking, pony trekking, rafting, tennis, golf, archery, mountain walks, climbing and mountaineering.

The winter season runs from mid-December to the end of April. The summer season is really only July and August, but with the road over the Petit St. Bernard Pass opening from June to October there are other tourists who stop in the resort overnight. (This area is very popular with motorcyclists.)

What type of visitors do you attract?

The visitors are mainly families, with the parents aged 35 to 50. This is due to the relatively easy, well-groomed slopes and the good facilities for the younger children. In winter, about 70% of the visitors are French, followed by the British, Belgian, Danish, German, Czech and Dutch visitors – in that order. In summer, almost all the visitors are French, due to the fact that tour companies don't offer summer holidays in La Rosière.

Why do you think La Rosière has become so popular?

The excellent snow record and good sunshine hours have always made it ideal for winter sports and activities. Until recently, however, the marketing for the resort wasn't really done on a professional basis. Most of the holidays, including those from abroad, were repeat business or through personal recommendation. This has had the advantage that the resort hasn't grown too fast, and its evolution has been controlled more easily.

More recently, however, with better marketing and advertising – coinciding with La Rosière being the type of resort people want today – the resort is becoming very popular. In the 2004/5 winter season, for example, we saw a growth of around 9%, whereas all the resorts around (Les Arcs, Val D'Isère, Tignes, La Plagne) had a decrease in numbers.

La Rosière is, in effect, a generation behind the bigger resorts. It still manages to retain its charm as a village, with many of the people who work in the resort actually living here. The tourists therefore find the same people here each year, and feel more at home. The role for all the people in the resort is to try and keep this 'welcome' without becoming too commercial.

How do you see the future of La Rosière?

In the winter there is already a tendency for people to spend less time on the slopes and more time on other mountain activities, as explained earlier.

Global warming may have an effect on tourism in Alpine resorts in general – especially resorts below 1800m. Other activities must be found, developing snowshoes, cultural walks, etc.

For the summer, La Rosière isn't ideally placed. It is a little too high, and so the weather plays an important role – it can snow even in July and August at 2000m. Our potential for the summer is relatively limited, but we will continue to offer our different activities, together with some newer ones.

In the last topic we looked at the features that are significant for special interest holidays and in this topic we go on to look at the providers of these types of holiday. By now, you will probably have collected a number of examples of providers of special interest holidays. In this topic we encourage you to classify these holiday providers, as follows:

- **Mass market and independent tour operators**
- **Specialists in tailor-made holidays**
- **Specialists in one destination, or market segment**
- **Transport principals.**

Clear identification of the type of provider, with examples, will improve your assessment grade.

Mass market and independent tour operators

Mass market tour operators have built their reputation on providing value for money holidays for the masses. So the specialist holidays that they will be interested in organising are those that will be bought by a large number of people – the larger niche markets. Can you guess what these might be?

Although the 'sun holiday' still dominates the market, this is changing as people's tastes shift – as we will see in the last two topics of this unit. Wedding and honeymoon packages and city centre tours have long been provided by holiday companies, but as the tourist market expands so the niche markets they provide for have increased too.

To see how they cater for this market, we will investigate some of the major tour operators and look at the type of special interest holidays they provide.

The only specialist area that First Choice particularly target is skiing. They aim to target those people who are first-time skiers – or perhaps just want everything organised for them. 'Ski and Snowboard Packs' are provided to make sure everything is ready on the guest's arrival in a resort, including lift pass, tuition and equipment hire. The main destinations are Andorra, Austria, Bulgaria, France, Italy Switzerland, but they also run trips to Canada and USA. First Choice also have a range of 'premier' holidays in four-star and five-star

hotels around the world – ideal locations for the honeymooners or golfers seeking a little luxury. Recognising the expansion of the health and fitness sector, some of the hotels are spa and Thalassotherapy centres. As part of the First Choice Group, 2wentys claim to offer some the best clubbing locations around the world for dance enthusiasts.

My Travel provides skiing holidays to France, Austria, Italy and Andorra. Like the other operators, they focus on the family, offering free child places as an incentive to book. They also have a well established cruise market, offering a vast array of destinations in the Canaries, Africa, Mediterranean, Caribbean, USA and Baltic fjords. As part of the My Travel Group, Bridge Travel provide tailor-made holidays and city breaks to many cultural locations such as Paris, Rome and Bruges, and offer river cruising. My Travel's range includes

Brazil, Caribbean, Barbados, Cuba, Dominican Republic, Jamaica – countries which have always been popular for honeymoons and weddings, but also facilitate diving holidays and golf trips. Descriptions of resorts in My Travel's brochures nearly always include a reference to their potential for a special interest holiday. In Cuba for example, Havana is described as 'steeped in history' with its Old Town a 'World Heritage Site'. Jibacoa has a 'coral reef excellent for snorkelling' and Varadero has 'a new golf course'.

Thomas Cook also provides ski holidays, but a large

market for them is cruises. They offer trips around the world and in particular to the traditional cruise areas of the Mediterranean, Florida and the Maldives. Active holidays and snow holidays are also catered for, with holidays such as mountain biking, dinghy sailing and windsurfing in Greece and some of the world's best diving in the Red Sea.

An example of a company that has created its reputation on catering for niche markets is Kuoni. They are clearly a major operator in the specialist holiday market, catering for a variety of special interests. They offer escorted tours on every continent, cruises, golf holidays, train journeys, diving holidays, safaris, weddings and honeymoons. In addition, Kuoni Sport Abroad is their specialist sports division offering a wide selection of holiday ideas fitted around sports. They also organise high quality supporters tours to selected major sporting events for cricket, rugby, motorsport and golf.

A Kuoni specialist holiday brochure

Independent tour operators are those that are smaller and act independently of the four main operators – TUI, Thomas Cook, My Travel and First Choice Holidays.

Specialists in tailor-made holidays

Tailor-made holidays are those that are designed to fit the needs of one person or group of people travelling together. This means that everything from leaving their home to returning is designed around their pre-selected needs – departure date and time, modes of transport, which airports, stations, etc., all destinations, duration of the trip, accommodation, and perhaps activities – and not forgetting the price.

Tailor-made holidays do not have to be luxury trips. More and more people are choosing to buy tailor-made holidays, due to their time constraints or personal circumstances. The extract below shows how Travelbag, one of the leading tailor-made specialists, presents itself.

Travelbag – travel created for you

We just don't sell holidays we plan them. Travelbag has always been about choice. About letting the traveller, rather than the travel agent, make the decisions about where to go and what to see.

Unlike other companies, we have Specialist Travel Consultants who specialise on specific destinations – this means that you get the facts about your chosen destination from someone who's actually been there. And because Travelbag is an independent travel company, the information and advice you receive from us is unbiased. So you receive the holiday most appropriate to your requirements without any bias towards a particular operator or airline.

Our Specialist Travel Consultants are there to assist you with your travel requirements from the start of your enquiries, until your departure. Our one-to-one service is tailored to the requirements of our customers, so you choose the order of destinations within your travel itinerary.

You know that you'll get value for money with Travelbag because we deal directly with our customers, cutting out the 'middle man' and lowering the cost of your holiday.

Source: www.travelbag.co.uk

activity

PROVIDERS OF A TAILOR-MADE HOLIDAY

Investigate at least three travel organisations that could provide a tailor-made trip for the following groups of people:

1 Amy and Gill, who are relatively fit and in their mid 40s, want to visit all the famous landmarks in Europe.

2 Mira and Jake, young American students, would like to experience a tour of the Far East, including China.

3 The Burne family with two teenage children are planning a once in a lifetime trip to Australia and want to learn how to scuba dive.

Specialists in one destination, or one market segment

Some very specialised companies focus on just one destination – Alaska, for example, or on just one market segment – bird watching, for example. Indeed, some companies only cater for one market segment in one destination. Frontier Travel, for example, only offers holidays based on animal watching in Canada – bears, whales, seals, birds and polar bears. (For more information visit www.frontiertravel.co.uk.)

There are many examples of companies that only sell holidays to one destination, promoting them across all areas of interest, as shown below.

Single destination tour operators

VFB Holidays Ltd is a well-established, and highly regarded French specialist tour operator offering city breaks to Paris, Lille, Bruges and Brussels, often including entrance to an exhibition or music festival. They also specialise in gastronomic tours, from river cruising to great value breaks in romantic chateau hotels.

Norwegian Coastal Voyage Limited employ a team of experienced personnel, who have travelled extensively in Norway and therefore have detailed local knowledge. The London office also has an extensive programme of holidays throughout Scandinavia, including city breaks, fly drives and skiing.

African Safari Air Holidays is one of the leading African tour operators. Established in 1993, its headquarters are in Kenya and it has a representative branch in the United Kingdom. Singles, couples, families, friends, or groups of people from all over the world are able to book holidays directly in Kenya, Zanzibar, Tanzania and other African countries, including flights and hotel bookings. The company provides three types of holiday in Africa:

1) Beach holidays – relaxing on the tropical beaches along the Indian Ocean.

2) Safari holidays – travelling in forests, parks and game reserves viewing the wildlife and landscapes.

3) Activity holidays – mountain climbing, leisure walks, hot air balloons, ocean diving, sport fishing, etc.

There are a number of companies that focus on one market segment. Ski holidays and cruises, as we have already seen, are market segments that are covered well by the mass-market operators as well as the smaller specialists. Providers for other less popular special interest activities often operate within the country of origin. For example, providers of flamenco dancing classes in Spain may be the same companies that provide dancing for the locals too.

Other market segments include those that target certain age groups. Saga Holidays, for example, who target the over 50s in the general tourist market, also provide special interest holidays that would interest this market, such as gardening and bridge holidays. Another example, at the younger end of the spectrum, is BUNAC, a company that targets young people to work in America (see case study below).

Summer Camp USA

"I knew I would love camp life and that I would have lots of fun but I had no idea how much I'd enjoy working with kids."

If you've got good, recent experience of working with children, this is your opportunity to enjoy the most amazing, fulfilling and challenging summer of a lifetime! Choose the best value camp counselling programme around! Pay the lowest upfront costs – it's just £67 to register with BUNAC. Bring home a salary of $820 or, if you're over 21, $880 minimum – that's more than any other camp counselling organisation can offer you.

Open to students and non-students aged between 18 and 35 who are available for at least nine weeks from May/June to mid-August. After camp, take to the road and visit all those places you've ever wanted to visit. Not just in the USA, but in Canada and Mexico as well.

The Summer Camp USA flight package isn't just a return flight ticket to America. It also includes:

- Your first night's accommodation in the US
- BUNAC support services in the UK and USA
- Informative orientation talk
- BUNAC reps at the airport on arrival and departure
- Moneywise Guide to North America
- T-shirt
- Phone card.

Source: www.bunac.org Courtesy of BUNAC

Read the case study on Summer Camp USA and discuss with a friend the advantages and disadvantages of the experience. Also discuss the places you would like to visit after the nine weeks is finished – you could draw your route on a map.

Transport principals

The Orient Express

Transport principals cover all forms of transport: airlines, rail companies, car and coach companies, ferry and cruise operators.

Unlike package holiday tourists, who never need to have any contact with the transport provider, independent travellers need to deal with various transport principals when arranging their flights, trains, buses, etc.

Airlines

The more remote the special interest destination, the less choice of transport operator. For example, a trip on a South African safari may start with a choice of airlines flying to Johannesburg, but then the traveller would have to take a local operator's flight to a smaller airport, such as Kruger Mpumalanga / Hoedspruit, before being taken by bus or taxi to their lodge.

Rail companies

As we have seen in the previous topic, some train operators operate across whole continents – not just countries. One of the best examples of this is the Orient Express. This company is world renowned for its luxurious train journeys across vast areas, appealing to people who enjoy travelling by train. But there is also a vast network of national rail lines in each country that interlink to provide transport for the traveller.

Car and coach companies

Road is still the most common means of transport and, for the most remote areas of the world, the only form of access. International car hire companies, such as Hertz and Avis, have hundreds of outlets and thousands of available cars, all over the world. The Greyhound bus line is the largest North American intercity bus company, with 16000 daily bus departures to 3100 destinations providing access to the United States, Canada and Mexico.

Ferry and cruise companies

Cruise companies such as Cunard, P&O and Swan Hellenic sell direct to the public as well as via other travel operators. Some operators focus on one region. Fred Olsen, for example, covers cruises around Scandinavia, and Royal Caribbean focuses on the Caribbean and South America. Ferry companies are relatively small in comparison to the international cruise companies, tending to concentrate on a few routes between specific countries.

Investigate one transport company from each of the sectors – airlines, rail, car and coach, ferry and cruise. On a map, identify the routes they service. If this is done as a group activity, each member could investigate a different organisation, and present their findings to the rest of the group.

In this topic we will first look at producing an itinerary, under the following headings:

> Who the itinerary is prepared for
>
> Dates
>
> Timing
>
> What is included, such as activities, excursions, and accommodation
>
> ▪ Contact details
>
> ▪ Other attractions
>
> ▪ Format and presentation.

In the second part of this topic we will go on to look at producing itineraries that meet the needs and circumstances of a variety of groups. These will include:

> ▪ Basic needs, such as education, leisure, sports, religious and relaxation.
>
> ▪ More complex needs, such as special travel arrangements, special facilities and services, alternative activities for different members of a group, standards, quality and exclusivity.

Who the itinerary is prepared for

An itinerary is a plan or schedule for a tourist or group of tourists to follow. The itinerary will vary according to a number of factors, but the type of customer and their special interest will dominate.

Planning an itinerary for an individual may be a lot easier than for a large group of people with assorted needs. A large ski party made up of a range of ages and skiing abilities will need an itinerary and destination that caters for them all. The destination may need access to appropriate slopes for the younger and more senior members of the group. An itinerary for an individual skier, on the other hand, will only need to consider their needs and their level of ability.

Dates

The seasons, with their different weather conditions, can have a big impact on the dates of a special interest holiday. For example, it is no good booking a deep-sea diving holiday to see the tropical fish on the

Great Barrier Reef during the rain and storm season in January, because the waters are too cloudy and visibility non-existent. Similarly, people would not want their ideal wedding to be in the hurricane season, or would choose to tour the English gardens in the winter.

For some special interest holidays, dates are less significant. For example, bridge and dancing holidays are available all year round, so too are trips to cities of heritage and culture, such as Prague or Florence.

Timing

It is vital to allow tourists ample time to pursue their special interest. For large groups, meeting times and the time allocated to certain activities is especially important. Waiting for one person before the rest can start can cause the organiser a real headache and also cause a lot of frustration amongst other guests. Everything from eating times to length of time doing the special interest needs to carefully calculated so that everything runs smoothly.

Activities, excursions and accommodation

Although the special interest may take up the predominant amount of time, often guests like to enjoy other activities during the course of each day. These may feature around meal times, such as a show by local dancers and musicians providing evening entertainment, or as additional daily excursions available during the trip. The activities, excursions and accommodation add to the holiday, as shown in the case study below on the itinerary for a diving holiday to the Red Sea.

Contact details

When arranging a trip, the first contact is likely to be a travel agent, although as more and more people are booking independently this could be a contact with the tour operator or transport company via the internet or telephone. Beyond the first contact others are likely to be with accommodation and transport providers.

Travel insurance is now a vital part of holidays, especially for the more adventurous, so an insurance contact is important. Other contacts may be for additional services such as car parking at the airport.

The more remote the trip and more independent the traveller then the more contact details become important, especially if the individual is covering rough terrain where reception for radio and telephones may be weak. A desert trek or walking holiday with only one guide will also require contact details, in case anything should happen to the guide. The more organised the trip, the more people involved, then it may be likely that only a few people in the group have all the contact details, but even then it is always worth ensuring everyone knows how to get help if it is needed.

Diving in the Red Sea

Situated on the Al Pasha Coast on the tip of the Sinai in a spectacular setting. Ideal for non-diving partners.

Location Just 15 minutes from the airport, the hotel is convenient for the resort centre and the main tourist attractions.

Facilities 24-hour reception, five restaurants, entertainment outlets, a fitness centre, health spa, massage, internet area, tennis, large swimming pool and hotel-operated watersports.

Activities For all of our diving we use the Aquarius Diving Club, based in the Sheraton Hotel. The dive centre has a swimming pool for skills sessions, a small shop, classroom facilities and a snack bar nearby.

After breakfast, which will be served in your hotel, you will be transported to the dive centre or boat. Certified divers will go straight from their hotel to the dive boat and enjoy one dive in the morning, and then lunch followed by another dive at a different site in the afternoon.

The dive boat accommodates up to 25 people and has a sundeck, saloon, shaded area and toilet. Non-certified divers must first complete their PADI Open Water course.

The Red Sea is ideal for snorkelling enthusiasts, since much of the underwater life exists in the first 10 metres. If members of your party do not wish to dive, they are welcome to join the dive boat and snorkel for a small daily charge.

Other activities (all bookable locally) Cairo and Luxor excursions; Camel safaris; Trip to Mount Sinai and St Catherine's Monastery; Quad biking; Trip to Coloured Canyon.

Source: www.thomascook.com

Itinerary for: **Mr B. Lunn and family**   **August 2005**

Tues 02	**0710** hrs	Depart Manchester	Flight KL1072
	0935 hrs	Arrive Amsterdam	Proceed for your flight to Cape Town
	1120 hrs	Depart Amsterdam	Flight KL597
	2255 hrs	Arrive Cape Town	

Upon arrival into the airport, you will be met and transferred to the Table Mountain Hotel, where you will stay for the following three nights – bed and breakfast basis.

Table Mountain Hotel is a gracious homestead nestled on the slopes of Signal Hill, offering breathtaking views of Table Mountain. All eight en-suite guest rooms are individually decorated, offering tea/coffee tray, satellite TV and direct-dial telephone. Relax and enjoy the views of Table Mountain on the terrace area by the swimming pool or enjoy a drink in the bar.

Wed 03	**0930** hrs	Europcar will deliver a Group 'O' hire car to the hotel for your use.

At leisure to explore Cape Town and the surrounding area. You might wish to take the 90-mile round trip scenic drive around the Cape Peninsula, to see Cape Point, where the Indian and Atlantic oceans meet. Stop at Boulders Beach, Simonstown to see the resident colony of jackass penguins, and the Kirstenbosch Botanical Gardens on the outskirts of Cape Town are also worth visiting. A full day touring the winelands should also be considered.

Fri 05		Return your hire car to the Europcar desk in time for your flight to Kruger International Airport.	
	0640 hrs	Depart Cape Town	Flight CE701
	0840 hrs	Arrive Johannesburg	Proceed for your flight to Hoedspruit
	1135 hrs	Depart Johannesburg	Flight SA1221
	1245 hrs	Arrive Hoedspruit	

Upon arrival into the airport you will be met and transferred to the Gomo Private Game Reserve, where you will stay for the following three nights on a full-board basis, including game viewing.

Accommodating a maximum of fourteen guests in five comfortable chalets and three East African style tents, all with private en-suite facilities, it overlooks the Laralumi River, where a variety of animals frequently come to drink.

Your private safari allows access to over 10,000 hectares of the finest big game country in the Timbavati Reserve, bordering the Kruger National Park, with lion, leopard, elephant and buffalo thriving alongside giraffe, zebra and a variety of antelope. Bird watching is wonderful, with various eagles, owls, francolins, kingfishers, rollers and weavers among the over 300 recorded species. Game drives are conducted by experienced rangers and Shangaan trackers in open 4X4 vehicles, with excellent photographic opportunities.

Guided bush walks provide an insight into nature's finer details and the chance to track game on foot.

Mon 08		The Gomo will transfer you back to the airport, where you will fly back to Johannesburg and on to Manchester	
	1240 hrs	Depart Hoedspruit	Flight SA592
	1450 hrs	Arrive Johannesburg	Proceed to International Departures for your flight to Amsterdam.

The facilities of the Rennies Premier Club Lounge are available with our compliments, whilst waiting for the departure of your flight.

	1940 hrs	Depart Johannesburg	Flight KL592

Tues 09	**0630** hrs	Arrive Amsterdam	Proceed for your flight to Manchester
	0830 hrs	Depart Amsterdam	Flight KL1081
	0850 hrs	Arrive Manchester	

Cost:	£1,520 per person sharing £1,725 per single room
Includes:	a) Flights as indicated, in economy class unless otherwise advised, including associated pre-payable taxes; b) Accommodation on a bed-and-breakfast basis unless otherwise indicated; c) Transfers as shown; d) Hire of a Europcar Group 'O' car (usually a Mercedes C180 automatic with air conditioning or similar); length of hire as indicated in the itinerary.

Additional information

Summer is generally hot and rainy with temperatures from about 15–30 °C. Winter is mostly warm and dry (5–23 °C) with sunny days and cold nights. In higher regions it may be colder than the averages shown.

Contact details

South African Adventures (Elise Shaw, Travel Consultant) Buckingham Street London SW1R 0RE Tel 020 8712 3255	Table Mountain Hotel Bloomsbury Road Signal Hill Cape Town South Africa Tel 72 83 90009	Gomo Private Game Reserve Hoedspruit Soshan South Africa Tel 09 76 88855	Europcar, Cape Town Tel 82 33 96669

Other attractions

Other attractions may be a bonus to a trip, but may add to the enjoyment and particularly to the individual's concept of value for money. This may be anything from local entertainment during mealtimes, to free access to facilities within the resort, such as fitness and spa facilities, etc.

Format and presentation of itineraries

Now that you have considered all the factors that contribute to an itinerary, you have to present your itinerary. An example is provided left. The customer must be able to clearly see what they are going to be doing, when they are going to be doing it, what they have paid for and what they have not. You also need to consider giving the customer guidance on things like check-in times at airports, transfer arrangements, etc.

activity

PLAN AN ITINERARY

Now it is your turn. Plan an itinerary for a special interest holiday of your choice. (Refer back to the start of Topic 1 if you need reminding of the different types of holiday.) Create your own itinerary, with all the relevant information.

Basic needs

People choose a special interest holiday for various reasons. But all hope that, in addition to being a holiday, it will meet their particular needs – educational, sporting or religious needs, for example. We will now go on to look at the implications for the itinerary of these 'basic needs' – the things that make special interest holidays 'special':

- Education
- Leisure
- Sports
- Religious
- Relaxation.

Education

Educational special interest holidays mostly target the younger end of the market – those in education, aged 10–21. These holidays are usually conducted under the supervision of staff – not parents. They have to be well organised and well planned with a detailed itinerary to ensure that students, staff and parents know what is to be expected before the holiday.

Often the holiday is based on part of the educational syllabus, such as French students going to France, or even Travel and Tourism students visiting New York

Pond dipping on an organised educational visit

(see overleaf). The itinerary must then fit the needs of the students' learning requirements and this will become the focus of the holiday. Additional activities will also be planned, particularly evening activities to keep the students occupied.

Other types of educational holiday include someone taking a special interest holiday to learn a new skill such as dancing, painting or cooking and these types of holidays also are well structured and focused on student learning.

Leisure

Leisure holidays include taking a break in a health and fitness centre or spa. Individuals or small groups often take this type of holiday, so the itinerary tends to be more focused on the individual needs. In fact, the itinerary may allow enough flexibility for the individual to choose their leisure pursuit as and when they wish during the holiday, but this will depend on the demand and size of the facility.

Sports

Sports holidays range from golf to skiing, to scuba-diving, sailing, etc. The list in endless, and the itinerary will depend on a number of factors. For example, organising the itinerary for a rugby tour of 40 people to Canada requires a very different itinerary compared to that for a couple of retired golfers going to Spain. Their requirements in terms of food and accommodation, activities and entertainment will be quite different. People on a sports holiday will require information on access to facilities, changing rooms, equipment hire and perhaps coaching services.

KUONI CONVENTION PACKAGE: NEW YORK STUDENT CONVENTION

Travel & Tourism (AS/A2 Level)

This 4-day study tour has been developed by practising teachers and lecturers to provide a simple off-the-shelf package to introduce tourism students to one of the world's leading tourist destinations.

Your Convention Package includes:

- Scheduled flights from London (or Manchester at a supplement) with BA, United or Virgin Atlantic
- 3 nights accommodation in deluxe self-catering apartments in the luxury Hotel Beacon on Broadway at 75th Street
- Lectures and seminars by leading UK and US industry professionals and educators
- An associated programme of 'backstage' and specialist visits
- Resident Convention Manager
- Student Information Booklets

- Discounted entry to many of the city's most famous tourist attractions
- Free places for accompanying staff.

The seminar programme

Every Convention includes a 2–3 hour seminar to enhance the visit and maximise students' educational experience in the city. We look in particular at issues of customer service and marketing, at how the events of 9/11 have impacted on the New York tourist industry and the development plans for Ground Zero. Speakers at our seminars are all leading professionals in their own field and mostly native New Yorkers.

Seminar venues

For groups of less than 100, the seminar is normally held in the Hotel Beacon's Seminar Room. For larger groups we have used very prestigious venues, such as the magnificent Theatre at Madison Square Gardens.

Hotel Beacon

Students will be accommodated in 1-bedroom suites with two double beds plus a convertible double bed-settee in the lounge. Being the tallest building in the area, many of the rooms offer fine views across the city.

Bringing New York alive!

Pre-book any of the following optional extras to enhance your visit to the city:

Guided sightseeing tour, Empire State Building, Circle Line boat tour, Radio City music hall, Yankee Stadium, NBC studio tour, Madison Square Gardens, theatre tickets, shopping, evening meals at themed restaurants.

Total package price: £349 (1:20 free place ratio)

Source: www.kuoni.co.uk

Similarly the itinerary may change dramatically in relation to the experience and skill of the tourists. An experienced sailor will require a completely different itinerary to that of a novice, and the latter will certainly need more support in terms of safety advice and emergency contacts, etc.

Religious

Religious special interest holidays can be for large organised groups – for example, a visit to Rome and a meeting with the Pope, or for an individual who wishes to make a personal pilgrimage to a destination such as Lourdes. The itinerary for both types of tourist may be quite different but the main focus of the trip will be the religious aspect.

Relaxation

Relaxation includes special interest holidays such as weddings and honeymoons or where the focus is on calm forms of activity such as meditation and yoga. These types of holiday are generally for individuals, couples or small groups, and focus on calmer activities where ultimately relaxation is the main part of the holiday – even if you are getting married. The itinerary will focus on what the individual or group want to do for the duration of their holiday.

Complex needs

Special travel arrangements

The need for special travel arrangements often arises because someone has special needs themselves. For example, they may be in a wheelchair or partially sighted, in which case the itinerary will have to based around their individual needs. Airports are particularly good at providing for special needs travellers, with wheelchairs and additional staff to assist people's transit.

Special facilities and services

Special facilities and services may include many things, dependent on the type of holiday. People travelling with young children may require access to baby-changing and bottle-warming facilities. Extra time may need to be added into the itinerary for stops on a bus tour for elderly guests, who may need access to toilet facilities on a regular basis.

Alternative activities for different members of a group

Providing activities for different members of a group can sometimes be the biggest headache for tour companies. But some have come to accept that it is necessary to have more than one itinerary. For example, some cities provide a choice of guided tours for the customer (often starting and finishing at the same place) so that different group members can choose the one that best suits their interest. Similarly, many sporting holidays provide a day of activity, such as golf, for one and an array of day trips for their partner. Companies recognise there is a market for this type of holiday. Obviously, the itinerary may have plenty of similarities, such as travel times, accommodation, etc. but the main daytime activities will differ.

Standards, quality, exclusivity

Standards, quality and exclusivity may cover a number of different types of special interest holiday, and there is certainly a growth in designer and exclusive holidays. These types of holiday generally cater for the individual or small group (unless it is a wedding or party for someone very rich) in a glamorous location. The itinerary will reflect the activity and the needs of the people taking the trip.

---

activity

DIFFERENT PEOPLE: ONE ITINERARY?

Design an itinerary that provides for the needs of the following family group:

John is a retired, but active, grandpa. He likes fishing and visiting museums. David (John's son) and his wife, Daphne, enjoy fine wines, good food and an evening at the theatre. Their 4-year-old twins, Jess and Tom, like to be entertained all day – but are good sleepers after 7.00 p.m. The family plans to take a week's holiday together.

What can you suggest? You can select any destination of your choice – at home or abroad – but ensure that you use a variety of resources in your research. Present your itinerary to the rest of the group.

The popularity of different holidays

In this topic we turn our attention to the popularity of different types of special interest holiday, looking at the following aspects:

Finding information

Analysing the information

Interpreting the data

Comparing the popularity

The significance of destinations and their features.

Finding information

Finding information about the types of special interest holidays on offer is easy. There is plenty of information in brochures, on travel programmes, in travel features and on the internet about the variety of holidays available and how to access them. It is more difficult, however, to find information about the

popularity of special interest holidays, but here are some suggestions:

- Staruk.org.uk is a very useful website for researching travel and tourism. It has information on a vast array of special interest holidays and would be a good place to start researching any project.

- Altis.ac.uk is another very useful website for the travel and tourism industry.

- The World Tourism Organisation is also a good source of information on a worldwide scale, and Europa for finding out information on Europe.

- The World Travel & Tourism Council (WTTC) is a membership organisation which undertakes research on specific countries and issues affecting the industry.

- The European Travel Commission's most recent research 'Megatrends of Tourism in Europe to 2005 and beyond, provides some interesting statistics, as shown in the case study (opposite).

- Individual countries have national internet sites,

such as www.visit.Norway.com and they are also useful sources of information.

- MORI is another research organisation that researches into national trends. The MORI 2002 survey conducted on behalf of ABTA, for instance, showed that the main reason Britons choose a holiday is to relax in a sunny environment, but that a growing number of people are buying activity packages and adventure holidays.

- The 2004 Passenger Shipping Association report announced, among other things, that UK passengers on cruises passed the one million mark in 2003.

- The Association of British Travel Agents, ABTA, 2004 report states, among other things, that 'seven nights and under' cruises are growing at 163%.

Analysing the information

'Analysing' means 'separating into parts in order to examine and interpret'.

Good analysis is presenting logical thought in successive sentences. It involves the writing of substantial paragraphs. Writing analytically requires thought and writing to be structured. The following may help:

1 **The point** – What is your point?

There are more people enjoying cruising holidays than ever before.

2 **Because** – Why is this true?

*This is **because** there are more cruising holidays available and their price is coming down.*

3 **Therefore** – Why does this point matter?

*The increasing demand for cruising will lead to a wider target market and **therefore** the appeal may broaden even further.*

Remember that the question 'why?' is vital in analysis, and when you are writing analytically you need to keep asking yourself 'why?'.

Interpreting the data

Interpreting the data often starts by looking for any common themes that the data show. For example, these may be just simply an increase in numbers of participants in a certain special interest holiday. Deeper analysis may require the data to be converted into percentages for ease of interpretation. These may be presented as graphs, tables or diagrams.

Megatrends of Tourism in Europe to 2005 and beyond

1 An ageing population will put more demand on relaxing entertainment facilities (e.g. golf courses) and for singles holidays (e.g. Saga Holidays for over 50s and other escorted tours).

2 There will be an increase in the demand for long-haul and short breaks, such as short cultural city breaks.

3 The increase in health consciousness will extend to more active holidays, as the demand for 'sun holidays' decreases. The demand for 'wellness' in particular spas and fitness centres is evident.

4 As the average level of education increases, so will the demand for holidays which involve the arts, culture and history.

5 Consumers are becoming more sophisticated and hence are looking for alternative ways to spend their money and experience different activities

6 As people's perceptions of their lifestyle change, they will move away from escorted tours and be more independent travellers.

7 There will be increasing specialisation by suppliers in relation to specific hobbies and interests, which will often be combined with holidaymaking.

8 The advances in the internet and other forms of ICT will make 'shopping' for holidays easier, and more people will put together their own packages.

9 As transportation continues to improve, so will access to the remoter parts of the world.

10 Environmental consciousness will continue to rise and so will those holidays linked to conservation and helping the developing world.

Source: www.abta.com

activity

ANALYSING THE MEGATRENDS

From reading the Megatrends findings, analyse the changes in the travel and tourism industry and how these will affect special interest holidays, by asking yourself the following questions:

1 What is the point?

2 Why is this true?

3 Why does it matter?

INTERPRETING THE TOP 20

Kuoni's Top Twenty

	1999	2000	2001	2002	2003	2004 (as at Jan 2004)
Thailand	1	1	1	1	2	1
Maldives	2	2	2	2	1	2
USA	5	3	4	6	5	3
Sri lanka	4	4	3	3	3	4
Egypt	7	5	5	4	4	5
Hong Kong	3	6	6	8	17	10
Dubai	11	7	9	5	6	6
Singapore	6	8	7	10	15	7
Malaysia	9	9	10	9	12	8
Kenya	10	10	8	7	11	11
Indonesia	8	11	11	16	-	-
Barbados	13	12	17	11	7	13
St Lucia	15	13	13	13	13	16
Mauritius	18	14	15	12	8	9
Mexico	14	15	12	15	14	18
Antigua	17	16	18	14	9	14
Australia	16	17	14	17	16	12
Cuba	12	18	20	19	10	17
China	19	19	19	20	-	-
India	20	20	16	-	20	15
Jamaica	-	-	-	18	18	20
South Africa	-	-	-	-	19	-
New Zealand	-	-	-	-	-	19

Source: Kuoni

Examine the data in the Top 20 holiday destinations table, and answer the following questions:

1 Explain the changes to the Top 5 from 1999 to 2004.

2 Why has Cuba gone from 12th to 17th and Australia from 16th to 12th in the rankings?

3 Why has Hong Kong gone from 3rd to 10th and Mauritius from 18th to 9th?

4 How could you have presented the information separately?

5 How do these trends effect special interest holidays?

Comparing the popularity

Comparisons may be made within the data or with data that has been collected in a different place or time. For example, the comparisons in rankings of countries over time as shown in the table above may be compared to another company's research on the popularity of their long-haul holiday destinations.

It may even be possible to compare the data with completely different data. For example, the Top 20 long-haul destinations could be compared with data showing the Top 20 short-haul destinations.

Obviously, the more dissimilar the data, the harder it will be to directly compare it. For example, the data will be probably be incompatible if it is recorded over different time periods.

The popularity of the more common types of special interest holiday is sometimes measured nationally. For example, a national newspaper or magazine such as *Holiday Which* may decide to survey the popularity of ski resorts and then publish the results in print. The case study below, for example, shows how *Holiday Which* has given a star rating to places it recommends to see on the Somme.

The Somme

If you have the time, or emotional strength, for only one battleground, the Somme is the best choice. It's easily accessible from Lille or Amiens, and a well-marked driving route, the Tour of Remembrance, links the main sights, all of which resonate with memories of lost men.

A good starting point is Peronne's excellent museum, the **Historical of the Great War****. Its informative, balanced approach displays period newspapers, weapons and soldiers' personal effects on three levels, representing Britain, France and Germany.

From here the tour passes through copses and cornfields to spots like **Delville Wood***, valiantly fought over by South African troops in July 1916, and now a verdant museum-memorial.

To the north, the most poignant monuments bring home the enormity of the events of 1 July 1916. On that single day, the British army suffered its worst ever casualty figures – 60,000 dead, wounded or missing. And all for a few yards of gained ground. Many men were never found: over 72,000 names are inscribed on the walls of Lutyen's memorial arch at **Thiepval****, a monolith that dominates the undulating landscape.

Just as heart-wrenching is the Canadian memorial park at **Beaumont-Hamel*****, where the Newfoundland Regiment lost 90% of its men in the first attack on 1 July. An eerie walking tour through the trenches and no man's land passes grassed-over shell holes and rusty poles that once supported barbed wire.

Unlovely **Albert*** has a good museum with old photos, war memorabilia, and realistic tableaux. Guided battlefield tours start at the station, which is useful if you are arriving by train.

Source: Holiday Which (Autumn 2002) comparison of things to see at the Somme

DESIGN A RATING SYSTEM

Read the report on the Somme. Select an area (preferably with historical or cultural appeal) that you are familiar with and design a rating system to judge the appeal of at least five places of interest within it. Explain your rating system and describe the main features of each place of interest. You may choose to focus this activity on your own town or region or any other area you are familiar with. Present your work to the rest of the group. Do they agree with your rating system and comments?

Comparing data can be difficult for some special interest holidays, such as ecological trips or those involving watching nature on safari as there are only small groups of people involved, and data may be limited.

The significance of destinations and their features

The significance of destinations and their features is important in establishing the popularity of a special interest holiday. For example, Bondi Beach has always had a reputation as one of the world's top surfing resorts, the African savannah for its animals, the Himalaya for their magnificent scenery – the list is endless. There are many places around the world that have become significant places to visit often because of the features of the resort. The features may be natural or man-made, but the features tend to give the holiday significance. For example, there is little point in deep-sea diving somewhere if there is nothing to see there.

The significance of a special interest holiday may change over time. For example, at the moment there is a growth in holiday weddings and honeymoons and cruising. Another growth area is for the more exclusive holidays as people recommend the experience to their friends. In fact, 'designer holidays' are a growth market, as the article below shows.

Trends: Designer and luxury holidays

People are continuing to spend money on top-end holidays and every week new luxury and boutique hotels – often now design-led and eco-friendly – are opening up. Bookings worth £2,500 or above for two people are considered to be in the luxury range. All these clients, whether they have time and money on their hands, or those who are increasingly cash-rich but time-poor, want both value for money and excellent service.

One of the top reasons clients buy luxury holidays is for a special occasion – whether that's a wedding, honeymoon, anniversary or landmark birthday.

Beaches for relaxation are the number one request for luxury seekers, but often clients are looking for something more exciting for secondary breaks. Big sporting events have become popular, along with luxury skiing, diving, sailing, golf and spa breaks. But increasingly 'experiential' holidays that are aspirational, exclusive and unknown are being sought.

The biggest growth area for luxury holidays is in the Indian Ocean with the Seychelles, Maldives and Mauritius all known for their increasingly good range in accommodation and dreamlike locations. Dubai's investment in luxury hotels has developed a new market, while the Caribbean, particularly Barbados and the smaller islands like the Grenadines and British Virgin Islands have always traditionally appealed to an elite market. Closer to home, designer hotels in our favourite destinations such as Mallorca and the Canaries are also becoming popular with the discerning pleasure seeker.

Trends was compiled by Frances Tuke of the ABTA Corporate Affairs Department, December 2004 © ABTA Ltd

In the final topic of this unit you will learn about the factors that have influenced the popularity and appeal of special interest holidays, and gain an understanding of why some are more popular that others. The factors are arranged under the following headings:

- Life–work changes
- Accessibility
- Availability of attractions and other tourist facilities
- Changing attitudes
- Increased awareness of cultural, environmental and health issues
- Increased health, wealth and fitness of retirees
- Increased interest in national sports, education and adventure
- Changing holiday patterns – increased demand for short breaks.

Life–work changes

The life–work balance has changed quite a lot for people over the last twenty or thirty years. People tend to work fewer hours a week, and have more days holiday. This has meant that many people now take more than one holiday a year (see chart). For example, a winter skiing holiday and a summer activity holiday, together with perhaps a weekend break to a cultural city is now a realistic annual total for lots of people – not only the rich and famous. All of these are examples of the types of special interest holidays that people could choose.

The nature of employment has also changed, with fewer people working for life for one company. Redundancies – through firm closure, 'restructuring' or relocation – have meant that people now have a less rigid life–work balance. In between jobs, they may have the opportunity to travel and perhaps experience something different, such as a working holiday or joining a conservation project for a couple of months. Breaks in employment have meant that these types of holiday are available to more people.

In addition, the working patterns have changed. Working from home has now become a reality for many, and employers have to consider this as an option, under the legal regulations on flexible working, if any employee requests it. So the rigid pattern of a five-day week has been altered with many people working more flexi-time or enjoying a four-day week. This means that the odd long week-end break is feasible too, without missing out on

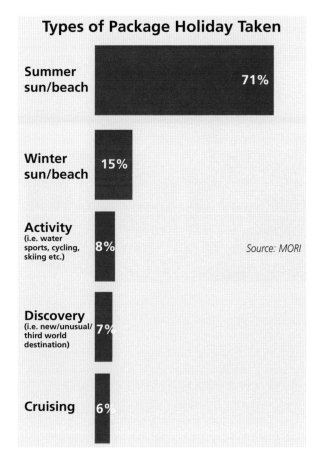

Types of Package Holiday Taken

Type	Percentage
Summer sun/beach	71%
Winter sun/beach	15%
Activity (i.e. water sports, cycling, skiing etc.)	8%
Discovery (i.e. new/unusual/ third world destination)	7%
Cruising	6%

Source: MORI

... And more often

1990	2000	2020
Main Holiday	Main Holiday	Main Holiday
Second Holiday	Second Holiday	Second Holiday
	Third Holiday	Third Holiday
		Fourth Holiday

work commitments. This again provides people with the opportunity to enjoy a cultural weekend in Prague or Barcelona, perhaps.

According to the European Travel Commission document Megatrends of Tourism in Europe to 2005 and Beyond 'modern society exerts increasing pressure on people's daily lives and stimulates the wish for more leisure time and relaxation'. The phrase 'money-rich, time-poor' is often applied to today's society. People are looking for quick ways to get away from the pressure of their lives, and hence the growth in short cultural breaks and visits to spa and fitness centres. The document also states that as the demand for sun-holidays decreases in line with people's growing fear of sun cancer, so active or activity holidays will increase – and the special interest sector will develop too.

activity

HOW THINGS HAVE CHANGED

There has been a growth in cultural breaks and visits to spa centres and fitness centres. Explain these trends in relation to life–work changes.

Accessibility

As access has improved, more people are travelling than ever before. High-speed trains and, in particular, low-cost air carriers have reduced accessibility problems throughout the world. One of the big growth areas in the special interest sector brought about by increased accessibility is city breaks – whether for historical, cultural or stag party reasons – as shown below.

City breaks

According to Ian Mounser, Sales Director at Superbreak Mini Holidays:

'As soon as clients have been to Paris, Amsterdam and Dublin, they look for alternatives, and while mid-haul is generally more expensive for flights it's often cheaper for accommodation and food and drink. With Paris, Amsterdam and Rome now firmly ticked off many people's wish-lists, holidaymakers are starting to put in the extra mile to land somewhere more exotic. Just two more airborne hours could have visitors swapping Madrid for Marrakesh, Rome for Riga or Innsbruck for Istanbul.'

Since the removal of the Iron Curtain the countries of Eastern Europe have become politically more accessible and have seen a huge increase in visitors as a result. This increase in popularity has more recently been fuelled by the growing number of cheap air flights to destinations like St Petersburg. In north Africa, destinations like Cairo have grown in appeal

Two distant but accessible special interest destinations

St Petersburg – 3 hours 45 mins

Cairo – 4 hours, 30 mins

Why go? Russia's old capital is an easily negotiable warren of squares, cobbled side streets and wide promenades, lined with spectacular baroque-style architecture. Then throw in some of the best ballet in the world, beef stroganov and cheap vodka. A winter wonderland during the miserable months, visitors can skate on Lake Neva and then escape the sub-zero temperatures (as low as –20°C) in one of the city's fabulous museums. In the summer, the gold-topped roofs glimmer in the sun and clients can take the hydrofoil to the Peterhof Palace and Gardens.

What not to miss? The Hermitage Museum, the Mariinsky Theatre – home to Russian ballet, the dome-topped St Isaac's Cathedral and the Pushkin Museum of Fine Arts.

Why go? There aren't many cities within four and a half hours' flying time of Heathrow where you can be totally immersed in a different climate, landscape and culture. Home to the only surviving wonder of the world, the Pyramids – voted one of the must-see attractions of a lifetime – history is the obvious attraction in the Egyptian capital, but there's also a relaxed café culture and many souks. The Nile is a focal point for day trips or for longer journeys to Aswan. Those who crave luxury can swim, play golf or drink cocktails overlooking the Pyramids.

What not to miss? The Pyramids, the Egyptian Museum, a cruise down the Nile and Cairo's café culture.

Source: Travel Weekly magazine

not only because of the shorter travelling times but also because of people's desire to experience something a little different.

activity

COMPARING ACCESSIBILITY

Select two special interest destinations, and compare their accessibility in terms of road, rail, sea and air transport.

Availability of attractions and other tourist facilities

The availability of attractions and other tourist facilities generally increases as the number of tourists increases. Many destinations which were originally developed to meet one area of special interest appeal, have since expanded to become resorts for other areas of special interest or other tourist activities. For

example, ski resorts that were been built for the sole purpose of providing quick and easy access to the slopes in the winter have become a paradise for walking, trekking and climbing enthusiasts in the summer. This year-long tourist season allows for the development of yet more attractions, drawing in yet more tourists and more facilities. Obviously there may be a greater choice of accommodation and restaurants but other tourist facilities also become viable, such as museums, theatres and galleries.

Special interest holidaymakers may choose a destination because, apart from providing for their special interest it has other attractions too. Certainly, if there is more than one person in the group, each with different interests, the availability of other attractions is even more significant. For example, a famous championship golf course may attract the keen golfers, but not as many perhaps as the golf course along the coast which has more attractions to suit their non-golfing partners.

AVAILABILITY OF ATTRACTIONS

Select two special interest holidays and compare the attractions and other tourist facilities that are provided. (You may use the case study on St Petersburg and Cairo, or find your own examples.)

Changing attitudes

Special interest holidays used to be considered a luxury for the rich and famous, or for those who had time on their hands. As we have seen, this is now not the case. With an increase in the overall wealth of the western world so people have changed their attitudes to holidays. It is now possible, and acceptable, for people to travel more and have frequent holidays.

There have been a number of factors that have caused this shift. The media, and in particular television, encourage people to want to visit foreign places and to experience different ways of life and culture. Surveys in the past have long shown Australia and New Zealand to be the places that most people would 'want to visit, if money were no object', but the fact is that, today, even these destinations are seen as perfectly accessible. Cycling around New Zealand or camping and touring around Australia are now a possibility for more and more tourists.

CHANGING ATTITUDES

For two types of special interest holidays, research and compare the changes in people's attitudes and the changes in their popularity. One type should be travelling-based (such as cruising or safaris) and one should be based at a single destination (such as culinary holidays or sporting events).

For a long time, long-haul destinations were considered just too far for ordinary people to consider travelling to. The two World Wars changed people's attitudes, as troops stationed overseas experienced a completely different culture for the first time. They were stationed in Africa, India, the Far East, and all over Europe, and they told stories about their travels when they returned. Society's attitudes towards travel and far away places slowly changed. Today there are many more flights available to long-haul destinations, and a lot of these destinations are much cheaper for the tourist to visit, so countries like Sri Lanka, Thailand, and India have become popular.

Increased awareness of cultural, environmental and health issues

Increased awareness of cultural, environmental and health issues has affected our choice of holiday over recent years.

Advances in communication have heightened our cultural awareness – people often say that 'the world is becoming a smaller place'. Television has given us the chance to see the different cultures of the world – and given us the desire to travel and experience them too. People are far more aware about the less developed countries of the world and what to expect if they choose to visit.

This appreciation of other cultures has certainly meant that the special interest holiday market has been able to expand to include a wider array of countries and interests. For example, living with tribal people or helping to build a village in New Guinea is now a possibility as a holiday experience, as shown in the account on the following page.

People's awareness of environmental issues has been heightened by many factors and probably one of the most influential has been global warming (see Topic 2 in Unit 8). This has led to a marked interest in issues such as preserving the rainforest, or protecting coastlines. In addition, the threatened wildlife have also become a focus of interest, with special interest holidays to see whales or mountain gorillas, for example, now being popular.

Health issues have also influenced people's choice of holiday. Avoidance of the sun – because of fear of skin cancer – has led to people taking fewer traditional 'sun holidays' and pursuing activity holidays instead. Rather than just vegetate on a beach, more people now want to be stimulated on their holidays, as it is better for their minds. Families want to spend time doing something together rather that just sitting by the pool which they see as similar to watching TV all day. Parents want to stimulate their children with experiences and skills that they may have for life, such as sailing, diving and snorkelling.

Visiting tribal people

Visiting tribal people has never been more popular. Proud and extravagantly decorated men and women who once only stared out at us from glossy magazines and TV documentaries are now accessible to intrepid travellers and tour companies.

We find ancient ways of life fascinating, and often of great romantic appeal. In today's world (supermarkets, fashions, celebrity culture, stressful jobs and lack of community) the ideal of people living simply together close to nature, in the same way that they have for thousands of years, is extremely appealing. For the tourist there is nothing like bridging centuries of modern development and making a connection with people whose lives are so very different from our own.

Although every community is different, many tribal cultures are extremely vulnerable to outside influences. It has been argued that tribal people need to be protected from tourists in order to preserve their unique cultures, and in many cases this is true. However we must remember that tribal communities have a right to make their own decisions about their development.

In many cases healthcare and education are a priority. Tourism can provide one way of earning money to provide for this. Many tribal communities have been marginalised and derided by other communities and governments as being primitive. For some of these communities, meeting people with a genuine interest and respect for them is important.

Whilst it is easy to say that we should leave tribal communities to make their own decision about how and when to invite tourists into their communities and lives, it is vital that they are able to make informed decisions. Many of us feel that developed countries, such as Spain, have made disastrous decisions about

some of their tourism development, and remote tribal communities experiencing tourism for the first time often need advice and support in assessing the pros and cons of tourism and how to manage it.

And so what advice for the tourist?

Travelling to visit tribal communities is fraught with difficulties for even the most responsible traveller. The best advice, beyond that below, is to be extremely sensitive to local people's reaction to your visit at all times, and be prepared to make changes to your itinerary.

The critical issue is that you should be confident that the community that you are visiting has extended an invitation to tourists. If you are in any doubt, the best advice is not to visit – there is nothing worse than feeling very unwelcome. Too often, tourism and tourists simply intrude with little thought.

Secondly, you should either travel with a local tour company with a proven track record (ask them for their written responsible tourism policy and references), or hire a guide from the local community to ensure that you benefit from their knowledge of what is, or is not, appropriate. Take time to read up on the people you are about to visit in a good guidebook, and remember at all times that you are a guest in somebody else's home.

In addition to ensuring that you minimise any negative impacts, you'll want to ensure that local people benefit from your visit. Trading for crafts, paying for the services of local guides, or for photographs, will benefit local people.

Begging poses difficulties for those of us keen to help, but not wanting to encourage begging. In some cases community funds have been created to support the marginalised and projects such as local schools. Enquire about these before you visit, and you might prefer to make a donation to ensure the economic benefits of your visit are spread throughout the community.

By Justin Francis

Source: Online travel agency www.responsibletravel.com

activity

VISTING TRIBAL PEOPLE

Read the case study above. Explain the factors that would make this type of special interest holiday popular.

Increased health, wealth and fitness of retirees

The UK has an ageing population with more people over the age of 65 than ever before. Life expectancy has also increased but so have the number of years that we can expect to live in poor health or with a disability. So people tend to want to make the most out of their holidays whilst they are able to do so.

The general health, wealth and fitness of retirees is improving all the time. According to the National Statistics Social Trends report 2004, the pre-tax income of pensioners in Great Britain rose by 26% in real terms between 1995 and 2003, compared with an increase of 13% in real average earnings. This means that retirees have more money to spend than ever before on holidays. The extract below from the *Travel Daily News* shows that the older generation are also keeping up with technology.

Older visitors to the top travel search engines

Mobissimo had the largest number of visitors over 55 (25%), compared to 18% of visitors to the Travel Agencies category. Hitwise research analysts note that as 'baby boomers' begin to retire and have more leisure time, this price-conscious group will become an increasingly powerful force on travel meta-search engines'.

Source: Travel Daily News, May 2005

Retirees at 60 or 65 are now quite fit, as they have generally enjoyed a better diet and better health care than previous generations, so they have more energy and desire to participate in a variety of special interest holidays. Saga Holidays targets this age group and, as well as cruises, provides a wide variety of special interest holidays, as shown below.

What do Saga offer?

- A diverse range of music-themed holidays, orchestral concerts, recitals, festivals and music-appreciation holidays.
- Walking holidays in the UK and overseas, catering for a range of abilities.
- Overseas art-appreciation holidays give you the perfect opportunity to learn more about a major artist or artistic movement.
- Our UK art-appreciation holidays explore the wide range of art in the galleries of major cities.
- Discover the legacies of ancient civilisations on a selection of holidays which include visits to ancient sites and world-class museums.
- Railway-themed holidays include a varied programme of railway journeys and visits to famous railway lines and museums.
- The historic houses and castles of England and Scotland offer a fascinating glimpse into the past, and gloriously landscaped gardens.
- Explore places of religious significance, accompanied by members of the clergy or senior lay people.

Source: www.saga.co.uk

Increased interest in national sports, education and adventure

Sport is beginning to be a major component of tourism as more and more people take a special interest in following sporting events. Today, all over the world, sporting activities are organised with little regard to national borders. Similarly, the enthusiastic supporter will travel anywhere to see their chosen spectacle.

The Olympic Games and other worldwide and continental sports competitions generate travel on a massive scale. This association between sport and tourism has been recognised by the major players on both sides. In 1999, the Olympic Committee and the World Travel Organisation signed a cooperation agreement, committing themselves to strengthening the links, which is a reflection of how important sport has become to the tourism industry. Hosting a major event can bring heavy investment in developing a destination, the effects of which remain long after the event is over. See the case study overleaf on the London 2012 Olympics.

Educational holidays are also popular as people see it as a chance to learn a new skill or acquire new knowledge. They may just enjoy the activity for the duration of the holiday or it may be something that they progress with and take into their lives. Examples

2012: The challenges for London

The Olympics have become events of such prestige and global significance that they have decisively changed previous winners. Japan can date its emergence from the shadow of war from the 1964 Tokyo Olympics. Seoul, too, marked a defining moment in Asia's growing power in 1988. Barcelona, four years later, projected a vibrant post-Franco image of a revived Spain. And Sydney is still basking in the reputation of organising the best games on record, a feat that has boosted Australia's global image and drawn millions of tourists to its shores.

London, too, now has a chance to buff its reputation as a world city and renew itself for the new century. But that chance must not be squandered. There is an immense task ahead, not only to build the facilities and regenerate a swathe of East London but also to overhaul ancient infrastructure. Huge demands will be made on power supplies, water, sewer systems, hotels and, above all, transport. London must spend at least £17 billion on trains, roads and the Underground. There must be no more bickering or planning delays: London must go to work now. Athens pulled it off at the last moment; but it was a close-run thing.

These games will involve everyone who makes up London's diversity: white, black, Asian, Muslim and Christian. All can, and should, find cause to rejoice in an enterprise that will be costly and also truly monumental. The IOC has set London its greatest challenge since the Blitz. A great city must rise to the occasion in Olympian fashion.

Source: Times Online 7 July 2005

of educational holidays range from learning how to play chess or bridge, to speaking a new language, cooking, dancing, taking photographs or painting. Many children get the chance to go on educational trips through their school or college. These can range from foreign exchange trips to improve their language skills to outward-bound courses to develop skills in a variety of outdoor activities.

Outward bound courses sometimes appeal to the more adventurous tourist as they tend to focus on things like abseiling, climbing and water sports. Adventure holidays do not just appeal to children, however. More and more people spend their working day at a desk which has heightened their desire to do something different in their holidays – something less boring and more active. They want to escape for a bit of adventure and experience something new and different.

activity

LONDON 2012

In the summer of 2012, London will become a special interest holiday destination when it hosts the Olympic Games. Explain the factors that will make this destination popular.

Changing holiday patterns – increased demand for short breaks

Low-cost flights and easy access have made short-break holidays far more popular. According to ABTA 2004, short breaks are very much part of the holiday landscape and have expanded the industry considerably. Paris, Amsterdam, Bruges and Rome were

2004's top four destinations, but there are many other cities that are opening up to become interesting new city-break destinations, such as Barcelona, Prague and other eastern European cities.

Bratislava, the Slovak capital, is just one of these. With new no-frills routes into the city and hotels investing in modernisation, Bratislava is set up to rival Prague. And it will be cheaper too! Bratislava's old town is compact and pedestrianised, with lots of outdoor cafés, while its baroque residential palaces and castle have breathtaking views across the Danube.

Other more unusual short breaks are also becoming popular such as a long weekend in Arctic Norway to watch pods of feeding orca whales, and perhaps see the Northern Lights (see the case study below).

Whale watching in Norway

each year between October and January to feed on the huge shoals of herrings that congregate here.

On this trip, from the safety of a boat, you could have the opportunity to see the orcas using their unique feeding pattern of rounding up the schools of herring into tight balls, and then stunning them with their powerful tails. Sea eagles, often in large numbers, feed on the herring at the same time, adding excitement to this unique trip. You will get close to these four-ton mammals – the most numerous of the whale species – in small zodiac boats. Furthermore, equipped with dry suits, snorkels, masks and fins, you can join these whales in the icy waters of the fjord, subject to sea conditions.

We have got together with Norway's leading orca whale expert, Tiu Simila, to offer you a fascinating whale-watching encounter, both from a small boat and, for the adventurous, a chance to snorkel with orcas – all over a long weekend!

The spectacular mountains of the fjords around the small town of Tysfjord, 60 miles north of the Arctic Circle, provide the perfect backdrop for orcas to gather

Source: Online travel agency www.responsibletravel.com

activity

FACTORS AFFECTING POPULARITY

Read the case study above on whale watching and explain how the factors listed below have contributed to its popularity as a short-break special interest holiday. Some of the factors may be more relevant than others.

Life–work changes

Accessibility

Availability of attractions and other tourist facilities

Changing attitudes

Increased awareness of cultural, environmental and health issues

Increased health, wealth and fitness of retirees

Increased interest in national sports, education, adventure

Changing holiday patterns – increased demand for short breaks.

How Unit 11 is assessed

The assessment evidence for this unit is in four distinct parts. It is suggested that they are presented in four sections within a portfolio. The sections should be titled:

(a) The geographical distribution of different types of special interest holiday
(b) An itinerary for a special interest holiday
(c) A comparison of two types of special interest holiday
(d) The factors influencing the popularity of two types of special interest holiday.

The assessment evidence could be in many different forms to allow for your learning preferences and strengths to be accommodated. There will at least be maps for task (a), and an itinerary for task (b) but there could also be written reports or witness testimonies of oral presentations or customer service role-plays with supporting notes.

The following guidance outlines how you can achieve the assessment criteria for each of the four parts.

Task (a) The geographical distribution of different types of special interest holiday

This section should show evidence of:

- maps showing the geographical distribution of different types of special interest holidays
- a description and explanation of the geographical distribution and providers of a range of special interest holidays.

(a.0) Introduction

Explain what a special interest holiday is, and the different types; those that take place in one destination and those that involve moving around.

(a.1) Geographical distribution

Produce at least six maps showing the distribution of six different types of special interest holiday.

(a.2) Features of Destinations

Describe the features of those selected areas in terms of the climate, landscape, transport routes and accessibility, accommodation, local services, natural and built attractions, events and entertainment, local culture and heritage, activities and facilities.

(a.3) Providers of special interest holidays

Explain who provides the holidays in the selected area. Providers include:

- Mass market and independent tour operators
- Specialists in tailor-made holidays
- Specialists in one destination or market segment
- Transport principals.

Task (b) An itinerary for a special interest holiday

This section should show evidence of an itinerary for a special interest holiday based at one destination, and an explanation of how the itinerary meets the needs of tourists as provided to you by your tutor in the form of a pen portrait.

(b.0) Introduction

Describe the special interest holiday selected.

(b.1) Who the itinerary is prepared for

Describe the customers, as given to you in the pen-portrait.

(b.2) Dates

State the dates of the holiday.

(b.3) Timings

Describe what is happening during each day, when and where.

(b.4) Activities, excursions and accommodation

Describe what is included in the holiday in terms of activities provided, excursions (including optional ones) and level of accommodation.

(b.5) Contact details

Provide the names, addresses and contact telephone numbers for the holiday.

(b.6) Features of the destination

Describe the features of the destination in terms of its attractions, such as the nightlife or restaurants.

(b.7) Justification for the recommendation

Justify your choice of holiday for the specified customers. Show that you understand the difference between 'basic' and 'complex' needs, including education, leisure, sports, religious, relaxation, special travel arrangements, special facilities and services, alternative activities for different members of a group, standards, quality, and exclusivity.

Task (c) A comparison of two types of special interest holiday

This section should show evidence of a comparison of features, tourist types and popularity of two different types of special interest holidays; one involving a tour and one based at one destination.

(c.0) Introduction

Describe the two different types of special interest holiday you have chosen to compare.

(c.1) Comparison of their features

A comparison of the features that make the two holidays appealing, to include the following: climate, landscape, transport routes and accessibility, accommodation, local services, natural and built attractions, events and entertainment, local culture and heritage, activities and facilities.

(c.2) Comparison of the tourist types they attract

A comparison of the types of customers the two holidays attract.

(c.3) Comparison of their popularity

A comparison of their popularity, based on statistical data and other sources.

(c.4) Bibliography

A referenced list of sources used to support the comparison of the two holidays.

Task (d) The factors influencing the popularity of two types of special interest holiday

This section should show evidence of an assessment of the factors influencing the popularity of two types of special interest holidays; one involving a tour and one based at one destination.

(d.0) Introduction

A description of the two types of special interest holiday selected.

(d.1) Comparison of the factors influencing the popularity of the two holidays

A comparison of the factors, to include the following: life–work changes, accessibility, availability of attractions and other tourist facilities, changing attitudes, increased awareness of cultural, environmental and health issues, increased health, wealth and fitness of retires, increased interest in national sports, education, adventure, changing holiday patterns and increased demand for short breaks.

Bibliography

List all of the sources of information that you have used to complete the assessment for this unit.

Appendices

Include any relevant supporting information in the appendices, such as examples of marketing materials, policies and procedures, etc.

This unit will look at the variety of travel organisations that make up this diverse and complex industry. We will look at the various sectors of travel and tourism and explore their connections with other sectors in the industry. The sectors we will look at are:

- Travel agents
- Tourist boards
- Attractions
- Tour operators
- Transport providers
- Accommodation providers.

The industry is changing out of all recognition. The advent of the internet and other technological advancements, such as digital communications, are set to shift the purchase of holidays away from the high street to the comfort of the traveller's home. Travel organisations have had to adapt to these changes in the way the industry operates. In this unit we will look at how each sector is adapting to these advances and how the changes are affecting their business.

We will also examine the legal and regulatory requirements of organisations in the sector and discover how these have affected their operations. These will include industry-specific regulations, such as the EU Package Directive, ABTA and ATOL, and the more generic legislation, such as Health and Safety, Equal Opportunities, Consumer Protection and Data Protection.

We will finish this unit by examining one travel organisation in depth, a company called African Pride. We will look at its scale and structure and also how it operates. The products and services of providing tailor-made trips to Africa will be investigated, along with the types of customers they are serving and how they cater for their varied needs. Any gaps in provision will be discussed with a view to recommending how these gaps may be covered in the future.

By the end of this unit you should have enough information to be able to select an organisation within the travel and tourism industry and investigate it for yourself, following the African Pride example.

This unit will include an industry focus interview with Melanie Wood, Marketing Director and part owner of Flamingo Land, in which she explains how she runs this unique attraction.

Traditionally, people see travel agents as the high street store where you can buy a holiday. They sell the products and services produced by the tour operators, cruise companies, airlines and hotel chains to the traveller or tourist who wants to buy them. They also provide ancillary services such as insurance and currency. In this topic we will look at the different types of travel agent and what they do, under the following headings:

- The role of the travel agent
- Multiples
- Miniples
- Independents
- E-agents
- Holiday hypermarket.

We will investigate the market share, turnover and profit of each sector, as well as their marketing objectives, to determine the key organisations in the sector and the degree of influence they have. But first let us determine what a travel agent does.

The role of the travel agent

A travel agency is an organisation that sells people travel, be it a package holiday or a train journey. They arrange trips for individuals or groups. They are the agent, or 'go-between', who liaises between the traveller and the travel company. Their role is to co-ordinate the holiday and book it for the customer.

A package holiday, refers to the pre-arranged combination of transport, accommodation or other tourist services, when sold or offered for sale at an inclusive price.

Travel agencies all belong to the private sector – companies whose prime motive is to make a profit and, if possible, to gain the largest share of their particular market. Current market leaders include TUI, Thomas Cook, My Travel and First Choice. These large

travel companies own travel agencies, but these are integrated with other sectors of the industry, such as tour operators and hotel chains.

In short, the large organisations have purchased the providers so as to ensure more control of the market. The majority of travel agents are members of the Association of British Travel Agents (ABTA). ABTA members are responsible for the sale of approximately 80% of all package holidays sold in the UK. This represents an annual turnover of over £28billion. Although it is called the Association of British Travel Agents, the membership also includes tour operators (who we will examine in Topic 4).

Travel agents are facing a difficult time with an increasing number of bookings being made directly with a tour operator or on the internet as the diagram opposite shows.

Changing Booking Methods

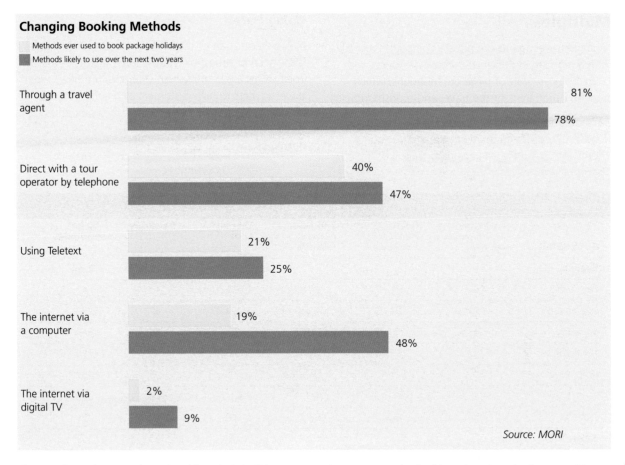

Methods ever used to book package holidays
Methods likely to use over the next two years

Through a travel agent: 81% / 78%

Direct with a tour operator by telephone: 40% / 47%

Using Teletext: 21% / 25%

The internet via a computer: 19% / 48%

The internet via digital TV: 2% / 9%

Source: MORI

The number of respondents booking their holiday through a travel agent has decreased by 18% over the last 12 years, as more and more people book over the internet. According to the Office for National Statistics: UK Labour Force Survey 2004, the internet could be accessed at home by 45% of UK households (11 million) in 2003, more than four times the proportion in 1999.

Traditionally, travel agents have always made their income through taking a commission from the travel companies they deal with. Different commission rates are paid by different sectors. For example, car-hire commission is usually higher than rail or cruise commission. But a lot of their revenue comes through selling package holidays. In the past, agents earned a basic 9% commission on an airline seat, but this has been cut to 7.5%, or even as low as 7% in the UK in the last few years, which has meant that many have been forced to charge 'service fees'. Service fees are charges made to the customer by the travel agent, at the time of booking.

In 2002, the ABTA Travel Agents Benchmarking Survey found that there had been a significant increase in the number of agents charging service fees – up from 38% in 2000 to 70% in 2002. The survey also suggested that those agents who had introduced service fees spent less time with people who were unlikely to make a booking.

The changes to the ways that travel agents conduct their business has also resulted in an increase in staff training costs – to an annual average of £345 per employee. In fact, the survey showed that there was a direct correlation between training and profit, as shown in the table below.

The link between training and profit (amount per employee)			
Training spend	More than £500	Average (£345)	Less than £200
Profit	£6,928	£5,311	£4,897
Turnover	£332,000	£313,000	£307,000

All these changes in the market – especially those involving the internet and direct sales – have meant that the customer now has a vast array of choice when choosing how, when and with whom to book their holiday. Some people say that this will lead to the death of the traditional travel agent, and it has certainly had an effect. The travel agencies have had to change and diversify – hence we have a number of different types of travel agent in the market place today.

Multiples

Multiple travel agents are private companies, usually with a high street presence in most UK towns and cities. They are part of large organisations, which trade in other areas of the travel and tourism industry.

According to BP Travel Marketing Services 2005 Report, the top three multiples are TUI (including Thomson), Going Places (including Travelworld) and Thomas Cook.

Going Places

Going Places, part of the MyTravel group of companies, is the second largest high street travel agents in the UK. Their stores are in many high streets with trained expert travel advisers to help customers plan and book their holiday or flight. Like many of the large companies, Going Places has an internet site which offers extra online discounts on tickets and holidays.

Major Multiples						
ABTA RETAIL	**First choice** (inc. Hypermarkets excl. Hays)	**Going Places** (inc. Travelworld)	**Thomson** (formerly Lunn Poly)	**Thomas Cook**	**Travelcare**	**Major Multiples**
Region:						Total
East Anglia	10	18	23	30	14	95
London & SE	105	184	209	192	82	772
Midlands	24	93	125	73	49	364
North East	19	105	109	84	78	395
North West	31	103	94	71	58	357
South West	75	55	70	51	19	270
Scotland	46	49	81	79	27	282
Wales	9	40	57	26	20	152
Norther Ireland	0	18	16	9	29	72
Republic of Ireland	0	0	0	2	0	2
TOTALS	**319**	**665**	**784**	**617**	**376**	**2761**

Source: BP Retail Marketing Services April 2005

---

activity

ANALYSING THE MULTIPLES

Study the table of multiples. Analyse the pattern of ownership of the multiples across the UK, identifying who has the strengths and weaknesses in each region.

TUI UK

TUI UK is the UK's largest holiday company and includes the leading UK brand of Thomson holidays. It employs approximately 9,000 people, 7,000 of whom work overseas in around 40 holiday destinations around the world. TUI UK also includes the travel agents Thomson Retail Shops (formerly Lunn Poly) – the UK's leading leisure travel retailer with over 750 retail stores including the award-winning flagship Superstore in Leicester. Thomson retail shops sell around 2.7m holidays and flights a year and account for over 20% of the total market.

Thomas Cook

Thomas Cook has over 600 stores and bureaux de change located throughout the UK and Ireland. It has carved its niche as one of the UK's biggest providers of foreign exchange, offering instant availability on all major currencies and nine different types of traveller's cheque.

Miniples

Miniple travel agents have more than one branch and usually a head office in a local area. The different branches may even trade under different names to keep their independence and maintain a sense of brand loyalty with the local community, such as Bath Travel, which also incorporates Tappers Travel.

According to BP Travel Marketing Services research, there are a number of miniples across the country, usually with around 30 branches (see table below). The largest is the the Co-op Travel Trading Group, which has a number of regional trading miniples such as the Leeds Co-op and the West Midlands Co-op, obviously with strong local loyalties to the organisation.

	ABTA Retail general branches	ABTA Retail business house branches	Other Outlets
MINIPLES			
Althams Travel Services	31	0	0
American Express	33	26	25
Bath Travel (inc. Tappers Travel)	70	0	2
BTI Hogg Robinson Travel Ltd	0	54	74
Callers Pegasus (owned by Thompson Travel Group)	20	0	0
Carlson Wagonlit Travel	0	43	48
Co-op Travel	95	0	1
Dawson & Sanderson	24	0	1
First Choice Holidays Hypermarkets	40	0	0
First Choice Travel Shops	279	0	2
Hays Travel Ltd (part owned by First choice)	121	0	1
Ilkeston Co-op	42	0	1
Leeds Co-op	21	0	0
Lets Go Travel	40	0	0
Midlands Co-op	97	0	2
Personal Service Travel	13	0	0
Premier Travel Agency	13	0	0
Travel House	23	0	0
Wardle Travel	37	0	0
West Midlands Co-op	0	0	0
Rest of CTTG	96	0	0

Source: BP Retail Marketing Services April 2005

Independents

Independent travel agents are private companies that may have only one or a few branches, often close to each other. They are often found in cities, towns and villages throughout the UK, and rely on repeat business from satisfied local customers. Others have diversified into niche markets that cater for a particular type of customer and their requirements. For example, African Pride – which we feature at the end of this unit – has built a reputation on providing holidays to Africa.

In the face of so much competition from the larger multiples and miniples, the small independents need to fight for their place in the market. The Campaign for Real Travel Agents (CARTA) has over 400 members from the independent travel agent sector. It was formed to promote choice and expose the vested interesst of the others in the industry. It is closely linked to the Association of Independent Tour Operators.

A lot of the independents are also members of the National Association of Independent Travel Agents, which trades under the brand name of Advantage Travel Centres. Currently they have over 800 members.

All the consortia organisations are reporting an increased interest in shop-fascia branding and national identity. ARTAC (Worldchoice and Advantage Travel Centres) insists on new members adopting the Worldchoice branded shop front, and currently has about 350 out of 850 outlets branded. Advantage claims that more agents than ever are branding their outlets, even though it is not compulsory. Industry observers feel that a strong brand within the local market is no longer enough, particularly as the multiples now own strong regional brands.

And, not only are independents competing in the high street with more branding they are also aligning themselves with major tour operators, as shown in the case study on page 254.

Business travel agents

Some independent agencies exist solely to offer travel services for business customers. An example of this is Key Travel, a business travel agency founded in 1980, which specialises in arranging travel for charity/non-profit organisations. The business has flourished because it understands this sector's special travel needs and has developed systems and training to ensure delivery of a high quality travel service. Key Travel is recognised in the industry and by all the major airlines as a leading agent in this field.

activity

INDEPENDENT CHANGES

Read the case study above and describe how the objectives of these organisations have changed over the last few years.

E-agents

The Mintel Report on Travel Agents 2002 states that although travel agencies themselves increasingly rely on technology to search for and buy travel products on behalf of their customers, the introduction of internet-based booking systems during the late 1990s has meant that technology is increasingly being used to remove travel agents from the purchase process. It is becoming ever easier for holidaymakers to make their own bookings, often directly purchasing separate elements with different providers.

People are increasingly turning to the internet to buy all sorts of products, and travel is one of the most popular. Airlines are realising the potential of the internet for lower-cost distribution.

Two years ago, no one would have predicted independent agents linking themselves to the vertically integrated companies. But since then, both of the independent ARTAC consortium's franchisees (Worldchoice and Advantage Travel Centres) have aligned themselves with the major operators.

In an increasingly polarised marketplace, where does this leave the rest of the independent agent and operator sector?

Cadogan Holidays has recognised that its distribution is threatened with the march of the multiples. It is now looking to form a group of 15 like-minded specialists that will work with a targeted 700 non-aligned agents. The retailers would be offered higher commission in exchange for guaranteed racking while both parties would embark on a joint marketing campaign, in-store training and educationals.

Cadogan managing director, Gary David, said: 'My business through the multiples is declining as they push in-house operators. It's the same for many specialist operators.'

CARTA chairman and managing director of Kirker Holidays, Chris Kirker, said: 'Specialist operators are finding it difficult to get their product racked on the shelf and will promote through CARTA. As far as Kirker Holidays is concerned, we have no wish to sell through the multiples anyway because they do not understand our product or the service we offer. CARTA agents do.'

AITO executive manager, Julia Hendry, stressed that the directional selling drive by the major operators is forcing more operators to review their distribution. 'For many the high street is out of play,' said Hendry. 'Operators are having to be selective and forge close relationships with independents who will happily sell their product. CARTA members fall into this category. Operators are also asked to pay prohibitive premium rates of commission by the multiples where the volume of sales does not warrant it.'

Some 350 travel agent branches and 56 AITO tour operators are now involved in the scheme – all of which pay a one-off joining fee and an annual subscription. For that, operators can promote through CARTA agents while retailers receive posters, window stickers and badges. In a bid to raise the profile of CARTA, national advertising in the form of a mini-directory is soon to begin, while a guide is being distributed to 300,000 consumers.

Source: www.travelweekly.co.uk

Agents such as Rosenbluth International have recognised this trend towards online purchasing, and recently bought the business travel agent website Biz Travel (www.biztravel.com). The site finds the best airline deals for subscribers and provides information for business travellers on topics such as connection times at airports, as well as delivering a regular email newsletter. Specialist online travel agents in the USA, such as Microsoft Expedia and the Sabre-owned Travelocity, have already recognised the potential of the UK market and introduced dedicated UK versions of their sites.

The internet is a major distribution channel for the travel industry. According to the latest Mintel report (Holidays on the Internet, 2004), the UK online travel market is expected to be worth £4.8bn by 2007, up from £1.4bn in 2002. (Source: ABTA 2004 Travel Statistics and Trends).

Following the popularity of auction sites like e-bay, some e-agents have come up with a new idea to attract business. The site details the holiday or flight on offer and shows the closing dates for bids. Confirmation is emailed to the successful bidder, and the customer is asked to pay by credit card or charge card via the internet, or over the telephone.

Thomson Holiday Auctions offers you the chance to join the bidding on their exclusive late deal package

holidays. Be the first to bid from only £1 on any auctions that have just opened, or snap up a bargain on an auction closing soon.

RoomAuction is a unique database of hotels, where you can find a better deal on accommodation rather than booking direct. Each hotel has its complete info together with their standard rates. All you need to do is decide how much you are willing to pay for a room and bid today! Hotels are likely to accept any reasonable offers when they wouldn't be able to sell rooms at standard rate.

GOING, GOING, GONE ON HOLIDAY

Discuss the appeal of an auction site. Analyse the advantages and disadvantages of buying and selling travel products in this way – for the customer, the organisation and the sector.

The internet is not the only form of new technology that is likely to impact upon the traditional travel agent. While not everyone has a PC and thus internet access in their home, most people have a television. As digital television inevitably increases its reach, so too will it pose an increasing threat to travel agents. Watching a travel programme and then deciding you want to book the featured holidays will soon become a reality when digital television providers offer the ability to purchase a host of products via your television set.

Holiday hypermarket

The holiday hypermarket offers the customer the opportunity to experience a new type of travel agent. Each store offers a themed experience, making you 'feel like you are on holiday before you even get there', claim First Choice, who provide a number of holiday hypermarkets around the country. They offer an extensive range of holidays and short breaks from all of the major holiday companies, as well as foreign exchange, car hire, airport parking, airport hotels and insurance. The stores have a very open-plan feel, often with a café area for the customers to relax in and view the brochures. Each section of the hypermarket is laid out like a supermarket, with all the brochures for each type of holiday in a particular area. For example, summer holiday brochures are in one area of the shop and ski brochures and cruising in others. In each section, a trained staff member related to the specific area of the store is there to provide a personalised tailor-made service for the customer.

255

Topic 1 Travel agents

COMPARING TYPES OF TRAVEL AGENTS

Create a comparative table, listing the advantages and disadvantages of each type of travel agent, for the customer, the organisation and the travel market. Consider each of the following: multiples, miniples, independents, e-agents and holiday hypermarkets.

Tourist boards

In the last topic we looked at travel agents, and in this one we look at tourist boards, which can be broken down into two main groups:

- **National tourist boards**
- **Regional tourist boards.**

National tourist boards

The United Kingdom has four national tourist boards:

- VisitBritain (formerly the English Tourism Council and the British Tourist Authority)
- VisitScotland (formerly the Scottish Tourist Board)
- The Northern Ireland Tourist Board (NITB)
- The Wales Tourist Board.

The British Tourist Authority (BTA) and the English Tourism Council (formerly the English Tourist Board), merged in 2003 to form VisitBritain. VisitScotland and the Wales Tourist Board were set up under the Development of Tourism Act in 1969. The Northern Ireland Tourist Board was set up under separate legislation. The aim was to co-ordinate the diverse interests that make up the tourism industry in each country and provide it with a single voice.

Each board reports to their own governing body. VisitBritain reports to the Department for Culture, Media and Sport (DCMS), the Wales Tourist Board reports to the National Assembly for Wales, VisitScotland reports to the Scottish Executive, and the NITB to the Northern Ireland Assembly.

As well as marketing England to the British, VistBritain has the responsibility of marketing all of Britain abroad. It maintains close links with all the other boards and their individual reporting authorities. The following government departments all have responsibilities for certain areas that link to the travel and tourism industry:

- Department for Transport – aviation, railways, roads, London underground

- Department for Education and Skills – sector skills councils, national training organisations
- Department for Environment, Food and Rural Affairs – food industry, forestry, sustainable development, climate change, environmental protection and water issues, wildlife and conservation, energy efficiency, rural affairs, countryside issues and inland waterways.
- Department for Trade and Industry – bank holidays, small and medium-sized businesses, e-commerce
- Office for the Deputy Prime Minister – building regulations and planning
- HM Treasury – taxation
- Home Office – liquor licensing.

VisitBritain works in partnership with the other national tourist boards in Northern Ireland, Scotland and Wales to promote an attractive image of Britain. It provides impartial tourism information and gathers essential market intelligence for the UK tourism industry. The goals of VisitBritain are shown opposite.

VisitBritain is funded by the Department for Culture, Media and Sport. In 2004/05 the net grant to promote Britain overseas as a tourist destination was £36m. The net grant to lead and co-ordinate England marketing was £14m, of which £4m was deployed directly through the Regional Development Agencies. A further £1.5m 'challenge fund' was available for domestic marketing subject to VisitBritain raising £3.5m partnership funding. VisitBritain also raises around £17m non-Government funding through partnerships and other activities.

Extensive research shows that in 2001, VisitBritain's activities generated £31 of overseas visitors' expenditure in Britain for every £1 of public money it spent.

VisitBritain operates a network of 25 offices, covering 31 key markets, and employs 450 staff, 60% of whom are based overseas in Britain's key tourism markets.

Overseas offices work closely with British diplomatic and cultural staff, the local travel trade and the media to stimulate interest in Britain. In the UK, VisitBritain has strategic partnerships with other organisations, namely the British Council, UKinbound, the British Hospitality Association and the UK Immigration Service.

There is a formal framework for cooperation between VisitBritain and the network of national tourist boards with powers to promote their own country, and the Mayor of London's remit to promote the capital overseas.

In addition to the national tourist boards, a number of statutory bodies have been established at the regional level with responsibility for developing tourism, including Regional Development Agencies and Regional Tourist Boards, as well as tourism partners for the Channel Islands and the Isle of Man.

VisitBritain provides a defined range of core services such as the provision of market intelligence, the maintenance of a contact centre, business tourism activities, press and PR activities, and work with the travel trade. In addition to this, VisitBritain offers the opportunity to buy into a menu of 'added-value' services – for example, dedicated campaign lines in the contact centre, translation services, warehousing of additional print, campaign fulfilment, etc.

Regional tourist boards

The regional tourist boards (RTBs) are not government agencies – they are funded from membership fees. These fees may come from a variety of sources, including local authorities, private businesses, National Tourist Boards, the DCMS and Regional Development Agencies (RDAs) – all with an interest in the region.

The structure and nature of the RTBs are currently being reviewed, in line with each region's individual strategy. In some regions, RTBs are working in partnership with Regional Development Agencies, whereas in others the

activity

REGIONAL TOURIST ORGANISATIONS

There are two main types of regional tourist organisation: Regional Tourist Boards, and Destination Management Organisations or Partnerships. Select one of each from the list below, and investigate the differences in their operations. Write a report on your findings.

- Tourism South East www.seeda.org.uk
- VisitLondon www.londontouristboard.com
- South West Tourism www.swtourism.co.uk
- East of England Tourist Board www.eetb.org.uk www.visiteastofengland.com
- North West Tourist Board www.visitnorthwet.com www.northwesttourism.net
- Heart of England Tourist Board www.visitheartofengland.com

- Northumbria Tourist Board www.visitnorthumbria.com
- Yorkshire Tourist Board www.ytb.org.uk
- Cumbria Tourist Board www.cumbria-the-lake-district.co.uk
- The Mersey Partnership www.visitliverpool.com
- Marketing Manchester www.destinationmanchester.com
- Cheshire and Warrington Tourism www.visit-cheshire.com
- Lancashire & Blackpool Tourist Board www.lancashiretoursim.com

Please note that these organisations are evolving and changing over the coming years – to identify recent changes visit www.culture.gov.uk.

role of the RTB is being taken over by the RDA. Alternatively, in some regions the RDAs have formed 'Destination Management Organisations' (or partnerships) which oversee the sub-regional development.

As an example of the work of one of these organisations let us look at the work done in London.

London plays a vital role in the UK's tourism industry, with over half of visitors to the UK coming via the capital. Promoting London as a tourist destination and as a 'gateway' to the rest of the UK is a statutory duty of the Mayor of London, who works through the London Development Agency in implementing his 'Tourism Strategy for London'. The DCMS has contributed £1.9m per year towards delivery of the strategy, with the initial emphasis being on developing the gateway role.

VisitLondon – a private company – was established in 1963 as the official tourist organisation for London. It currently employs about 70 staff in its offices near London Bridge, and is funded by partnership subscriptions and commercial activity. It also receives public funding from the DCMS, via the Mayor of London, and from the London Development Agency and the Association of London Government.

Visit London's role is to:
1. Promote and market London to leisure and business visitors.
2. Advocate quality improvements to tourism infrastructure and services.
3. Work to maximise the benefits of tourism for Londoners and the local economy.

Working closely with a number of key partners, VisitLondon's key activities are:
- Public affairs – tourism strategy, developmental issues, research.
- Marketing – campaigns and marketing strategy, VisitLondon publications, trade shows.
- Partnership – activity and opportunities.
- Travel trade – publications and exhibitions.
- Press – VisitLondon and London News, press photo library.

Regional tourist boards operate in Northern Ireland, Wales and Scotland too. In Wales, four Regional Tourism Partnerships (RTPs) were set up in 2002 to cover North, Mid, South-West and South-East Wales (see map).Their principal role is to lead the implementation of four regional tourism strategies, which seek to improve the competitive performance of tourism so that it makes a better contribution to the economic and social prosperity of Wales. The RTPs will work in

partnership with the Wales Tourist Board, local authorities, tourism businesses and with other organisations to undertake a range of marketing, product investment and business support activities on behalf of the tourism industry. The Wales Tourist Board is devolving a greater level of funding to the RTPs to support the strategically led activities they deliver and work closely with them to ensure that resources are used effectively for the benefit of the tourism industry and the economy of Wales.

Tourism is one of Scotland's most important industries, employing 9% of the workforce (200,000 jobs) and generating £4.4b per year. It is recognised as an area for real potential growth in coming years if Scotland can capitalise on its tourism assets and respond to market trends. The Scottish Executive's ambition to increase visitor spend in Scotland by 50% by 2015 shows their commitment to the industry. Scottish Enterprise is Scotland's main development agency and is funded by the Scottish Executive. Scottish Enterprise works with VisitScotland and their regions (see map) to promote this at a regional level.

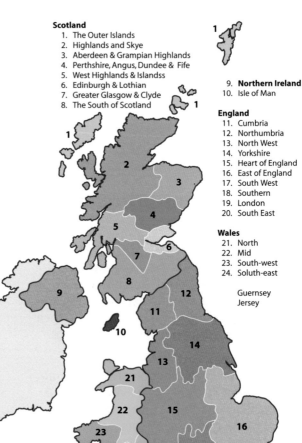

Scotland
1. The Outer Islands
2. Highlands and Skye
3. Aberdeen & Grampian Highlands
4. Perthshire, Angus, Dundee & Fife
5. West Highlands & Islandss
6. Edinburgh & Lothian
7. Greater Glasgow & Clyde
8. The South of Scotland

9. **Northern Ireland**
10. Isle of Man

England
11. Cumbria
12. Northumbria
13. North West
14. Yorkshire
15. Heart of England
16. East of England
17. South West
18. Southern
19. London
20. South East

Wales
21. North
22. Mid
23. South-west
24. Soluth-east

Guernsey
Jersey

There are over 2000 tourism-related businesses in Northern Ireland, 26 local authorities (each with a mandate for tourism development, visitor servicing and promotion), as well as private sector and community associations, funding agencies and training bodies – all actively involved in tourism. To manage and coordinate tourism interests at this level, the Northern Ireland Tourist Board (NITB) is proposing the establishment of Regional Tourism Partnerships. The NITB identified ten 'action programmes' in its *Strategic Framework for Action 2004–07*. To translate and deliver these action programmes at regional level, NITB proposed the creation of four or five Regional Tourism Partnerships, representing appropriate local stakeholders, e.g. local authorities, industry associations, funding agencies, private sector training organisations and government agencies.

Currently, there are five Regional Tourism Organisations (RTOs) in Northern Ireland, primarily responsible for marketing and, in some instances, visitor servicing. The proposed RTPs will build upon the current RTO structure. Their key roles will vary according to regional priorities and needs, but will cover the following:

Communications RTPs will be a conduit of information between Tourism Ireland, NITB and the local tourism industry. This includes disseminating market intelligence, marketing/business development opportunities, policy and strategy. Communication should be a two-way process.

Marketing Where appropriate, RTPs will support NITB and Tourism Ireland to market Northern Ireland to the best-prospect segments. In particular, RTPs will play an important role in markets closer to home.

Visitor servicing Visitors require a range of services on the ground – information services, booking facilities, events, entertainment, accommodation and signage. Many of the services at present are managed through the local councils via tourist information centres. NITB is

proposing, through RTPs, that councils, with the private sector and other public sector agencies, work collectively at regional level to provide greater, coordinated visitor care, and create a unique and seamless experience.

Product development RTPs will play an important role in auditing product availability, identifying product gaps, channelling local and national resources into filling identified gaps, packaging products appropriately for different market segments and assisting NITB to monitor quality/visitor satisfaction of regional product offer. NITB has also identified five 'signature projects' within the *Strategic Framework for Action*:

- Christian Heritage/Saint Patrick
- Giant's Causeway /Antrim and Causeway Coast area
- Mournes National Park
- Titanic (Maritme)/Belfast
- The Walled City of Derry

In addition, Fermanagh has been identified as a potential sixth signature project. RTPs will play an important role, not only in the development of the signature projects, but also by creating opportunities on behalf of the greater region.

Industry capability Through the establishment of Tourism Ireland and the support from central government and European Funding programmes, Northern Ireland has been 'fast tracked' up the ladder as an international tourism destination. Visitor numbers have grown significantly over the past decade, but this also has an impact on the industry's capability to deliver. Northern Ireland's tourism industry not only operates in a global market but must also meet international standards. RTPs have the potential to channel local and national training resources into addressing regionally identified skills gaps – giving the industry what they want and need.

Commercialism NITB, in recognising that tourism structures in Northern Ireland will not always have European Funding to rely on, are seeking new ways in which delivery mechanisms can generate income over and above public sector contributions.

---

activity

CHANGES IN NORTHERN IRELAND

Read the case study and analyse the changes that the Northern Ireland tourism industry faces and how the NITB is trying to address these issues by restructuring in the future.

Topic 3 Attractions

Tourist attractions can be in many forms, but for the purpose of this topic we will focus on them under the following headings:

- **Heritage**
- **Cultural**
- **Educational**
- **Entertainment**
- **Multi-function (conference facilities and special events).**

Heritage attractions

The UK's attractions are at the very heart of the tourism industry, with the top twenty paid attractions accounting for 45 million visits a year (2003). The UK has almost 6,500 visitor attractions, including country parks and farms, historic properties, theme parks, zoos, gardens, museums, galleries, and places of worship. They offer a wealth of unique experiences for international and domestic visitors alike. Attractions act as a major draw for visitors, generating income for local and regional economies – and for other sectors. such as hospitality, transport, retail, etc.

The Department for Culture Media and Sport works in partnership with the attractions sector to improve and enhance the quality of its product, to develop the skills base of those working in the sector, to generate better data for analysis and decision-making, and to promote and market UK visitor attractions domestically and internationally.

Heritage is our legacy from the past, what we live with today, and what we pass on to future generations. Heritage organisations operate in the public, private and voluntary sectors of the tourism industry.

The Historic Houses Association (HHA) represents the interests of Britain's historic houses, castles and gardens that remain in private ownership. The Association represents over 1500 such properties, the majority of which provide some form of public access. Around 350 open regularly to the public on a commercial basis, attracting between them over 12 million visitors each year. Many more open on an occasional basis.

The HHA represents more privately owned houses open to the public than those in the care of the National Trust, English Heritage and their equivalents in Scotland, Wales and Northern Ireland, put together.

These properties collectively make a massive contribution to rural economies through tourism and other commercial activities. Their contribution is estimated at £1.2b per year and they employ around 10,000 people. Successive governments have recognised the private owner as the most economic and effective guardians of these properties – not only the buildings themselves but also their contents, works of art, gardens, parks and archives.

The HHA is an association of these private owners, together with enthusiasts who want to visit the properties and help maintain this important element of Britain's built heritage.

Other guardians of our national heritage are the National Trust and English Heritage which are covered in detail in Unit 7.

The World Heritage List

'World heritage site' is the designation for places all over the world that have been judged by UNESCO (United Nations Educational, Scientific and Cultural Organisation) to be of outstanding universal value to humanity, and have been placed on the World Heritage List so that they will be protected for future generations to appreciate and enjoy. Places as diverse and unique as the Pyramids of Egypt, the Great Barrier Reef in Australia, the Galapagos Islands in the Pacific, the Taj Mahal in India, the Grand Canyon in the USA, or the Acropolis in Greece, are examples of the 788 natural and cultural places put on the World Heritage List to date.

A place on the World Heritage List and the resulting prestige often helps raise awareness among citizens and governments for heritage preservation. A country may also receive financial assistance and expert advice from the World Heritage Committee to support activities for the preservation of its sites.

Kew Gardens became a world heritage site in 2003, listed because of its uninterrupted contributions to botanical and environmental science since 1759, together with its unique collection of plants from all over the world, and its international influence on the history of landscape and garden design.

Major historic properties: visitor numbers

Attraction	2002	2001	% change
Tower of London	1,940,000	2,020,000	−3.9
Edinburgh Castle	1,155,000	1,125,	+2.4
Windsor Castle	930,000	905,000	+3.0
Roman Baths	845,000	865,000	−2.2
Stonehenge	760,000	675,000	+12.2
Chatsworth	620,000	520,000	+19.4
Tatton Park	565,000E	340,000E	+65.6
Hampton Court Palace	525,000	570,000	−7.9
Blenheim Palace	465,000	410,000	+13.2

Notes: *Excludes one attraction where operator did not authorise figures for publication. E = estimate.*

Source: www.staruk.org.uk

Cultural attractions

Cultural attractions are made up of a mixture of public, private and charitable organisations. Cultural organisations cover the arts, theatre, museums, etc. as shown in the table below. The National Gallery had nearly 5 million visitors in 2002 closely followed by the British Museum.

Major museum and art galleries: visitor numbers

Attraction	2002	2001	% change
Tate Modern	4,620,000	3,550,000	+30.0
British Museum	4,605,000	4,800,000	−4.0
National Gallery	4,130,000E	4,920,000E	−16.0
Natural History Museum*	2.960,000	1,695,000	+74.4
Victoria & Albert Museum*	2,660,000	1,445,000	+84.0
Science Museum*	2,630,000	1,355,000	+94.3
National Portrait Gallery	1,485,000	1,270,000	+16.9
Tate Britain	1,180,000	1,010,000	+16.5
Kelvingrove Art Gallery & Museum	955,000E	1,030,000	−7.3
The Lowry	810,000E	815,000E	−0.7

Notes: * *National Museums and Galleries that changed admission policy from paid admission to free admission in 2000 or 2001. Excludes one attraction where operator did not authorise figures for publication. E = estimate.*

Source: www.staruk.org.uk

a c t i v i t y

RECENT GENERAL TRENDS

Read the extract below on the general trends to visitors attractions and analyse the factors that have affected the various UK attractions over the last few years. Why do you think some have fared better than others?

Survey of visits to visitors attractions: general trends

The annual survey of visits to visitor attractions (2002) reveals a positive picture for tourism. The main trend according to the report, reveals a leap in visits to farms, gardens and countryside attractions as tourism recovered from the Foot and Mouth outbreak: farm visits are up 50% having been down 20% in 2001; country parks are up 13% having been down 10%; wildlife attractions are up 13% having been down 5%; and historic properties are up 8% having been down 6%.

Major attractions illustrating this trend are: Chester Zoo with 1.13 million visitors through the door last year, a 7% increase, and 75,000 visitors ahead of where they were in 2001; Chatsworth and Blenheim Palace saw increases of 19%, up to 620,210, and 13%, up to 465,562, respectively; Stonehenge welcomed a 12% increase in visitors, taking numbers up to just under 760,000.

The survey shows that the impact of free entry has helped to drive visits to museums and art galleries, particularly those in London. Visits to the Science

Museum increased 94% to 2.63 million; to the Victoria & Albert Museum 84% to 2.66 million; and to the Natural History Museum 74% to 2.9 million.

However, some historic properties in London and the South East are still suffering, as overseas visitors have not fully recovered to pre-Foot and Mouth levels, e.g. Tower of London, Canterbury Cathedral and St Paul's Cathedral, all of whom saw a slight drop in their visitor numbers. Yet many of the newer attractions have enjoyed consistent increase over the last few years. In 2002: British Airways London Eye received 4.09 million people, a 6% increase; the Eden Project received 1.83 million, an 8% increase; Tate Modern received 4.62 million, a 30% increase. The Deep in Hull opened last year and enters the survey with an estimated 750,000 visitors.

Blackpool Pleasure Beach remains the most popular attraction with 6.2 million visitors.

Source: www.staruk.org.uk

In 2001 the government scrapped the entry charges to all the country's national museums. Three years after the turnstiles were removed, visits were up 75% nationally with nearly 6 million more visitors. Visits to the Royal Armouries in Leeds had risen by 147%, to National Museums Liverpool by 94% and to the National Railway Museum in York by 57%.

Many principal museums gain funding through national and local government. According to the DCMS, the government's aim (2005) is to:

- Broaden access for all to all museums and galleries, including through free access to our sponsored museums and galleries.
- Ensure that our sponsored museums and galleries continue to retain their reputation as world-class institutions in terms of research and collections care.
- Develop and promote the educational potential of all museums and galleries, including those we do not fund directly, working in partnership with the Department for Education and Skills.
- Improve standards of training and encourage diversity in the museums workforce.
- Ensure an adequate skills supply for the museum and gallery sector.
- Promote best practice in the museum and gallery sector in all areas.

Educational attractions

Attractions that are educational are varied and include organisations such as:

- Activity holiday and summer school providers
- Educational institutions and language schools
- Country homes and gardens
- Farm parks
- Wildlife attractions, zoos, etc.

Activity holiday centres, such as PGL, provide activity holidays for children aged 7 to 17 and for families, offering a wide range of activities from kayaking, golfing, football to dancing and art. PGL have 15 centres in the UK, and now some in France.

Educational institutions also provide summer schools – not just for students to learn languages but also many sporting and other activities. According to the star uk 2001 survey on major paid admission attractions, the Eden Project, run by the Eden Charitable Trust, is the third most popular attraction in the country. It claims to be 'all about education but isn't like school', as shown in the case study above, right:

Country homes and gardens provide many keen gardeners the chance to admire and learn form these magnificent properties. Kew Gardens has nearly a

The Eden Project: education and communication

What's in it?
Over 100,000 plants representing 5,000 species from many of the climatic zones of the world. Many of these can grow in the mild conditions of Cornwall, but others demand greenhouses, and that is where Eden's two gigantic conservatories come in. The Humid Tropics Biome – the world's largest greenhouse – is home to the plants of the rainforest – bananas, rubber, cocoa, coffee, teak and mahogany. The Warm Temperate Biome, meanwhile, is filled with the plants of the Mediterranean regions of the world – South Africa, California and the Med itself. Outside, sunflowers, hemp, tea and a host of other plants from our own region grow.

Is it for scientific people or will the general public find it interesting?
Eden is all about making plant-based issues interesting to the ordinary person. Maybe 3 million people in this country are already signed up to environmental groups in some way. Eden welcomes them, of course, but is actually more interested in the 53 million others who are not – those who feel that the environment is of no relevance to them, or that they are too 'small' to effect any real change.

Is there anything for kids?
Schools are literally queuing up to experience the Eden magic. There are no white-knuckle rides, but at every turn there is something to engage and entertain children of all ages.

Where is it?
Eden is set amongst Cornwall's china clay country near St Austell – about 270 miles west of London. Just 50 miles further west is Land's End.

Are there any animals?
In the controlled environment of the biomes there are insects, butterflies and some lizards but there are no plans for any other animals – that is not what Eden is about.

Isn't it all just a big green theme park?
To many it will indeed be a green theme park. But the real difference lies in the scientific integrity and talent which underpins the whole enterprise – the academic excellence on site and the many partnerships we have set up with institutes, universities and individuals right across the world.

Source: www.edenproject.com

activity
ANALYSIS OF SUCCESS

Analyse what has made the Eden Project so successful as an attraction. What type of person do you think that it would not appeal to, and why? Can you make any suggestions as to how the project may be improved in the future?

million visitors a year, but there are many others that are popular around the country, as shown in the table below.

Major gardens: visitor numbers

Attraction	2002	2001	% change
Eden Project	1,830,000E	1,700,000	+7.8
Kew Gardens	970,000	990,000	–2.0
Edinburgh Royal Botanic Garden (F)	650,000	645,000E	+0.4
Wisley Garden	650,000	625,000	+3.9
Belfast Botanic Gardens (F)	620,000E	600,000E	+3.3
Cardwell Nursery/Garden Centre Gourock (F)	495,000	DK	na
Glasgow Botanic Gardens (F)	400,000E	400,000E	0.0
Wakehurst Place	320,000	290,000	+10.6
Stourhead Garden	305,000	270,000	+13.6

Notes: *Excludes one attraction where operator did not authorise figures for publication.(F) = Free. DK=data not provided. E = estimate.*

Source: Staruk.org.uk

Farm tourism is a rapidly growing sector and is particularly popular with families with young children. Horton Park Children's Farm in Surrey is just one of many that offer a 'hands-on' experience of feeding and touching the animals. Here the children are encouraged to hold baby chicks, ducklings and lambs.

Horton Park Children's Farm, Surrey

In the past, zoos and aquariums were the traditional place that children and families visited to see animals, but over recent years their popularity has declined as people have become less happy about seeing animals in captivity. These organisations now have to work harder than ever to encourage customers – as seen in the Blue Planet Aquarium at Ellesmere Port. At the heart of the aquarium is a 70-metre-long Aquatunnel (one of the longest in the world) with a moving walkway providing a spectacular underwater view, as ten different species of shark pass overhead.

In particular, organisations need to embrace the principles of green or eco-tourism and show that their activities are actively supporting the environment, rather than damaging it. This aspect of tourism development is dealt with in further detail in Unit 7.

Entertainment attractions

Entertainment attractions include all the big rides at leisure/theme parks such as Alton Towers – the largest theme park attraction in the UK. However, the UK's most popular entertainment attraction is the British Airways London Eye, with nearly 4 million visitors a year. Flamingo Land in North Yorkshire offers the opportunity to visit a theme park and zoo on the one site (see the Industry Focus interview on page 276).

Whilst a few of the attractions are privately owned, more and more are part of large international organisations – because attractions are big business. For example, the Tussauds Group is one of the world's leading visitor attraction and entertainment businesses, built on the strength of a balanced portfolio of brands with 15 million customers a year visiting international icons like Madame Tussauds and the British Airways London Eye, national leaders like Alton Towers or precisely targeted regional leaders like Thorpe Park, Heide Park, Chessington World of Adventures and Warwick Castle.

activity

BEING PART OF A LARGE ORGANISATION

Analyse the advantages of a single visitor attraction being a part of a large organisation such as the Tussauds Group. Can you think of any disadvantages?

Multi-function attractions

Multi-function attractions are facilities that offer more than one attraction on a single site. For example, the large entertainment centres – mostly on the outskirts of large towns and cities – that have been built around the country, offer a variety of attractions from conference centres to events. The 'ExCeL London' international exhibition and conference centre hosts a vast range of events throughout the year, from international travel trade exhibitions, to sporting events, as well as product launches, conferences and corporate hospitality functions. It is located by Canary Wharf – with its bars, pubs, cafés, restaurants and hotels – and is accessible by all modes of transport.

---
activity

MULTI-FUNCTION ATTRACTIONS

1 Research a specific multi-function attraction to discover what they offer the tourism customer. Which type of customer would they appeal to and why? (You may like to visit the ExCel London website.)

2 Analyse why multi-function attractions have increased around the country.

---
activity

RELATIONSHIPS BETWEEN SECTORS

As a final activity for the first part of this unit, you could visit a local organisation in one of the travel and tourism sectors – a travel agent, tour operator, tourist board, attraction, transport provider or accommodation provider. Investigate the relationship the organisation has with all the other sectors. Present your findings to the rest of the group.

Melanie Wood

Marketing Director (and joint owner), Flamingo Land, Yorkshire

Can you tell me about your job and how you came to get it?

My father purchased Flamingo Park in 1978, when I was 5 years old. Whilst I have no official qualifications in marketing, over the years I have worked in every department at the park – catering, bars, admissions, retail, holiday village and even the zoo. In my role as Marketing Director, my strength, therefore, is that I know the park and its customers extremely well. The fact that I am also joint owner adds a financial reason for me to do well at my job. I feel, therefore, that I am probably better at marketing Flamingo Land than someone who has a marketing degree but no connections to its ownership. (This is not to say, however, that such graduates or people with marketing experience would not benefit the company in a positive way.)

Can you tell me a little about the history of Flamingo Land?

Flamingo Park first opened in 1962. It started out as a very small zoo with camels, some monkeys, and polar bears – and, of course, flamingos. It was sold in 1971 to Scotia Investments, who also owned bingo halls, nightclubs and casinos all over the UK. Scotia added a few attractions to the park in the following few years, including a small fairground with rides such as dodgems, a carousel, a ghost train and a haunted house. The major new attraction, however, was dolphins, which they introduced in 1974. Whilst these additions improved the numbers, by 1977 Flamingo Park was losing money, and went up for sale yet again. One of the Directors of Scotia, Robert Gibb, my father, then purchased the park in 1978.

The first change he made was to rename it 'Flamingo Land Theme Park and Zoo'. Gradually new attractions were added, including, in 1991, the Bullet Rollercoaster – the first in Europe – which really put Flamingo Land on the map. Visitor numbers increased, reaching one million visitors in 1993.

What are the main aims for Flamingo Land?

With 1.4 million visitors (2003) Flamingo Land is currently the number one theme park in the north, and the third in the country, according to the BTA tables. Despite being the only privately owned

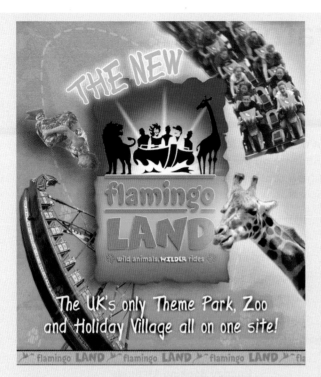

The UK's only Theme Park, Zoo and Holiday Village all on one site!

theme park in the top five, we still strive to be number two and then, in time, number one – a big ambition but, we believe, achievable.

Has Flamingo Land any unique selling points?

It is the only theme park with a zoo and a holiday village attached. It boasts over 100 rides and attractions and can accommodate up to 4,000 people in its holiday village – in tents, touring caravans, luxury static caravans or log cabins.

What forms of promotion do you use?

Flamingo Land is involved in a lot of promotions every year, including television, radio, magazines, newspapers and outdoor advertising. In total we have a budget of £650,000. In addition, marketing agencies invite us to participate in Days Out promotions that they are putting together for one of their clients. This means offering a discount – two admissions for the price of one, for example.

In 2000 Yorkshire and Tyne Tees Television produced a fly-on-the-wall documentary called 'Theme Park' which showed us preparing for the opening of our new season. Whilst we could not tell how many people visited the park as a direct result, what better way to advertise new attractions than to talk about them for half an hour once a week – during the summer holidays – on the two major regional television stations closest to the park. The series was very well received, and another series was produced two years later.

Can you tell us about your future plans for the resort?

Every winter we reinvest around £6 million back into Flamingo Land. This covers new ride purchases and new animal enclosures (around £4m), painting of rides and buildings (£500,0000) and in some years the purchasing of brand new luxury caravans (£1.3m) or new log cabins (£600,000). .

Over the past few years we have invested more and more into the zoo. In 2004 we launched our Lost River Ride which is a family flume ride that meanders through the grasslands of the Lost Kingdom, allowing the passengers to view the wild animals up close.

2006 brings a new suspended, looping rollercoaster, and two more examples of bringing our theme park and animals together: Old McDonald's Farm, a tractor ride for younger visitors which meanders through a 'farm' full of livestock, and Safari Ride which travels through the Lost Kingdom.

The Flamingo Land dancers

Topic 4   Tour operators

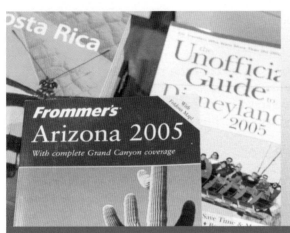

In this topic we look at tour operators and their influence on the travel and tourism industry. After a brief consideration of the role of the tour operator, we will investigate the following types:

- **Specialist**
- **Independent**
- **Integrated and mass market**
- **Outgoing**
- **Incoming**
- **Domestic.**

Tour operators are the organisers and providers of package holidays. Working with hotels, airlines and transport providers, it is the tour operators who put together the whole holiday packages. They then market the holidays to the public through travel agents, advertising, printed brochures and websites.

The chart to the right shows that the number of people choosing to book holidays via a tour operator is increasing. According to the ABTA Travel Statistics and Trends 2004, tour operators generate an annual turnover of £13bn by selling package holidays.

Specialist tour operators

Specialist tour operators are those companies that specialise in certain types of holiday, from cruising to mountain trekking. There are a number of specialist tour operators in Britain offering a wide range of holidays.

The Association of Independent Tour Operators (AITO) is an organisation representing around 160 of Britain's best specialist tour operators, and they are all listed on their website, www.aito.co.uk. AITO members are independent companies, most of them owner-managed, specialising in particular destinations or types of holiday. Every AITO member is passionate about their chosen destinations or activities and keen to share that enthusiasm with discerning holidaymakers.

The common aim of all AITO members is to provide the highest level of customer satisfaction by concentrating on choice, quality and service – as promised in the association's 'Quality Charter'. It is a source of pride to the Association that AITO

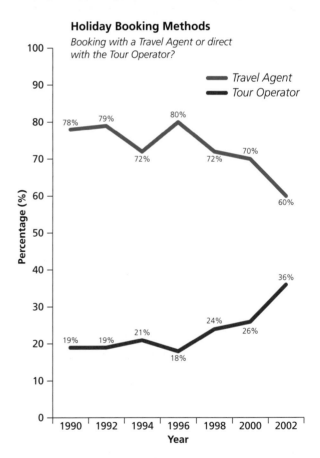

Holiday Booking Methods

Booking with a Travel Agent or direct with the Tour Operator?

— Travel Agent
— Tour Operator

companies dominate the consumer-voted travel awards every year, in various categories.

Companies admitted to AITO are not only vetted and fully bonded for clients' protection, in compliance with UK and European regulations. They are also bound by AITO's own code of business practice, which includes provisions for the clear and accurate description of holidays, and the use of customer questionnaires for monitoring standards. AITO members are also encouraged to participate in raising awareness among staff, customers and suppliers of the importance of responsible tourism.

Many of the tour operators are members the Federation of Tour Operators (FTO) which works as the voice of the industry for all tour operators, and aims to ensure the continued long-term success of all air-inclusive holidays by influencing governments and opinion formers.

activity

RESEARCH A SPECIALIST TOUR OPERATOR

Research a specialist tour operator of your choice (or use the case study on Exodus Travel) and then analyse the advantages and disadvantages of taking a holiday with them. (www.aito.co.uk has a list of the specialist tour operators.)

Independent tour operators

A lot of independent tour operators are members of AITO, as described above, and provide holidays for niche markets. However, others provide independent travel to a certain country or region. For example, Balkan Tours provides holidays to Bulgaria, and Baltic Travel provides holidays to the Baltic region, including Lithuania, Estonia and Latvia. There are many independent travel companies that operate around the world focusing in this way.

Others focus on a particular market segment – such as the luxury end of the market. An example is one of the world's oldest travel companies, Cox & Kings, founded in 1758. It organises high-quality group tours – such as 'Japan's Cultural Treasures' and 'Grand Tour of Northern India' – and private tailor-made trips, from the luxurious to the adventurous.

Integrated and mass market tour operators

Integrated tour operators are integrated with other parts of the industry – a retail travel agent or transport provider, perhaps. There are two types of integration – vertical and horizontal – as shown below.

Vertical integration occurs when the connections are made along the distribution chain, for example when an airline acquires (or forms) its own tour operations company. Vertical integration cuts out the middleman, saving on commission fees.

Horizontal integration occurs when two similar organisations – smaller tour operators, for example – merge or are amalgamated, or where one is taken over and absorbed by the other.

Horizontal integration cuts operating cost, especially if merged companies can use just one administration centre. Integration of this type is always subject to the monopoly and merger laws. The company formed must not be so big that it totally dominates the market, leaving no room for competition.

There are four big integrated companies in the UK market – TUI, Thomas Cook, First Choice and MyTravel. The dynamics of each organisation is shown in the table overleaf. The holidays they offer tend to be based around the sun, sand and sea, and are based on high-volume, low-cost packages. They are known as 'mass market tour operators' because each year they send millions of people to hundreds of destinations worldwide – and, as a result, have become household names.

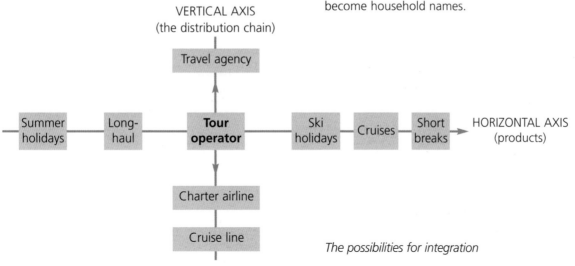

The possibilities for integration

The' big four' integrated companies

Company (Nationality)	Tour operator brands	Distribution brands	Airlines (and other integrated services)
TUI (previously named Thomson) (German)	Club Freestyle Just Jetsave Jersey Travel Tropical Places Skytours Something Special OSL Simply Travel Magic Travel Group Crystal International Thomson Breakaway Thomson Ski and Snowboarding/Lakes and Mountains Thomson Direct Portland Direct	Thomson (previously Lunn Poly) Callers Pegasus Team Lincoln (teletext and internet) Thomson TV (previously Lunn Poly TV)	Thomsonfly (previously Britannia) (and hotels)
Thomas Cook (briefly re-named JMC) (German)	Thomas Cook JMC Club 18–30 Signature Neilson Sunset Sunworld Style Cultura	Thomas Cook Thomas Cook TV	Thomas Cook Airlines (and many interests such as hotels)
First Choice (British)	First Choice Unijet 2wentys Sunquest Sovereign Eclipse Falcon Sunstart Hayes and Jarvis Meon Villas Exodus Citalia	Holiday Hypermarkets First Choice Travel	First Choice Airways (and Suncars car hire, First4extras airport parking)
MyTravel (previously called Airtours) (British)	Airtours Aspro Cresta Direct Holidays Escapades Manos Panorama Tradewinds Bridge	MyTravel Going Places Holidayline The Cruise Store MyTravel TV Late escapes.com	MyTravel Airways (previously Airtours International and Premiair) MyTravel Lite (and International Hotels, White Horse Insurance)

activity

ONE OF THE 'BIG FOUR'

Investigate one of the big four organisations, and analyse the relationship between the tour operator, distribution brands, and airlines within the group. For example, how do they ensure that their brands are marketed together on their websites?

Outgoing tour operators

Outgoing tour operators provide for the tourist travelling out of their resident country. For UK residents the most popular destination for travellers is Spain and other areas of the Mediterranean. The package holiday is still the preferred holiday for those leaving Britain, although long-haul and specialist activity holidays are growing in popularity.

The four major players dominate the outbound sector: TUI, Thomas Cook, MyTravel and First Choice (see left). The remainder of the market is shared by small and medium-sized operators, many serving specialist segments of the market.

activity

AN OUTGOING TOUR OPERATOR

Research one of the major outgoing tour operators. Describe the scale and structure of the organisation, and the products and services it provides. Can you identify any gaps in its provision of products and services?

Incoming tour operators

Incoming tour operators provide for the tourists coming into a country. UKinbound (formerly the British Incoming Tour Operators Association) is the official trade body representing the UK inbound tourism industry. It provides travel trade professionals and visitors from around the world with comprehensive information about the UK tourism industry. UKinbound represents over 270 major companies and organisations in all sectors of the travel and tourism industry in the UK.

According to VisitBritain – the national body responsible for the promotion of Britain abroad – in 2003 there were 24.8 million overseas visitors to the UK (up 3% on 2002) who spent £11.9b (up 1%). The USA is the biggest single exporter of tourists to Britain and therefore crucial to the success of inbound tourism. To attract tourism from America, VisitBritain has been concentrating on some 'niche' campaigns, promoting our heritage and cultural cities.

Examples of tour operators that run trips to the UK include large and small organisations. The Globus group of travel companies, founded in 1928, is today the world's most successful operator of escorted tours all around the world, including the UK. Cosmos is part of the Globus Group and arranges holiday packages to the UK, such as 'The Best of Southern England' and 'Bonnie Scotland'. Another group, Trafalgar Tours, offer tours such as 'Taste of Britain', 'Best of Scotland' and 'Irish Highlights'.

Contiki Tours, the 'world's largest travel company for 18–35 year olds', runs a trip around the UK, taking in London, Liverpool, Glasgow, the Highlands, Edinburgh, York and Oxford. At the other end of the scale, Abercrombie & Kent provide local guides, high quality accommodations, comfortable transportation and a choice of activities as they take travellers around Britain 'in style'.

Domestic tour operators

Domestic tour operators provide for people who wish to stay and holiday in their own country. According to VisitBritain, UK residents made 135 million visits within England in 2002 (up 2% on 2001), spending £21b (up 2.5%). The domestic market accounted for 74% of all tourist trips/visits by UK residents, but only 47% of nights away from home.

Most domestic tourist trips in the UK are made for holiday purposes, but business trips and visits to friends or relatives (VFR) are both growing in importance. Between 1998 and 2002, the number of business trips increased by 24% and the number of VFR trips rose by 19%, compared with an increase of only 11% in the number of holiday trips. The foot-and-mouth outbreak led to an overall reduction in demand in 2001, but business travel was affected less because business trips are more likely to be undertaken to urban areas than rural ones.

There are a number of domestic tour operators which operate in the UK. Many are small companies working in niche markets, such as Haggis, specialising in Scottish day tours.

Superbreak is the largest provider of UK (and European) short breaks. (More information on Superbreaks can be found on pages 89 and 92 of the AS Travel and Tourism book, or by logging on to their website www.superbreak.co.uk.)

activity

ONE INCOMING, ONE DOMESTIC

Investigate one incoming tour operator and one domestic tour operator.

1 Describe the scale and structure of each organisation.

2 Describe the products and services each organization provides.

3 Explain how the products and services meet the needs of customers.

4 Identify any gaps in provision, and explain how the organisation could fill the gaps and meet the needs of the customer.

In the last topic we looked at tour operators and their role in the travel and tourism industry. In this topic we go on to look at the role of transport providers, under the following headings:

- **Airline companies**
- **Rail operators**
- **Ferry and cruise operators**
- **Car and coach companies.**

Airline companies

Airline companies are those that provide flights into and out of the UK via airports across the country. There are two main types of airline service – scheduled flights and charter flights.

Scheduled flights

Scheduled flights fly to a published timetable on fixed routes, such as the frequent services between London and Paris, or the transatlantic flights from London to New York. The flights are usually at convenient times (i.e. not leaving or arriving in the middle of the night) and are from and to the best located airports. The no-frills airlines operate scheduled flights too.

Around 600 airline companies around the world provide scheduled flights. British Airways is the UK's largest international scheduled airline, flying to over 550 destinations. BMI is the UK's second largest, with its main operational base at Heathrow. It holds 12% of all Heathrow's take-off and landing slots and operates 1,700 flights a week with a fleet of 41 jet aircraft. In 2004 BMI flew 10.5 million passengers.

Virgin Atlantic, launched in 1984, is the second largest long-haul airline in the UK, and the third largest European carrier over the North Atlantic. Virgin's route network has grown rapidly to include destinations in the USA, Caribbean, Far East, India and Africa, and they have won virtually every award the travel industry has to offer. In 2003 they flew 3.8 million passengers.

As an independent airline, Virgin Atlantic successfully competes on all of its routes with most of the industry's major national carriers. These include British Airways, BMI, American Airlines, Continental, Delta and United on transatlantic routes; British Airways and South African Airways to South Africa; British Airways and Cathay Pacific to the Far East.

The market changed considerably when the cheap no-frills airlines entered the competitive arena in the late 1990s. EasyJet was the first company to change the airline market with its concept of no-frills flights and online booking (see the case study below). Today easyJet operates 210 routes across 63 key European airports. Other companies in the cheap flight market include Ryan Air and bmibaby.

There are many other smaller airlines operating around the country and regions. For example, Aer Lingus is Ireland's main airline, operating flights between Ireland and Great Britain. Smaller specialist airlines include City Jet, connecting London City airport with Dublin, and Emerald Airways operating between Liverpool and the Isle of Man.

Charter flights

Charter flights fly to specific destinations for tourism purposes, e.g. taking holidaymakers on package trips in the summer to Spain and Greece. Charter airlines often belong to the larger tourism companies, giving them full control of destinations, times and frequency. Charters flights are mostly seasonal – to Malaga in the summer, for example, and to Geneva for skiing in the

The easyJet airline was founded by Stelios Haji-Ioannou, and the family remains the major shareholder. It keeps costs low by eliminating the unnecessary costs and 'frills' which characterise 'traditional' airlines. The airline's headquarters, for example, is called 'easyLand'. In an industry where big city corporate HQs are generally the ultimate status symbol, this bright orange building next to the main taxiway at Luton Airport represents perfectly the easyJet low-cost ethos.

easyJet was one of the first airlines to embrace the opportunity of the internet when it sold its first seat online in April 1998. Now, approximately 95% of all seats are sold online, making easyJet one of Europe's biggest internet retailers. This helps to reduce significantly the cost of issuing, distributing, processing and reconciling millions of tickets each year.

Eliminating free onboard catering reduces costs, unnecessary bureaucracy and management. Passengers can, however, purchase food onboard.

The concept of a 'simple service model' eliminates other unnecessary, complex-to-manage and costly services, such as pre-assigned seats, interline connections with other airlines and cargo/freight carriage.

Efficient use of airports also cuts costs. Although easyJet flies to main destination airports throughout Europe, it gains efficiencies through rapid turnaround times – 30 minutes and below – allowing it to achieve extra rotations on the high-frequency routes, and make the most of its aircraft.

easyJet favours an informal company culture. Ties are banned – except for pilots! Remote working and 'hot-desking' have been characteristic of easyJet since the beginning.

winter – but some destinations are year round, such as Florida and the Canaries. At airports, charters have to use the 'landing slots' that are left before, after (and sometimes between) the fixed scheduled flights. This means that they often fly at 'unsocial' hours (but it also keeps costs down).

Charter fares tend to vary depending on supply and demand. To keep costs to a minimum, tour operators will always try to fill their aircraft and will discount to the extent of selling below cost to fill their allocations. Prices can soar at certain times of the year when

EASYJET AND OTHER AIRLINES

1 Read the easyJet case study and analyse the changes that they have brought to the airline market, for example in terms of new ticketing arrangements or fare structure.

2 Research and compare the changes made to the services offered by other airline companies over recent years. Explain the advantages and disadvantages of flying with easyJet compared to a scheduled flight with British Airways.

many people want or need to travel, e.g. school holidays, bank holidays and Christmas.

The Charter Airline Group of the UK (CAG) represents the UK's five largest charter airlines, First Choice Airways, Britannia Airways, Monarch, MyTravel and Thomas Cook Airlines. Collectively they carry 32 million passengers per year, employ 11,000 people and operate 145 aircraft.

Rail operators

In the UK there is one 'track operator' and several 'train-operating companies'. Network Rail has the task of providing and maintaining all the stations and the 21,000 miles of track across the country. The various train-operating companies run all the services for different parts of the country.

Trains provide a vital link in the travel industry, and they are often the first experience that the incoming tourist has of the UK. The Heathrow Express and the Gatwick Express ferry thousands of visitors from their inbound flights into London every day. Other train routes then provide access to the rest of the country. GNER, for example, provide high-speed services along Britain's East Coast main line, linking England and Scotland along a route of almost 1,000 miles. Virgin Rail operates InterCity and Express services linking over 130 stations across England, Scotland and Wales, including the new fast inter-city trains from London to Manchester (see page 272).

In addition to the national railway lines there are a number of local transport rail systems in major cities. The largest of these is the London Underground, with a system of 275 stations carrying over 3 million passengers a day, using 500 trains at peak times. Eleven separate lines criss-cross the capital and in the middle of London the lines are underground. This is a very popular mode of transport for visitors.

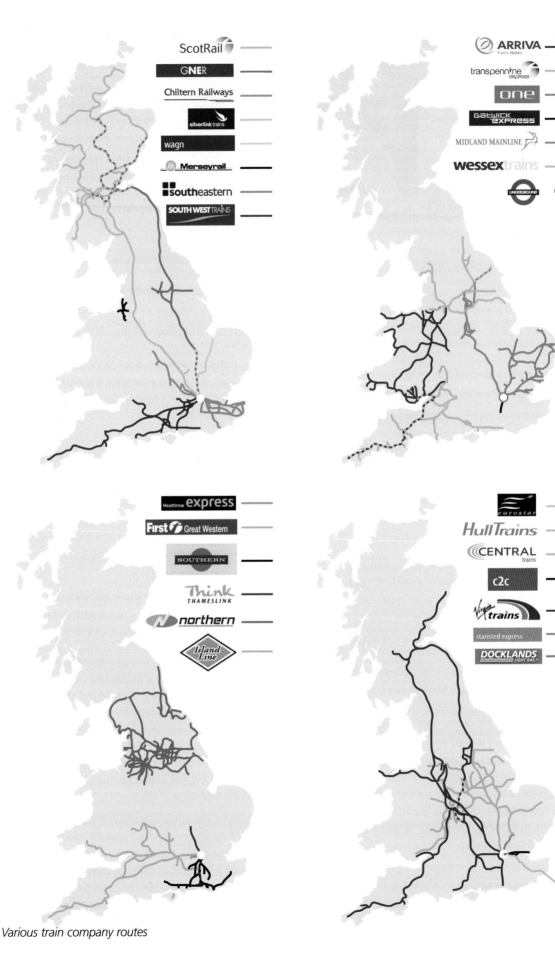

Various train company routes

Virgin Trains is putting airline competition to flight in speed, frequency, cost and convenience between London and Manchester, with train passenger numbers soaring since the launch of faster and more frequent services. A 29% increase in passenger numbers has followed the introduction of a half-hourly train service, with the train journey taking around two hours 16 minutes.

Virgin Trains has doubled frequency with its fleet of 125mph tilting Pendolino trains and now provides 33 weekday services each way compared to a total of 19 flights between Heathrow and Manchester, split between rival airlines.

Virgin Trains runs services at least every 30 minutes out of London Euston to Manchester between 07:05 and 20:05, with further services before and after these times. In contrast, air passengers must choose between five airlines using four London airports and, if they miss a flight, may have to wait up to eight hours for the next service with the same carrier.

Charles Belcher, managing director of the West Coast Mainline franchise, said: 'It has never been easier or quicker to catch the train between these

key cities. Passengers clearly value a short, seamless journey without speed cameras, airport check-ins, congestion charges and the hassle of transferring to and from the city centre.

Pendolino travellers can enjoy the convenience of First Class direct travel to and from city centres, at-seat catering and a spacious working environment. Also, a wide range of audio entertainment is available for moments of relaxation.

Business travellers also now benefit from the Business Advance First Class return fare from £225, which can be booked up to 18:00 on the day before travel and is significantly cheaper than British Airways' £285 Traveller Flexible fare.

Source: Virgin website www.virgintrains.co.uk, Jan. 2005

TRAIN OR PLANE?

Explain the advantages of travelling by Virgin Train rather than by British Airways for a business traveller.

Ferry and cruise operators

The ferry and cruise companies operate two quite different types of service. The ferry companies provide transport for passengers, cars and freight on fixed routes within the British Isles or to the other parts of Europe. If accommodation is offered it tends to be just overnight, as the passengers sail to a distant port so that they can start their holiday. Cruise companies, on the other hand, allow the passengers to travel in style for a much longer period – providing on-board accommodation, food and entertainment over several days or even weeks. For these passengers, the 'journey' is the holiday.

Ferry companies

The two main ferry companies operating around our shores are P&O and Brittany Ferries. Smaller ferry

companies, such as Caledonian MacBrayne (CalMac) and Swansea–Cork Ferries connect Great Britain with other islands. On the short Channel crossings, Hoverspeed and Hover Travel offer faster alternatives to the traditional ferry. Seacats make the crossing between Dover and Calais in less than an hour compared to the normal one and a half hour crossing by ferry.

P&O Ferries boasts the largest fleet of ships offering a wide range of services and facilities, the most comprehensive route network (see map) and the most frequent passenger and freight services to the continent.

Brittany Ferries, formed in 1972, operates one of the most modern fleets on the Channel, with eight ships and over 2,500 employees. It accounts for over 50% of the traffic on the Western Channel, carrying in excess of 2.6 million passengers, 780,000 cars and 170,000 lorries a year.

Cruise line companies

There are a number of cruise line companies that have become established in the UK, the largest being P&O Cruises, which is owned by Carnival plc – the third largest cruise company in the world by revenue. It includes Princess Cruises – the North American

P&O and Brittany Ferries routes

WHERE DO FERRIES GO?

Research the routes of at least six of the following UK ferry companies: Brittany Ferries; CalMac; Color Line; Condor Ferry; Hover Travel; Hoverspeed; Irish Ferries; Red Funnel Ferries; Scandinavian Seaways; Sea France; Stena; Swansea–Cork; Wightlink Ferries.

A new trend in cruising

easyCruise is aimed at the younger, more independently minded traveller –people in their 20s, 30s and 40s, who might not be interested in the traditional style of cruising. It is one of the latest ventures launched by Stelios (www.stelios.com), founder of the easyGroup.

Their first ship, easyCruiseOne, is based in the French and Italian Rivieras in the summer, and Barbados and the surrounding Caribbean Islands in the winter. Unlike traditional cruising, the ship will stay in port in the afternoon and evening to encourage people to have fun ashore and then sail late at night for the next destination. The flexible one-week itineraries allow for the travellers to embark and depart at any port on the route, provided they stay on board for at least two nights.

premium brand; Aida Cruises, one of Germany's fastest growing cruise companies; the successful P&O Cruises (Australia); Swan Hellenic in the UK; Ocean Village ('informal cruising'); and A'ROSA in Germany.

In contrast to the long-established P&O company, one of the newest entrants to the cruise line business is easyCruise (see below, left).

The Passenger Shipping Association, which aims to ensure that passengers travel in a safe, healthy and secure environment, has 34 cruise line companies as members, including:

Carnival Cruise Lines www.carnivalcruise.co.uk
Crystal Cruises www.crystalcruises.com
Cunard Line www.cunard.co.uk
Fred. Olsen Cruise Lines www.fredolsencruises.co.uk
Hebridean Island Cruises www.hebridean.co.uk
Norwegian Cruise Line www.uk.ncl.com
Ocean Village www.oceanvillageholidays.co.uk
Orient Lines www.orientlines.co.uk
P&O Cruises www.pocruises.com
Princess Cruises www.princess.com
Radisson Seven Seas Cruises www.rssc.co.uk
Swan Hellenic www.swanhellenic.com
Thomson Cruises www.thomson-cruises.co.uk
Voyages Of Discovery www.voyagesofdiscovery.com

RESEARCHING A CRUISE COMPANY

Select one of the cruise companies listed above and investigate their operation, researching the following points:

1 The size of the company and its ownership

2 The type of cruises it offers, and to which locations

3 The prices and additional costs.

Car and coach companies

According to the United Kingdom Tourism Survey (2002) 73% of all trips are made by car. For most people this is most likely to be in their own car. However, the inbound tourist often relies on hiring a car. More often than not they hire the vehicle from one of the transport gateways, such as an airport or railway station. In addition, each major town or city has a hire company depot – if not two or three. Well-recognised international car companies include Alamo, Avis, Europcar, Hertz, and National Car Rental.

Coach companies vary from those providing scheduled services from destination to destination, such as National Express and Stagecoach, to those that provide all-inclusive tours, such as Wallace Arnold Coaches and Shearings. The coach companies' place in the tourism market, however, is likely to change in the future (see below).

Other major players in the transport of tourists around the country are to be found in the popular tourist cities, especially London. In addition to the thousands of buses and taxis, the rickshaw is now breaking through as a mode of transport for tourists, as shown at the bottom of the page.

The future of the coaching industry

The Coaching Holidays report by market research company Mintel has predicted that the coaching sector will dramatically reduce in the future, with 'small family businesses falling by the wayside'. It follows the recent announcement of a merger between coach operators Wallace Arnold and Shearings, still to be approved by the Office of Fair Trading. The new company will carry one million passengers annually.

Mintel experts believe that larger coach companies could purchase hotels and niche transport firms to increase their position in the market. It said operators need to target specific sectors of the market – such as luxury or budget tours – to remain competitive. More worrying for coach firms, the report predicts that it will be difficult for operators to expand their customer base. Its poll found only 15% of holidaymakers who have not been on a coach holiday would consider going on one.

Sales through travel agents are also set to decline with more consumers booking direct, according to Mintel. However, internet bookings only make up a maximum 5% of coach bookings. Despite this, the future for the coach market is not all bad news, with growth predicted for this year. The total number of coach holidays predicted [for 2005] stands at 8.2 million – 5.9 million in the UK and 2.3 million abroad. This compares to a total of 7.9 million last year – 5.8 million in the UK and 2.1 million abroad. Mintel described the predicted rise as a 'tentative comeback' for the sector.

Destinations likely to see growth in this market include Eastern Europe. 'Eastern European destinations such as the Czech Republic, Hungary, Poland and Slovakia offer new experiences and a sense of adventure as well as low prices,' said the report.

Source: www.travelweekly.co.uk/Article 20645

activity

THE COACH INDUSTRY

Read the Mintel report and describe the changes predicted that will affect the coach industry. Explain the identified gaps in provision within the market.

The 'bloody nuisance' loved by tourists

Pedicabs – London's pedal-powered rickshaws – loved by tourists but loathed by taxi drivers, are gridlocking streets around the capital's West End nightlife hotspots. Pedicabs have soared in numbers over the last six years. London has an estimated 350 rickshaws, and they have also sprung up in Oxford, Manchester and Edinburgh. There are believed to be seven companies operating them in the capital, although nobody is sure of the exact number because they are not subject to any rules.

Taxi drivers went to court last year in an attempt to get pedicabs outlawed, claiming they were breaching an 1869 Act of Parliament which gave black cabs a monopoly on soliciting for passengers on London's streets.

But a high court judge threw out the challenge, ruling instead that a rickshaw amounted to a 'stagecoach', and was legal as long as it charged individual fares for each passenger.

But the Licensed Taxi Drivers Association has vowed to fight them off the streets. Its general secretary, Bob Oddy, believes rickshaws are 'deathtraps' which tip over if they touch the kerb or take corners at speed. He said: 'It's just a question of time before somebody gets killed.'

Mr Oddy said rickshaws did not represent a commercial threat to London's 30,000 black taxis. He said: 'They're not a challenge to us, and they clearly never will be. We don't want them because they're a bloody nuisance.'

Source: Guardian, 1 November 2004

We looked at transport providers in the last topic and reviewed the large variety of carriers that we have in the UK. But accommodation is also an important sector in the travel and tourism industry, and in this topic we will focus on the providers, under the following headings:

- **Hotels and motels**
- **Bed and Breakfast and guesthouses**
- **Self-catering accommodation**
- **Holiday centres**
- **Caravanning and camping**
- **Standards of accommodation.**

Hotels and motels

The basic difference between a hotel and a motel is that a hotel is a building where rooms and meals are provided for the traveller, whereas a motel is a building of furnished rooms, built to provide accommodation for the motorist and his/her vehicle.

Hotels and motels are still ranked as the most popular form of accommodation, along with guesthouses, with visitors from overseas; 45% stay in hotels and motels according to the United Kingdom Tourism Survey (2002). In fact 26% of UK residents stayed in a hotel in 2002, second in terms of accommodation behind staying with friends and relatives.

Accommodation Used by UK Residents in the UK

	2002	
	% of Trip	% of Spending
Hotel/Motel/Guesthouse	26	40
B&B/Farmhouse B&B	7	8
Rented House/Flat/Chalet	6	9
Hostel/University/School	1	1
Friends/Relatives Home	47	27
Second Home/Timeshare	1	1
Camping	2	1
Towed Caravan	3	2
Other	11	10

Source: United Kingdom Tourism Survey (UKTS)
Note: UKTS accomodation category definitions. Figures may over add dues to more than one accommodation type being used.

Accommodation Used by Overseas Residents in the UK by Visits

	2002	
	% of Trip	% of Spending
Hotels etc	45	46
Bed & Breakfast	5	4
Camping/Mobile Home	1	1
Hostel	4	6
Holiday Village/Centre	0	0
Rented House	3	6
Paying Guest	3	4
Free Guest	39	28
Own Home	2	3
Other	5	2

Source: International Passenger Survey (IPS)
Note: IPS accommodation category definitions

---

activity

UNDERSTANDING THE FIGURES

Examine the tables above, and explain what they show. Explain the differences in the figures for domestic and incoming visitors on the percentage of trips and their spending.

The major hotel chains have established themselves in the major cities around the UK – especially, of course, in London. This is where you will find the popular hotel chains such as the Ramada Jarvis, Radisson, Express By, Holiday Inn, Marriott and Best Western hotels.

Whitbread, owner of the Marriott and Premier Travel Inn brands, is the UK's largest hotel chain, with about 500 sites and 37,000 bedrooms, as shown in this table of the market leaders:

Hotel market leaders

Operator	Brands	Bedrooms
Whitbread	Marriott, Premier Travel Inn	37,100
InterContinental	InterContinental, Crowne Plaza, Holiday Inn, Express by Holiday Inn	29,100
Hilton International	Hilton	16,000
Permira	Travelodge	13,300
Accor Hotels	Sofitel, Novotel, Mercure, Ibis, Etap, Formule 1	11,300
Thistle Hotels	Thistle	10,100
Choice Hotels	Quality, Comfort, Sleep, Clarion	7,000

Source: BHA Trends and Statistics, 2004

In the last twenty years, Travelodge has taken the UK market by storm. Now with 271 lodges around the country, the company continues to grow – focusing more on town and city centres, including central and greater London. The lodges are located along the main road network across the UK and are aimed at the business traveller and families. They sell themselves on a friendly welcome and a clean and comfortable room, all from only £26 a night, as shown below.

easyHotels – found in cities in over 100 countries – represent the easyGroup's entry into the competitive budget hotel sector. They are targeting short-stay customers, who can book their rooms online – paying less the earlier they book.

Smaller hotel chains operate on a local or regional basis with maybe two or three in an area. These are often privately owned and offer individual style and service to the customer. Also, small family-run hotels still exist up and down the country, particularly in the traditional seaside resorts and rural villages, where there is not enough trade to interest a large hotel chain but enough to provide a good business for smaller ones. Indeed many 'country house hotels' offer an alternative to the larger hotels often with the same facilities but in a more scenic country setting. Old large converted country houses with a swimming pool, spa and golf course are popular with tourists at home and abroad.

Bed and Breakfast and guesthouses

B&Bs and guesthouses are often run by individuals in their own home. 'Bed and Breakfast' accommodation offers simply a room and breakfast, whereas a guesthouse can offer the option of up to three full meals a day, and often provides visitors with a communal sitting as well as a bedroom.

Both of these types of accommodation often provide supplementary income to the household and are more often than not run by the householder. These businesses are firmly set in the private sector, and range across a spectrum of country houses, cottages, village houses, farmhouses, town houses, manor houses, and even castles. They usually provide cheaper accommodation than hotels and motels, and

A good night's sleep at Travelodge

At Travelodge, we provide everything you need for a comfortable night's sleep, whether you're on the road for business, or enjoying a city break with your family.

Every room has: king-sized bed with cosy duvet; en-suite bathroom; remote-control colour TV; tea and coffee-making facilities; direct dial phone; internet access; in-room films.

We also offer: family rooms; smoking and non-smoking rooms; rooms with disabled facilities; 24-hour reception; fast check in – no check out; breakfast; drinks and snacks vending.

Many are also sited next to a fast food outlet, making access to meals easy for the traveller. Some even offer a delivery service to your room.

Source: www.travelodge.co.uk

tend to be located off the main road network. In some rural areas, farmers supplement their income by offering travellers bed and breakfast – providing invaluable accommodation in the more remote areas of the country. Tourist Information Offices often provide a list of local B&Bs and guesthouses, or they may advertise in the local area and in listing magazines.

Self-catering accommodation

Self-catering accommodation can range from renting a flat, house or chalet to the more unusual buildings, such as a church or lighthouse. Self-catering accommodation may be owned by individuals or a consortium of individuals but is mainly privately owned.

Large companies, however, are often involved with the marketing and promotion of the properties. For example, Cottages4you is an internet company that offers 9000 properties across the UK and 30,000 properties across the rest of Europe. It invites home-owners to advertise their property on their website. Holiday Cottages Group, part of Cendant VRG, has grown to become the premier cottage rental agency in the UK since entering the market in the 1970s. They operate under a number of different brand names, to appeal to every kind of holidaymaker, such as Country Cottages, English Country Cottages, Irish Country Cottages, Scottish Country Cottages, Blakes, Chez Nous and many others.

Hoseasons claim to offer the widest choice of self-catering holidays and short breaks throughout Britain, Ireland and Europe (see below).

WHAT ACCOMMODATION?

1 Read the case study on Hoseasons and then write a short report describing the variety of accommodation that the company provides.

2 Which type of accommodation would you recommend for the groups below. Justify your reasoning.

(a) Ceris and Wilf are aged 5 and 3, and are going on holiday with their grandparents.

(b) Sam and Rob are two teenage boys who with their Mum and Dad want to experience a change in their normal family holiday.

(c) Wynn and Colin are retired and looking to take a relaxing holiday in the UK.

Holiday centres

Holiday centres – or holiday parks – offer a complete package of accommodation and entertainment. Sometimes food is also offered, but self-catering accommodation and a choice of restaurants tend to be more common. There is plenty of entertainment and activities, often centred around a pool and sporting activities, with plenty for children to do. Holiday centres tend to attract families with children and, indeed, many will not allow single-sex groups of young adults to stay in the accommodation at all.

In 1936, Billy Butlin created a new holiday concept for the British holidaymaker – Butlins holiday camps. The first

Hoseasons

Hoseasons Holiday Lodges and Parks offer the widest choice of self-catering holiday rentals in British and Irish country locations, from secluded forest lodges to seaside holiday parks with swimming pools and entertainment. Whichever holiday centre you choose our well-equipped accommodation – in lodges, caravans, bungalows, apartments, chalets or cottages – is designed to give you the very best.

A Hoseasons Country Cottage can provide luxury accommodation in a perfect coast, country or village setting. Choose from cottages all over UK and Ireland – from the rugged Highlands of Scotland or the hills of rural Wales to the beautiful countryside of England. Hoseasons can help you find the perfect retreat for your holiday or short break – whether you're looking for an English country cottage, a rural farmhouse, a Scottish bothy, a rustic Welsh barn conversion or an Irish castle holiday home.

A Hoseasons Boating Holiday lets you explore the rivers and canals of England or Europe at a relaxing pace. Rent a self-drive cruiser and delight in the Norfolk Broads, the historic River Thames, the scenic Scottish Lochs or even the waterways of France, Germany, Italy or Ireland. Or discover the historic canals of England and Wales aboard your own narrowboat.

Discover Europe from the comfort of your own holiday park, apartment or villa. Over 120 holiday villages, parcs, centres and resorts give you the choice of lodges, apartments, bungalows and cottages in Holland, Germany, Belgium, France, Italy, Spain, Denmark, Norway and Sweden.

Source: Hoseasons Holidays

resort opened in Skegness, with fun and entertainment (led by the famous 'Redcoats') the backbone of the holiday. The Butlins 'camps' have had to change with the times, and they have now branched out to provide theme holidays and corporate hospitality, as well as hosting TV shows and competitions like 'Britain's Strongest Man'. Pontin's is another company that offers a similar type of holiday experience (but with 'Bluecoats' leading the entertainment). They also have a position in the market, with eight sites around the country

Haven Holidays (see below) are the largest holiday park company in the UK, owning 35 parks with a choice of self-catering and half-board accommodation (and some parks even have ground for caravans and camping). Center Parcs (see right) is a relatively new type of holiday park in Britain.

activity

PARK OR PARC: ANALYSING DIFFERENCES

From reading the comments above and by researching their websites, analyse the differences between Haven Holiday parks and Center Parcs. Explain which would appeal to which type of customer, and why.

Center Parcs in the UK

Center Parcs has four UK sites, each based around a central covered 'subtropical' water-sports area, including shops and restaurants. All four sites are set in beautiful locations: Longleat Forest in Wiltshire, Sherwood Forest in Nottinghamshire, Oasis Whinfell Forest in Cumbria, and Elveden Forest in Suffolk. The natural setting yields activities that fulfil all kinds of individual needs, whether it's sailing on the lake, getting quietly close to nature or taking up a new physical challenge such as a '3-G Swing' from a 13-metre climbing tower.

If sport isn't your thing, you can opt for pastimes as various and creative as flower arranging at Longleat, a bird of prey demonstration at Elveden, watercolour painting at Sherwood or a Hawk Walk at Oasis Whinfell. Or relaxing in the spa whilst the children are looked after in the children's club may be more appealing.

On arrival you park your car, and from then on transport within the village is by bicycle or on foot. Nature is the backdrop to everything, and the Villages are full of surprises. Set in forests with hides for wildlife, heathland glades, and wildflower meadows, their aim is for peace and relaxation.

www.centreparcs.co.uk

Caravanning and camping

As we have seen, caravan and camping accommodation is often associated with holiday parks, as it offers an alternative and cheaper form of accommodation. Caravanning and camping involve the tourists taking their own accommodation on holiday – in the form of a caravan or tent – plus their own beds and bedding and cooking facilities.

Caravan and camping sites range from a small area of ground – perhaps in a farmer's field or alongside some waterfront – with the bare minimum of facilities, to quite luxurious camping facilities with swimming pools and other entertainment, such as that found at Wildrose Caravan Park (see next page).

Standards for caravan and camping parks around Britain are ensured by the 'Best of British' which is a network of 'independent premier caravan, camping and holiday parks situated in some of the finest locations in the UK' (see map overleaf). Every park which is graded 'Excellent' by the Tourist Board, provides the 'Best of British' guarantee of quality.

'Best of British' site map

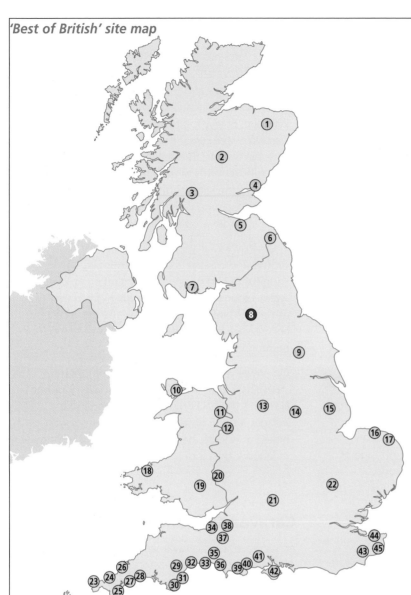

1. Huntly Castle Caravan Park
2. Blair Castle Caravan Park
3. Trossachs Holiday Park
4. Riverview Caravan Park
5. Drum Mohr Caravan Park
6. Ord House Country Park
7. Brighouse Bay Holiday Park
8. **Wild Rose Park**
9. Goosewood Holiday Park
10. Home Farm Caravan Park, Wales
11. The Plassey Leisure Park
12. Beaconsfield Caravan Park
13. Lime Tree Park
14. Shardaroba Caravan Park
15. Bainland Country Park
16. The Old Brick Kilns Caravan & Camping Park
17. Two Mills Touring Park
18. Cenarth Falls Holiday Park
19. Brynich Caravan Park
20. Poston Mill Park
21. Lincoln Farm Park
22. Highfield Farm Touring Park
23. Polmanter Touring Park
24. Trevella
25. Carnon Downs Caravan Park
26. Wooda Farm Park
27. Seaview International
28. Sun Valley Holiday Park
29. Dornafield
30. Beverley Park
31. Ross Park
32. Oakdown Touring & Holiday Home Park
33. Wood Farm Caravan & C P
34. Home Farm Holiday Park, Somerset
35. Golden Cap Holiday Park
36. Highlands End Holiday Park
37. The Old Oaks Touring Park
38. Bath Chew Valley Caravan Park
39. Wareham Forest Touring Park
40. Merley Court Touring Park
41. Sandy Balls Holiday Centre
42. The Orchards Holiday Caravan & Camping Park
43. Broadhembury Holiday Park
44. Quex Caravan Park
45. Hawthorn Farm Caravan Park

Wild Rose Caravan Park – a 'Best of British' site

Wild Rose is a family park in quiet countryside near the historic market town of Appleby-in-Westmorland. Caravans, motorhomes and tents welcome. Grass and hardstanding pitches available, some fully serviced with their own electric, water and TV hook-up points. Washing facilities and laundry. All facilities maintained to an exceptionally high standard.

Other facilities:
- Fully licensed restaurant and take away
- Shop
- Indoor TV and games rooms
- Outdoor heated swimming pool

Standards of accommodation

How do tourists know the standard of the accommodation they may be booking? National quality assurance schemes are a guide to the levels of quality you can expect at assessed properties. Visitbritain have assessed well over 10,000 hotels and B&Bs in England, and rated them according to quality, services and the facilities they offer. In fact, there are over 23,000 assessed accommodation providers in England in total. Hotels are rated between one and five stars and smaller establishments such as B&Bs, inns or farmhouses are graded between one and five diamonds. In both cases, five is the highest grade on the scale. Gold and silver awards are also awarded to those establishments that not only achieve the overall quality required for their rating but also reach the highest levels in key areas of guest comfort and service.

Scotland and Wales have their own quality assurance schemes, grading all types of accommodation on a one to five star rating, taking into account the quality, services and the facilities provided.

WHO SHOULD GO WHERE?

The following groups of customers are looking to find suitable accommodation in Penrith. Which accommodation would you recommend to each group, and why?

1 The Clark family (two adults and three boys aged 10 to 15) are going for a weekend orienteering in the Lakes and they would like to take their dog, but can leave him at home if necessary.

2 Graham and Ruth Hunt are looking to experience a relaxing week walking and enjoying the local hostelries. They are not limited by funds and enjoy fine wines and food.

3 The Glegg family (2 adults and four children under 10) are looking to visit the Lakes and attend a family wedding in Carlisle.

4 Jo and Elise want to spend the weekend getting to know the local area and to experience the local culture.

A selection of places to stay near Penrith

Brackenrigg Inn ◆◆◆◆

Overlooking Ullswater, award-winning food, fine wines and local ales, Les Routiers, family friendly, AA 4-Diamonds, dogs welcome in some rooms, spacious suites, 4-posters available.

£56.00 – £222.00 per double room per night, breakfast included

The White House Experience Guest House ◆◆◆◆

Comfortable and welcoming family-run licensed country guest house, set in half an acre of lovely gardens. Ample secure parking within the grounds. Children and pets welcome.

£60.00 – £80.00 per double room per night, room only

Brantwood Country Hotel

Country House Hotel ★★

Brantwood, originally being the principal building of a small estate, is an attractive country residence, dating from the early eighteenth century.

£66.00 – £90.00 per double room per night, breakfast included

Cove Park

Camping and Caravan Site
★★★★★

A small and peaceful caravan park for all Lakeland activities. Well-maintained with superb facilities.

From £13 per caravan per night

Meaburn Hill Farm ◆◆◆◆

Beautiful 16th century West Morlang longhouse with centrally-heated, en-suite rooms.Family-run with home cooking. Special diets catered for.

£65 – £75 per double room per night, breakfast included. Dogs £3 per night

In the last six topics we looked in detail at the various travel organisations in the travel and tourism industry. In the next three topics we will look at the legal and regulatory requirements that these organisations must adhere to. This topic considers those specific to the travel and tourism industry (or a sector within it) under the following headings:

■ **EU Package Directive**

■ **ABTA Code of Conduct**

■ **ATOL.**

We will investigate how these affect an organisation's operations and the products and services it provides. Then we will analyse the extent to which organisations have adapted their operations to meet the legal requirements.

EU Package Directive

From the 1960s to the early 1990s, ABTA had given protection for most holidaymakers, but a few large company collapses (and an increasing number of non-ABTA niche-market providers) prompted the EU chiefs to try and create a better protection system. The European Union (EU) Package Travel Directive came into force in 1990 as a consumer-protection measure, and was incorporated into UK law in December 1992.

The EU Directive defines the responsibilities of tourism operators in relation to 'packages' which they sell or promote. A 'package' is a pre-arranged combination of two or more of the following:

• transport

• accommodation

• other tourist services which account for a significant proportion of the package.

In addition, the package must be offered at an inclusive price and cover a period of at least 24 hours or overnight accommodation.

The law relating to package travel requires the tour operator to:

• provide full and accurate details about packages, including terms and conditions

• provide guarantees for any advance booking monies until the trip has taken place

• be liable as well as responsible for the services supplied by their sub-contractors.

For the customer this legislation should provide security in a variety of ways, not least of which is protection of deposits and late changes in arrangements. Tour operators must provide financial security of prepayments in one of three ways:

• bonding – setting up a form of business guarantee usually through an association such as ABTOT (The Association of Bonded Travel Organisations Trust Ltd)

• insurance – an individual policy for each customer

• trust accounts – lodging prepayments in a secure account until the package has been taken.

The directive means that tours now have to be licensed, a fund has to be created to cover contingencies, and travel agents are liable for incorrect information in brochures. The directive also restricts the use of 'additional surcharges' on package holidays. (Note, however, that flight-only sales are not covered by the legislation.)

EU member countries still retain their own consumer protection, but the regulations harmonise applications to travel throughout Europe. They create civil and

WHO IS LIABLE?

Under the EU Package Directive, who is liable for what has gone wrong in the following situations?

1 George and Martha booked a package holiday with a hire car through their local travel agent, but the car repeatedly broke down and was unavailable for half of the holiday.

2 Sam arrived at her hotel and realised it was too remote to stay in all week so she booked and paid for a number of local excursions with a local tour operator. Two were cancelled and no refund was given.

3 The Cammish family booked direct with a tour operator over the internet for a Florida holiday with all the theme park tickets and hire car. On arrival they found the pool too filthy to use and the hotel restaurant closed for maintenance.

4 Jo and Alice booked a flight to Dublin on the internet, and then the firm went bankrupt.

criminal liability for tour operators (wholesalers) and travel agents (retailers) for failures of the holiday or component parts such as hoteliers, airlines, airports and transfer companies. The official wording says: 'the organiser shall be liable to the consumer for the proper performance of all obligations under the contract [booking]'. This puts a lot of responsibility on

the organisation that has organised the package. Examples of breaches of the regulations are:

- Swimming pool closed because it is dirty
- A leaking pipe in a bathroom is left unattended despite telling the manager and resort rep repeatedly.
- Food served in a hotel causes illness.

However, there are certain situations that the tour organiser is not responsible for, such as:

- When an accident happens due to drunkenness or bravado
- When an accident is due to a third party – a local motorist, for example
- When 'force majeure' occurs – such as war, riots or natural disasters
- Excursions bought in the resort.

So, in short, if the organiser has sold a customer an inclusive deal, containing transport and accommodation and covering more that a 24-hour period, this legislation comes into effect. The travel organiser if also liable to provide customers with all additional advice as necessary, such as visa and health requirements, details of all connections, plus insurance and safety advice.

WHAT SHOULD THE COMPANY HAVE DONE?

Read the case study below. Discuss in a group how you think Airtours should have reacted. Discuss why they failed to provide adequate compensation straight away.

£5,400 holiday was a disaster

In January 2001, John and Meryl booked a summer holiday at a resort in Crete that had nearby nightlife for their 17 year-old twins. They specifically requested two adjacent luxury seafront bungalows, so that the twins would be free to come and go without disturbing their parents. The holiday was booked through Airtours at a total cost of £5,406.

Three weeks before departure, they were told that the bungalows were no longer being offered. They contacted Airtours and told them that they were not prepared to settle for a single villa. Airtours promised to investigate, and three days before departure, told them that it had indeed found them two bungalows.

However, on arrival they were allocated a single villa with one bedroom and extra sleeping in the

lounge/kitchen. While John and Meryl had the bedroom, the twins occupied the lounge/kitchen. This was precisely the arrangement they wanted to avoid, because the youngsters were heading for bed as their parents woke up in the morning. Not surprisingly, the holiday was a disaster.

Upon return, John wrote to Airtours, which offered a £200 holiday voucher. John asked 'Which' for help. 'Which' wrote to Airtours, arguing that is was in breach of the Package Travel Regulations. Airtours then offered to increase its offer to £696, which was considered inadequate. They then upped the offer to £1,336. The subsequent offer of £1,750 was accepted.

Source: Holiday Which, Spring 2002

ABTA Code of Conduct

The Association of British Travel Agents (ABTA) is the UK's main trade association for tour operators and travel agents. In January 2005 its members included 1052 tour operators and 6310 travel agency offices – accounting for 85% of UK-sold holidays, and a turnover of £26 billion.

If a company or firm is selling in the UK or the Republic of Ireland and is engaged in retail business (i.e. acting as a travel agent) and/or engaged in principal business (i.e. acting as a tour operator) it can join ABTA as a member.

Being a part of ABTA sends strong signals to a company's customers – telling them that the business is committed to high standards and practices, and that the customers' money is protected.

To protect consumer's monies and holidays, ABTA paid out £2.2 million in respect of travel agents' failures

A summary of the ABTA Code of Conduct

- ABTA members must not mislead customers with their advertising and must include all compulsory charges in their prices. It is a requirement of all ABTA members to include their ABTA number in all their advertisements.

- When a customer books with an ABTA member they must receive accurate information to help them choose the travel arrangements that are right for them.

- ABTA members must follow all the necessary legal requirements such as the ATOL Regulations and must make the customer aware of the terms and conditions that apply.

- ABTA members must also give the customer guidance about any health requirements and the passport and visa requirements for the customer's travel arrangements.

- If a customer has any special requests concerning a disability or other medical condition, ABTA members must ensure that these are dealt with properly and confidentially. ABTA members must also give information about travel insurance.

- Before completing a booking, ABTA members must tell the customer if the Foreign and Commonwealth Office has issued advice about the destination.

- ABTA members must notify the customer as soon as possible if it is necessary to change or cancel the travel arrangements. An ABTA member cannot cancel the booking after the date for payment of the full price unless it is necessary to do so for reasons outside its control. If this happens, the ABTA member must offer the customer the choice of having all their money back or choosing alternative travel arrangements.

- If an ABTA member makes a significant change to the customer's travel arrangements they must offer them the choice of accepting the changed travel arrangements or having their money back.

- If an ABTA member does cancel the booking or makes a significant change to the travel arrangements after the date for payment of the full price they must offer compensation unless the reason for the cancellation or change was outside of their control.

- An ABTA member must notify the customer as soon as possible of any serious building works at their destination. If they wish, the customer can transfer to another holiday or cancel and have their money back.

- If a customer has a complaint about travel arrangements they should write to the ABTA member concerned. They must provide the customer a full reply within 28 days. If the customer remains dissatisfied they should write again pointing out the areas of dispute. Again the ABTA member must respond within 28 days.

- If the customer fails to reach a satisfactory position with the ABTA member they can have the matter resolved through the ABTA Arbitration Scheme.

- A Code of Conduct Committee, which has independent representation, considers any cases. Their decisions could result in companies being reprimanded, fined or even expelled from ABTA.

(2001) and £90,000 in respect of tour operators failures. They have a procedure for handling complaints and settling with customers. In 2003, ABTA dealt with nearly 17,000 complaints. Of these, over 1,200 went to ABTA's independent arbitration scheme, an alternative to a small claims court.

As a regulatory body, ABTA maintains a strict Code of Conduct (see below, left) which aims to ensure that consumers receive the best possible service from ABTA travel agents and tour operators.

activity

HAVE YOU THOUGHT ABOUT JOINING ABTA?

Explain, as if to a newly established travel agent, the advantages and disadvantages of being an ABTA member. Explain how it will affect their operation – including their administration procedures and the way they deal with customers.

If a customer believes that their tour operator has broken the Code of Conduct, it is up to them to pursue a claim against the company. But for the claim to succeed it's not enough that the customer didn't enjoy the holiday, as there may be many reasons for this – bad weather, a wrong choice of holiday, or things beyond the tour operator's control.

The customer has a legal duty to prove that the tour operator has broken the terms of the holiday contract. These are known as 'express' or 'implied' terms. Examples of express terms are where the brochure promises full board or water-skiing. Implied terms are those which you would reasonably expect, even though they aren't actually spelt out in the contract – for example, your holiday should be of a reasonable standard, bearing in mind the price you paid.

The complaint may not succeed if the customer did not complain as soon as possible – on the spot while in resort – and give the tour operator every reasonable opportunity to put things right, or if they didn't accept any reasonable attempts by the company to sort out the problem at the time. It's rare to get the whole holiday cost back. Only if the holiday was a total disaster from start to finish or if the customer's disappointment and expenses were substantial can they expect a full refund.

ATOL

The 'Air Travel Organiser's Licence' (ATOL) system is a protection scheme for flights and air holidays, managed by the Civil Aviation Authority (CAA). Most firms who sell air travel in the UK are required by law to hold a licence called an ATOL. The ATOL travel protection scheme is the UK's biggest by far, protecting 28 million passengers every year, and covering virtually all flights and holidays sold by travel firms in the UK, including telephone and internet bookings.

ATOL protects the customer from being stranded abroad or losing money when a tour operator goes out of business. ATOL protection is included in the price of a holiday booked with an ATOL holder, and there's a government-backed fund called the Air Travel Trust that steps in if any ATOL bond isn't enough to look after everyone affected by a failure.

Between January 1986 and March 2001:

- 303 licensed companies failed to provide 4.9 million holidays.

- 181,814 people were abroad when their tour operator failed, and arrangements were made at a cost of £28.8 million for them to complete their holidays and return home.

- A further 1,069,107 people were given refunds of advance payments totalling £126.9 million from bonds and the Air Travel Trust.

As a customer, if you pay any money – even a deposit – to a travel firm in the UK for a flight or a package holiday by air, the sale usually has to be ATOL protected unless you get a scheduled air ticket straight away. A travel agent may not have its own ATOL, but it must book you with a firm that holds one, and tell the customer which ATOL they are protected by. As soon as the customer pays any money, they must be given a special 'ATOL receipt'. An ATOL receipt gives the name of the licensed firm the passenger has booked with, and its ATOL number. It must honour the booking, even if the agent goes out of business or if it goes bust itself.

The exceptions to the ATOL rules are if a customer:

- buys a scheduled airline ticket from a travel agent

- books direct with an airline, rather than with a travel firm

- books from outside the UK (in most cases).

Health and safety and equal opportunities legislation

In the last topic we looked at legislation specific to the travel and tourism industry. The next two topics look at how more generic legislation applies to travel and tourism organisations. This topic considers regulations concerned with health and safety, and with equal opportunities, under the following headings:

- **The Health and Safety at Work Act 1974**
- **EU Working Time Directive**
- **Equal opportunities legislation**
- **The Disability Discrimination Act 1995**
- **The Sex Discrimination Act 1975**
- **The Race Relations Act 1976**
- **Age discrimination.**

The Health and Safety at Work Act 1974

Health and safety is a big issue in most industries and none more so than travel and tourism. Travel organisations have to make sure that their customers are protected – but also their staff.

The Health and Safety at Work Act 1974 is the principal piece of health and safety legislation in this country. Under the 1974 Act, both employers and employees have duties. Employers' duties are to:

- ensure, so far as is 'reasonably practicable', the health, safety and welfare of all employees and any other people who may use their premises or be affected by their business.

- produce a written policy statement explaining how they intend to do this.

- provide appropriate training, instruction, supervision and information.

Employees' duties are to:

- cooperate with employer's arrangements for ensuring health and safety.

- take reasonable care of the health and safety of themselves and others.

Employers' duties to protect the 'health, safety and welfare' at work of all their employees are qualified with the words 'so far as is reasonably practicable'. This means that employers can argue that the costs of a particular safety measure are not justified by the reduction in risk that the measure would produce.

The Act allows the government to issue Regulations, Guidance and Approved Codes of Practice for employers, enforced by an inspectorate – the Health and Safety Executive – who can issue penalties against employers if they do not obey the law. Where risk of injury to health – from whatever cause – is high, employers are also required to carry out a risk assessment.

activity

HEALTH AND SAFETY RISKS

In groups, choose a specific sector of the travel and tourism industry and discuss the possible health and safety risks that are likely to arise.

EU Working Time Directive

The EU Working Time Directive provides guidance on the working time permissible for an individual within the workplace. The directive:

1. Lays down minimum safety and health requirements for the organisation of working time.

2. Lays down requirements about minimum periods of daily rest, weekly rest and annual leave, breaks and maximum weekly working time; and certain aspects of night work, shift work and patterns of work.

3. Applies to all sectors of activity, both public and private, with the exception of air, rail, road, sea, inland waterway and lake transport (and sea fishing, other work at sea and doctors in training).

So clearly the working time directive applies to some parts of the travel and tourism industry and not others. For example, this directive does not cover security and surveillance personnel who protect property and persons, or dock or airport workers. Also it does not cover people who work in an environment where there is a foreseeable surge of activity. This is particularly relevant in travel and tourism, with its seasonal patterns.

Equal opportunities legislation

Equal opportunities is about treating everyone equally and giving everyone the same opportunity – regardless of their age, sex, race, religion, disability, sexual orientation, etc.

Equal opportunities in travel and tourism is about making tourism possible for everyone – whether you are young, old, a mum pushing a buggy, a wheelchair user, a visually or hearing-impaired person, a carer or someone recovering from an accident or an illness.

For travel and tourism organisations, equal opportunities legislation consists of a range of laws that outline how they are to operate. The Equal Opportunities Commission (EOC) provides companies with guidelines (see below). The EOC is the organisation responsible for overseeing the relevant legislation. Employment law outlaws discrimination at

Examples of EOC guidelines for employers

Getting staff

- Ask applicants for details that will tell you if they can do the job
- Don't ask questions unrelated to the job
- Adapt your methods of recruitment to enable disabled people to apply
- Ensure starting pay is set fairly and equitably

Keeping staff

- Keep open channel of communication with all staff
- Make sure opportunities for promotion are made known and open to all staff

Harassment/bullying

- Make it clear with all staff that harassment and bullying are not tolerated
- Don't be tempted to blame the person who is being harassed or bullied – don't discipline or sack them
- Don't' ignore the situation – it won't go away

Discipline/grievances

- Have procedures in place for handling discipline and grievances
- Apply action fairly and consistently, regardless of race, sex, disability, sexual orientation, religion, belief or age.

Flexibility/reasonable adjustments

- Make reasonable adjustments to overcome physical and non-physical barriers for people, such as disabled people, older people or people with pushchairs.

Maternity/paternity law

When an employee becomes pregnant an employer must:

- Allow her paid time for antenatal care
- Provide additional health and safety protection for her and her child during her pregnancy and whilst she is a new mother, or as long as she is breastfeeding
- Allow her to return to her job after a period of maternity leave
- You must not dismiss her because she is pregnant or penalise her in any way – no matter how short a time she has been working for you and regardless of how few hours she works.
- Fathers who have been working for you for at least a year are entitled to take two weeks paid paternity leave when their child is born.

Equal pay

- Equal pay means providing the same pay and condition for men and women doing the same job. They should be paid the same hourly rate whether a man or a woman does it, and whether it is done full-time or part-time.

work on the grounds of sex, sexual orientation, religion, race and disability. Women and men have a right to be paid equally for doing the same job or for doing work of equal value.

Unequal pay usually comes in two forms:

- women being paid less than men for the same or a similar job
- women being paid less than men for doing work of equal value, that is, doing a job that is different but requires the same levels of skill, knowledge, effort and responsibility.

The right to equal pay comes regardless of your type of contract and covers basic pay, bonuses, overtime, holiday pay, sick pay, performance-related pay and occupational pensions.

The Disability Discrimination Act 1995

You will already be aware of the Disability Discrimination Act 1995 (DDA) from your AS course. The DDA was introduced to prevent discrimination against disabled people. The Act means that accommodation providers, including small hotels and guest accommodation providers, have to make reasonable adjustments to the way in which they deliver their services so that they do not discriminate against disabled people and are better able meet disabled people's requirements. Taking no action potentially leaves an organisation open to legal action.

The DDA uses a broad definition of disability that embraces people with a range of impairments, including people who

- are blind or partially sighted
- are deaf or hard of hearing
- have heart conditions
- have epilepsy

- have problems with continence
- have insulin-dependent diabetes
- have Downs Syndrome
- are dyslexic
- have arthritis
- are wheelchair users
- have experienced mental health problems
- have learning difficulties.

Since 1995 it has been illegal to refuse to serve somebody on the grounds that they have a disability. For example, it would be illegal to refuse to take a booking from a guest simply because they had a guide dog.

The Act also covers deliberately providing a poorer quality of service to disabled people, for example taking longer to serve a disabled person, or applying terms that are unreasonable, such as asking for a higher deposit or charging a disabled customer more than non-disabled guests.

Since October 2004 the DDA has also expected all service providers to take reasonable measures to remove, alter or provide a reasonable means of avoiding any physical barriers to accessing and using their premises.

Equal opportunities are important because they also make good business sense. There are at least 8.5 million disabled people in the UK alone, with an annual spend of over £40bn. Of these, we know at least 2.5million travel regularly, but we also know that many do not, because the facilities are not there. At present only 2% of accommodation in the UK has been assessed as being accessible to people with disabilities.

By 2009, there will be 2 million more people over 60 in the UK than there are today. There is a similar trend across the rest of Europe. While these groups live longer, and are better off than previous generations, age brings an increasing chance of a disability, although many people may not identify themselves as 'disabled'.

Increasingly, conference organisers and those hosting international events will not book venues unless there is sufficient accessibility. Visitors with high expectations of accessibility from countries like the US expect to find similar facilities when they book overseas.

Most retail sector businesses reporting back to the Disability Rights Commission (DRC) on alterations made to their premises have stated that their primary motivation was 'moral' – making their premises more accessible was the right thing to do. However, the majority also reported that the investment was repaid in increased business.

1 Check if public telephones are fitted with inductive couplers so that people who use hearing aids can use the handset. Most modern phones have this facility.

2 Ensure that at least some telephones are available with large buttons and a flashing light when the phone rings.

3 Have a portable 'vibrating alarm' available on request for guests who may have difficulty in responding to an audible fire alarm.

4 Specialist equipment required by guests with a disability is often available locally for hire through Social Services, the Red Cross or Disability Information Advice Line (DIAL).

5 Ensure that there is at least one copy of the menu in large print, and offer to read the menu if appropriate.

6 At a reception/entrance desk, paper and pen should be available for guests with hearing difficulties.

7 Use large-print guest information and registration forms.

8 Accept assistance dogs (for both visual and hearing impaired people) in bedrooms and public areas.

9 Use coloured glassware and jugs to make it easier for visually impaired people to see what they are using.

10 When changing signage, incorporate clear typeface, contrasting colours, non-reflective and well-lit information. Easy to read, head-height wall signs not only assist people who are partially sighted, you also make it easier for people who cannot easily hear or make themselves understood at busy reception times. Tactile and Braille information should be at a height that can be reached.

11 When decorating, ensure that door surrounds/frames are in contrast with the wall and door, and that there is contrasting door furniture. Ensure that steps are distinguishable through contrasting brightness.

12 Where there is not a low reception, ensure that a low desk is made available and that reception staff approach the guest rather than leaning over the desk.

13 Avoid an all-white finish in bathrooms and public toilets. Provide coloured towels where there is white furniture so that visually impaired guests can find them more easily.

14 Ensure that blocks are available for raising the height of beds.

15 Trim any overhanging plants or hedges along pathways.

16 If appropriate to your reception/entrance area, display a 'hoot car horn for attention' sign.

17 When talking to a wheelchair user, don't lean on the wheelchair as this is part of the user's personal space.

18 If someone looks as if they need assistance, offer it, but wait for them to accept before you help.

19 When taking bookings, always ask about a guest's particular requirements that you might need to know – for example, do they need a vegetarian or other special diet, do they have a disability, will they be arriving early? In this way, taking care of a disabled guest is simply an extension of the way you take care of all guests.

20 Disabled people are individuals like everyone else. Don't make assumptions about their abilities or needs.

Source: www.tourismforall.org.uk

Cornish owner pleased with his bookings

'We have a two-bedroom self-catering cottage with disabled access. We're registered in the National Accessible Scheme and we've been pleasantly surprised by the number of bookings,' says the owner. 'In our first year of business, families with a disabled or elderly person have accounted for 35% of our bookings. What's more, most of them have told us that they would recommend our accommodation to others.' The owner is so pleased with bookings that he is looking at building a second cottage for up to four guests.

Source: www.tourismforall.org.uk

activity

PLANNING FOR EASY ACCESS

Read the Cornish owner story and the top tips to easy access. The accommodation in Cornwall is to be expanded for more disabled guests by building another self-catering cottage alongside the first. The new cottage is to be built next to a wide area of off-road car parking, and will consist of two bedrooms, kitchen, sitting room and bathroom – all on one floor. Write a complete list of the things the owner needs to consider when building and decorating this new cottage. You may find it useful to include a plan in your answer.

The Sex Discrimination Act 1975

The Sex Discrimination Act (SDA) prohibits sex discrimination against individuals in the areas of employment, education, and the provision of goods, facilities and services, and in the disposal or management of premises. It also prohibits discrimination in employment against married people. It is not unlawful to discriminate against someone because they are not married. Victimisation because someone has tried to exercise their rights under the SDA (or Equal Pay Act) is prohibited. The SDA applies to women and men of any age, including children.

The SDA prohibits 'direct' and 'indirect' sex discrimination. Direct sex discrimination is where someone is treated less favourably, because of their sex, than a person of the opposite sex in comparable circumstances. Types of direct sex discrimination include sexual harassment and treating a woman adversely because she is pregnant. Indirect sex discrimination is where a condition or practice is applied to both sexes – but it adversely affects a considerably larger proportion of one sex than the other, and it is not justifiable, irrespective of sex, to apply that condition or practice. For example, an unnecessary requirement to be under 5' 10' in height would discriminate against men; a requirement to work full-time might be unlawful discrimination against women.

Discriminatory advertisements are unlawful, but only the Equal Opportunities Commission can take action against advertisers.

In general, it is unlawful for an employer to discriminate directly or indirectly on grounds of sex or marriage in:

- Recruitment (although sex discrimination will be lawful if one of the defined genuine occupational requirements applies – for example, the job needs to be held by a man to preserve privacy and decency, or a role in a performance needs to be held by a woman for reasons of authenticity).
- Treatment at work (but note that claims relating to discrimination in contractual pay and benefits are brought under the Equal Pay Act).

The Race Relations Act 1976

The Race Relations Act is concerned with people's actions and the effects of their actions, not their opinions or beliefs. Racial discrimination is not the same as racial prejudice.

It is not necessary to prove that the other person intended to discriminate against you: you only have to show that you received less favourable treatment as a result of what they did.

The Race Relations Act makes it unlawful for a person to discriminate on racial grounds against another and defines racial grounds as including race, colour, nationality or ethnic or national origins.

Discrimination occurs when someone is treated less favourably on grounds of their colour, race, nationality, or ethnic or national origin. From the individual's point of view it is not necessary to prove that someone intended to discriminate against them: it is sufficient only to show that the outcome of their action was that the individual received less favourable treatment.

The Race Relations Act identifies three main types of racial discrimination:

Direct racial discrimination

This occurs when a person has been treated less favourably on racial grounds than others in similar circumstances. Racist abuse and harassment are forms of direct discrimination .The law considers this to have the effect of violating that person's dignity, or of creating an intimidating, hostile, degrading, humiliating or offensive environment for that person.

Indirect racial discrimination

Indirect racial discrimination may fall into one of two categories. The first is 'on grounds of colour or nationality' under the original definition in the Race Relations Act. This occurs when an apparently non-discriminatory requirement or condition which applies equally to everyone:

- can only be met by a considerably smaller proportion of people from a particular racial group; and
- which is to the detriment of a person from that group because he or she cannot meet it; and
- the requirement or condition cannot be justified on non-racial grounds.

For example, a rule that employees must not wear headgear could exclude Sikh men who wear a turban, or Jewish men who wear a yarmulka, in accordance with practice within their racial group.

The second category – introduced by the Race Relations Act (Amendment) Regulations 2003, to comply with the EC Race Directive – is indirect discrimination based 'on race, ethnic or national origin'. This occurs when a provision, criterion or practice which, on the face of it, has nothing to do with race and is applied equally to everyone:

- puts, or would put, people of the same race or ethnic or national origins at a particular disadvantage when compared with others; and
- puts a person of that race or ethnic or national origin at that disadvantage; and cannot be shown to be a proportionate means of achieving a legitimate aim.

This second, newer, category is, in general terms, broader than the first category. As a result, it may be easier to establish indirect racial discrimination than previously.

Victimisation

Victimisation has a special legal meaning under the Race Relations Act. It occurs if a person is treated less favourably because they have complained about racial discrimination, or supported someone else who has.

Racist incidents – ranging from criminal harassment and abuse to physical violence – are offences under the criminal law. Inciting racial hatred is also a criminal offence. Publishing and disseminating materials such as leaflets and newspapers that are likely to incite racial hatred are also criminal offences and should be reported to the police.

Racially offensive material in the media contravenes media codes of practice. Complaints can be made to the Press Complaints Commission or the Broadcasting Standards Authority. Complaints about racially offensive advertisements should be made to the Advertising Standards Authority.

Age discrimination

Discriminating against workers on the basis of their age can be unfair to individuals and harmful to the economy. In particular, the assumption that someone is 'too old' to be sufficiently adaptable to do a job as well as a younger person wastes talent and potential in many workplaces.

In 2000, the EU passed a new directive requiring governments to introduce equality in employment legislation, including age discrimination. The UK plans to introduce the legislation in October 2006. The directive sets very broad minimum requirements, obliging countries to prohibit age discrimination with respect to the labour market, including access to training as well as to jobs. It leaves many matters of detail up to governments.

Holiday spirit

Sarah was looking for a new job, and applied to work for a firm in Greater Manchester as a receptionist in a hotel. She was invited to go for an interview, but when she got home she received a call from the firm to ask her whether or not she was Jewish.

She stated that yes, she was Jewish – the company then went on to ask her whether she intended to take all the Jewish holidays. She explained that she planned to take only one Jewish holiday, as leave. The person that she spoke to said that the company 'had nothing against Jewish people'.

Four days later, when she had still not heard whether she was successful in her application, she rang the company who said that she had not been offered the job. She was told that the successful candidate 'had different circumstances'. This message was confirmed in writing a few days later.

Sarah felt that she had suffered discrimination on the grounds of her race, and came to the Commission for Racial Equality for advice. Before her case could be heard at employment tribunal, the company settled out of court for a four-figure sum.

Source: www.cre.gov.uk

activity

WHAT WENT WRONG?

Read the 'Holiday spirit' story and explain how the hotel company contravened the Race Relations Act. How should they have acted to avoid the situation occurring?

activity

YOU ARE THE LEGAL EXPERT

Mr Habib is planning to set up a travel agents in his home town. It is your job to advise him about the following legislation:

- The Disability Discrimination Act
- The Sex Discrimination Act
- The Race Relations Act
- Age discrimination.

Research how each will affect Mr Habib's new business. Role-play the scenario of you meeting Mr Habib to advise him on the steps he should take to ensure that his new business trades within the boundaries of the law.

Topic 9 Consumer and data protection

In the last topic we looked at how health and safety and equal opportunities legislation applies to travel and tourism organisations. This topic considers further generic legislation, this time concerned with consumer protection and data protection, under the following headings:

- **The Trades Description Act 1968**
- **The Sale of Goods Act 1979**
- **The Supply of Goods and Services Act 1982**
- **The Data Protection Act 1984/1988.**

The Trades Description Act 1968

In the early days of tourism, consumers had very little protection against fraud, or poor quality travel or holiday experiences. Gradually legislation has been introduced to ensure that if standards are low or experiences not as advertised or expected then there is a mechanism in place to protect the customer. This may lead to the customer getting a refund or some form of compensation. (Consumer protection in relation to sales and promotion is covered in Unit 10 – here we focus on how legislation affects an organisation's operation.)

The Trade Descriptions Act makes it an offence for a trader to make false or misleading statements about goods or services. The Act makes it an offence if the trader:

- Applies a false trade description to any goods.
- Supplies (or offers to supply) any goods to which a false trade description is applied
- Makes certain kinds of false statement about the provision of any services, accommodation or facilities.

An example of a 'false trade description' would be if a product or service is described or shown in a brochure

Not quite what was expected

Jeff and his wife Mo are in their fifties. They chose a 4-star hotel in Illetas from the Cadogan Holidays brochure, and paid £1,708 for half board for a week. The brochure and photographs failed to mention that the 'Garden Rooms' were some distance from the main hotel and its facilities. To reach them you had to use circuitous routes involving various permutations of underground corridors, 200-step hilly ascents and busy roads. To make matters worse, the adjacent building was undergoing loud building work. Their rooms overlooked a noisy road and there was a stagnant pool directly below their window.

When Geoff complained, he was offered a room on the next level of the same apartments. To salvage the situation he forked out another £1,968 to move to another hotel.

Once home, Jeff wrote to Cadogan Holidays, but to no avail. Finally he asked Which to help. We wrote on Jeff's behalf and they replied, arguing that the hotel's luscious tropical gardens and 28 Garden Rooms were referred to in the brochure. It also disputed the details regarding the inconvenience of the suite's location and claimed that the construction work was not building work but finishing touches to a refurbishment scheme.

We pointed to the brochures of rival operators, which described the rooms' location. Cadogan offered £700, which Jeff rejected. The operator insisted the hotel was 5-star and so they had experienced a superior product, but upped its offer to £1,000, which Jeff accepted.

Source: Holiday Which, Spring 2003

Read the *Holiday Which* account and answer the following questions:

1 Analyse the situation from the points of view of the customer and the company.

2 Why did Cadogan Holidays argue their case so vehemently?

3 Explain why you think they offered compensation in the end.

Are the following situations covered under the Sale of Goods Act?

1 A holiday is described by the agent as 'ideal for children' but the accommodation is above a night club.

2 A hotel is described as 'having wheelchair access' but clearly does not.

3 A ticket states that it is for 'first class' travel, but there is no room left in the first class accommodation.

to be of a particular standard – and actually isn't. If you expect a 5-star hotel room according to the promotional brochure and you get a 2-star hotel room, this would come under the Trade Descriptions Act as misleading the customer. The Act carries criminal penalties and is enforced by local authorities' Trading Standards Officers.

The Sale Of Goods Act 1979

The main aim of the Sale of Goods Act is to protect consumers from the sale of faulty goods or falsely labelled goods. Wherever goods are bought they must 'conform to contract'. This means that they must be:

- 'As described' – if the travel agent states 5-star luxury travel then it should have all the attributes of 5-star luxury travel.

- 'Fit for purpose' – if the holiday brochure states that the boats are unsinkable they should be unsinkable.

- 'Of satisfactory quality' – the quality should be in line with the price paid and the description of the product or service.

If consumers discover that products do not meet these requirements they can reject them and ask for their money back, providing they do so quickly. Alternatively, they can request a repair or replacement, or claim compensation. A little known fact is that it is the seller, not the manufacturer, who is responsible if goods do not conform to contract. For up to six years after purchase (five years from discovery in Scotland) purchasers can demand damages – which a court would equate to the cost of a repair or replacement. In general, the onus is on all purchasers to prove that the goods did not conform to contract (because they were inherently faulty, perhaps) and should have reasonably lasted until this point in time (perishable goods, for example, would not be expected to last for years).

The Supply Of Goods And Services Act 1982

The Supply of Goods and Services Act 1982 requires tradesmen and professionals to provide services to a proper standard of workmanship. Also, any materials used or goods supplied in providing the service must be of satisfactory quality. The law treats failure to meet these obligations as a breach of contract, and consumers would be entitled to seek redress, if necessary through the civil courts.

The travel and tourism business is highly dependent on the service it provides to customers – it is a service industry. For example, tour guides, travel representatives, travel agents and all service providers are covered by this Act. If their service is not to a satisfactory quality, then they can be taken to court.

The Data Protection Act 1984/1988

Data protection was brought in to protect customers, staff and members of an organisation from having data on them used unethically or unscrupulously. The first Act, introduced in 1984, was updated in 1998. The 1998 Act seeks to strike a balance between the rights of the individuals and the sometimes-competing interests of those with legitimate reasons for using personal information.

Anyone processing personal information must notify the Information Commissioner's Office (ICO) that they are doing so (unless their processing is exempt). They must also comply with the eight enforceable principles of good information handling practice, which state that data must be:

- Fairly and lawfully processed (see below)
- Processed for limited purposes
- Adequate, relevant and not excessive
- Accurate and up to date
- Not kept longer then necessary
- Processed in accordance with the individuals rights
- Secure
- Not transferred to countries outside the European Economic area unless the country has adequate protection for the individual.

Six conditions

At least one of the following six conditions must be met for personal information to be considered 'fairly processed':

- The individual has consented to the processing
- Processing is necessary for the performance of a contract with the individual
- Processing is required under a legal obligation (other than one imposed by the contract)
- Processing is necessary to protect the vital interests of the individual
- Processing is necessary to carry out public functions, e.g. administration of justice
- Processing is necessary in order to pursue the legitimate interest of the data controller or third parties (unless it could unjustifiably prejudice the interests of the individual).

Specific provision is made under the Act for processing sensitive personal information. This includes racial or ethnic origin, political opinions, religious or other beliefs, trade union membership, physical or mental health condition, sex life, criminal proceedings or convictions.

The Act (see below) gives individuals certain rights regarding information held about them. It places obligations on those who process information (data controllers) while giving rights to those who are the subject of that data (data subjects). Personal information covers both facts and opinions about the individual.

A number of criminal offences are created by the Act, including:

- Notification offences – This is where processing is being undertaken by a data controller who has not notified the Commissioner either of the processing being undertaken or of any changes that have been made to that processing.
- Procuring and selling offences – It is an offence to knowingly or recklessly obtain, disclose or procure the disclosure of personal information without the consent of the data controller. There are some exceptions to this – for example, where such obtaining or disclosure was necessary for crime prevention/detection.

Seven rights

There are seven rights under the Data Protection Act that the individual has, as follows:

- The right to subject access – This allows people to find out what information is held about them, on computer and within some manual records.
- The right to prevent processing – Anyone can ask a data controller not to process information relating to him or her that causes substantial and unwarranted damage or distress to them or anyone else.
- The right to prevent processing for direct marketing – Anyone can ask a data controller not to process information relating to him or her for direct marketing purposes.
- Rights in relation to automated decision-taking – Individuals have a right to object to decisions made only by automatic means, that is, there is not human involvement.
- The right to compensation – An individual can claim compensation from a data controller for damage and distress caused by any breach of the Act. Compensation for distress alone can only be claimed in limited circumstances.
- The right to rectification, blocking, erasure and destruction – Individuals can apply to the court to order a data controller to rectify, block or destroy personal details if they are inaccurate or contain expressions or opinions based on inaccurate information.
- The right to ask the Commissioner (ICO) to assess whether the Act has been contravened.

Electronic marketing communications

The Privacy and Electronic Communication (EC Directive) Regulations 2003 cover, amongst other things, unsolicited electronic marketing communications. Unsolicited marketing calls should not be made to individual subscribers who have opted out either directly of by registering with the central 'stop list', the Telephone Preference Service (TPS), or to corporate subscribers (e.g. companies) who have objected either directly or by registering on the Corporate TPS.

Unsolicited marketing faxes should not be sent to individuals without their prior consent or to any subscriber who has objected, either directly or by registering on the Fax Preference Service (FPS).

Unsolicited marketing emails should not be sent to any individual subscriber who has not consented, unless the email address was collected in the context of a commercial relationship. For example, if a customer consents to having information sent from other areas of the company they cannot complain when they are approached by them.

Wholly automated marketing calls – where a recorded message is played and the recipient does not speak to a human being – can only be made where the subscriber concerned (whether individual or corporate) has consented.

For more information visit the Information Commissioner's Office website www.informationcommissioner.gov.uk

activity

WHAT IT MEANS FOR A TRAVEL ORGANISATION

Write a short report on how the Data Protection Act will affect the way that a selected travel organisation collects, stores and uses personal information in relation to their staff and their customers. You may decide to conduct this research as an interview with a local travel and tourism company.

With the advances in technology one of the problems that customers and travel organisations have to face is fraud over the internet. In particular, people fear that their personal details are not protected. Although paying online is becoming more and more common, some people still do not like giving personal details over the internet. An example of how Travelcare try to handle their customer's fears is shown above, right.

TRAVELCARE SECURITY NOTICE

How do we make sure that others do not have access to your credit card information?

Credit/debit card payments will automatically be encrypted using Secure Sockets Layer (SSL). This technology ensures that your credit/debit card numbers are not accessible by any unauthorised persons and are as safe as possible. This means the credit and debit card numbers are securely processed into code when sent to us. Only the scrambled encoded data is then sent over the internet, which Travelcare receives and decodes.

Furthermore, as required by the UK Data Protection Act of 1998, we follow strict security procedures in the storage and disclosure of information that you have given us, to prevent unauthorised access. Our security procedures mean that we may occasionally request proof of identity before we are able to disclose sensitive information to you. We absolutely retain the right to refuse any booking made via our site.

When you are entering the secure area of the site you will see a padlock symbol at the bottom of your screen and the letter 's' after the word http in our website name showing in your browser window.

www.travelcare.co.uk

activity

LEGISLATION AND THE TRAVEL AND TOURISM INDUSTRY

Legislation has a great effect on the travel and tourism industry. Make sure that you have read the last three topics about all the relevant legislation. Then, create a table to show, for each piece of the following pieces of legislation, its main aims, and how it affects the travel and tourism industry: EU Package Directive, ABTA Code of Conduct, ATOL scheme, Health and Safety at Work Act, EU Working Time Directives, Disability Discrimination Act, Sex Discrimination Act, Race Relations Act, Age Discrimination Act, Trade Descriptions Act, Sale of Goods Act, Supply of Goods and Services Act, Data Protection Act.

African Pride – an independent travel company

This unit has been all about travel organisations. In this final topic we will look in detail at just one organisation – an independent tour operator called African Pride. It specialises in creating bespoke (tailor-made) holidays for discerning travellers to southern and East Africa. Unlike many tour operators, African Pride concentrates only on African holidays, and takes no commission on payment to hotels, lodges or safari operators, so preserving its reputation for being truly independent. We will study this organisation under the following headings:

- Scale and structure
- Operating business systems
- The products and services it provides
- How it meets the needs of different types of customer
- Any gaps in its provision for new products or services.

Let us now look at this bespoke company in more detail.

Scale and structure

African Pride was established in 1999, in York, by three experienced travel managers. It now employs twelve staff – eight 'travel consultants' and four administration staff. It has established itself as a niche-market tour operator creating individual travel itineraries for customers all across the country. Whereas a lot of tour operators operating trips to Africa have targeted the business and very expensive

Fly–drive – a great way to see South Africa

Day 1: Evening flight from Heathrow

Day 2: On arrival in Cape Town, transfer to Table Mountain Lodge in the city for a stay of 3 nights (B&B)

Days 3 and 4: At leisure for local sightseeing

Day 5: Europcar delivered to your hotel. Drive through winelands to Mossell Bay and then to Eight Bells Mountain Inn for 2 nights (B&B)

Day 6: Visit an ostrich farm or Cango Caves or have a day of leisure

Day 7: Drive the 'Garden Route' to Plettenberg Bay. Stay at Bosavern Guest House for 2 nights (B&B)

Day 8: Explore the 'Garden Route' or walk through Tsitsikamma Forest

Day 9: Drive along the coast to Port Elizabeth and stay overnight at the Beach Hotel

Day 10: Return the car to the airport and depart on flight to Johannesburg. Connect with flight to Nelspruit. On arrival, collect another self-drive car and drive to Rissington Inn, Hazyview for 3 nights

Day 11: Day for touring the 'Panorama Route'

Day 12: Day of leisure and viewing in the Kruger National Park

Day 13: Drive to Hoedspruit and return the car. Transfer to Gomo Gomo Private Game reserve for a 3-day/2-nights safari.

Day 14: Day spent viewing game

Day 15: Early morning game viewing. Early afternoon flight to Johannesburg. Evening flight to London

Day 16: Arrive Heathrow early morning.

Source: www.africanpride.co.uk

luxury holidays, African Pride are unique in that they create holidays for the middle to upper end of the market. For example, a popular first-time visitor trip is a 16-day fly–drive safari to South Africa, as shown below, which costs between £1,745 and £2,435 (2006) depending on the date of travel.

The team of eight travel consultants each create about 250 itineraries a year, which is approximately 2,000 bespoke holidays in total. Every itinerary sold is different. They have contacts and experience throughout Africa, which enables them to provide advice on everything from accommodation to transport to tours, etc.

Eighty per cent of African Pride's business is via independent travel agents –Bath Travel or Ryedale Travel, for example. These companies contact African Pride if they have a customer wanting to travel to Africa with an independent itinerary – something more than just a package holiday. If the customer buys the holiday then the travel agent takes a 12.5% commission.

The other twenty per cent of African Pride's business is through direct sales to the customer – via the internet, telephone or post.

Operating business systems

The business operates with the use of technology in the form of computers and of course the internet. But, the individual travel consultant creates each itinerary. Each component of the holiday is individually sourced and priced and added to the holiday. The company are therefore not fully computerised like some large tour operators, that can create an itinerary at the flick of a switch. This 'hands on' individual approach is what makes them so successful in creating the individual package to suit the customer's requirements.

When someone makes an enquiry there are a number of steps that the consultant goes through before the holiday is booked:

- The customer makes contact with African Pride usually via telephone, internet or email. The travel consultant asks various questions to establish whether the customer already has an itinerary in mind and, if necessary, makes suggestions about the kinds of holiday they might have. They then send out a brochure.

- Various options are discussed, and the consultant constructs a 'sample itinerary', which is then posted or emailed to the customer, with the relevant leaflets.

- The customer generally then changes the sample itinerary to suit their particular requirements, such as an upgrade in accommodation or more nights spent in one place and fewer in another.

- When the customer is happy with the itinerary and agrees that they want to go ahead on that basis, a deposit of £150 per person is required.

- The travel consultant will then try and make all the necessary reservations. If certain hotels are full, alternatives have to be found to keep within the itinerary.

- The final itinerary is then confirmed with the customer and an Order Confirmation and Invoice are sent to the customer. The Order Confirmation confirms timings, flights, ABTA regulations, class of travel, accommodation, transfers, tours, car hire, etc. In addition, there are notes on visas, medical requirements and general travel information on the country.

- The Invoice must be paid 8 weeks before departure.

- African Pride pre-pay the hotels etc, one month before departure.

- Two to three weeks before departure, tickets are issued and details of hotel addresses and driving directions sent to the customer.

- On return the travel consultant contacts the customer to see if they have had a good holiday, even if this is only via the travel agent.

The products and services it provides

We have already seen the type of bespoke services that African Pride provide for their customers. These are complemented by the products – the holidays – that they provide. Below is a table showing the popularity of the various holidays, by country.

Popularity of African Pride holidays by country (%)	
South Africa	65
Kenya and Tanzania	15
Botswana	8
Mauritius	6
Zambia and Namibia	4
Seychelles	2

The holidays cover a wide range: Battlefields of Kwa-zulu (Natal), golf tours, short escorted coach tour, Garden Route tours, fly–drive suggestions and accommodation, plus safaris throughout South Africa, Zambia, Botswana, Namibia, Kenya and Tanzania.

The fly–drive holiday to South Africa is probably one of the more popular types of trips, a sample of which we have seen above. Next in popularity are the safaris to Kenya and Tanzania. African Pride find that their beach destinations – Mauritius or the Seychelles – are often chosen by their customers in combination with a more active holiday.

How it meets the needs of different types of customer

When a customer is considering a trip to Africa they are obviously looking for something a little different from a sun, sea and sand two-week holiday on the Costa del Sol, Spain. There are some package tours to Africa operated by the larger travel companies such as Thomas Cook and Going Places, but independent tour operators often meet the needs of the customers better, because they can arrange an itinerary that fits their needs more precisely.

African Pride caters for a number of different customer groups. The majority are best categorised as couples who are aged 50+. But their holidays are also popular with honeymooners and, increasingly, with families and people looking for a different type of holiday. They can also cater for disabled travellers.

The needs of the customer have not noticeably changed over time but customers are now more confident to book in advance, as the political stability of South Africa has improved.

Any gaps in its provision for new products or services

If there are any gaps in provision, it would be for groups of travellers, ranging from sports groups who require a tour to the increasing number of families who want to holiday in southern Africa. African Pride

recognise that these are gaps in the market which they could address.

Further gaps are provided by the advances in technology, and particularly the internet. Although direct sales over the internet are more profitable for the company (as they do not have to pay 12.5% commission to the travel agent), they are also often more time consuming. Customers often get African Pride, with all their experience of the country, to do the research and make all the suggestions and then they take the itinerary and try and book it for themselves, hoping to save money. However, they often find that they cannot match African Pride's rates – because the company has built up good relations over the years and can get good discounts. In addition, the customer, working alone, is not covered if any of the companies go bust, whereas African Pride is a recognised tour operator with ABTA and ATOL bonding.

Acknowledgement

The information for this topic is based on an interview with Liz Lund, Senior Tours Consultant with African Pride. Liz took a degree in Recreational Management at Sheffield Polytechnic, before working in a hotel as an Assistant Manager. She then worked for South African Travel, before joining Austravel and finally working for African Pride.

How Unit 12 is assessed

You are required to investigate one sector of the travel and tourism industry and one organisation within that sector. The assessment evidence for this unit is in four distinct parts. It is suggested that they are presented in four sections within a portfolio:

(a) The organisation
(b) The proposal for a new or adapted product, service or facility
(c) Legal and regulatory requirements affecting the organisation
(d) An evaluation of the sector.

The assessment evidence could be in many different forms to allow for your learning preferences and strengths to be accommodated. Tasks could be evidenced through written reports or witness testimonies of oral presentations with supporting notes. For task (b) there may also be diagrams or images used.

The following guidance outlines how you can achieve the assessment criteria for each of the sections.

Task (a) The organisation

(a.0) Introduction
Describe the organisation and its position in the chosen sector. Give a brief history of the organisation.

(a.1) Type of organisation
Describe the type of organisation.

(a.2) Scale of the organisation
Describe the size and scale of the organisation.

(a.3) Structure of the organisation
Describe how the organisation is structured.

(a.4) Products and services
Explain the products and services that the organisation provides, and how they meet the needs of the different types of customers.

(a.5) Gaps in provision
Identify any gaps in the organisation's provision of products and services.

Task (b) The proposal for a new or adapted product, service or facility

This section should include your proposal for a new or adapted product, service or facility for your selected organisation to fill the gap(s) identified in task (a). It should include a detailed description of your proposal and an explanation of how it meets customer needs.

(b.0) Introduction
Describe the gap(s) in the organisation's provision.

(b.1) The proposal
Provide a detailed explanation of your proposal for the product, service or facility.

(b.2) Meeting the customers' needs
Explain how the proposal meets the needs of the customers. Identify the customers clearly.

Task (c) Legal and regulatory requirements affecting the organisation

This section should show evidence of research undertaken to complete all tasks and an analysis of the extent to which legal and regulatory requirements have affected the operation of the chosen sector of the industry.

(c.0) Introduction
Describe the type of legal and regulatory requirements that may affect the operation of the chosen sector.

(c.1) Legal and regulatory requirements
An explanation of the legal and regulatory requirements affecting your chosen sector, to include detail on the following, as applicable: EU Package Directive, ABTA Code of Conduct, ATOL, health and safety, equal opportunities, consumer protection, data protection.

(c.2) Bibliography
A list of sources used as evidence of your research.

Task (d) An evaluation of the sector

This section should show evidence of an evaluation of the degree of influence held by key organisations in the sector and the connections between the sector and others in the travel and tourism industry.

(d.0) Introduction
A description of the key organisations in the sector.

(d.1) The influence of the key organisations
An evaluation of the degree of influence held by the key organisations, to include statistical data regarding market share, turnover and profit.

(d.2) Connections between the sector and the rest of the industry
An explanation of the connections between the sector and others in the travel and tourism industry.

Bibliography

List all of the sources of information that you have used to complete the assessment for this unit.

Appendices

Include any relevant supporting information in the appendices, such as examples of marketing materials, policies and procedures, etc.

Index

Index